The ASQ Certified Medical Device Auditor Handbook

Fourth Edition

ASQ Medical Device Division
Scott A. Laman, Editor

Supports preparation for the ASQ Certified Medical Device Auditor (CMDA) certification

ASQExcellence
Milwaukee, Wisconsin

Published by ASQExcellence, Milwaukee, WI
Produced and distributed by Quality Press, ASQ, Milwaukee, WI

Publisher's Library of Congress Cataloging-in-Publication data

Names: Laman, Scott, editor.
Title: The ASQ certified medical device auditor handbook , fourth edition / ASQ Medical Device Division , Scott A. Laman, editor
Description: Includes bibliographical references and index. | Milwaukee, WI: ASQExcellence, 2021.
Identifiers: LCCN: 2020952290 | ISBN: 978-1-952236-09-9 (Hardcover) | 978-1-953079-96-1 (Hardcover) | 978-1-952236-10-5 (epub) | 978-1-953079-98-5 (epub) | 978-1-952236-11-2 (pdf) | 978-1-953079-97-8 (pdf)
Subjects: LCSH Medical instruments and apparatus—Standards. | Medical instruments and apparatus—Safety regulations. | Medical instruments and apparatus industry—Quality control. | Medical instruments and apparatus—Design and construction—Quality control. | BISAC BUSINESS & ECONOMICS / Auditing | BUSINESS & ECONOMICS / Industries / Manufacturing
Classification: LCC R856.6 A77 2021 | DDC 610.28—dc23

ASQ and ASQExcellence advance individual, organizational, and community excellence worldwide through learning, quality improvement, and knowledge exchange.

Attention bookstores, wholesalers, schools, and corporations: Quality Press and ASQExcellence books are available at quantity discounts with bulk purchases for business, trade, or educational uses. For information, please contact Quality Press at 800-248-1946 or books@asq.org.

To place orders or browse the selection of ASQExcellence and Quality Press titles, visit our website at: http://www.asq.org/quality-press.

25 24 23 LS 5 4 3 2

Quality Press
600 N. Plankinton Ave.
Milwaukee, WI 53203-2914
Email: books@asq.org

Excellence Through Quality™

Inspire Excellence

Table of Contents

Part IV: Quality Tools and Techniques

Part V: Appendices

List of Figures and Tables

Preface

The ASQ Certified Medical Device Auditor Handbook (formerly *The Biomedical Quality Auditor Handbook)* was developed by the American Society for Quality (ASQ) Medical Device Division (formerly Biomedical Division) in support of its mission to promote the awareness and use of quality principles, concepts, and technologies in the medical device community. It principally serves as a resource to candidates preparing for the Certified Medical Device Auditor (CMDA) certification exam.

The original Certified Biomedical Auditor (CBA) certification was initially introduced as an add-on to the Certified Quality Auditor (CQA) certification in 2000 and became the stand-alone CBA certification in 2005. In 2020, recognizing that the membership of the division is better represented by the description "medical device" than by "biomedical," division leadership proposed and the ASQ Board of Directors approved the name change to Medical Device Division. For consistency and to attract appropriate candidates for certification, the ASQ Certification Board followed suit with a change to the name of the certification exam to Certified Medical Device Auditor.

Obtaining the CMDA credential establishes the competence of an auditor in the medical device industry, with the CMDA described as understanding the principles of standards, regulations, directives, and guidance for auditing a medical device quality system. The CMDA certification exam is supported by its Body of Knowledge (BoK) and reference list that define the exam scope, with both elements maintained concurrently and generally updated every five years.

Regulations and guidance affecting the medical device industry continually evolve. Although new or updated requirements may be introduced at any time, revisions to the exam BoK, reference list, and exam maintain their five-year review cycle. Consequently, contents of this handbook and CMDA certification differ from the current state of the medical device industry.

The fourth edition of *The ASQ Certified Medical Device Auditor Handbook,* as a primary source of information for certification exam preparation, correlates to the 2020 certification exam BoK and reference list. This edition has been reorganized to align more closely with the BoK and includes a significant amount of brand-new material. As a result, the number of chapters in the fourth edition has increased from 24 to 28. Many other chapters and parts of chapters have been substantially rewritten, and all have been reviewed for accuracy and to reference current versions of the standards and regulations.

Each chapter of the third edition was initially compared to the requirements of the 2020 BoK via a gap analysis. Existing chapters were classified as:

- Review and update as necessary when there were no changes to the BoK topic addressed, or if there were only minor changes to content.
- Update the new BoK when there were significant content changes to the BoK topic addressed.
- Write new content when the new BoK covered a subject that was not in the third edition.

Part I on Auditing contains new content on data privacy, data integrity principles, and the Medical Device Single Audit Program (MDSAP).

Part II on Medical Device Quality Management System Requirements contains an entirely new Chapter 6, as the subject of "The EU Medical Device Regulation" has replaced "The EU Medical Device Directives." Chapters 4 and 5 have been switched to be consistent with the sequencing in the 2020 BoK. Chapter 4 has been rewritten and enhanced with new content on various codes of federal regulations that were not in the third edition. Chapter 8 on In Vitro Diagnostic (IVD) devices has also been substantially rewritten.

Part III on Technical Medical Device Knowledge contains new content for Chapter 13 (Human Factors and Usability Engineering), Chapter 16 (General Safety and Performance Requirements, 18 (Labeling), and Chapter 22 (Validation). Chapter 12 (Risk Management) has been rewritten to cover ISO 14971:2019 and the risk management requirements in IEC 62366 for usability engineering and ISO 13485 for quality system risk management. Chapter 17 (Software Development and Maintenance for Products) has been rewritten with additional content on the applicable guidances, as well as cybersecurity considerations.

Part IV on Quality Tools and Techniques has been improved with additional details and explanations. New content includes 5 Whys, is/is not (Kepner-Tregoe), setting alert and action limits, levels of measurement, and sampling. A related subject, test method validation and measurement systems analysis, is covered in Chapter 22 as part of validation.

Topics in this handbook are described in summary fashion and are not intended as a stand-alone tool for exam preparation. It is suggested that exam candidates read and understand the reference material to have a complete background in any one topic. The combination of this publication and reference materials is intended to provide a well-rounded background in medical device auditing.

The ASQ Medical Device Division believes this handbook will be a useful resource to those medical device professionals preparing for the CMDA exam.

Scott A. Laman
General Editor, Fourth Edition

Acknowledgments

Many people contributed to the fourth edition of this book, including some who were involved in the development of previous editions.

First, an effort of this magnitude begins with obtaining the wisdom and advice of previous editors of similar handbooks. Initial discussions with Grace Duffy, Mark Durivage, and Heather Crawford were immensely valuable to provide direction and, more importantly, instill vision and confidence that the task was achievable.

The ASQ Medical Device Division leadership has been fully supportive and involved with recommendations for contributors and stepping up to do some of the hands-on work themselves. The book name change that followed from the division name change originated from the vision of division leaders such as the following who requested the name change from "Biomedical Division" to "Medical Device Division" in January 2020.

Karen Brozowski, chair (2020)

Jim Shore, past chair (2019)

Teresa Cherry, past chair (2018)

Shreya Chandrasekhar, treasurer (2020)

Lisa Grosskopf, chair elect (2020)

The editor and the ASQ Medical Device Division would like to thank the following authors who reviewed, updated, and, as necessary, wrote new content:

Scott Blood, MEDIcept, for updated content on requirements for IVD devices and international standards for quality systems

Karen Brozowski, NeedleTech Products, Inc., for updated and new content on QSR requirements

Cinta Burgos, The Biotech Box, for new content on data integrity principles, MDR, and general safety and performance requirements

Teresa Cherry, Cherry Tree Quality Consulting, LLC, for updated content on controlled environments, utility systems, reprocessing/reuse/cleaning, medical device directives and standards, and sources for new and evolving standards

Barry Craner, CQA-Associates, for updated content on ISO 14971 risk management

Mark Durivage, Quality Systems Compliance LLC, for updated and new content on auditing fundamentals, ethical/legal/professional issues, and validation

Bruce Haggar, MedQSystems Consulting, for updated and new content on Health Canada and other international agencies, IEC 62366, ISO 13485 risk management, human factors and usability engineering, biological evaluation, packaging, and labeling

David Manalan, INQC Consulting, for updated content on FDA CFR, FD&C Act, IVD devices, and software development and maintenance for products

Jim Shore, Quality Lean Solutions, for updated and new content on audit preparation and planning, audit performance, audit report, and audit follow-up and closure

Sandra Storli, QRC Compliance LLC, for review and updated content on auditing fundamentals, ethical/legal/professional issues, audit procedural references, and labeling

Bob Turocy, consultant, for updated content on international guidelines for auditing: ISO 19011:2018, QSIT, FDA CPGM 7382.845, and MDSAP

Steven Walfish, U.S. Pharmacopeia, for updated and new content on quality tools and techniques, process improvement techniques, and data types and sampling

Peer reviewers who provided valuable review and input for this edition were:

Elizabeth Nichols, retired, Abbott Laboratories

Srikanto H. Paul, PhD, ConvaTec Group

Stephen E. Kappesser, Terumo Cardiovascular Systems

Contributors to the previous editions of this book set the foundation for the current work. See previous editions for acknowledgments of Paul Brooks, M. Elizabeth Bierman, Elizabeth Blackwood, David Dunn, Sue Jacobs, Don Johnson, Dan Olivier, Susan Reilly, Mark Roberts, Steve Thompson, and Jim Wood.

Finally, I would like to thank my wife, Krista, for her support throughout 2020, as this book took a tremendous amount of time with so much going on personally, at work, in the family, and throughout the world.

Part I

Auditing

Chapter 1
Auditing Fundamentals

AUDITS BY PURPOSE

Organizations conduct quality audits for a wide variety of reasons, including the assessment of the effectiveness, efficiency, and compliance of systems, processes, subprocesses, tasks, subtasks, products, assemblies, subassemblies, components, materials, and services. The reasons organizations undertake auditing activities vary. Some organizations perform audits merely to comply with regulations, standards, and guidances. Other organizations embrace auditing as part of a proactive risk management program, which is perceived within the organization as being a value-added activity through identifying previously unidentified risks, seeking opportunities for improving effectiveness and efficiency, ensuring compliance, and verifying the effectiveness of corrective actions from previously identified issues. See Figure 1.1 for further explanation of the differences between effectiveness and efficiency.

Effectiveness vs. Efficiency

Effectiveness measures the ability of a process to achieve its intended result—Doing the right things.

Efficiency measures the utilization of resources required for a process to achieve its intended result, the relationship between inputs and outputs, and how successfully the inputs are being transformed into outputs—Doing things right.

Figure 1.1 Effectiveness vs. efficiency.

Internal auditing activities may also be performed to assess medical device and facility registration status. The medical device registration status will usually review the associated design history file (DHF) of the medical device to assess whether significant changes or modifications in the design, components, method of manufacture, or intended use require an updated device registration.

Audits can also be used to assess the capability of potential suppliers, reassess current suppliers, evaluate future supplier partnerships, and ensure supplier corrective actions have been effectively implemented.

Certification audits are usually used by organizations to obtain ISO registration, for example, ISO 13485, and normally consist of an initial certification audit, surveillance audits (partial system audits) following years one and two, and a full recertification audit in year three.

Regulatory inspections are performed by regulatory agencies and competent authorities to determine the organization's level of compliance with regulations including marketing authorization, post-market surveillance activities, and quality management system (QMS) requirements. U.S. FDA regulatory inspections can be used for: routine inspections, pre-market product approvals (PMAs), for-cause inspections, or compliance follow-up activities.

Routine FDA regulatory inspections are mandated by law to be expected every two years for manufacturers of Class II or Class III medical devices. The purpose of routine regulatory inspections is to assess whether the organization is in compliance with requirements. Routine FDA inspections target the four major subsystems of the quality management system including:

- Corrective and preventive actions (CAPA)
- Design controls (if applicable)
- Management controls
- Production and process controls

PMA preapproval and post-market inspections assess the organization's systems, methods, and procedures for the specific PMA devices to ensure the firm's quality management system is effectively established (defined, documented, and implemented).

For-cause regulatory inspections are generally performed when regulatory authorities perceive a public health threat, detect or suspect any fraudulent activity, detect or suspect counterfeit products, recognize a trend in reportable activities or adverse events, or are acting on a formal whistleblower complaint.

Regulatory compliance follow-up inspections are performed when the organization was issued significant 483 observations or a warning letter. The FDA will verify that the actions taken in response to those observations were adequately corrected.

Due diligence audits are performed by organizations when considering mergers and acquisitions to assess the degree of regulatory compliance, including facility registrations and marketing authorizations.

Audits can be used for a variety of reasons, including the assessment of organizational effectiveness, system efficiency, business performance, process effectiveness, risk management, regulatory compliance, supplier qualification, compliance with standards (certification and surveillance), and supporting mergers and acquisitions. Regardless of the reason for performing an audit, a risk-based process should always be employed.

AUDITS BY METHOD

There are several types of audits as defined by ISO 19011:2018 *Guidelines for auditing management systems.* The three primary types of audits include first, second, and third party.

First Party

First-party audits are usually referred to as internal audits. Internal audits are performed on behalf of the organization either by trained internal auditors or a qualified consultant to audit a product, process, or system to ensure compliance with standards, regulations, product, and internal requirements. Internal audits typically look for problematic areas, procedural misalignments, opportunities for improvement, and the overall effectiveness of the quality management system.

Internal audits are generally more in depth than the other audits and are used as a tool to foster continuous improvement.

External audits include those generally called second- and third-party audits. Second-party audits are conducted by parties who have an interest in the organization, such as customers, or by other individuals on their behalf. Third-party audits are conducted by independent auditing organizations, such as those providing certification/registration of conformity or governmental agencies.

Second Party

A second-party audit is when an organization performs an audit of a supplier to ensure that specified requirements are met. These requirements may include process validations, continuous process monitoring, traceability of materials, components, subassemblies, assemblies and parts, requirements for special cleanliness standards, requirements for specific documentation, and good manufacturing practices. Service suppliers may be evaluated for the ability to meet contractual requirements, maintain documentation, and follow procedural requirements.

Second-party audits can also be used as part of a supplier qualification and monitoring program. For monitoring programs, these audits can be done off-site through a review of documents and records submitted by the supplier. When initially qualifying a supplier, these audits should be performed on-site.

Third Party

Third-party audit occurs when an organization wants to acquire third-party registration, certification, or accreditation to a particular QMS. Third-party audits are conducted by independent agencies to verify that the organization has successfully established, implemented, and maintains a compliant QMS.

Audits are further characterized by what is being audited, such as products, processes, and systems (Figure 1.2). Product audits assess whether products are meeting requirements. Process audits evaluate whether processes are operating properly. System audits assess the adequacy of the QMS.

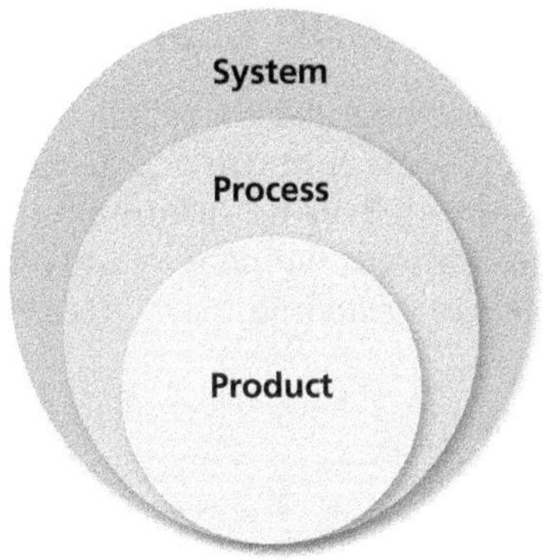

Figure 1.2 Types of audits.

Process approach audits are detailed audits that evaluate how a process is performing through its life cycle from input and processing, to output and improvement.

AUDIT ROLES AND RESPONSIBILITIES

Audits are authorized and/or requested by the client. The client is the organization or person requesting an audit. In the case of an internal audit, the audit client can also be the auditee or the person managing the audit program. Requests for external audit can come from sources such as regulators, contracting parties, or potential clients. The auditor is the individual(s) conducting the audit. The auditee is the organization that is being audited.

Each audit will have a least one auditor, who is referred to as the lead auditor. For more complex audits, an audit team overseen by the lead auditor may be required. The audit team may consist of one or more additional auditors (including auditor trainees) as well as technical experts. Technical experts may be used to provide specific knowledge or expertise related to the organization, activity, process, product, service, or discipline to be audited. Additionally, technical experts may help address cultural and language issues. Regardless of the purpose for using a technical expert, they do not act as auditors unless they are specifically trained and part of the audit team.

During the audit, the auditee (the organization being audited) may request to provide a guide. Guides should aid the audit team and act at the request of the audit team. Guides are responsible for assisting auditors in identifying individuals to participate in interviews and confirming timings and locations. They ensure that rules concerning location-specific arrangements for access, health and safety, environmental, security, confidentiality, and other issues are known and respected by the audit team and any potential risks are addressed. Guides witness the audit on behalf of the auditee, and, when appropriate, provide clarification or assist in collecting information.

PROFESSIONAL CONDUCT AND RESPONSIBILITIES

Objective auditing is characterized by a reliance on seven key principles. These principles help ensure the audit program and audits are effective tools in support of management policies by delivering information that can be used to identify issues and opportunities for improvement and to enhance performance.

ISO 19011:2018 *Guidelines for auditing management systems* provides the following key principles:

- Integrity
- Fair presentation
- Due professional care
- Confidentiality
- Independence
- Evidence-based approach
- Risk-based approach

Auditors and audit program management should perform their work with honesty, diligence, and responsibility; observe and comply with any applicable legal requirements; demonstrate their competence while performing their work; and perform their work in an impartial manner by remaining fair and unbiased.

Auditors and audit program management should not get drawn into company/department politics and should be sensitive to any influences that may be exerted on their judgement while carrying out an audit.

Audit findings, audit conclusions, and audit reports must be unbiased and must accurately and objectively reflect the activities of the audit. Obstacles encountered during the audit and unresolved issues between the audit team and the auditee should be documented and reported.

Auditors must exercise due professional care. Due professional care is having the ability to make reasoned judgements in all audit situations.

Auditors are usually required to sign a non-disclosure agreement (NDA). This should be done before the audit in case a legal review of the agreement is needed prior to the audit.

Auditors must be independent of the activity being audited wherever practicable and in all cases act in a manner that is free from bias and conflict of interest. For internal audits, auditors should be independent from the operating managers of the function being audited. Auditors should maintain objectivity throughout the audit process to ensure the audit findings and conclusions are based only on the audit evidence.

For small organizations, it may not be possible for internal auditors to be fully independent of the activity being audited, but every effort should be made to remove bias and encourage objectivity.

Audit evidence should be verifiable. Audits are generally based on a sampling of the information available, since an audit is conducted during a finite period and with finite resources. An appropriate use of sampling should be applied, since this is closely related to the confidence that can be placed in the audit conclusions.

An audit approach that considers risks and opportunities should be employed by auditors and audit program management. A risk-based approach should influence the planning, conducting, and reporting of audits to ensure that audits are focused on matters that are significant.

The ASQ Code of Ethics establishes global standards of conduct and behavior for its members, certification holders, and anyone else who may represent or be perceived to represent ASQ. The ASQ Code of Ethics requires individuals to act with integrity and honesty; demonstrate responsibility, respect, and fairness; and safeguard proprietary information and avoid conflicts of interest.

LEGAL CONSEQUENCES AND LIABILITY

Liabilities of an auditor for negligence and misfeasance (breach of duty or trust) can involve civil and criminal penalties. An auditor is in a contractual relationship with a client. If the auditor does not perform the audit according to contract terms, the client can sue for breach of contract. A client may seek remedies for breach of contract for: (1) specific performance; (2) general monetary damages for losses incurred as a result of the breach; and (3) consequential damages that occur indirectly as a result of the breach.

DATA PRIVACY

Maintaining confidentiality of any personal information that is reviewed during audits is essential for maintaining the integrity of the auditor and the audit program. As a medical device auditor, there may be times that the data encountered are subject to the U.S. Health Insurance Portability and Accountability Act (HIPPA) and EU General Data Protection Regulation 2016/679 (GDPR).

HIPPA gives patients control over the use of their health information and defines boundaries for the use/disclosure of health records by covered entities. HIPPA helps to limit the use of personal health information (PHI) with the aim of minimizing inappropriate disclosure.

GDPR is a regulation in the European Union (EU) pertaining to data protection and privacy, and addresses the transfer of personal data outside the EU. The GDPR gives control to individuals over their personal data. GDPR applies to any enterprise—regardless of its location and the data subjects' citizenship or residence—that is processing the personal information of data on subjects inside the EU.

Auditors must exercise discretion in the use and protection of information that is acquired during the audit. Audit information should not be used inappropriately for personal gain by the auditor or the audit client, or in a manner detrimental to the legitimate interests of the auditee. This concept includes the handling of sensitive or confidential information including copyrights, patents, trademarks, products, processes, clients, and customers.

Chapter 2

Auditing and Inspection Processes

AUDIT PREPARATION AND PLANNING

Audit Purpose and Scope

During the planning stages of the audit, the auditing organization, the auditor, or the audit team must define and document the audit purpose and scope. Defining the objectives and scope enables efficient use of time and resources. The objectives define what is to be accomplished. The scope establishes boundaries and identifies what is to be examined. The following should be considered when establishing the audit scope:

- Medical devices manufactured
- Quality system requirements
- Type of audit (initial, surveillance, special, or unannounced)
- Physical location of activities and documentation
- Regulations, standards, and company-specific requirements

If applicable and appropriate, the audit purpose and scope should be provided to the auditee for review and approval. It is feasible that during the audit the objectives and/or scope may change based on audit observations and nonconformances noted. Whenever possible, it is customary to share the audit agenda at least two weeks prior to the audit. This will allow the proper review and preparation by the auditee, as well as ensure that the appropriate people will be available for the audit.

Resources

To ensure reliable audit results and conclusions, there must be adequate resources (for example, competent staff, financial support, time, technical information, external expertise) dedicated to the audit process and associated auditing activities.

Competence of the Audit Team

A lead auditor with the competence to plan and manage an audit, as well as direct team members, must be included on the audit team. If the team consists of only one auditor, then this individual will be the lead.

If the lead auditor determines that the area being audited requires a technical or subject matter expert (SME), then the SME should be identified before the audit date. The SME should be trained on auditing techniques and understand how much time is required for planning purposes. Specific documents may be requested prior to the audit, which will help the SME become familiar with the processes.

The audit team must possess the necessary professional and technical competence to cover the scope of the audit. The team should be competent with respect to understanding:

- Applicable regulatory, statutory, and safety requirements
- Appropriate device technologies and processes
- Auditing of medical device manufacturers' quality systems

Other areas to consider in assessing competence include professional qualifications, education, skills, training, experience, and personal attributes. If the necessary technical competence is not present within the audit team, additional experts in processes and technology relevant to the scope of the audit may be included, or team members may be provided specialized training.

Records to demonstrate the competence of auditors must be maintained by the auditing organization. A copy of their certification should be available to the auditee upon request.

Independence

The audit process should ensure objectivity and impartiality. The auditing organization and its auditors should perform their duties in an independent, objective manner and avoid any potential conflict of interest. Auditors should not audit their own work and must be unbiased and independent of the area being audited to permit objective completion of the audit. Independence should be regularly assessed. Factors to consider include personal relationships, financial interests, and prior job assignments and responsibilities.

If anyone on the audit team has a conflict of interest, he or she should immediately notify the lead auditor. That person may be able to perform a portion of the audit that is outside that conflict or may need to be replaced. These decisions must be made well in advance of the audit.

Written Procedures

To ensure consistency of audits, the audit process—including the responsibilities and requirements for managing, planning, and conducting audits, reporting results, and maintaining records—should be defined and documented. These procedures must address applicable regulatory and quality requirements. Auditing organizations should implement and maintain a quality system to ensure the audits conducted are of the highest quality and to facilitate continuous improvement.

Adequacy of Audit Documentation

The auditor or audit team needs to obtain documented evidence to achieve the audit objectives effectively. Documentation associated with each audit should include any information that is required by government regulations or regulatory authorities. Procedures should be in place to ensure adequate retention of the documentation for a time sufficient to satisfy legal, professional, and organizational requirements. The retention of these records must follow the auditing company's policy regarding record retention as well as the regulations.

Documentation maintained may include a record of the audit:

- Scope and objectives
- Program
- Process
- Evidence gathered
- Findings and conclusion
- Report and responses to findings, which may include actions to be taken and due dates

There may be documents that are identified as the objective evidence during the audit that may not be allowed to be removed or copied due to the auditee's policy or may violate intellectual property concerns. If that is the case, the auditor must document the specifics as well as possible so the auditee will understand the report and/or finding.

Audit Process

While experts have described the audit process in many ways, it has traditionally been divided into phases or stages, as shown in Figure 2.1.

Stage 1: Audit Preparation

The stages of the process are notification, preparation, preview of quality system documented information, audit plan, audit plan changes, audit team assignments, and working documents. Portions of the audit preparation process, such as notification and preview of quality system documented information, are not applicable to those situations where unannounced audits are deemed necessary by the auditing organization. These unannounced audits apply to audits of those companies that have a CE mark and are conducted by notified bodies.

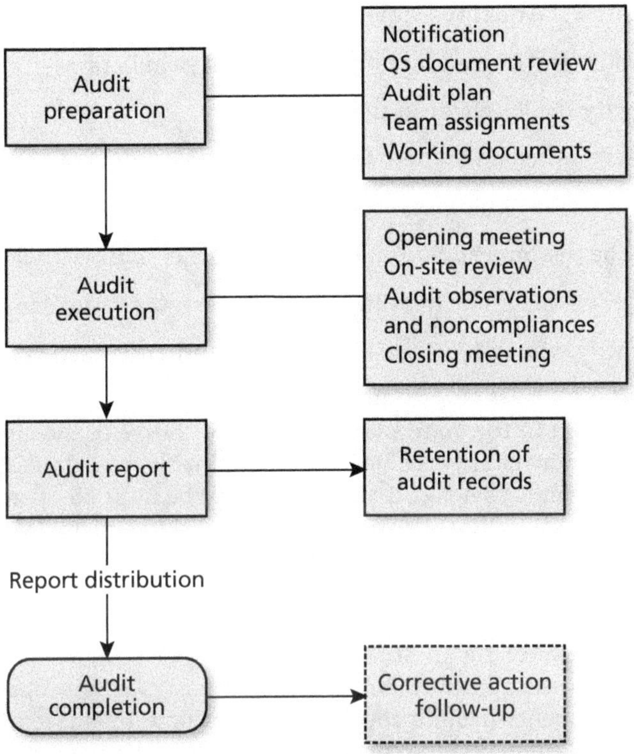

Figure 2.1 Audit process.

Unless regulatory requirements mandate otherwise, the auditee should be notified in advance that an audit is to be conducted. Before the on-site examination, the lead auditor should conduct a desk audit of the documented information to determine whether the quality system is aligned with regulatory requirements. This can be accomplished by reviewing the quality manual and, if applicable, top-level standard operating procedures (SOPs). Although this preview is done during the preparation stages, it is actually part of audit execution. If it becomes obvious during the review that the documented system is inadequate, then a conversation with the auditee should be held about potentially suspending the on-site audit until necessary corrective actions are made.

The lead auditor must develop an audit plan. Where permitted by regulations, the documented plan should be submitted to the auditee for approval before the site visit. The audit plan should:

- Define the objectives and scope of the audit
- Identify the manufacturer's management team having direct responsibility for the audit scope and purpose
- Identify the applicable audit standards and other reference documents to be utilized

- Identify the quality elements that will be audited
- Identify the lead auditor and other team members
- Specify the language of the audit
- Specify when and where the audit will be conducted
- Identify the organizational units and areas that will be audited
- Define the time and duration for each major audit activity
- Schedule meetings to be held with the manufacturer's management
- Identify who will get the final audit report and when

It is important to note that audit plans are subject to change, and this possibility should be stated in the audit plan. During the course of the audit, the objectives and/or scope may change, or become unattainable, based on audit observations and nonconformances noted. The auditee must be notified of any changes.

It is the lead auditor's responsibility to assign specific tasks to audit team members. These tasks should be assigned according to the participants' qualifications and expertise.

Working documents are required when performing an audit to international auditing guidelines. Again, it is the lead auditor's responsibility to prepare the working documents; team members should assist as appropriate. Examples of working documents include checklists (to evaluate the system elements against regulatory requirements) and forms (to record observations and collect supporting evidence).

AUDIT PERFORMANCE

Stage 2: Audit Execution

The audit execution stage should start with an opening meeting with the auditee's senior management. The purpose of this meeting is to:

- Introduce the audit team
- Restate, and clarify if necessary, the audit scope, objectives, plan, and schedule
- Review the methods and procedures to be used during the audit
- Confirm that the necessary resources and facilities to support the audit process are available
- Establish communication links
- Make any adjustments to the audit plan based on personnel availability or to witness certain activities that are identified on the audit plan

During the on-site assessment, applicable elements of the quality system are evaluated. Objective evidence is collected by:

- Interviewing and questioning personnel
- Reviewing records and documents
- Visually observing activities and conditions

Wherever possible, evidence collected through personnel interviews should be confirmed by other means. Documents or copies of records collected, or any photographs taken, should be noted by the auditors and acknowledged by the auditee. Sampling of records and documents should be appropriate to the risks associated with the device, the complexity of manufacturing technologies, and available post-market surveillance data.

Upon evaluation of the objective evidence collected, auditors must document their quality audit observations (a statement of fact made during a quality audit and substantiated by objective evidence). Nonconformities (nonfulfillment of specified requirements within the planned arrangements), and quality audit observations that have the potential to become nonconformities, should be reviewed with the auditee as they are noted.

Nonconformities must be supported by the evidence collected and must identify the requirements that have been violated. One or more major nonconformities may indicate that the auditee does not comply with the regulatory requirements. The following are examples of quality audit observations that may be considered nonconformities:

- Lack of or failure to implement a quality system requirement
- Product safety or performance is/may be compromised
- Large number of minor nonconformances against a quality system requirement
- Failure to implement appropriate corrective and preventive actions
- Repeat observations

An exit or closing meeting is held at the completion of the on-site evaluation. The purpose of this meeting is for the lead auditor to discuss quality audit observations, nonconformities, severity of the nonconformities including the classification criteria, and overall conclusions with the auditee's senior management, and those individuals responsible for the areas audited, before a final report is prepared. The audit team then presents a list of audit observations and nonconformities to the management team.

It is customary to thank the auditee and their team for their support of the audit. In addition, any areas that were positive or people who were helpful should be identified as well.

AUDIT REPORTING

Stage 3: Audit Report

The audit report is the method of formally communicating the audit scope and objectives, audit plan, standards and methodology utilized, objective evidence collected, and quality audit observations, nonconformities, and conclusions. The audit findings and conclusions should be consistent, accurate, and supported by the evidence gathered throughout the audit process.

The lead auditor is responsible for preparing, dating, signing, and submitting the audit report to the auditee. It is very important that this report be completed and sent to the auditee in a timely manner. Otherwise, the delay may compromise the integrity of the audit program and may be perceived negatively by the auditee.

Nonconformities identified in the audit report should be specific in nature and should include the following:

- Requirements of the internal or external standard
- Severity with respect to the requirements
- Confirmable (traceable and verified) nonconformities

The audit report timing and distribution should be determined prior to the audit. If the report cannot be made available to the auditee within the agreed period, the auditing organization must provide the reason for the delay and notify the auditee of the new issue date.

AUDIT FOLLOW-UP AND CLOSURE

Stage 4: Audit Completion

The audit is considered complete upon transmittal of the final audit report to the auditee; however, some organizations do not consider an audit complete until the auditing organization approves the corrective action plans, including timelines. The auditing organization may require the root cause and corrective action plan to be submitted within a defined timeframe. The implementation of the corrective action may or may not be required within a certain time depending upon the severity of the nonconformity

The auditee is expected to take actions to correct identified nonconformities. The auditing organization and the auditee should agree on a plan for completing the necessary corrective actions and, if required, reaudits to verify that corrective actions were taken. Periodic reports may also be requested by the auditing organization to determine the status of the necessary corrective actions. Documented information prepared for and resulting from the audit should be retained at least until audit completion, or as specified by the audit program, and as agreed by the audit participants.

DATA INTEGRITY PRINCIPLES

Data integrity refers to the accuracy, completeness, and reliability of data throughout their life cycle. It is a critical aspect of the design, implementation, and usage of any system that stores, processes, or retrieves data.

Data integrity for medical devices consists of physical integrity, logical integrity, ALCOA (attributable, legible, contemporaneously recorded, original, and accurate) principles, metadata, and audit trails.

Compliance with current good manufacturing practices (CGMPs) requires companies to record, track, manage, store, and easily access documents such as SOPs, batch records, test data, and logbooks. Regulations also require manufacturers to monitor electronic records and data to ensure they are reliable, trustworthy, traceable, and verifiable to conform with U.S. FDA's 21 CFR Part 11, EudraLex Volume 4, and MHRA GXP Data Integrity Guidance and Definitions.

The process to ensure data integrity includes:

- Procedures or instructions for completion of records and record retention
- Procedures for good documentation practice (GDP)
- Staff training and authorization for data generation and approval
- System(s) designed to consider how data are generated, recorded, processed, retained, and used, and effectively controlling risks or vulnerabilities
- Routine data verification
- Periodic surveillance

Physical Integrity

Physical integrity deals with challenges associated with correctly storing and retrieving the data to ensure the quality, preservation, and integrity of the information stored.

Considerations for a paper-based system include:

- A company signature log for GxP documents
- A decision whether digital images of a person's handwritten signature are permitted
- Data recorded in permanent, indelible ink
- GMP forms or bound notebooks that are controlled through generation, distribution, review, and retention
- Original records that are readily available for inspection
- Record retention and disposal

Considerations for an electronic-based system include:

- The system has a unique user login with electronic signatures
- Staff is trained to never disclose their username or passwords
- The system automatically generates a timestamp when data are entered.
- Data are transferred between systems
- Records and data are backed up

Logical Integrity

Logical integrity is concerned with the correctness of a piece of data for a particular context and time.

Considerations for a paper-based system include:

- Staff is trained in GDP
- Qualification/validation activities are performed on original preapproved protocols

Considerations for an electronic-based system include:

- Software is validated
- Stored data are reviewed for readability
- Audit trails are convertible to an intelligible form
- The system prevents unauthorized changes or deletion of original data
- Metadata are periodically reviewed

ALCOA

The ALCOA acronym was first coined by Stan W. Woollen from the FDA's Office of Enforcement in the 1990s. ALCOA is used by regulated industries as a framework for ensuring data integrity and is essential to ensuring GDPs. ALCOA applies to paper and electronic data. ALCOA principles are essential for a compliant paper and/or electronic data management life-cycle system, complying with GDPs and GMPs, and driving data integrity initiatives.

The five ALCOA principles are:

- ***Attributable.*** It should be clear who collected the data and when. All paper and electronic data must be attributable to the person generating the data, including who performed an action and when. This can be accomplished by recording manually such as by initialing and dating a paper record or by audit trail in an electronic system. To ensure GDPs, all data collected must be signed and dated by the individual collecting/entering the data, unless noted.

- ***Legible.*** All paper and electronic data must be legible and permanent. Ensuring records are legible and permanent assists with accessibility throughout the data life cycle, including the storage of paper and electronic data. Any changes to entries should be made to not obscure the original entry. A single line that is then dated and initialed is required to support the changes, along with a reason for the change, by the person making the entry. For example, there might be a transcription error at the time of recording, a write over, or a miscalculation.
- ***Contemporaneous.*** Contemporaneous means to record the paper or electronic data at the time the data are generated. Date and time stamps should flow in order of execution for the data to be credible. Data should never be back dated, or forms completed with expected results prior to execution.
- ***Original.*** Original data is the paper or electronic medium on or in which the data point is initially recorded including protocol, form, notebooks, spreadsheet, database, or software application. Even data collected on items such as paper towels, gloves, and sleeves of lab coats are included and archived. Understanding where the original data are generated ensures content and meaning are preserved.
- ***Accurate (true and complete observations).*** For paper and electronic data to be accurate, the data should be free from errors, complete, truthful, and reflective of the observation. Editing should only be performed by using the principles of GDPs.

CCEA (complete, consistent, enduring, and available) was added to ALCOA in 2010. ALCOA-CCEA is more commonly known as ALCOA-C or ALCOA+. The following information defines ALCOA-C or ALCOA+:

- ***Complete.*** All paper and electronic data, including original test results and repeat tests results, must be properly recorded, clearly identifying the person performing the test as well as when the test was performed.
- ***Consistent.*** The data sequence of events should be in the expected sequence of operations and appropriately date or time stamped to demonstrate the data are contemporaneous.
- ***Enduring.*** Paper and electronic data are appropriately recorded in laboratory notebooks or in validated software systems including spreadsheets and databases.
- ***Available.*** Paper and electronic data are required to be readily available for review, audits, or inspections for the required lifetime of the record. Paper and electronic data should be clearly indexed and/or appropriately labeled to facilitate retrieval.

Metadata

The term *metadata* refers to data that describe the attributes of other data and provide context and meaning. Typically, these are data that describe the structure, data elements, interrelationships, and other characteristics of data. It also permits data to be attributable to an individual. Metadata forms an integral part of the original record. Without metadata, the data themselves have no meaning. Metadata is the extent to which all data are complete, consistent, and accurate throughout the data life cycle. Data integrity steps must ensure the accuracy, completeness, content, and meaning of data are retained throughout the data life cycle.

Audit Trails

An audit trail in electronic systems can be considered the who, what, where, when, and why of a record. The FDA defines audit trails in electronic/computerized systems as: a secure, computer-generated, time-stamped electronic record that allows for reconstruction of the course of events relating to the creation, modification, or deletion of an electronic record. For example, an audit trail should detail at what time and location an authorized user entered, deleted, or made changes to a specific dataset, as well as the justification for the modification. Audit trails should be periodically reviewed.

Data Integrity Standards and Regulations

The following standards directly or indirectly cover principles of data integrity:

- FDA Guidance on Data Integrity—CGMP data integrity requirements emphasized by the FDA in this guidance include: Part 211.68—Backup data should be "exact and complete" and "secure from alteration, inadvertent erasures, or loss". ... Part 212.110(b)—Data should be "stored to prevent deterioration or loss." The agency's expectations can be applied to medical devices.
- EudraLex Volume 4 Annex 11 Computerized Systems
- MHRA GxP Data Integrity Guidance and Definitions
- WHO Technical Report 996:2016 Guidance on good data and record management practices[1]
- 21 CFR 820.30(g) Design Validation
- 21 CFR Part 11 Guidance for Industry Electronic Records; Electronic Signatures
- ISO 13485 section 4.2.5 Control of Records
- ISO 14155: *Clinical investigation of medical devices for human subjects—Good clinical practice*

- Draft U.S. FDA Guidance: Content of Premarket Submissions for Management of Cybersecurity in Medical Devices
- ISO/WD 4669: *Document management—Controlled sharing of digital documents*
- ISO 11506: *Document management applications—Computer output microform (COM)/Computer output laser disc (COLD)*
- ISO 12651, parts 1&2: Electronic document management
- ISO 17797: *Electronic archiving—Selection of digital storage media for long-term preservation*

Chapter 3

Audit Procedural References

Standards and guidance are made available by organizations including the International Organization for Standardization (ISO) and U.S. Food and Drug Administration (FDA). In this chapter, the following standards are summarized: Guidelines for auditing management systems (ISO 19011:2018), FDA Quality System Inspection Technique (QSIT), FDA Compliance Program Guidance Manual (CPGM) 7382.845, and the Medical Device Single Audit Program (MDSAP). These reference standards are an excellent source of information and will enhance one's access to valuable information.

ISO 19011:2018

ISO 19011:2018: *Guidelines for Auditing Management Systems* was prepared by Project Committee (PC) 302, Guidelines for Auditing Management Systems. Currently, the third edition cancels and replaces the second edition, which was ISO 19011:2011. The main differences from the second edition are as follows:

- The 2018 edition uses a risk-based approach to principles of auditing.
- The guidance on managing the audit program, including program risk, was expanded.
- This guidance places an emphasis on audit planning.
- Auditor generic confidence requirements were expanded.
- The terminology was adjusted to reflect the process and not the object.
- The requirements for auditing specific management system disciplines were removed from the annex containing competence.
- Annex A was expanded to provide guidance on auditing new concepts such as organizational context, leadership, and commitment, (FDA) audits, compliance, and supply chain status.

Knowing and following ISO 19011 auditing concepts and attributes will greatly enhance an auditor's ability to perform an ethical, fair, independent, and factual management system audit. It is highly recommended to read, understand, and recall the entire standard because it provides a solid foundation for conducting a management system audit. This "guide" establishes the foundation of auditing techniques for many organizations.

Risk-based thinking has its roots in ISO 9001:2015 as well as ISO 13485 and IATF 16949. Please note that ISO 19011 is a "guide" and an auditing organization or manufacturer performing audits should establish their own auditing program. Following are the various sections of ISO 19011.

Introduction

The ISO 19011:2018 standard is guidance for management to utilize results of audits in business planning, product and process improvements identified and implemented, and any other related manufacturing activities. Audits have the potential to be conducted against many aspects of a quality management system, including standards, policies, and other requirements from interested parties, statutory and regulatory requirements, processes identified by the organization or other parties, and management system plans related to specific outputs.

ISO 19011:2018 focuses on three audit types: internal audits (also known as first-party audits), audits conducted by organizations on their external providers and other external interested parties (also known as second-party audits), and, finally, certification or accreditation audits and statutory, regulatory, and similar audits (also known as third-party audits).

This guidance document applies to many different potential users, including auditors, organizations executing quality management systems, and organizations needing to conduct management system audits for regulatory or contract rationale. This guidance can also be used for self-declaration and useful to organizations involved in auditor training of personnel requiring certification.

ISO 19011:2018 is intended to be flexible. It addresses the complexity of organizations to be audited as well as the objectives and scope of the audit to be conducted. This document includes a combined risk-based audit approach where two or more management systems of different groups are audited together. It also provides guidance on management of an audit program, on the planning and execution of management systems audits, and on auditor or audit team education and their evaluation.

Guidelines for Auditing Management Systems

ISO19011:2018 identifies its own scope for organizations that are required to plan audits, implement either internal or external audits, or manage an audit program. Direction is provided for auditing management systems, including principles of auditing, managing, and conducting management system audits, as well as the evaluation of individuals. The audit process includes auditors, audit teams, and individuals managing the audit program. Normative references are not part of this standard because it is not industry specific. Many terms and definitions are provided within this guidance that are based on ISO 9000:2015 definitions or may have been slightly modified. Being familiar with the concepts and knowing the terms or definitions contributes toward an effective and thorough audit.

Principles of Auditing

The following are condensed principles of auditing displayed in ISO 19011 section 4:

- The foundation of professionalism (integrity)
- The obligation to report truthfully and accurately (fair presentation)
- The application of diligence and judgment in auditing (due professional care)
- Security of information (confidentiality)
- The basis for impartiality of the audit and objectivity of the audit conclusions (independence)
- The rational method reaching reliable and reproducible audit conclusions in a systematic audit process (evidence-based approach)
- An audit approach that considers risks and opportunities (risk-based approach)

The audit should be a reliable and effective tool supporting management's policies and controls to continually improve products or processes. Auditors should maximize and utilize the principles defined in this guidance.

Managing an Audit Program

Following is a summary of the principles for managing an audit program. The plan-do-check-act (PDCA) cycle, which was defined by Dr. W. Edwards Deming in the 1950s, is followed to portray audit program management as a continuous improvement process. See also ISO 19011:2018, section 5.1, Figure 1—Process flow for the management of an audit program, which is a pictorial representation of this cycle. The audit program should be based on management system standards or specified requirements and should include adequate resources necessary to perform an audit meeting the requirements within reasonable time frames.

The following paragraphs are highlights from ISO 19011, sections 5.2-5.7 for establishing an audit program. One should see ISO 19011:2018 for a detailed and complete presentation of information in these paragraphs. The audit program should be implemented effectively per the planned objectives.

Establishing the objectives of an audit program. The people managing the audit program should ensure that roles and responsibilities are understood. Competence of individuals should be based on audit principles and standards. The person managing the audit program should establish the extent of the program, which has the potential to be different from audit to audit. Resources such as finances and manpower should be taken into consideration when establishing an audit program.

Determining and evaluating audit program risks and opportunities. There are risks and opportunities related to the context of the auditee that can be associated with an audit program and can affect the achievement of its objectives. The individuals managing the audit program should identify and present to the audit client the risks and opportunities considered when developing the audit program and the resource requirements so they can be addressed appropriately.

Establishing the audit program. The roles and responsibilities of individuals managing the audit program must be identified, the competence of individuals managing the audit program must be specified, the extent of the audit program should be established, and the resources of the audit program need to be determined.

Implementing the audit program. Implementing the audit program is dependent on the established resources and planned activities previously defined. The person managing the audit should establish the audit method meeting the criteria, scope, and objectives. He or she should also determine the requirements and competence of auditors, including technical experts or translators, to meet the requirements of the audit. The responsibilities should define the team and individual(s) responsibilities. The person managing the audit program (team leader) should maintain the audit records (schedule, auditees' identity, reports, findings, corrective actions, follow-up).

Monitoring the audit program. The person managing the audit program should ensure schedules are being met and feedback is provided to the auditee.

Reviewing and improving the audit program. The lead managing the audit program should review the results with the auditee to ensure objectives have been met. In addition, improvements to the audit program should be reviewed and implemented if necessary.

Conducting an Audit

Following are highlights from ISO 19011, sections 6.1-6.7 for conducting an audit. One should see ISO 19011:2018 for a detailed and complete presentation of the paragraphs. Also, see ISO 19011:2018, section 5.1, Figure 1—Process flow for the management of an audit program for Sections 6.2-6.7, which shows the steps for conducting an audit and how the PDCA cycle applies to these clauses.

Initiating the audit. The audit team leader is responsible for communication with the auditee and establishing feasibility of the audit. He or she ensures the contract is understood and agreed upon before implementing the audit. Arrangements, attributes, and details are established and agreed to prior to audit execution.

Preparing audit activities. Documented policies, procedures, and other relevant information should be secured from the auditee. A risk-based approach should be included in the audit preparation. Planning should incorporate objectives, scope, audit criteria, previous reports, communications, corrective actions, and follow-ups. The audit team leader should assign responsibilities to the audit team per the auditor's ability and background. The audit checklist, sampling strategy, and audio/visual information should be prepared for the audit. This information should be retained per documented procedure or at least until the audit is completed.

Conducting audit activities. See ISO 19011:2018 section 6.4.7, Figure 2—Overview of a typical process of collecting and verifying information. Roles and responsibilities of guides and observers should be assigned and in agreement with the auditee. The opening meeting should be confirmed and agreed to by the auditee. Audit communication should be either formal or informal. Exchange of information between audit team members may be necessary to identify risks or opportunities. Information critical to the audit is accessed via established procedure as to its location, when available, and how to use the information. Information should be reviewed during the audit to determine management system conformity. Information should be collected and verified via applicable sampling plans. The team leader should generate audit findings, determine conclusions, prepare the audit closing meeting agenda, and conduct the closing meeting.

Preparing and distributing the audit report. The audit team leader should report conclusions per the audit plan and according to the audit program. The report should be neat, accurate, complete, and clearly understood. The confidential report should be distributed within the agreed-upon time frame and to the designated individuals.

Completing the audit. After planned activities are completed, the confidential audit report should be distributed per agreement with the auditee. Risks and opportunities from the audit have the potential to benefit the auditee's management system.

Conducting audit follow-up. The audit outcome can be processed depending on the audit. If necessary, corrective action agreed to during the closing meeting will be verified at the agreed time-to-complete date. The verification of completion and effectiveness should be documented.

Competence and Evaluation of Auditors

Following are highlights from ISO 19011, section 7 for competence and evaluation of auditors.

General. Attaining the audit objective and having confidence in the audit team leader and auditors are paramount. Competence of the audit team is based on education, training, experience, and communication skills, and evaluated on an established frequency.

Determining auditor competence. An auditor's current knowledge and skills should be evaluated relative to the knowledge of standards to be audited, education, audit process, risk and opportunities, process experience, and product knowledge necessary to meet audit objectives. Desirable auditor traits include good personal behavior, honesty, fairness, ethical, observant, ability to be flexible, motivation to further education, and willingness to improve. They should have general skills of auditors and the willingness to accept a team leadership responsibility. They should be knowledgeable of legal terms, general contract statements, and liability. Working with and for an experienced audit team leader will enhance an auditor's competence.

Establishing auditor evaluation criteria. Criteria should incorporate education, training, audits performed, training days/hours, and number of audits performed.

Selecting the appropriate auditor evaluation method. The evaluation should utilize two or more of the following: record review, feedback, interview, observation, testing, or post-audit reviews.

Conducting auditor evaluation. Auditors should be evaluated relative to the knowledge and skills necessary to achieve the intended output that the auditor is expected to perform. General competence, along with a level of discipline, skills, and sector-specific knowledge, should be evaluated. The audit team leadership should have additional knowledge and skills necessary to provide leadership to the team.

Maintaining and improving auditor competence. Auditing organizations and auditors must continually improve their performance, especially their competence. Improvement is achieved through work experience, training, private study, coaching, sharing information, formal education, sharing best practices, and attending seminars and conferences. There are many reasons for improving competence, including revision to standards or procedures, product changes, and facility additions.

Appendix A

The appendix provides supplemental information and additional guidance for auditors planning and conducting audits, as previously discussed in the preceding clauses of this standard. Many different methods can be applied to implement an audit. Audit methods depend on a few criteria, such as objectives, scope, and the location(s) and duration of the audit. Auditor competence, education, training, and experience within an industry are key components to ensuring the audit is effective.

Management systems audits can be performed either on-site or virtually. On-site audits will involve in-person interaction, whereas virtual audits require no in-person interaction. On-site audits can be performed at the auditee's location(s). Virtual audits can occur at any location.

The process approach to auditing is a requirement for all ISO management system standards in accordance with ISO/IEC directives. Auditors should understand that the output of one department is the input to another department. Auditors must understand the PDCA process, which involves the following: people, methods, materials, measures, equipment, and environment. Auditors should apply professional judgment during the audit process and focus on successful implementation of the quality management system rather than searching for specific words from the standard. Professional judgment should be utilized to determine whether the intent of the clause has been met. Process output is important. However, the results of the management system and its performance are what really counts.

Audit objective evidence will demonstrate whether the requirements of the management system are being met. Sampling is implemented when it is not cost effective or practical to examine all information from a process. In other words, the total amount of information may be too much to sample every item of the population. Judgment-based sampling relies on the experience of the audit team and is not statistically based. When statistical sampling is used, auditors should document the work performed. This should include a description of the population to be sampled, the sampling criterion used for the evaluation (for example, what is an acceptable sample), statistical parameters and methods that were utilized, the number of samples evaluated, and the results attained.

MEDICAL DEVICE SINGLE AUDIT PROGRAM (MDSAP)

MDSAP is a program that permits the consolidation of global inspections over different international regulatory bodies. MDSAP is intended to reduce the resources required for auditing the medical device community. MDSAP offers a single audit that is used in lieu of multiple separate audits or inspections by participating regulatory authorities or their representatives. Therefore, for many medical device manufacturers, MDSAP reduces the overall number of audits or inspections and optimizes the time and resources expended on audit activities.

Currently, there are five countries that are actively participating in MDSAP. These countries include Australia, Brazil, Canada, Japan, and the United States. Manufacturers must ensure their auditing organization is authorized to utilize the MDSAP audit and seek answers to the questions required in the audit process. The MDSAP process will focus on risk management, beginning with management and then including processes, design and development, and document control, similar to an ISO audit.

Australia. The Therapeutic Goods Administration (TGA) will accept an MDSAP certificate to show conformance with ISO 13485. However, it could seek additional supporting information.

Brazil. The ANVISA accepts an MDSAP certificate as an alternative to ANVISA inspection only if a previous ANVISA inspection was in conformance.

Canada. As of January 1, 2019, it is required to attain an MDSAP certificate for Class II, III, and IV medical devices. The Canadian Medical Device Conformity Assessment System (CMDCAS) was transferred to MDSAP. MDSAP is now mandatory in Canada.

Japan. The MDSAP report/certificate can be submitted during pre- and post-market QMS inspection, which exempts some manufacturing locations from on-site inspections and/or permits the manufacturer's marketing holder (MAH) to substitute an MDSAP repot/certificate for a portion of the inspection requirements.

United States. MDSAP reports/certificates are accepted as an alternative to FDA inspections. However, PMA and combination product inspections are excluded from the MDSAP program.

Over three years, the MDSAP cycle is as follows:

Initial audit. This involves the review of documentation in accordance with ISO 13485 and applicable regulations of the specific country. This is also known or identified as a Stage 1 audit. A few weeks after a Stage 1 audit, a Stage 2 audit is executed to review records identified in the manufacturer's procedures. This ensures the products are safe and effective, and conform with applicable performance specifications. A first Stage 1 audit consists of a documentation review and the evaluation of the readiness of the manufacturer to undergo a Stage 2 audit. The purpose of a Stage 2 audit is to determine if all applicable QMS requirements of ISO 13485 and all other applicable regulatory requirements from participating regulatory authorities have been effectively implemented.

Surveillance audit. The initial audit is followed by partial surveillance audits conducted once per year for two consecutive years. This is implemented to ensure conformance of the QMS and to applicable standards and regulations.

Recertification audit. The cycle begins again with a complete re-audit, also referred to as a recertification audit, in the third year. Upon successful certification or recertification audits, auditing organizations will issue MDSAP-specific certification documents stating compliance to ISO 13485 and applicable regulatory requirements.

Remedial action. The auditing organization grades the nonconformances of the audit on a scale of 1-5, where grade 5 is most critical. If the audit identified one or more grade 5 nonconformities, or more than two grade 4 nonconformities, a public health threat, or any fraudulent activity or counterfeit product, the auditing organization shall inform the regulatory authorities within five working days. For grade 4 or 5 nonconformities, manufacturers are expected to provide evidence to the auditing organization of implementation of the remediation actions addressing any grade 4 or 5 nonconformity within 30 days of the audit end date. Auditing organizations are subsequently expected to provide the audit package, which includes the NC grading and exchange form, to a recognizing regulatory authority within 45 days of the end of the audit. MDSAP auditors will perform a follow-up unannounced audit within six to nine months later to verify that the appropriate corrective actions have been effectively implemented, and subsequent follow-up visits are then scheduled.

QUALITY SYSTEM INSPECTION TECHNIQUE (QSIT)

When the quality system regulation became effective June 1, 1997, the FDA recognized the need to change its inspection method and considered a "systems approach" to evaluate a firm's level of compliance. The August 1999 document titled *Guide to Inspections of Quality Systems* was the final output from a two-year reengineering effort that changed the way the FDA conducts inspections of medical device manufacturers. The FDA recognized the need to improve the efficiency and effectiveness of inspections while also maximizing FDA resources and reducing inspection time by conducting more-focused inspections. This inspection strategy is called the quality system inspection technique (QSIT). Under the QSIT approach, an inspection should be completed within four to five days, significantly less than previous inspection times.

Often referred to as a "top-down" approach that evaluates a firm's overall ability to address quality (as opposed to a "bottom-up" approach that begins by looking at one or more individual problems that may point to a failure in the quality system), QSIT breaks the quality system regulation into seven subsystems, of which four subsystems are considered major and three are considered minor. QSIT directs the inspector to focus on specific elements within each major subsystem considered to be key indicators that place responsibility on the firm to self-monitor compliance and take appropriate and timely action to correct product, process, and quality system problems. The FDA concludes the inspection with an overall evaluation of the implemented quality system where managers with executive responsibility are accountable to have demonstrated that they comply with the requirements of the regulation, oversee implementation, provide adequate resources, and ensure the quality system is effectively implemented and maintained.

Applicability

The FDA uses QSIT to conduct medical device quality system/good manufacturing practice (GMP) inspections for both domestic and foreign manufacturers. While the *Guide to Inspections of Quality Systems* provides specific instructions for the inspector, it is designed for use in conjunction with the following FDA references:

- *Compliance Program Guidance Manual for Inspection of Medical Device Manufacturers* (CPGM 7382.845)
- *Investigations Operations Manual* (IOM)
- 21 CFR Parts 820, 803, and 821
- Compliance Policy Guides (CPG) for devices (Subchapter 300)
- *Process Validation: General Principles and Practices,* FDA, January 2011 (currently replaced with GHTF/SG3/N99-10:2004 (Edition 2))

QSIT inspections are preannounced inspections where the FDA may request documentation in advance to minimize on-site inspection time. In the spirit of cooperation with the agency, and to minimize the disruption of an extended on-site inspection, manufacturers are encouraged to provide the documentation for the inspector to review in advance. Documentation requested in advance will be returned to the manufacturer when the on-site inspection begins.

While the primary purpose of the QSIT is for use by the FDA inspector, device manufacturers also use QSIT to conduct internal assessments of their quality system. QSIT does not evaluate every aspect of a firm's quality system and, as a result, is not considered a full quality system audit. QSIT can be an excellent tool to determine a firm's "inspection readiness" but should not be considered an alternative to, or substitute for, internal quality system audits.

Subsystems

The FDA's *Guide to Inspections of Quality Systems* breaks the Quality System Regulation (QSR) into seven subsystems with satellite subsystems under CAPA and production and process controls as applicable. The seven subsystems are categorized as major and minor subsystems as follows:

Major subsystems

1. Management controls
2. Design controls
3. Corrective and preventive action (CAPA)
   a. Medical device reporting
   b. Reports of corrections and removals
   c. Medical device tracking

4. Production and process controls
   a. Sterilization process controls

Minor subsystems

5. Material controls
6. Records/documents/change controls
7. Facility and equipment controls

Management controls, design controls, CAPA, and production and process controls are considered the four major subsystems and are recognized as the foundation of the quality system. An evaluation of the four major subsystems will include the three remaining subsystems (material controls, records/documents/change controls, and facility and equipment controls) depending on their relationship to the activity or process being evaluated.

Each subsystem contains inspectional objectives, a decision flowchart, and narrative discussion for each objective. The narrative states the basic purpose/importance for the subsystem and guides the inspector through each objective in terms of the type of records to review. Links to related subsystems are noted, as well as references to specific FDA policies and compliance programs.

A QSIT inspection will begin and end with management controls. Demonstrating the top-down approach, QSIT directs the inspector to first interview the management representative (or designee) "to obtain an overall view of the management controls subsystem as well as a feel for management's knowledge and understanding of the subsystem." This interview will set the tone for the inspection. Objective 7 under management controls instructs the inspector to stop the review of the management system until the remaining subsystems have been evaluated. The order in which the remaining subsystems are reviewed is also specific: design controls, followed by CAPA, and concluding with production and process controls. Design controls and CAPA intentionally precede production and process controls because the records and data reviewed are factors the inspector will consider when selecting a process to evaluate under the production and process controls subsystem.

Sampling Tables

The *Guide to Inspections of Quality Systems* provides information for using binomial sampling plans, which are included in the document. The inspector is instructed to select a table from the guide based on the level of confidence appropriate to the risk of the device or the records being sampled (that is, Table 1 for 95 percent confidence level, or Table 2 for 99 percent confidence level). While both the bottom-up and the top-down approaches include a review of records, under QSIT the record review is conducted in a more controlled manner.

FDA COMPLIANCE PROGRAM GUIDANCE MANUAL (CPGM) 7382.845

The FDA provides instructions to the field—investigators and compliance officers—using compliance programs. The compliance program for medical devices is contained in the CPGM 7382.845, *Inspection of Medical Device Manufacturers.* This particular compliance program directs when to inspect medical manufacturers, what criteria to use in the inspection, what areas to look into, and what to do if the manufacturer is not compliant. It is important for industry to understand the program to react properly in the event of an inspection. The guidance is also helpful for internal and supplier auditors to help them focus on the same areas as the regulatory agency.

The document described in this chapter is continually being modified. The following generally describe the contents of each section, but it is very important to review the most current version and become familiar with its contents. Significant changes may occur without notification.

Major Sections

This section outlines each major section of the compliance program and discusses key elements.

Part I gives a general overview of the compliance program. Specifically, it discusses the QSR, medical device reporting (MDR) regulation, medical device tracking regulation, corrections and removals regulation, and the registration and listing regulation. Each reporting requirement is described in detail in this manual.

Part II covers the implementation of objectives and program management instructions. Each regulation is further discussed, objectives of each regulation are outlined, and inspection scheduling is described. The guidance breaks inspections into priorities, with the priority given to premarket and preclearance inspections, Class III devices manufacturers previously not inspected, compliance follow-up/for-cause inspections, manufacturers of devices considered high risk, and reprocessors of devices originally labeled for single use. Highest priority is given to premarket and preclearance inspections, as well as to Class III device manufacturers that have never been inspected. Class I device manufacturers should receive the lowest inspection priority unless the inspection is for-cause or there is an apparent health hazard. This manual provides a reference to pre-announcement of inspections, how a manufacturer chose the annotation of the FDA 483, and resource instructions.

Part III provides comprehensive and detailed inspectional strategy for determining compliance with the QSR. Inspections should generally be conducted in accordance with QSIT. This part also provides inspection levels as referenced to inspection type and guidance for conducting the inspection. Inspection Level 1 describes an abbreviated inspection consisting of two QSIT major subsystems, that is, CAPA plus production and process controls or design controls. Inspection Level 2 correlates to a comprehensive inspection consisting of all four major QSIT subsystems. Inspection Level 3 for compliance follow-up, special inspections for-cause, and special inspections per the FDA's risk-based work plan are directed by CDRH inspection assignment and elements of QSIT.

Part IV of the compliance program manual describes analytical laboratories, analysis to be conducted, and methods to be used. The FDA has specialist laboratories throughout the country, and laboratories are chosen based on the type of medical device to be tested. This section also outlines sampling plans for sterility.

Part V is the regulatory/administrative follow-up section. It outlines the action to be taken if the inspection has identified noncompliance. Typical regulatory actions include warning letters; however, depending on history, injunctions, citations, detention of product, and civil penalties are possibilities. In addition, a manufacturer in this position will have premarket approvals held until resolution. The following are addressed: quality system regulation, MDR, tracking, corrections and removals, registration and listing, radiation-emitting devices, and exports.

Part VI provides references, program contacts, select FDA organizational charts, and summaries for MDR, tracking, corrections and removals, and sterilization reporting requirements. This manual also provides sources of information, where to obtain the information forms, as well as where to submit the information.

Part II

Medical Device Quality Management System Requirements

Chapter 4

FDA—Code of Federal Regulations (CFR) Title 21

CODE OF FEDERAL REGULATIONS (CFR)[2]

The FDA's legal authority to regulate both medical devices and electronic radiation-emitting products is the Federal Food, Drug, and Cosmetic Act (FD&C Act). The FD&C Act contains provisions, that is, regulatory requirements, that define the FDA's level of control over these products. To fulfill the provisions of the FD&C Act that apply to medical devices and radiation-emitting products, the FDA develops, publishes, and implements regulations.

The *Federal Register* is the official daily publication for rules, proposed rules, and notices of federal agencies and organizations, as well as executive orders and other presidential documents. Proposed rules are initially published in the *Federal Register* for public comment and subsequently published in the Code of Federal Regulations (CFR) after the rule is final. Final regulations published in the *Federal Register* are subsequently placed or codified into the printed edition of the CFR on an annual basis.

The CFR is a codification of the general and permanent rules that were published in the *Federal Register* by the executive departments and agencies of the federal government. It is divided into 50 titles that represent broad areas subject to federal regulation. Most of the FDA's medical device and radiation-emitting product regulations are in Title 21 CFR Parts 800-1299. These final regulations codified in the CFR cover various aspects of design, clinical evaluation, manufacturing, packaging, labeling, and post-market surveillance of medical devices. In addition, the regulations address standards and product reports that apply to radiation-emitting products.

The regulations covered in this chapter are:

4—Regulation of combination products

7—Enforcement policy

11—Electronic records; signatures

58—Good laboratory practice for nonclinical laboratory studies

801—Labeling

803—Medical device reporting

806—Medical devices; reports of corrections and removals

807—Establishment registration and device listing for manufacturers and initial importers of devices

820—Quality system regulation

821—Medical device tracking requirements

830—Unique device identification

21 CFR 4 CURRENT GOOD MANUFACTURING PRACTICE REQUIREMENTS FOR COMBINATION PRODUCTS[3]

A combination product is a product composed of two or more different types of medical products (that is, a combination of a drug, device, and/or biological product with one another). The drugs, devices, and biological products included in combination products are referred to as "constituent parts" of the combination product.

Under 21 CFR 3.2(e), a combination product includes:

- A product comprising two or more regulated components, that is, drug/device, biologic/device, drug/biologic, or drug/device/biologic, that are physically, chemically, or otherwise combined or mixed and produced as a single entity (a "single entity" combination product, such as a prefilled syringe or drug-eluting stent);
- Two or more separate products packaged together in a single package or as a unit and composed of drug and device products, device and biological products, or biological and drug products (a "copackaged" combination product, such as a surgical or first-aid kit);
- A drug, device, or biological product packaged separately that according to its investigational plan or proposed labeling is intended for use only with an approved, individually specified drug, device, or biological product where both are required to achieve the intended use, indication, or effect and where upon approval of the proposed product, the labeling of the approved product would need to be changed (for example, to reflect a change in intended use, dosage form, strength, route of administration, or significant change in dose) (a "cross-labeled" combination product, as might be the case for a light-emitting device and a light-activated drug); or
- Any investigational drug, device, or biological product packaged separately that according to its proposed labeling is for use only with another individually specified investigational drug, device, or biological product where both are required to achieve the intended use, indication, or effect (another type of cross-labeled combination product).

One of the FDA's goals is to ensure the availability of quality drugs, biologics, devices, and combination products that consistently meet applicable requirements and specifications. The drug CGMP and device Quality System Regulation (QSR), as well as the CGMPs for biologics and current good tissue practices for human cells, tissues, or cellular or tissue-based products (HCT/Ps), provide a framework of minimum requirements to help assure product quality. In addition, these regulations call for ongoing assessment of systems and the implementation of corrective actions where appropriate.

For single-entity combination products and copackaged combination products, Part 4 identifies two ways to demonstrate compliance with CGMP requirements. Under the first option, manufacturers demonstrate compliance with all CGMP regulations applicable to each of the constituent parts included in the combination product. Under the second option, manufacturers implement a streamlined approach for combination products that include both a drug and a device by demonstrating compliance with either the drug CGMPs (21 CFR parts 210 and 211) or the device QSR (21 CFR part 820) and also demonstrating compliance with specified provisions from the other of these two sets of CGMP requirements. In addition, for a combination product that includes a biological product, the manufacturer must demonstrate compliance with the CGMP requirements specific to biological products in parts 600 through 680 (21 CFR parts 600 through 680). For a combination product that includes any HCT/P, the manufacturer must demonstrate compliance with the regulations in part 1271 (21 CFR part 1271)—including the current good tissue practice (CGTP) requirements and donor eligibility requirements.

If a streamlined approach is used, the manufacturer must demonstrate compliance with all the relevant provisions of either the drug CGMPs or device QSR, and the provisions specified in 21 CFR 4.4(b) for the other set(s) of CGMP requirements applicable to the product.

Relevant provisions:

- The drug CGMPs and the following provisions from the device QSR in accordance with 21 CFR 4.4(b)(1) (drug CGMP-based streamlined approach):
    - (i) 21 CFR 820.20 Management responsibility
    - (ii) 1 CFR 820.30 Design controls
    - (iii) 21 CFR 820.50 Purchasing controls
    - (iv) 21 CFR 820.100 Corrective and preventive action
    - (v) 21 CFR 820.170 Installation
    - (vi) 21 CFR 820.200 Servicing

Or

- The device QSR and the following provisions from the drug CGMPs in accordance with 21 CFR 4.4(b)(2) (device QSR-based streamlined approach):
    - (i) 21 CFR 211.84 Testing and approval or rejection of components, drug product containers, and closures
    - (ii) 21 CFR 211.103 Calculation of yield

(iii) 21 CFR 211.132 Tamper-evident packaging requirements for over-the-counter (OTC) human drug products
(iv) 21 CFR 211.137 Expiration dating
(v) 21 CFR 211.165 Testing and release for distribution
(vi) 21 CFR 211.166 Stability testing
(vii) 21 CFR 211.167 Special testing requirements
(viii) 21 CFR 211.170 Reserve samples

21 CFR 7 ENFORCEMENT POLICY[4,5]

FDA enforcement policy primarily applies to voluntary recalls of products subject to the FDA's jurisdiction, including any food, drug, and device intended for human or animal use, any cosmetic and biological product intended for human use, and any tobacco product intended for human use.

It is critical for firms in a product distribution chain to be "recall ready," to help minimize public exposure to products that are in violation of the FD&C Act and other laws administered by the FDA.

As appropriate and applicable to its operations, the FDA recommends that a firm make the following preparations:

- *Identify appropriate personnel.* Specific employees should, and sometimes must, be assigned recall-related responsibilities and possess the authority to take the steps needed to implement a product recall when necessary.
- *Train personnel on their responsibilities.* Employees who have been identified to perform recall activities should be trained so they have a thorough understanding of the recall procedures they are being asked to perform.
- *Establish a recall communications plan.* Such a plan should address internal communications, communications with the FDA, and communications to direct accounts or the public in the event that a recall is deemed necessary.
- *Identify any reporting requirements associated with the products.* A firm should know in advance whether its product is associated with any legal or regulatory requirements to make a report to the FDA, or to report a product removal or correction to the FDA.
- *Use adequate product coding.* Medical devices generally have a unique device identifier (UDI) requirement.
- *Maintain distribution records.* Medical devices are required to maintain distribution records.

In addition to these preparations, the FDA recommends that firms consider preparing and maintaining written recall initiation procedures. Written recall initiation procedures help to minimize delays created by uncertainty as to the appropriate actions to take when a decision is made to initiate a recall, help ensure that necessary actions are not overlooked, and may minimize the disruptive effect a recall can have on a firm's business. Such procedures should be considered as part of a more comprehensive "written contingency plan for use in initiating and effecting a recall in accordance with [21 CFR] §§ 7.40 through 7.49, 7.53, and 7.55." (21 CFR 7.59(a)).

A firm's written recall initiation procedures should assign responsibility and describe the steps to perform all actions related to initiating a recall, including the following, as appropriate to the firm or facility:

- Ceasing distribution, shipment, and/or sales of affected product(s).
- Developing a recall strategy. In accordance with 21 CFR 7.42, a recall should be initiated according to a strategy developed by the recalling firm after considering various factors, including, but not limited to, the potential risk to those exposed to the product and the ease in identifying the product.
- Notifying direct accounts about the product being recalled, including what should be done with respect to the recalled product.
- When appropriate, notifying the public about a product that presents a health hazard.

FDA officials may conduct discussions with a firm about a product problem. When the FDA determines that a distributed product violates the law, it may inform the firm and may recommend that it cease distribution and recall the product in accordance with 21 CFR part 7, Subpart C and agency procedures. If the firm voluntarily decides under any circumstances to recall the product, then the action is considered a firm-initiated recall under 21 CFR 7.46.

Under certain circumstances, the FDA may also request a firm to initiate a recall under 21 CFR 7.45. An FDA-requested recall is generally pursued after conducting discussions with a firm. The FDA must make all the following determinations before requesting a recall under 21 CFR 7.45:

1. That a product that has been distributed presents a risk of illness or injury or gross consumer deception;
2. That the firm has not initiated a recall of the product; and
3. That an agency action is necessary to protect the public health and welfare.

21 CFR 11 ELECTRONIC RECORDS; ELECTRONIC SIGNATURES[6]

In March of 1997, the FDA issued final part 11 regulations that provide criteria for acceptance by the FDA, under certain circumstances, of electronic records, electronic signatures, and handwritten signatures executed to electronic records as equivalent to paper records and handwritten signatures executed on paper. These regulations, which apply to all FDA program areas, were intended to permit the widest possible use of electronic technology, compatible with the FDA's responsibility to protect the public health. It is important to realize that the FDA considers records and documents to generally be the same, whereas ISO 13485:2016 defines records as a special type of document.

After part 11 became effective in August 1997, significant discussions ensued among industry, contractors, and the agency concerning the interpretation and implementation of the regulations.

In 2003, the FDA announced the withdrawal of the draft guidance for industry, *21 CFR Part 11; Electronic Records; Electronic Signatures, Electronic Copies of Electronic Records* and withdrawal of the part 11 draft guidance documents on validation, glossary of terms, time stamps, maintenance of electronic records, and CPG 7153.17. The FDA does not intend to reissue these draft guidance documents or the CPG.

Current FDA Approach to Part 11 Requirements

Part 11 will be interpreted narrowly. The FDA is now clarifying that fewer records will be considered subject to part 11. For those records that remain subject to part 11, the FDA intends to exercise enforcement discretion with regard to part 11 requirements for validation, audit trails, record retention, and record copying in the manner described in this guidance and with regard to all part 11 requirements for systems that were operational before the effective date of part 11 (also known as legacy systems).

The FDA will enforce all predicate rule requirements, including predicate rule record and recordkeeping requirements related to the following controls and requirements detailed in §§ 11.10:

- Limiting system access to authorized individuals
- Use of operational system checks
- Use of authority checks
- Use of device checks
- Determination that persons who develop, maintain, or use electronic systems have the education, training, and experience to perform their assigned tasks
- Establishment of and adherence to written policies that hold individuals accountable for actions initiated under their electronic signatures
- Appropriate controls over systems documentation
- Controls for open systems corresponding to controls for closed systems bulleted above (§ 11.30)
- Requirements related to electronic signatures (e.g., §§ 11.50, 11.70, 11.100, 11.200, and 11.300)

Under the narrow interpretation of the scope of part 11, with respect to records required to be maintained under predicate rules or submitted to the FDA, when persons choose to use records in electronic format in place of paper format, part 11 would apply. On the other hand, when persons use computers to generate paper printouts of electronic records, and those paper records meet all the requirements of the applicable predicate rules and persons rely on the paper records to perform their regulated activities, the FDA would generally not consider persons to be "using electronic records in lieu of paper records" under §§ 11.2(a) and 11.2(b). Under this narrow interpretation, the FDA considers part 11 to be applicable to the following records or signatures in electronic format (part 11 records or signatures):

Records that are required to be maintained under predicate rule requirements and that are maintained in electronic format in place of paper format are part 11 records. On the other hand, records (and any associated signatures) that are not required to be retained under predicate rules, but that are nonetheless maintained in electronic format, are not part 11 records. The FDA recommends determining, based on the predicate rules, whether specific records are part 11 records. The FDA recommends documenting such decisions.

In some cases, actual business practices may dictate whether you are using electronic records instead of paper records under § 11.2(a). For example, if a record is required to be maintained under a predicate rule and you use a computer to generate a paper printout of the electronic records, but you nonetheless rely on the electronic record to perform regulated activities, the agency may consider you to be using the electronic record instead of the paper record. That is, the agency may take your business practices into account in determining whether part 11 applies. Accordingly, the FDA recommends that, for each record required to be maintained under predicate rules, you determine in advance whether you plan to rely on the electronic record or paper record to perform regulated activities. The FDA recommends documenting this decision (for example, in a standard operating procedure (SOP), or specification document).

Records submitted to the FDA, under predicate rules (even if such records are not specifically identified in agency regulations) in electronic format are part 11 records. However, a record that is not itself submitted, but is used in generating a submission, is not a part 11 record unless it is otherwise required to be maintained under a predicate rule, and it is maintained in electronic format.

Electronic signatures that are intended to be the equivalent of handwritten signatures, initials, and other general signings required by predicate rules are part 11 signatures. Part 11 signatures include electronic signatures that are used, for example, to document the fact that certain events or actions occurred in accordance with the predicate rule (for example, approved, reviewed, and verified).

Electronic Signatures

Each electronic signature must be unique to one individual and must not be reused by, or reassigned to, anyone else. The identity of the individual must be verified. Persons using electronic signatures must certify to the FDA that the electronic signatures in their system are intended to be the legally binding equivalent of traditional handwritten signatures. The certification is submitted in paper form and signed with a traditional handwritten signature.

Signature Manifestations

Signed electronic records must contain: (1) the name of the signer; (2) the date and time of the signing; and (3) the meaning of the signature, such as author, reviewer, or approver. This information is also to be provided with all readable forms of the electronic records that are accessible electronically or in printed form.

Signature/Record Linking

Electronic signatures and handwritten signatures that are executed to electronic records must be linked to the record to ensure they cannot be copied or deleted.

Many commercial systems are being offered today to support electronic records and electronic signatures. It is recommended that the requirements of 21 CFR Part 11 be used to evaluate potential vendors to see how well their systems satisfy these requirements. As the use of electronic signatures adds additional requirements, most companies have elected to comply first with the electronic record elements and address electronic signature in subsequent phases of implementation.

21 CFR 58 GOOD LABORATORY PRACTICE FOR NONCLINICAL LABORATORY STUDIES[7]

The preamble to part 58 generally discusses when good laboratory practice (GLP) for nonclinical laboratory studies applies and lists certain limitations regarding the scope, including the following:

1. GLP applies only to nonclinical laboratory studies submitted in support of a research or marketing application for a regulated product;
2. GLP does not apply to studies utilizing human subjects, human specimens, clinical studies, or field trials in animals;
3. The scope is limited to safety studies (functionality studies are excluded); and
4. The scope is confined to studies performed on animals, plants, microorganisms, or subparts thereof.

The GLP regulations apply to nonclinical laboratory studies supporting research or marketing applications for FDA-regulated products (21 CFR 58.1). These regulations set forth the minimum basic requirements for study conduct, personnel, facilities, equipment, written protocols, operating procedures, study reports, and a system of quality assurance oversight for each study to help assure the safety of FDA-regulated products.

A nonclinical laboratory study is an in-vivo or in-vitro experiment in which a test article is studied prospectively in a test system under laboratory conditions to determine its safety (21 CFR 58.3(d)). A test article is a medical device for human use, or any other article subject to regulation under the FD&C Act or under sections 351 and 354-360F of the Public Health Service Act. A test system is any animal, plant, microorganism, or subparts thereof to which the test or control article is administered or added for study. Examples of nonclinical laboratory studies include in-vitro and in-vivo biocompatibility testing and animal studies used to evaluate the potential for adverse responses to a medical device. Bench tests, such as chemical or physical testing, and any other studies that do not involve use of an animal, plant, or microorganism, are not included. GLP regulations include nonclinical laboratory studies that support research or marketing applications across medical products, including devices marketed under section 510(k) of the FD&C Act, PMAs, and product development protocols under section 515 of the FD&C Act and HDEs and IDEs under section 520 of the FD&C Act.

The GLP regulations sets out details in the following areas:

- General provisions, including scope, definitions, applicability, and inspection
- Organization and personnel, including testing facility management, study director, and quality assurance unit
- Facilities related to animal care, handling test and control articles, laboratory operation areas, and specimen and data storage
- Equipment design and maintenance/calibration of equipment
- Testing facilities operation with SOPs, reagents and solutions, and animal care
- Test and control articles characterization, handling, and mixtures of articles with carriers
- Protocol for and conduct of a nonclinical laboratory study
- Records and reports of nonclinical laboratory study results, storage and retrieval of records, and retention of records
- The disqualification of testing facilities and their reinstatement

21 CFR 801 LABELING[8,9,10,11]

The general labeling requirements for medical devices are contained in 21 CFR Part 801, Subpart A. Subparts B, C, D, E, and H specify the requirements for unique device identification, over-the counter devices, exemptions, and special requirements for specific devices; additionally, subparts F through G are reserved. Subpart H—Special Requirements for Specific Devices is not covered under the scope of this manual. Labeling of in-vitro diagnostic products is addressed in 21 CFR § 809.10 and in other parts this handbook.

- Subpart A—General Labeling Provisions, deals with general definitions and label requirements.
- Subpart B—Labeling Requirements for Unique Device Identification, deals with the UDI Information on a label.

- Subpart C—Labeling Requirements for Over-the-Counter Devices, specifies items related to the principal display panel, identity, net quantity, and warning for ozone-depleting propellants.
- Subpart D—Exemptions from Adequate Directions for Use, details information about prescription devices, IVD products, devices for research or analysis, and expiration of exemptions.
- Subpart E—Other Exemptions, addresses devices for processing, labeling, or repacking.

Subpart A—General Labeling Provisions

The label of a device shall contain the name and place of business of the manufacturer, packer, or distributor, including the street address, city, state, and zip code. If the firm's street address is in the local telephone directory, the street address can be omitted. If the firm listed on the label is not the manufacturer, the firm information must be qualified by an appropriate statement such as "Manufactured for…" or "Distributed by…." The detailed regulation should be consulted for assurance of compliance.

Meaning of "Intended Uses"

The words "intended uses" or words of similar import in § 801.5, 801.119, and 801.122 refer to the objective intent of the persons legally responsible for the labeling of devices. Intended use defines what the labeling says the device is to be used for, while indications for use defines under what circumstances or conditions one would use that particular product. The intent is determined by such persons' expressions or may be shown by the circumstances surrounding the distribution of the article. This objective intent may, for example, be shown by labeling claims, advertising matter, or oral or written statements by such persons or their representatives. It may be shown by the circumstances that the article is, with the knowledge of such persons or their representatives, offered and used for a purpose for which it is neither labeled nor advertised. The intended uses of an article may change after it has been introduced into interstate commerce by its manufacturer. If, for example, a packer, distributor, or seller intends an article for different uses than those intended by the person from whom the devices were received, such packer, distributor, or seller is required to supply adequate labeling in accordance with the new intended uses. But if a manufacturer knows, or has knowledge of, facts that would give him or her notice that a device introduced into interstate commerce by him or her is to be used for conditions, purposes, or uses other than the ones for which he or she offers it, he or she is required to provide adequate labeling for such a device that accords with such other uses to which the article is to be put.

Adequate Directions for Use

"Adequate directions for use" means directions under which the layman can use a device safely and for the purposes for which it is intended. Directions for use may be inadequate because they insufficiently describe the indications for use, including dosage, frequency and duration, route or method, cleaning and reuse or single use and disposal. Subpart D provides exemptions from the requirement for adequate directions for use. Generally, the exemption is for Rx or prescription devices, or devices for which directions for use are not needed.

Misleading Statements

A device is misbranded if it makes a false or misleading statement or is labeled incorrectly.

Prominence of Required Label Statements

A word, statement, or other required information may lack the required prominence and conspicuousness for the following reasons:

- If it fails to appear on the part or panel that is displayed under customary conditions of purchase
- If the package contains sufficient space and the required information fails to appear on two or more panels, each of which is designed to render it likely to be displayed under customary conditions of purchase
- Failure to extend required labeling over package space provided
- Lack of sufficient label space for required labeling due to placement of nonrequired labeling of the package
- Smallness or style of type, insufficient contrast between labeling and package background, designs that obscure labeling, or overcrowding of labeling renders it unreadable

Regulatory Requirement 21 CFR § 801.16 Medical Devices; Spanish-Language Version of Certain Required Statements

If devices restricted to prescription use only are labeled solely in Spanish for distribution in the Commonwealth of Puerto Rico where Spanish is the predominant language, such labeling is authorized under 21 CFR § 801.15(c).

Format of Dates Provided on a Medical Device Label

In general, whenever the label of a medical device includes a printed expiration date, date of manufacture, or any other date intended to be brought to the attention of the user of the device, the date must be presented in the following format: The year, using four digits; followed by the month, using two digits; followed by the day, using two digits; each separated by hyphens. For example, January 2, 2014, must be presented as 2014-01-02.

Subpart B—Labeling Requirements for Unique Device Identification

In general, the label of every medical device shall bear a unique device identifier (UDI) that meets the requirements of this subpart and part 830 of this chapter, and every device package shall bear a UDI that meets the requirements of this subpart and part 830 of this chapter.

A UDI is a unique numeric or alphanumeric code that generally consists of a device identifier (DI) and a production identifier (PI). The DI is a mandatory, fixed portion of a UDI that identifies the labeler and the specific version or model of a device.

The PI is a conditional, variable portion of a UDI that identifies one or more of the following when included on the label of a device:

- Lot or batch number within which a device was manufactured
- Serial number of a specific device
- Expiration date of a specific device
- Date a specific device was manufactured
- Distinct identification code required by § 1271.290(c) for a human cell, tissue, or cellular and tissue-based product (HCT/P) regulated as a device

The device labeler must provide the UDI in two forms on labels and packages:

- Easily readable plain text
- Machine-readable form that uses automatic identification and data capture (AIDC) technology

The UDI rule also requires specified product information be submitted to the FDA's Global Unique Device Identification Database (GUDID). Most of this information in GUDID will be made available to the public. GUDID includes a standard set of basic identifying elements for each device with a UDI and contains ONLY the DI, which serves as the key to obtain device information in the database. GUDID does not include the PI.

Subpart C—Labeling Requirements for Over-the-Counter Devices

The term principal display panel, as it applies to over-the-counter devices in package form and as used in this part, means the part of a label that is most likely to be displayed, presented, shown, or examined under customary conditions of display for retail sale. The principal display panel of an over-the-counter device in package form shall bear as one of its principal features a statement of the identity of the commodity.

The label of an over-the-counter device in package form shall bear a declaration of the net quantity of contents. This shall be expressed in the terms of weight, measure, numerical count, or a combination of numerical count and weight, measure, or size.

All over-the-counter devices containing or manufactured with chlorofluorocarbons, halons, carbon tetrachloride, methyl chloride, or any other Class 1 substance designated by the Environmental Protection Agency (EPA) shall carry warnings.

Subpart D—Exemptions from Adequate Directions for Use

A device is exempt from requirements for adequate directions for use when all the following conditions are met:

- The device is in the possession of a person, or his or her agents or employees, regularly and lawfully engaged in the manufacture, transportation, storage, or wholesale or retail distribution of such device; or in the possession of a practitioner, such as physicians, dentists, and veterinarians, licensed by law to use or order the use of such device; and is to be sold only to or on the prescription or other order of such practitioner for use in the course of his or her professional practice.
- The label of the device, other than surgical instruments, bears the symbol statement "Rx only" or "[rx] only" or the statement "Caution: Federal law restricts this device to sale by or on the order of a ___", the blank to be filled with the word "physician," "dentist," "veterinarian," or with the descriptive designation of any other practitioner licensed by the law of the state in which the practitioner practices to use or order the use of the device; and the method of its application or use.
- Labeling on or within the package from which the device is to be dispensed bears information for use, including indications, effects, routes, methods, and frequency and duration of administration, and any relevant hazards, contraindications, side effects, and precautions under which practitioners licensed by law to administer the device can use the device safely and for the purpose for which it is intended, including all purposes for which it is advertised or represented. Such information may be omitted from the dispensing package only if the article is a device for which directions, hazards, warnings, and other information are commonly known to practitioners licensed by law to use the device.

A device shall be exempt from section 502(f)(1) of the act insofar as adequate directions for common uses thereof are known to the ordinary individual.

A device intended for processing, repacking, or use in the manufacture of another drug or device shall be exempt from section 502(f)(1) of the act if its label bears the statement "Caution: For manufacturing, processing, or repacking" (See also 21 CFR 801.150).

A device subject to 801.109 shall be exempt from section 502(f)(1) of this act if shipped or sold to, or in the possession of, persons regularly and lawfully engaged in instruction in pharmacy, chemistry, or medicine not involving clinical use, or engaged in law enforcement, or in research not involving clinical use, or in chemical analysis, or physical testing, and is to be used only for such instruction, law enforcement, research, analysis, or testing.

Subpart E—Other Exemptions

A shipment or other delivery of a device that is to be processed, labeled, or repacked, in substantial quantity at an establishment other than that where originally processed or packed, shall be exempt, during the time of introduction into and movement in interstate commerce and the time of holding in such establishment, from compliance with the labeling and packaging requirements if various conditions are met, including that such shipment or delivery is made to such establishment under a written agreement. Additional details of such agreements are found in 801.150 (b) to 801.150 (e).

Advertising

According to an appellate court decision: "Most, if not all advertising, is labeling. The term 'labeling' is defined in the FD&C Act as including all printed matter accompanying any article. Congress did not, and we cannot, exclude from the definition printed matter which constitutes advertising."

21 CFR 803 MEDICAL DEVICE REPORTING[12,13,14,15]

The statutory authority for the medical device reporting (MDR, not to be confused with the EU's medical device regulation) regulation is section 519(a) of the FD&C Act. The final MDR regulation for user facilities was published in the *Federal Register* on December 11, 1995. On July 31, 1996, the new MDR regulation became effective for user facilities and device manufacturers. The FDA Modernization Act of 1997 (FDAMA) changes to medical device adverse event reporting became effective on February 19, 1998. On January 26, 2000, the changes to the implementing regulations, 21 CFR § 803, were published in the *Federal Register* to reflect these amendments in the act.

The MDR regulation provides a mechanism that allows the FDA, as well as the device manufacturer, to identify and monitor adverse events (deaths and serious injuries) and certain malfunctions involving medical devices. The MDR regulation also includes adverse event reporting and recordkeeping requirements for medical device user facilities (for example, a hospital, ambulatory surgical facility, nursing home, outpatient diagnostic facility, outpatient treatment facility), importers of medical devices, and medical device distributors.

Manufacturers, including foreign manufacturers, of legally marketed medical devices in the United States, are required to:

- Submit to the FDA reports of MDR reportable events involving their medical devices [21 CFR 803.10(c) and 803.50]
- Develop, maintain, and implement written procedures for the identification and evaluation of all medical device events (for example, malfunctions, serious injuries, and deaths) to determine whether the event is an MDR reportable event [21 CFR 803.17]
- Establish and maintain complete files for all complaints concerning medical device events [21 CFR 803.18]

A manufacturer of medical devices is required to submit reports to the FDA of a reportable death, serious injury, or device malfunction [21 CFR 803.10(c)]. A reportable death, serious injury, or malfunction is based on information a manufacturer receives or otherwise becomes aware of, from any source, that reasonably suggests that one of its marketed devices:

- May have caused or contributed to a death or serious injury [21 CFR 803.3 and 803.50]
- Malfunctioned, and the malfunction of the device or a similar device marketed by the manufacturer would be likely to cause or contribute to a death or serious injury if the malfunction were to recur [21 CFR 803.3 and 803.50].

MDR reportable events generally must be submitted to the FDA within 30 calendar days after the day one becomes aware of the event [21 CFR 803.10 and 803.50] and are referred to in this guidance document as "30-day reports" or "initial reports." Under some circumstances, a medical device report is required to be submitted within five work days after the day one becomes aware of the need to submit such a report [21 CFR 803.10 (c)(2) and 803.53].

Reports required to be submitted within five work days are referred to as "five-day reports." A "work day" is Monday through Friday, except federal holidays [21 CFR 803.3]. A "manufacturer" is any person who manufactures, prepares, propagates, compounds, assembles, or processes a device by chemical, physical, biological, or other procedure [21 CFR 803.3]. The term includes any person who:

- Repackages or otherwise changes the container, wrapper, or labeling of a device in furtherance of the distribution of the device from the original place of manufacture;
- Initiates specifications for devices manufactured by a second party for subsequent distribution by the person initiating the specifications; or
- Manufactures components or accessories that are medical devices and that are: (1) ready to be used and are intended to be commercially distributed and intended to be used as is, or (2) processed by a licensed practitioner or other qualified person to meet the needs of a particular patient.

All manufacturers of legally marketed medical devices in the United States, including foreign manufacturers who export devices to the United States, are subject to the MDR regulation and must submit required reports. U.S. manufacturers of medical devices that are not cleared or approved in the United States, but are exported to foreign locations, are also subject to the MDR regulation. Any person who reprocesses a single-use device for reuse in human beings becomes the manufacturer of the device and is subject to all the requirements applicable to the original manufacturer, including the requirements of the MDR regulation.

Following are excerpts from the MDR regulation:

As a manufacturer, you are considered to have "become aware" of an event whenever [21 CFR 803.3]:

- Any of your employees become aware of information that reasonably suggests that an event is required to be reported in a 30-day report or in a five-day report that we have requested from you; or
- Any of your employees with management or supervisory responsibilities over persons with regulatory, scientific, or technical responsibilities (including consultants or contractors) or whose duties relate to the collection and reporting of adverse events, becomes aware from any information (including any trend analysis) that an MDR reportable event(s) necessitates remedial action to prevent an unreasonable risk of substantial harm to the public health. In this case, you must submit a report no later than five work days after the day you become aware.

MDR procedures should identify the roles and responsibilities of contractors or consultants who review and process complaints.

The Quality System Regulation (QSR) requires manufacturers to have a formally designated unit to receive, review, and evaluate complaints [21 CFR 820.198(a)]. Manufacturers who are subject to the QSR should ask all their employees to forward device-related complaints to that unit in a timely manner. All device-related complaints must be reviewed to determine whether the complaint represents an MDR reportable event [21 CFR 803.18(e) and 820.198].

Information that "reasonably suggests" that an MDR reportable event has occurred means any information, including professional, scientific, or medical facts, observations, or opinions, that would result in a reasonable conclusion that a device has caused or may have caused or contributed to an MDR reportable event [21 CFR 803.20(c)]. "Caused or contributed" to a death or serious injury means that a death or serious injury was or may have been attributed to a medical device or that a medical device was or may have been a factor in a death or serious injury, including events occurring as a result of [21 CFR 803.3]:

1. Failure;
2. Malfunction;
3. Improper or inadequate design;
4. Manufacture;
5. Labeling; or
6. User error.

An MDR submission must use an electronic equivalent of Form 3500A that is approved by the FDA [21 CFR 803.11 and 803.14] and must include all information that is able to be obtained. If the MDR report omits any required information, it must explain why this information was not provided and the steps taken to attempt to obtain this information.

Adverse Event Codes[16]

The FDA MDR adverse event codes are collectively a system of codes, terms, and definitions used to describe and categorize medical device adverse events. They are primarily used to complete MDRs. They are divided into six separate types, each of which is organized hierarchically. In addition, the FDA MDR adverse event codes are related to two other coding systems: the National Cancer Institute Thesaurus (NCIt) and the International Medical Device Regulators Forum (IMDRF) Adverse Event Reporting terminologies.

The FDA believes manufacturers have a responsibility to inform all employees, including marketing, sales, engineering, manufacturing, regulatory, legal, installation, and service personnel, to immediately forward adverse event information to the appropriate person appointed by those entities to submit MDR reports. Thus, the FDA generally considers that a manufacturer becomes aware of an adverse event whenever any employee becomes aware of an adverse event. Employees should be trained to properly identify, collect, and report complaints to a formally designated complaint handling unit.

If the complaint information requires further investigation to determine if the event is MDR reportable, then an investigation should be conducted for the purpose of gathering enough evidence to support the decision to submit or not to submit an MDR report. This should be completed in a timely manner. Once a determination is made that the event is MDR reportable, it must be submitted within the required time frame.

An injury must meet the definition of "serious injury" in 21 CFR 803.3 for an event to be reportable as a serious injury. A serious injury is an injury or illness that [21 CFR 803.3]:

- Is life threatening;
- Results in permanent impairment of a body function or permanent damage to a body structure; or
- Necessitates medical or surgical intervention to preclude permanent impairment of a body function or permanent damage to a body structure.

"Permanent" means irreversible impairment or damage to a body structure or function, excluding trivial impairment or damage [21 CFR 803.3]. Note that not all cosmetic damage will be considered trivial. Furthermore, a life-threatening injury meets the definition of serious injury, regardless of whether the threat was "temporary."

It should also be noted that a device does not have to malfunction for it to cause or contribute to a serious injury. Even though a device may function properly, it can still cause or contribute to a death or serious injury.

"Malfunction" means the failure of a device to meet its performance specifications or otherwise perform as intended [21 CFR 803.3]. Performance specifications include all claims made in the labeling for the device.

The FDA presumes that once a malfunction has occurred it will recur. In the preamble to the 1995 MDR final rule, the FDA stated that a malfunction is reportable if any one of the following is true:

- The chance of a death or serious injury occurring as a result of a recurrence of the malfunction is not remote;
- The consequences of the malfunction affect the device in a catastrophic manner that may lead to a death or serious injury;
- The malfunction results in the failure of the device to perform its essential function and compromises the device's therapeutic, monitoring, or diagnostic effectiveness, which could cause or contribute to a death or serious injury or other significant adverse device experiences required by regulation. (The essential function of a device refers not only to the device's labeled use but also to any use widely prescribed within the practice of medicine.);
- The malfunction involves:
  - a long-term implantor;
  - a device that is considered to be life supporting or life sustaining and thus is essential to maintaining human life; or
  - the manufacturer takes, or would be required to take, an action under section 518 or 519(g)10 of the FD&C Act as a result of the malfunction of the device or other similar devices.

The malfunction of a long-term implant is reportable only when the malfunction would be likely to cause or contribute to a death or serious injury if it were to recur.

Malfunctions that are not likely to cause or contribute to a death or serious injury if they recur do not have to be reported.

A malfunction that is or can be corrected during routine service or device maintenance is considered to be an MDR reportable event if the recurrence of the malfunction is likely to cause or contribute to a death or serious injury. The fact that such a malfunction may be corrected does not change the fact that the device failed to meet its performance specifications or otherwise perform as intended.

The FDA generally considers a device to be "similar" to another device if the devices have the same:

- Basic design and performance characteristics related to device safety and effectiveness; and
- Intended use and function; and
- Device classification and product code.

Devices that differ only in minor features unrelated to safety or effectiveness can be considered similar devices. Other factors that are used to determine whether devices are similar include: brand name, common name, and whether the devices were introduced into commercial distribution under the same premarket notification 510(k) (see 21 CFR Part 807) or the same premarket approval (PMA) application number (see 21 CFR Part 814).

The FDA considers the failure of a diagnostic device to be reportable when it indirectly causes or contributes to, or is a factor in, a death or serious injury, or would be likely to, if the failure were to recur.

Basic Requirements for Importers

An "importer" is any person who imports a device into the United States and who furthers the marketing of the device from the original place of manufacture to the person who makes final delivery or sale to the ultimate user of the device. It should be noted, however, that a person who repackages or otherwise changes the container, wrapper, or labeling of the device or device package is considered to be a manufacturer of the device [21 CFR 803.3].

Importers are required to submit MDR reportable events within 30 calendar days after the day they become aware of a reportable event, as follows:

- Reports of device-related deaths and serious injuries must be reported to the FDA and to the manufacturer [21 CFR 803.10 and 21 CFR 803.40]; and
- Reports of device-related malfunctions must be reported only to the manufacturer [21 CFR 803.10 and 21 CFR 803.40].

Importers are also required to:

- Develop, maintain, and implement written MDR procedures [21 CFR 803.17]; and
- Maintain files related to medical device adverse events [21 CFR 803.18].

Basic Requirements for Distributors

A "distributor" is any person, other than the manufacturer or importer, who furthers the marketing of a device from the original place of manufacture to the person who makes final delivery or sale to the ultimate user [21 CFR 803.3]. It should be noted, however, that, as is the case with importers, a person who repackages or otherwise changes the container, wrapper, or labeling of the device is considered to be a manufacturer of the device. Distributors are only required to establish and maintain device complaint records (files) [21 CFR 803.18(d)].

21 CFR 806 CORRECTIONS AND REMOVALS[17]

Under 21 CFR 806, Medical Devices; Reports of Corrections and Removals, manufacturers and importers are required to make a report to the FDA of any correction or removal of a medical device(s) if the correction or removal was initiated to reduce a risk to health posed by the device or to remedy a violation of the act caused by the device that may present a risk to health. A report must be made even if the event was caused by use error. A report is not required if the information has already been provided to the FDA under Medical Device Reporting (21 CFR 803) or Repurchase, Repairs or Replacement of Electronic Products (21 CFR 1004) or if the corrective or removal action was initiated by an FDA order under Medical Device Recall Authority (21 CFR 810).

Manufacturers and importers must keep records of those corrections and removals that are not required to be reported to the FDA. However, if a report is not required under 21 CFR 806, the firm may voluntarily report under 21 CFR 7.

The definition of "risk to health" under 21 CFR 806 tracks the definitions of Class I and Class II recalls in 21 CFR 7.3(m). Therefore, reports of corrections and removals are required for Class I and Class II recalls. Under 21 CFR 806, manufacturers and importers need not report events categorized as Class III recalls under 21 CFR §7; only record keeping requirements would apply.

The following actions are exempt from the reporting requirements:

Actions taken by device manufacturers or importers to improve the performance or quality of a device but that do not reduce a risk to health posed by the device or remedy a violation of the act caused by the device:

- Market withdrawals (§ 806.2(h))
- Routine servicing (§ 806.2(k))
- Stock recoveries (§ 806.2(l))

Who Must Report

Manufacturers and importers are required to report a correction or removal of a product if it involves a risk to health. Only the person who initiates the correction or removal is required to report.

When to Report

The report must be submitted to the FDA within 10 working days from the time the firm initiates the correction or removal. If there is not a "risk to health" involved, a report to the FDA is not required, but the manufacturer or importer must keep a record of the correction or removal.

What to Report—§ 806.10(c)

This section of the regulation identifies the specific information to report including registration number, contact details, device name and intended use, model/lot/serial number, associated illness/injury, actions taken, and a description of the event.

Where to Report

The report may be submitted via the FDA electronic submission software.

Amendments

If, after submitting a report, a manufacturer or importer determines that the same correction or removal should be extended to additional lots or batches of the same device, the manufacturer or importer must amend the original report by submitting an amendment within 10 working days of initiating the extension of the correction or removal [21 CFR 806.10(d)]. The amendment should cite the original report number assigned, all the information required by 21 CFR 806.10(c)(2), and any information required by 21 CFR 806.10(c)(3) through (c)(12) that is different from the information submitted in the original report. The manufacturer or importer must also state what required information is not readily available and a date for when it will be submitted.

Recordkeeping Requirements

The device manufacturer or importer that initiates a correction or removal of a device that is not required to be reported to the FDA (recordable action) must maintain records of the correction or removal. Records must contain brand name, model/lot/serial number, description of event, justification for not reporting, and a copy of all communications regarding the correction or removal.

21 CFR 807 ESTABLISHMENT REGISTRATION AND DEVICE LISTING FOR MANUFACTURERS AND INITIAL IMPORTERS OF DEVICES[18,19,20]

Owners or operators of places of business (also called establishments or facilities) that are involved in the production and distribution of medical devices intended for use in the United States are required to register annually with the FDA. This process is known as establishment registration (Title 21 CFR Part 807).

Congress has authorized the FDA to collect an annual establishment registration fee for device establishments. A detailed list of the types of device establishments that are required to register and pay the fee can be found at "Who Must Register, List and Pay the Fee." The establishment registration fee is not eligible for a reduced small business fee.

Most establishments that are required to register with the FDA are also required to list the devices that are made there and the activities that are performed on those devices. If a device requires premarket approval or notification before being marketed in the United States, then the owner/operator should also provide the FDA premarket submission number (510(k), PMA, PDP, HDE, De Novo).

All registration and listing information must be submitted electronically unless a waiver has been granted.

Registration and listing provide the FDA with the location of medical device establishments and the devices manufactured at those establishments. Knowing where devices are made increases the nation's ability to prepare for and respond to public health emergencies.

The following organizations are required to register per Title 21 CFR Part 807.

Domestic

- Manufacturers/remanufacturers and kit assemblers
- Repackagers/relabelers
- Contract manufacturers/sterilizers

- Specification developers
- Reprocessors of single-use devices
- Complaint handlers
- Initial importers (initial distributors)

Note: In contrast, domestic distributors do not register.

Foreign

- Manufacturers/remanufacturers and kit assemblers
- Repackagers/relabelers
- Contract manufacturers/sterilizers
- Specification developers
- Reprocessors of single-use devices
- Complaint handlers
- Foreign exporters and private label distributors

Note: Applies only if devices are sold in the United States.

Exemptions from Registration and Listing Requirements

- Component manufacturers that provide raw materials and/or components used in the manufacture or assembly of a device
- Manufacturers of devices used solely for veterinary purposes
- Licensed practitioners who manufacture/alter devices solely for use in their practice may not distribute to other practitioners to keep exemption
- Retail establishments that provide devices directly to end users, including pharmacies, surgical supply outlets, etc.

  Note: Shipments must be properly labeled.
- Manufacturers whose devices are used solely in research, teaching, or analysis and not introduced into commercial distribution

When to Register and List

- Initial/first-time registration
  - Domestic establishments—within 30 days of putting a device into commercial distribution
  - Foreign establishments*—prior to exporting to the United States for the first time

    ** Failure to do so may result in shipment detention by Customs/Border Patrol.*

- Initial importers*—prior to importing to the United States for the first time
  - □ only register; do not list
  - □ must identify the manufacturer of each device imported

  ** Failure to do so may result in shipment detention by Customs/Border Patrol.*

- Annual registration and listing certification
  - Establishments must certify that their registration information is complete and accurate
    - □ must be done annually—between October 1 through December 31 of each year
    - □ make any changes as necessary
  - Information may be updated at any time
    - □ strongly recommend if plan to discontinue, resume, or begin marketing/distributing of a device
- For all establishments (domestic/foreign)
  - Pay the annual registration user fee
  - Register the establishment in the FDA Unified Registration and Listing Systems (FURLS)
  - Provide information about the establishment, owner operator, and official correspondent (name, address, phone, email, etc.)
  - Create at least one listing at time of initial registration
    - □ not required for initial importers
    - □ for devices that require a premarket submission, may not do this step until the device is legally marketed
  - Identify all proprietary names under which the product is marketed in the United States
- For foreign establishments only
  - Identify all persons you know of who import or who offer to import your product into the United States
  - Identify a U.S. agent
- For initial importers only
  - Identify manufacturers of the product you import by establishment name, address, establishment registration number, or device listing number
  - All establishments that must register also must list their devices, except initial importers/distributors do not list

    Foreign establishments must list a device before it can be imported into the United States
  - Manufacturer or specification developers must list the device first; then the contract manufacturer or sterilizer may list

- For combination products, identify the type of combination
  - □ for example, device-biologic; device-drug, etc.

Registration and Listing Information

For exempt/pre-amendments devices:

- Product code for the device
- Activities performed at the establishment for the device (for example, manufacture, relabel, etc.)
- Proprietary or brand names under which the device is marketed—may be marked confidential

For devices that require FDA premarket submission:

- Submission number from your clearance/approval letter (for example, K123456, P123456)
- Activities performed at the establishment for the device (manufacture, relabel, etc.)
- Proprietary or brand names under which the device is marketed

Each successfully created listing generates a unique listing number, and all the establishments under an owner operator share the same listing number.

FDA's Unified Registration and Listing System (FURLS) Device Registration and Listing Module (DRLM)

DRLM is a web-based system. All establishments must use the online system unless waiver of electronic entry is granted.

21 CFR § 807 SUBPART E—PREMARKET NOTIFICATION PROCEDURES

Each person who wants to market in the United States, a Class I, II, and III device intended for human use, for which a PMA is not required, must submit a 510(k) to the FDA unless the device is exempt from 510(k) requirements of the FD&C Act and does not exceed the limitations of exemptions in .9 of the device classification regulation chapters (for example, 21 CFR 862.9, 21 CFR 864.9, etc.). There is no 510(k) form; however, 21 CFR 807 Subpart E describes requirements for a 510(k) submission. Before marketing a device, each submitter must receive an order, in the form of a letter, from the FDA that finds the device to be substantially equivalent (SE) and states that the device can be marketed in the United States. This order "clears" the device for commercial distribution (see The 510(k) Program Guidance (/regulatory-information/search-fda-guidance-documents/510k-program-evaluating-substantialequivalence-premarket-notifications-510k)).

A 510(k) is a premarket submission made to the FDA to demonstrate that the device to be marketed is as safe and effective, that is, substantially equivalent, to a legally marketed device (section 513(i)(1)(A) FD&C Act). Submitters must compare their device to one or more similar legally marketed devices and make and support their substantial equivalence claims. A legally marketed device is a device that was legally marketed prior to May 28, 1976 (pre-amendments device), or a device that has been reclassified from Class III to Class II or I, a device that has been found SE through the 510(k) process, or a device that was granted marketing authorization via the De Novo classification process under section 513(f)(2) of the FD&C Act that is not exempt from premarket notification requirements. The legally marketed device(s) to which equivalence is drawn is commonly known as the "predicate." Although devices recently cleared under 510(k) are often selected as the predicate to which equivalence is claimed, any legally marketed device may be used as a predicate. Legally marketed also means the predicate cannot be one that is in violation of the FD&C Act.

Until the submitter receives an order declaring a device SE, the submitter may not proceed to market the device. Once the device is determined to be SE, it can then be marketed in the United States. The SE determination is usually made within 90 days and is made based on the information submitted by the submitter.

Substantial Equivalence

A 510(k) requires demonstration of substantial equivalence to another legally U.S. marketed device. Substantial equivalence means that the new device is as safe and effective as the predicate.

A device is substantially equivalent if, in comparison to a predicate, it:

- has the same intended use as the predicate; and
- has the same technological characteristics as the predicate; or
- has the same intended use as the predicate; and
- has different technological characteristics and does not raise different questions of safety and effectiveness; and
- the information submitted to the FDA demonstrates that the device is as safe and effective as the legally marketed device.

A claim of substantial equivalence does not mean the new and predicate devices need to be identical. The FDA first establishes that the new and predicate devices have the same intended use and any differences in technological characteristics do not raise different questions of safety and effectiveness. The FDA then determines whether the device is as safe and effective as the predicate device by reviewing the scientific methods used to evaluate differences in technological characteristics and performance data. This performance data can include clinical data and non-clinical bench performance data, including engineering performance testing, sterility, electromagnetic compatibility, software validation, biocompatibility evaluation, among other data.

If the FDA determines that a device is not substantially equivalent, the applicant may:

- resubmit another 510(k) with new data, or
- request a Class I or II designation through the De Novo Classification (/medicaldevices/premarket-submissions/de-novo-classification-request) process because the device is considered a Class III, or
- file a reclassification petition, or
- submit a premarket approval application (PMA).

The decision-making flowchart for evaluating substantial equivalence in premarket notifications is shown in Figure 4.1.[21]

The FD&C Act and the 510(k) regulation (807.3) do not specify who must submit a 510(k). Instead, they specify which actions, such as introducing a device to the U.S. market, require a 510(k) submission.

The following four categories of parties must submit a 510(k) to the FDA:

1. *Domestic manufacturers introducing a device to the U.S. market.*

   Finished device manufacturers must submit a 510(k) if they manufacture a device according to their own specifications and market it in the United States. Accessories to finished devices that are sold to the end user are also considered finished devices. However, manufacturers of device components are not required to submit a 510(k) unless such components are promoted for sale to an end user as replacement parts. Contract manufacturers, those firms that manufacture devices under contract according to someone else's specifications, are not required to submit a 510(k).

2. *Specification developers introducing a device to the U.S. market.*

   A specification developer develops the specifications for a finished device but has the device manufactured under contract by another firm or entity. The specification developer submits the 510(k), not the contract manufacturer.

3. *Repackers or relabelers who make labeling changes or whose operations significantly affect the device.*

   Repackagers or relabelers may be required to submit a 510(k) if they significantly change the labeling or otherwise affect any condition of the device. Significant labeling changes may include modification of manuals, such as adding a new intended use, deleting or adding warnings, contraindications, etc. Operations, such as sterilization, could alter the condition of the device. However, most repackagers or relabelers are not required to submit a 510(k).

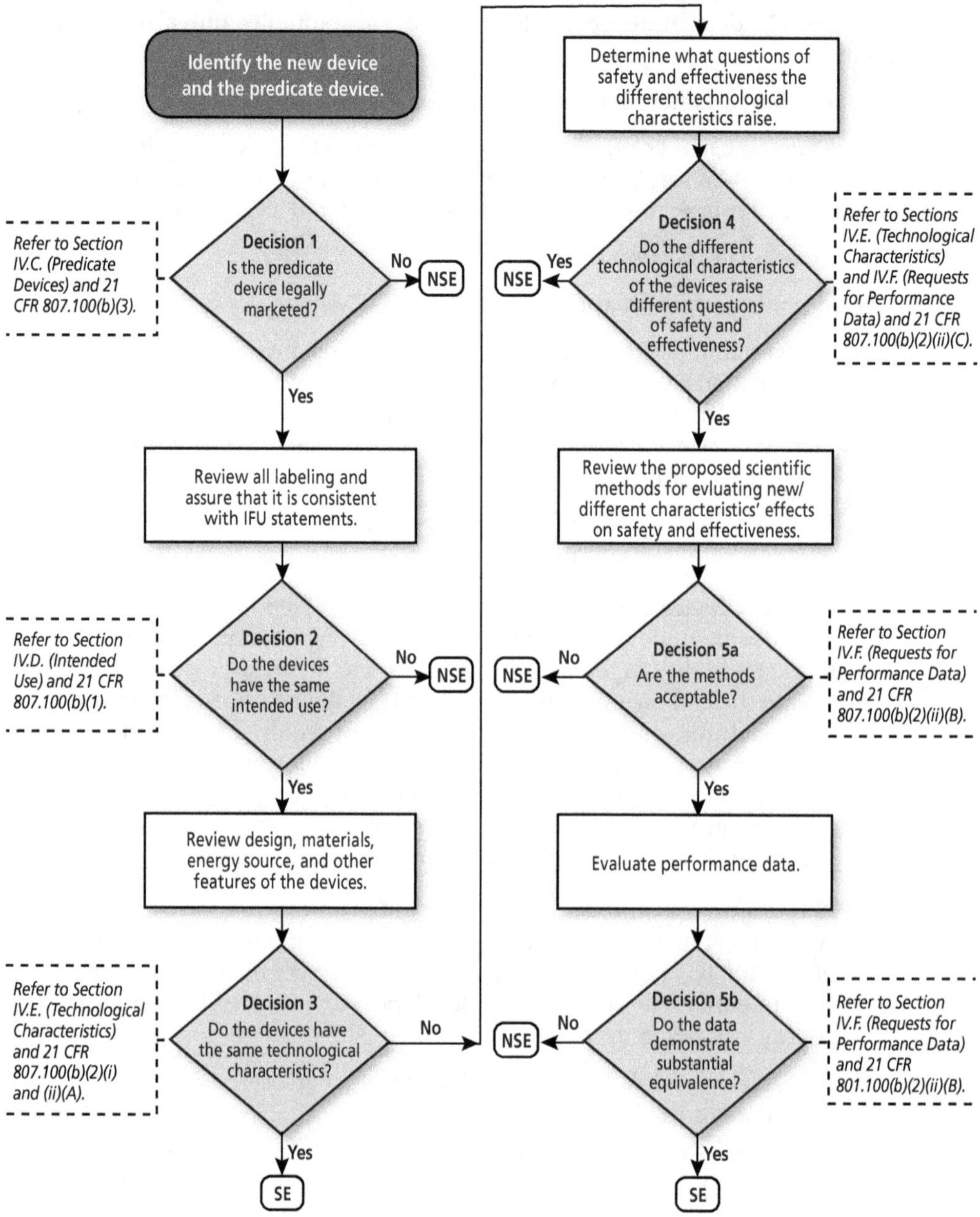

SE = "Substantially Equivalent"
NSE = "Not Substantially Equivalent"
IFU = "Indications For Use"

This flowchart is not intended to be used as a 'standalone' document and should be considered in conjunction with the accompanying text in this guidance.

Figure 4.1 510(k) decision-making flowchart.

4. *Foreign manufacturers/exporters or U.S. representatives of foreign manufacturers/exporters introducing a device to the U.S. market.*

   Please note that all manufacturers (including specification developers) of Class II and III devices and select Class I devices are required to follow design controls (21 CFR 820.30) during the development of their device. The holder of a 510(k) must have design control documentation available for FDA review during a site inspection. In addition, any changes to the device specifications or manufacturing processes must be made in accordance with the QSR (21 CFR 820) and may be subject to a new 510(k). Additional information is found on the web page: "Is a new 510(k) required for a modification to the device?" (/medical-devices/premarket-notification-510k/new-510k-required-modification-device).

510(k) Required

A 510(k) is required when:

1. Unless exempt, introducing a device into commercial distribution (marketing) for the first time. After May 28, 1976 (effective date of the medical device amendments to the FD&C Act), anyone who wants to sell a device in the United States is required to make a 510(k) submission at least 90 days prior to offering the device for sale, even though it may have been under development or clinical investigation before that date. If your device was not marketed by your firm before May 28, 1976, a 510(k) is required.
2. There is a change or modification to a legally marketed device and that change could significantly affect its safety or effectiveness. The burden is on the 510(k) holder to decide whether a modification could significantly affect safety or effectiveness of the device. Any modifications must be made in accordance with the QSR, 21 CFR 820, and recorded in the device master record and change control records. It is recommended that the justification for submitting or not submitting a new 510(k) be recorded in the change control records.

A new 510(k) submission is required for changes or modifications to an existing device, where the modifications could significantly affect the safety or effectiveness of the device or the device is to be marketed for a new or different intended use. See "Is a new 510(k) required for a modification to the device?" (/medical-devices/premarket-notification-510k/new-510k-required-modification-device) for additional information.

510(k) Not Required

The following are examples of when a 510(k) is not required.

1. You sell unfinished devices to another firm for further processing or sell components to be used in the assembling of devices by other firms.

However, if your components are to be sold directly to end users as replacement parts, a 510(k) is required.

2. Your device is not being marketed or commercially distributed. You do not need a 510(k) to develop, evaluate, or test a device. This includes clinical evaluation. Please note that if you perform clinical trials with your device, you are subject to the investigational device exemption (IDE) regulation (21 CFR 812).
3. You distribute another firm's domestically manufactured device. You may place a label on the device, "Distributed by ABC Firm" or "Manufactured for ABC Firm," and sell it to end users without submission of a 510(k).
4. In most cases, if you are a repackager or a relabeler and the existing labeling or condition of the device is not significantly changed. The labeling should be consistent with the labeling submitted in the 510(k) with the same indications for use and warnings and contraindications.
5. Your device was legally in commercial distribution before May 28, 1976, and has not been significantly changed or modified in design, components, method of manufacture, or intended use. These devices are "grandfathered," and you have pre-amendment status documentation to prove this.
6. The device is made outside the United States, and you are an importer of the foreign-made medical device. A 510(k) is not required if a 510(k) has been submitted by the foreign manufacturer and has received marketing clearance. Once the foreign manufacturer has received 510(k) clearance for the device, the foreign manufacturer may export the device to any U.S. importer.
7. Your device is exempted from 510(k) by regulation (21 CFR 862-892). That is, certain Class I or II devices can be marketed for the first time without having to submit a 510(k). A list of the Class I and II exempted devices can be found in "Medical Device Exemptions 510(k) and GMP Requirements." However, if the device exceeds the limitations of exemptions in .9 of the device classification regulation chapters (for example, 21 CFR 862.9, 21 CFR 864.9), such as the device has a different intended use or operates using a different fundamental scientific technology than a legally marketed device in that generic type of device, or the device is a reprocessed single-use device, then a 510(k) must be submitted to market the new device.

21 CFR 820 QUALITY SYSTEM REGULATION

The Quality System Regulation (QSR), promulgated as 21 CFR 820, became effective June 1, 1997, replacing the 1978 Good Manufacturing Practice (GMP) requirements for medical devices. The regulation provides a framework of basic requirements for manufacturers to follow and includes requirements related to methods used in, and facilities and controls used for, the design, manufacture, packaging, labeling, storage, installation, and servicing of medical devices for human use. Refer to Chapter 10 for detailed discussion of the QSR.

21 CFR 821 MEDICAL DEVICE TRACKING REQUIREMENTS[22,23]

Summary

Manufacturers are required to track certain devices from their manufacture through the distribution chain when they receive an order from the FDA to implement a tracking system for a certain type of device. The purpose of device tracking is to ensure manufacturers of certain devices establish tracking systems that will enable them to promptly locate devices in commercial distribution. Tracking information may be used to facilitate notifications and recalls ordered by the FDA in the case of serious risks to health presented by the devices.

Introduction

Manufacturers must adopt a method of tracking devices whose failure would be reasonably likely to have serious, adverse health consequences; or which is intended to be implanted in the human body for more than one year; or are life-sustaining or life-supporting devices used outside of a device user facility. The required tracking information for a manufacturer of a tracked device is identified at 21 CFR 821.25. The required tracking information for a distributor of a tracked device is identified at 21 CFR 821.30.

Effective, February 19, 1998, the tracking requirement was changed to eliminate automatic mandatory tracking for certain devices; instead, the FDA has discretion to order manufacturers of certain types of Class II or Class III devices to initiate a program to track their medical devices down to the patient level. The tracking provision is intended to ensure manufacturers can expeditiously remove potentially dangerous or defective devices from the market and/or notify patients of significant device problems. Tracking augments the FDA's authority to order mandatory recalls and require notification of health professionals and patients regarding unreasonable risk of substantial harm associated with a device.

Requirements

Manufacturers of a tracked device must establish a written standard operating procedure (SOP), which includes a method for tracking the device throughout distribution and a quality assurance program including audit procedures. Final distributors of these devices will be required to provide manufacturers with patient information. Device tracking is required for the useful life of the device.

The types of devices subject to a tracking order may include any Class II or Class III device:

> The failure of which would be reasonably likely to have serious adverse health consequences; which is intended to be implanted in the human body for more than one year; or which is intended to be a life-sustaining or life-supporting device used outside a device user facility.

Patients who received a tracked device may refuse to release, or refuse permission to release, their name, address, social security number, or other identifying information for the purpose of tracking.

When a new device receives FDA clearance or approval for marketing, and is on the tracked devices list, the FDA will issue tracking orders to the manufacturer to confirm the tracking requirements for that device. No tracking obligations exist unless tracking orders have been issued.

The FDA will notify applicable manufacturers, in writing, when a device gets released from tracking requirements.

Manufacturers must have written SOPs that define a method of tracking that will produce the information required by regulation. Tracking methods must provide certain critical information about the location of a tracked device within a short time frame. Manufacturers will have three working days to provide critical information about devices that have not yet been distributed to a patient and 10 working days for devices that have been distributed to patients.

Manufacturers must make sure the tracking program works. Manufacturers must perform audits at six-month intervals for the first three years after receiving tracking orders and then annually after the three years. Audits should verify that the tracking method actually works and that the information collected is accurate so, in the event of a recall, the right persons are notified in a timely fashion. A recognized statistical sampling plan should be used. Audits may be conducted through on-site visits or through some other effective way of communication with the distributors, professionals, and patients.

Tracking methods are subject to FDA inspection, which may include a review of the tracking system. The FDA may review your tracking program to ensure the tracking method actually tracks your device to the end user.

Tracking is no longer required when you have evidence to confirm: (a) that the device has been returned, destroyed, or explanted; or (b) that the patient died.

Refurbishers and remanufacturers of tracked devices that remain in domestic commercial distribution are also subject to tracking requirements and should be able to ensure that the original manufacturer can promptly locate the devices. For devices with an approved PMA that are also subject to a tracking order, the need for continued tracking may be reassessed, at the sponsor's request or by the agency's initiative, 10 years from the date of the original PMA's approval.

While the primary responsibility for assuring a functional tracking system rests with the device manufacturer, any other person, including a device importer or distributer (whether final distributor or multiple distributor) who fails or causes others to fail to comply with the tracking requirements would be considered to be violating sections 301(e) and 301(q)(1)(B) of the FD&C Act.

A manufacturer or distributor that goes out of business is required to notify the FDA at the same time that it notifies any government agency, court, or supplier of the business shutdown. With the notification to the FDA, the manufacturer or distributor must provide the FDA with a complete set of its tracking records and information.

The FDA considers a kit or system assembler to be a distributor. Distributors must notify the manufacturer when a tracked device has been received. Distributors should also ensure, when appropriate, that anyone who receives the kit or system knows that it contains a tracked device. The manufacturer's original labeling should remain on every tracked device included in a kit or system.

User facilities, such as hospitals and nursing homes, have responsibilities as a final distributor when the device is for single use and otherwise have responsibilities as a multiple distributor when the device is for multiple use. For example, a hospital that implants single-use tracked devices is the final distributor of those devices. A hospital outpatient clinic that rents, leases, or loans a multiple-use tracked device is the multiple distributor of those devices.

Patients, but not user facilities, may refuse to provide personal information gathered for device tracking. Such refusals should be documented by the product, model and serial number, and the information provided to the manufacturer. The manufacturer must maintain this record for the useful life of the device. A patient's refusal does not relieve the manufacturer of its obligation to account for the tracked device.

Information on implementation of the medical device tracking regulation, along with a list of devices the FDA ordered to be tracked, can be found in the guidance "Medical Device Tracking—Guidance for Industry and Food and Drug Administration Staff" (March 27, 2014). The current list of devices to be tracked can be found on the FDA's website.

21 CFR 830 UNIQUE DEVICE IDENTIFICATION[24,25,26]

UDI involves both 21 CFR 801 and 21 CFR 830.

Requirements for a Unique Device Identifier

The UDI rule requires a UDI on every device label and package. There are general exceptions to this requirement. Each UDI must be in both easily readable plaintext and in a form that uses automatic identification and data capture (AIDC) technology. The "labeler" has the responsibility for complying with the UDI label, data submission, and records requirements.

Device Identifier (DI)

The device identifier (DI) is a mandatory, fixed portion of the UDI that identifies: (1) the labeler, and (2) the specific model or version of the device. The DI is used to look up information about the device in the database administered by the FDA called the GUDID. Each DI is used to identify only one version or model. A new DI must be assigned if a change is made to the device.

Production Identifier (PI)

A production identifier (PI) is a conditional, variable portion of the UDI. If the following information is included in the device label, that information must also be included in the PI portion of the UDI:

(a) The lot or batch within which a device was manufactured

(b) The serial number of a specific device

(c) The expiration date of a specific device

(d) The date a specific device was manufactured

(e) For an HCT/P regulated as a device, the distinct identification code required by 21 CFR 1271.290(c)

In vitro diagnostic products must comply with both UDI label requirements and the label requirements in 21 CFR 809.10. See Chapter 8 for more details. There are very specific technical requirements for UDIs. FDA-accredited issuing agencies (IAs) are required to issue UDIs that conform to the following ISO standards:

(a) ISO/IEC 15459-2:2006(E), Information technology—Unique identifiers—Part 2: Registration procedures (second edition; March 1, 2006)

(b) ISO/IEC 15459-4:2008(E), Information technology—Unique identifiers—Part 4: Individual items (second edition; July 15, 2008)

(c) ISO/IEC 15459-6:2007(E), Information technology—Unique identifiers—Part 6: Unique identifier for product groupings (first edition; June 15, 2007)

The UDI may use only characters and numbers from the invariant character set of ISO/IEC 646:1991(E), Information technology—ISO 7-bit-coded character set for information interchange (third edition; December 15, 1991).

Format for Dates Provided on a Label (21 CFR 801.18)

If your device label includes a printed expiration date, date of manufacture, or any other date you want brought to the attention of the user, the dates must be presented in a specified format that is consistent with international standards and international practice. This format is: the year, using four digits; followed by the month, using two digits; followed by the day, using two digits; each separated by hyphens. For example, January 2, 2014, must be presented as 2014-01-02.

There are some limited exceptions pertaining to combination products and radiation-emitting products that are listed in 21 CFR 801.18(b). Figure 4.2 is an example of a UDI.

Permanent UDI (21 CFR 801.45)

If your device is intended to be used more than once and intended to be reprocessed before each use, your device must have the UDI permanently marked on the device itself. This permanent UDI may be identical to the UDI that appears on the device label, or it may be a different UDI to distinguish the device from its packaging. The permanent UDI must be in: (1) easily readable plaintext; and/or (2) AIDC form or alternative technology that will provide the UDI of the device on demand.

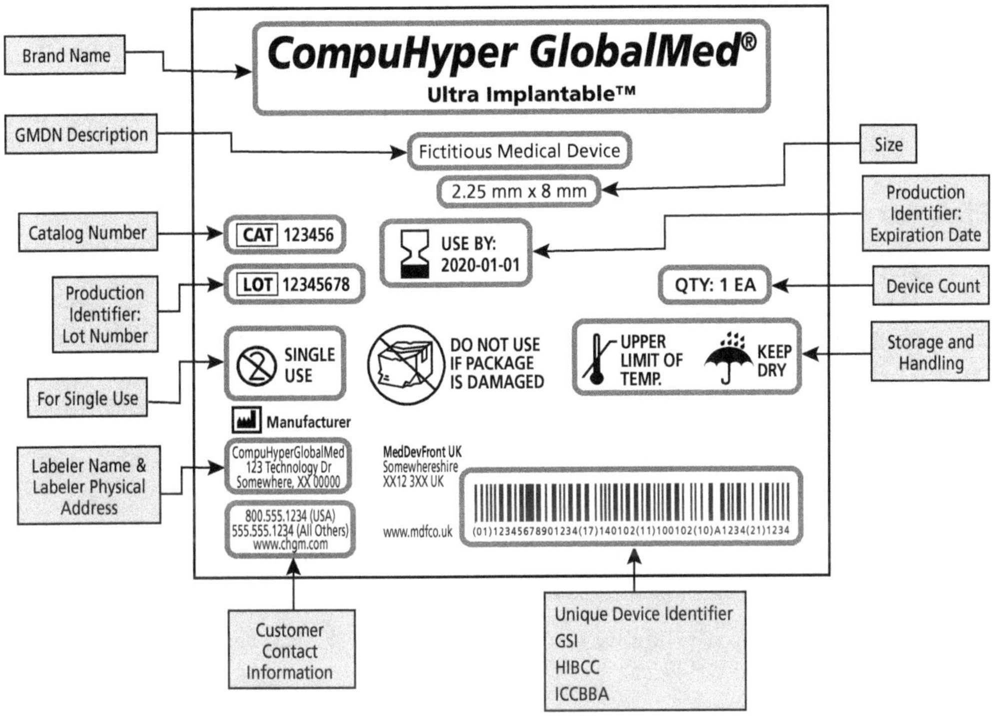

Figure 4.2 Format for unique device identification.

The permanent UDI requirement does not apply if your device that is intended to be used more than once and intended to be reprocessed before each use meets any of the following criteria:

(1) Any type of direct marking would interfere with the safety and effectiveness of the device.

(2) It is not technologically feasible to directly mark the device.

(3) The device is cleared/approved as a single-use device.

(4) The device already has a permanent UDI directly marked on the device.

The basis for the decision must be documented in the design history file required by 21 CFR 820.30(j).

Stand-Alone Software (21 CFR 801.50)

There are no UDI special requirements for a device that contains software as a component of the device, but stand-alone software must be labeled with a UDI. If the stand-alone software is distributed in packaged form, it is subject to the same UDI labeling requirements as any other medical device.

Stand-alone software that is not distributed in packaged form (for example, when downloaded from a website) must also convey the version number in its production identifier.

Stand-alone software that is distributed in both packaged form and in a form that is not packaged may be identified with the same DI.

FDA Accreditation of an Issuing Agency

UDI systems must be operated by an FDA-accredited IA. An IA may charge a labeler a fee for use of the IA for the issuance of UDIs. Each IA operates a system for assignment of UDIs that meets the requirements listed in technical requirements for a UDI (21 CFR 830.20). An IA makes available information concerning its system for assigning UDIs, maintains a list of labelers that use its system for the assignment of UDIs, provides an annual list of labelers to the FDA, and upon request provides the FDA with information on a labeler that employs the IA's system for assigning UDIs.

The FDA accredits IAs. The eligibility and accreditation criteria are set out in 21 CFR 830.100. A private organization may apply for accreditation. The FDA may accredit an organization if the system employed by the organization will:

1. Conform with the ISO standards listed in technical requirements for a UDI (21 CFR 830.20)
2. Be available to all users according to a single set of consistent, fair, and reasonable terms and conditions
3. Protect against conflicts of interests between the organization and labelers

The procedure for FDA initial accreditation and renewal is outlined in 21 CFR 830.110. The initial term of accreditation is three years with renewal terms of seven years. The FDA may suspend or revoke an IA's accreditation if the FDA finds that the IA was guilty of fraud in obtaining its accreditation, failed to fulfill the responsibilities required by the UDI rule, failed to protect against conflicts of interest or has engaged in anticompetitive activity, or has violated the UDI rule or related regulation.

FDA as an Issuing Agency

Under 830.200, under certain conditions, the FDA may act as an IA. When the FDA acts as an IA, any labeler may use the IA services, not only small businesses.

Global Unique Device Identification Database

In general, if a UDI is required for a device or device package, it is required to submit the information to the GUDID electronically.

Information Required (21 CFR 830.310)

For each version or model of a device required to have a UDI on its label, there is a defined list of information to be submitted.

FDA Rejection or Removal of Submitted Information

The FDA may reject or delete that information from GUDID if it does not conform with requirements. It may also reject or remove any device identification data if it has suspended the accreditation of the IA that was used. This does not apply if the IA relinquishes or does not renew its accreditation.

Correction (21 CFR 830.350)

The FDA may provide notification and delete or correct any information submitted to the GUDID that appears to be incorrect or potentially misleading. Corrected information, or an explanation why the information is correct, must be submitted within 30 days from receipt of the notice.

Modifications to Other 21 CFR Provisions

The UDI rule modifies additional sections of 21 CFR so other 21 CFR provisions remain consistent with the provisions, definitions, and language of the UDI rule. Table 4.1 describes modifications made by the UDI rule to other CFR sections that have not otherwise been mentioned.

Table 4.1 UDI modifications to 21 CFR.

Section modified	Modification
803.32	User facilities must include the UDI on the device label or on the device package in individual adverse event report submissions.
803.33	User facility must submit in annual reports the UDI that appears on the device label or the device package.
803.42	Importers must include the UDI on the device label or on the device package in individual adverse event report submissions.
803.52	Manufacturers must include the UDI on the device label or on the device package in individual adverse event report submissions.
806.10	The manufacturer or importer must include on reports of corrections and removals: the UDI that appears on the device label or on the device package, or the device identifier, universal product code (UPC), model, catalog, or code number of the device and the manufacturing lot or serial number of the device or other identification number.

(continued)

Table 4.1 UDI modifications to 21 CFR. *(continued)*

Section modified	Modification
806.20	Records of corrections and removals not required to be reported to the FDA shall contain the UDI, or the device identifier, UPC, model, catalog, or code number of the device and the manufacturing lot or serial number of the device or other identification number.
810.10	The FDA will include the UDI that appears on the device label or on the device package in its cease distribution and notification order.
814.84	The holder of an approved premarket approval shall identify in its periodic report each device identifier currently in use for the device, and each device identifier for the device that has been discontinued since the previous periodic report.
820.120	Labeling shall not be released for storage or use until a designated individual(s) has examined the labeling for accuracy including, where applicable, the correct UDI or UPC, expiration date, control number, storage instructions, handling instructions, and any additional processing instructions.
820.184	Device history records must include any UDI or UPC, and any other device identification(s) and control number(s) used.
820.198	Manufacturers must include in their complaint files any UDI or UPC, and any other device identification(s) and control number(s) used.
820.200	Service reports that represent an event that must be reported to the FDA must include any UDI or UPC and any other device identification(s) and control number(s) used.
821.25	A manufacturer of a tracked device must include the UDI, lot number, batch number, model number, or serial number of the device or other identifier necessary to provide for effective tracking of these devices.
821.30	Persons other than device manufacturers and distributors must include the UDI, lot number, batch number, model number, or serial number of the device or other identifier used by the manufacturer to track the device.
822.9	Class II and III device manufacturers required to conduct post-market surveillance must include both premarket application/submission number and device identifiers in the post-market surveillance plan submission.

Chapter 5

U.S. Requirements (FD&C Act, 201, 301-304, 501-502, 510, 513, 518, 522, 704)

INTRODUCTION

The Federal Food, Drug, and Cosmetic Act (FD&C Act) allows for extensive regulation of medical devices. The FD&C Act currently governs the entire life span of a device, from premarket clearance or approval, through the manufacturing process, subsequent release to the market, and use by a healthcare professional or patient.

The Pure Food and Drug Act, promulgated in 1906, regulated only drugs and not medical devices. After repealing the act in 1938, Congress recast it as the FD&C Act, adding specific provisions for enforcement actions concerning devices. However, the actions were limited to policing post-market activity through prohibition of adulteration and misbranding. The 1938 act did not provide for premarket review or post-market surveillance of devices.

With the passage of the Medical Device Amendments of 1976 (MDA), Congress expanded the FDA's authority to regulate devices. One significant change was a broadened definition of "device." The term included "implement, machine, implant, in vitro reagent, and other similar or related article."[27] Additionally, the MDA increased the conditions that qualified a device for regulation under the FD&C Act. Inclusion in the National Formulary or the U.S. Pharmacopeia (USP), or any supplemental documents, became qualifying criteria. The definition of "device" was also fine-tuned by adding limitations that a device must neither: (1) "achieve any of its principal intended purposes through chemical action within or on the body of man or other animals," nor (2) be "dependent upon being metabolized for the achievement of any of its principal intended purposes."[28]

The MDA gave the FDA the authority to inspect device manufacturers. This authority included new requirements for device manufacturers or importers to maintain records and provide reports to ensure devices are safe and effective. Additionally, the FDA representatives were authorized to physically inspect "any factory, warehouse, or establishment" in which devices "are manufactured, processed, packed, or held" and to enter any vehicle being used to transport devices.[29]

The MDA also granted the FDA the power to control the release of medical devices into interstate commerce. The amendments created a three-tiered scheme for premarket regulation and post-market review. For this purpose, devices were divided into three classes based on their perceived safety risk. Class I devices, those deemed to pose the least risk of harm, were to be the least regulated, while

Class III devices, which present the highest risk, would be the most heavily regulated.

The MDA provided two procedures by which Class II and III devices could be authorized for distribution in interstate commerce. They were 510(k) premarket notifications and premarket approval applications (PMAs). The FDA was also granted the authority to impose performance standards and to ban devices entirely.

More than 10 years later, Congress passed the Safe Medical Devices Act of 1990 (SMDA) to enhance the FDA's regulation of devices. This new legislation followed in the wake of criticism by congressional investigators and others of the limits of the earlier act. The SMDA imposed more-stringent premarket and post-market requirements, as well as new mechanisms for enforcement. Now the FDA must issue an order declaring a device to be substantially equivalent to a legally marketed predicate device before a manufacturer can market a device pursuant to a 510(k) notification.[30] The SMDA also added the authority for the FDA to set performance standards. Further, it included a provision allowing post-market surveillance of Class II or III devices that may pose serious health risks, that are life supporting or sustaining, or that are meant to be implanted in humans for more than one year. Additionally, the FD&C Act added civil penalties to the FDA's enforcement options.

The device statutes of the FD&C Act had two further revisions in the 1990s. The Medical Device Amendments of 1992 did not include major changes to existing device law. However, the FDA Modernization Act of 1997 (FDAMA) is notable for two of its provisions. The first provision provided a safe harbor for device manufacturers and distributors in which to disseminate certain information to medical practitioners concerning new uses for devices already in commercial distribution, provided that the company committed to file, within a specified time frame, a supplemental application to establish the safety and effectiveness of the unapproved use. The provision was controversial, however, because many in the device industry believed it was too restrictive. The provision ceased to be effective on September 30, 2006, due to a sunset provision.[31] Because the provision was no longer effective, in 2009 the FDA issued a guidance document on dissemination of journal articles and medical/scientific publications on unapproved new uses of approved drugs and approved or cleared devices.[32] The other FDAMA provision allows shipment of investigational devices in emergency situations or to combat serious conditions.[33] The law further enables patients being treated by licensed physicians to request and receive these devices directly from the manufacturer or distributor. Although industry believed the FDAMA provision on dissemination of information was too restrictive, both of these FDAMA provisions reflected a shift for the FD&C Act. Since its inception, the amendments to the FD&C Act imposed tighter restrictions on distribution of devices in the interest of safety. Here, the countervailing interest of allowing greater access to medical advances and information regarding new uses of approved or cleared devices began to be balanced against the FD&C Act's primary safety concerns.

In 2012 the Food and Drug Administration Safety and Innovation Act (FDASIA) expanded the FDA's authority to collect user fees from industry to fund reviews of innovator drugs, medical devices, generic drugs, and biosimilar biological products; promote innovation to speed patient access to safe and effective products; increase stakeholder involvement in FDA processes; and enhance the safety of the drug supply chain. As part of FDASIA, the Medical Device User Fee and Modernization Act (MDUFMA III) reauthorizes user fees from industry to fund reviews of medical devices in exchange for the FDA to meet certain performance goals.

FD&C ACT CHAPTER II: DEFINITIONS

Section 201—Definitions

Section 201 of the FD&C Act provides definitions for terms used throughout the quality system regulation. Many of these terms will be discussed in other chapters where they are applicable to the regulation subpart.

(b) The term *interstate commerce* means:

   (1) commerce between any state or territory and any place outside thereof; and

   (2) commerce within the District of Columbia or within any other territory not organized with a legislative body.

(h) The term *device* means an instrument, apparatus, implement, machine, contrivance, implant, in vitro reagent, or other similar or related article, including any component, part, or accessory, that is:

   (1) recognized in the official National Formulary or the U.S. Pharmacopeia, or any supplement to them;

   (2) intended for use in the diagnosis of disease or other conditions, or in the cure, mitigation, treatment, or prevention of disease, in man or other animals; or

   (3) intended to affect the structure or any function of the body of man or other animals, and which does not achieve its primary intended purposes through chemical action within or on the body of man or other animals and that is not dependent upon being metabolized for the achievement of its primary intended purposes. The term "device" does not include software functions excluded pursuant to section 520(o).

(k) The term *label* means a display of written, printed, or graphic matter upon the immediate container of any article; and a requirement made by or under the authority of this act that any word, statement, or other information on the label shall not be considered to be complied with unless such word, statement, or other information also appears on the outside container or wrapper, if any there be, of the retail package of such article, or is easily legible through the outside container or wrapper.

(l) The term *immediate container* does not include package liners.

(m) The term *labeling* means all labels and other written, printed, or graphic matter:

(1) upon any article or any of its containers or wrappers, or

(2) accompanying such article.

FD&C ACT CHAPTER III: PROHIBITED ACTS AND PENALTIES

Section 301—Prohibited Acts

Section 301 of the FD&C Act[34] specifies acts related to any food, drug, device, tobacco product, or cosmetic that are prohibited, and the causing of such act is also prohibited. Prohibited acts related to medical devices include:

(a) Introducing or causing introduction into interstate commerce of an adulterated or misbranded device

(b) Adulteration or misbranding of a device in interstate commerce

(c) The receipt in interstate commerce of any device that is adulterated or misbranded, and the delivery or proffered delivery thereof for pay or otherwise

(d) The introduction or delivery for introduction into interstate commerce of any article in violation of section 404, 415, 505, or 564

(e) Refusal to allow access to or copying a required record, failure to establish or maintain a required record, or make any report required by another FD&C Act section as specified

(f) Refusal to permit entry or inspection authorized under FD&C Act section 704, factory inspection

(g) Manufacture of an adulterated or misbranded device

(h) Giving a guaranty or undertaking referred to in FD&C Act section 303(c)(2) or 303(c)(3), which is false

(j) Using or revealing trade secret information for personal advantage. This does not authorize withholding information from Congress or authorized committee

(k) Altering, mutilating, destroying, obliterating, or removing whole or part of labeling after shipment into interstate commerce that results in the device being adulterated or misbranded

(n) Use or reference to any report issued per FD&C Act section 704 factory inspection in labeling, advertising, or other sales promotion

(p) Failure to register in accordance with FD&C Act section 510, failure to provide device listing information or notice required by FD&C Act sections 510(j) or 510(j)(2), or failure to provide information required by FD&C Act section 510(k) premarket notification

(q) Failure or refusal to comply with a requirement under FD&C Act section 518 concerning notification or section 520(g) regarding investigational device use; failure to notify or provide information required by FD&C Act section 519 concerning adverse event reporting or section 520(g); failure to comply with a post-market surveillance requirement under FD&C Act section 522; or submitting a report that is false or misleading in material

(r) Movement of a device subject to a detention order, or removal/alteration of mark/label required identifying a detained device

(w) Knowingly making a false statement, failure to submit a required certificate of analysis, or failure to maintain or submit required records required under FD&C Act section 801 regarding imports and exports

(x) Falsifying a declaration of conformity to a performance standard, or failure/refusal to provide data/information requested under FD&C Act section 514 regarding provision of standards

(y) Submission of a false/misleading report or recommendation, disclosure of confidential information or trade secret without written consent, or receipt of a bribe or other corrupt act by an accredited person as described under FD&C Act section 523

(z) Disseminating information in violation of FD&C Act section 551, regarding treatment information for devices

(ff) Importing or offering to import when there is a failure to submit requested establishment registration information

(gg) Failure of an accredited person to report, include false information, or failure to include material facts in an inspection report, a condition observed during inspection that could cause or contribute to an unreasonable risk to public health

(jj) Failure to submit certification or clinical trial information required by Public Health Service Act section 402(j); knowingly submitting false or misleading information regarding clinical trials

Section 302—Injunction Proceedings

A court-ordered injunction requires an individual or corporation to either do or refrain from performing a specific act. The FDA may seek an injunction to prevent an individual or corporation from violating or causing violation of the act. A court or jury shall try an individual or corporation in violation of an injunction or restraining order issued under section 302.

Section 303—Penalties

Civil penalties may be levied against any person who violates a requirement related to devices. Such penalty shall not exceed $15,000 for each violation related to devices and not exceed $1,000,000 for all violations adjudicated in a single proceeding.

Section 304—Seizure

Seizure is intended to remove specific violative goods from commerce. This action may be brought against an FDA-regulated product that is adulterated and/or misbranded. Additionally, an officer or qualified FDA employee may order a device be detained for a reasonable period up to 20 days, or up to 30 days if the action requires more than 20 days.

FD&C ACT CHAPTER V: DRUGS AND DEVICES

Section 501—Adulterated Drugs and Devices

Adulteration laws are intended to ensure that a Class III device has the required approval and that all devices are manufactured in accordance with applicable quality requirements. Adulteration regulations generally are intended to ensure that marketed medical devices conform to FDA quality requirements. A device is considered adulterated if it is actually or potentially unclean or injurious to health.[35] To safeguard against adulterated devices, the regulations address the conditions under which a device was manufactured, as well as its post-market condition.

Adulteration laws and regulations concern general safety issues. For example, the FD&C Act empowers the FDA to impose good manufacturing practice (GMP) requirements to ensure the safety and effectiveness of devices. The GMPs, referred to as the Quality System Regulation (QSR), govern device manufacture and control, including design validation, and packing, storage, and installation of devices.[36] Nonconforming devices are considered adulterated. Similarly, devices that the FDA has banned are also considered adulterated.[37] Adulteration laws extend to product containers, which are adulterated if composed in whole or part of any poisonous or deleterious substance that may render the contents injurious to health.[38]

Some adulteration laws focus on the cleanliness of devices. A device is considered adulterated if it contains any filthy, putrid, or decomposed substances. Devices are also adulterated if they have been prepared, packed, or held under[39] unsanitary conditions where they may have become filthy or rendered injurious to health.[40]

Other adulteration regulations address performance. The FDA enforces two types of performance standards: those established by the FDA and those established by other organizations and recognized by the FDA. A device that is obligated to meet either of these standards will be considered adulterated if it does not conform to the standard in every respect.[41]

Finally, if a Class III device is marketed without submission and approval of a required premarket approval application, or if a premarket approval has been denied, suspended, or withdrawn, or is otherwise ineffective, the device will be considered adulterated under the FD&C Act.[42]

Section 502—Misbranded Drugs and Devices

Misbranding regulations protect against the sale of devices manufactured in facilities that have not been registered, as well as against false, misleading, or insufficient statements appearing in device labeling or advertisements. Through misbranding statutes, device manufacturers are prohibited from making misrepresentations about the device and are required to disclose specific types of information to potential users, as well as to the FDA. The laws forbid the inclusion of false or misleading information in device labeling and advertisements. Additionally, these materials must identify the product manufacturer, packer, or distributor, and include uniform device descriptions and instructions for safe use. Finally, misbranding statutes may require manufacturers and distributors of certain devices to issue notifications of unreasonable risks or to conduct post-market surveillance.

Misbranding provisions protect the public from purchasing devices that have not been properly registered and listed with the FDA. A device may be characterized as misbranded if it is disseminated without identifying the manufacturer, packer, or distributor, or if it originates from a manufacturer that has failed either to register its facilities or to list a device with the agency.[43] FDA requires that the device label identify the name and place of business of the device manufacturer, packer, and/or distributor.[44] In addition, to avoid being considered misbranded, a device: (1) must be manufactured, prepared, propagated, compounded, and/or processed in a facility registered in compliance with FD&C Act regulations;[45] (2) be included on the facility's registered list of devices for commercial distribution;[46] and (3) comply with applicable performance standards and premarket approval requirements prior to introduction into interstate commerce.[47]

In addition, the misbranding restrictions also forbid inclusion of false or misleading information in device labeling or advertisements.[48] A device is misbranded if it is dangerous when used in the manner, frequency, or duration suggested, prescribed, or recommended in its labeling.[49] If the device is a restricted one, the prohibition against false or misleading statements extends to advertisements.[50]

The FD&C Act also includes a duty to submit device labeling for review by the FDA. The amount of material to be submitted depends on whether the device is restricted or is subject to a performance standard or premarket approval requirements. Manufacturers and distributors of devices that do not fall into those categories are simply obliged to provide the FDA with the label and package insert, as well as a representative sampling of any other labeling.[51] All other manufacturers and distributors have the greater obligation of providing a copy of all device labeling.[52] Those manufacturing and distributing restricted devices must submit a representative sample of product advertisements and, upon good cause, the FDA may request that they provide a copy of all device advertisements.[53]

In addition to outlawing false statements, the FDA requires the inclusion of statements that create greater uniformity in labeling. For example, device packaging must accurately state the weight, measure, or numerical count of its contents.[54] It must also include symbols from the FDA's uniform system of identification of devices.[55] Any information required under the FD&C Act must be prominently and conspicuously placed on a device's labeling so an ordinary individual "under customary conditions of purchase and use" would be likely to read and understand it.[56]

Other mandatory labeling requirements are intended to promote safe use of the device. Device labeling must include adequate directions for users and adequate warnings against potentially hazardous misuse, or against unsafe dosage or methods or duration of use.[57] Labeling for devices subject to a performance standard may be required to prescribe the proper installation, maintenance, and operation of the device.[58] All advertisements and promotional materials for restricted devices must include safety information consisting of a brief statement of the device's intended uses, and relevant warnings, precautions, and side effects.[59] In special instances, where the FDA finds it necessary to protect public health, the agency may require a full description of a device's components or formula, including the quantity of each ingredient.[60] In extraordinary circumstances, the FDA can even require prior approval of an ad's content.[61]

Finally, misbranding laws impose notification and monitoring obligations on manufacturers and distributors of devices presenting a high risk of harm to users. Upon determining that a device presents an unreasonable risk of substantial harm to public health, the FDA may require a producer to issue notification of the risk to all prescribing health professionals.[62] Failure to issue the notification renders the device misbranded. Similarly, the FDA may order a manufacturer to conduct post-market surveillance of the following types of Class II or III devices: (1) those likely to have serious adverse health consequences upon failure; (2) those implanted in humans for more than a year; and (3) those that sustain or support life and are used outside of a controlled facility.[63] Devices that are not monitored in compliance with this provision are also deemed misbranded.

Section 510—Registration of Producers of Drugs and Devices

Any person who owns or operates a U.S. establishment engaged in the manufacture, preparation, propagation, compounding, or processing of a medical device shall register annually between October 1 and December 31. Any establishment located outside the United States that performs any of the listed activities for a device imported or offered for import into the United States is also required to register.

With the exception of initial importers, an establishment subject to registration requirements is also required to provide a listing of devices manufactured, prepared, propagated, compounded, or processed.

Initial registration and listing information must be submitted by U.S. establishments within 30 days of beginning a regulated activity or putting a medical device into commercial distribution. Establishments outside the United States must register and/or list before exporting devices to the United States. If the device requires 510(k) premarket notification clearance or premarket application (PMA) approval, its regulatory application must be cleared/approved before registration and listing.

Section 510 establishes that registered firms engaged in the manufacture, propagation, compounding, or processing of a Class II or Class III device are to be inspected biennially. Section 510 also requires firms to provide premarket notification to the FDA at least 90 days before marketing a device, unless the device is a Class I device and not of substantial importance to human health or an unreasonable risk of illness or injury.

Section 513—Classification of Devices Intended for Human Use

Each generic device type is categorized into one of 16 classification panels that are organized by clinical medicine and fundamental sciences, such as cardiovascular, neurology, or orthopedic. These panels are codified in Parts 862 to 892 of Title 21 of the Code of Federal Regulations (CFR), and specify those human-use devices subject to general controls, special controls, or premarket approval.

Devices intended for human use are further classified into one of three classes (that is, Class I, Class II, Class III) based on the level of control necessary to assure device safety and effectiveness. Classification is based on the risk to patient and/or user posed by the device where Class I devices present the lowest risk, and Class III present the highest risk. Device classification determines the type of premarket submission/application required to legally market the device. The classifications are described as:

- Class I, General Controls: Controls authorized by the act are sufficient to provide reasonable assurance of device safety and effectiveness. These devices are are not life supporting or life sustaining, or do not have substantial importance in preventing health impairment. Class I devices do not present a potential unreasonable risk of illness or injury and are typically exempt from premarket regulatory requirements.
  - General controls include adulteration; misbranding; establishment registration and device listing; premarket notification; banned devices; notification and repair, replacement, and refund; records and reports; restricted devices; and GMPs.
- Class II, General Controls and Special Controls: General controls alone are not sufficient to provide reasonable assurance of device safety and effectiveness. Special controls are necessary to provide reasonable assurance. Class II devices typically require 510(k) premarket clearance from the FDA prior to commercialization.
  - Special controls are typically device-specific and may include performance standards, post-market surveillance, patient registries, premarket data requirements, and FDA guidance documents.
- Class III, General Controls and Premarket Approval: Devices classified as Class III have insufficient information to determine if general and/or special controls would adequately provide reasonable assurance of safety and effectiveness. These devices are characterized as being

life sustaining, life supporting, or have substantial importance in preventing health impairment, and present a potentially unreasonable risk of illness or injury. A Class III device generally requires premarket approval from the FDA, and potentially a human clinical trial, prior to legally commercializing the device.

A device may be reclassified on the basis of valid scientific evidence including the health benefit of the device, nature and incidence of risk (if known), and why controls associated with the proposed classification are sufficient to provide a reasonable assurance of safety and effectiveness. Proposed reclassification orders are published in the *Federal Register.*

Section 518—Notification and Other Remedies

Under section 518 of the FD&C Act,[64] the FDA can issue three types of orders for resolving problems with medical devices. The three main types of orders in ascending order of seriousness are:

- Notification
- Repair, replacement, or refund
- Recall

Note that separate provisions of the FD&C Act apply to electronic products.[65] Section 518 was originally included in the original Medical Device Amendments of 1976.[66] Since that time, this section has been amended twice.

The first change was in 1990 when the SMDA added subsection (e), which gave the FDA explicit authority to order device recalls.[67] Two years later, the Medical Device Amendments of 1992 modified the wording of the provision relating to repair, replacement, or refund.[68] In 1996, the FDA issued regulations implementing the mandatory recall provisions of section 518(e).[69]

Notification Orders

If there is a problem with a medical device, the FDA might issue a notification order. The order will be issued if the FDA determines that the device "presents an unreasonable risk of substantial harm to the public health, that the notification will be necessary to eliminate the specific risk, and that no more practical means is available to eliminate the risk." As provided by section 518(a):[70]

If the Secretary determines that:

1. A device intended for human use that is introduced or delivered for introduction into interstate commerce for commercial distribution presents an unreasonable risk of substantial harm to the public health, and
2. Notification under this subsection is necessary to eliminate the unreasonable risk of such harm and no more practicable means is available under the provisions of this chapter (other than this section)

> to eliminate such risk, the Secretary may issue such order as may be necessary to assure that adequate notification is provided in an appropriate form, by the persons and means best suited under the circumstances involved, to all health professionals who prescribe or use the device and to any other person (including manufacturers, importers, distributors, retailers, and device users) who should properly receive such notification in order to eliminate such risk.

An order under this subsection shall require that the individuals subject to the risk with respect to which the order is to be issued be included in the persons to be notified of the risk unless the Secretary determines that notice to such individuals would present a greater danger to the health of such individuals than no such notification.

If the Secretary makes such a determination with respect to such individuals, the order shall require that the health professionals who prescribe or use the device provide for the notification of the individuals whom the health professionals treated with the device of the risk presented by the device and of any action that may be taken by or on behalf of such individuals to eliminate or reduce such risk. Before issuing an order under this subsection, the Secretary shall consult with the persons who are to give notice under the order.

Neither the statute nor any of the regulations define what constitutes "an unreasonable risk of substantial harm to public health." But a 1984 draft, *Medical Device Notification and Voluntary Safety Alert Guideline,* defined the phrase to mean "actual or possible nonserious harm to a large number of persons as well as actual/ or possible serious harm to a few individuals."

Unlike other orders under section 518, an "informal hearing" is not required before the FDA issues an order under this section. But the statute directs that the secretary "shall consult with the persons who are to give notice under the order." As a matter of practice, the FDA will notify the company and give it 10 days to consult with the FDA. The company then has the opportunity to negotiate the terms of the notification based on the nature of the risk as well as the scope of the affected patient group.

The notice of the risk must be given either to the healthcare providers who prescribed the device or to the individuals who are users of the device. But if the FDA decides that the notification would present a greater danger to the health of such individuals, then "the order shall require that the health professionals who prescribe or use the device provide for the notification of the individuals whom the health professionals treated."

The statute uses the phrase "provide for the notification" rather than "notify" since individuals other than health professionals may be the appropriate persons to provide notification.[71] The FDA may also require notification of any other party, including manufacturers, importers, distributors, and device users, if it decides that the notification will help to eliminate the risk. The content of the notification must be "in an appropriate form," and generally should include information about the risk and about any action that may be taken to eliminate or reduce the risk.

As a matter of procedure, the FDA relies on voluntary notifications called "safety alerts" or "safety communications."[72] The 1984 Draft Guideline states that the purpose of the safety alert is to "inform health professionals and other appropriate persons of a situation that may present an unreasonable risk of substantial harm to the public health presented by a device in commercial distribution and intended for human use, in order to reduce or eliminate the risk."

The manufacturer can develop these without FDA comment but, as always, the FDA will consider the content and effectiveness of the alert to determine whether any other notification should be ordered. If a company does issue a safety alert, the FDA may classify it as a recall within the meaning of 21 CFR Part 7, as well as publish the alert as a recall in the weekly FDA Enforcement Report. Enforcement Reports are archived online at: www.fda.gov/%20Safety/Recalls/EnforcementReports/default.htm.

If the manufacturer issues a safety alert, the FDA requires that it review its efforts to ensure the notification reached its intended audience.

Repair, Replacement, or Refund Orders

The next most serious regulatory power for dealing with a problem with a medical device is an order by the FDA that directs the manufacturer to repair, refund, or replace the device.[73] The applicable statute is 21 USC § 360h(b), which was enacted in 1976 but has never been used. The procedure reveals the difficulties the FDA would have if it were to take enforcement action under this section:

(b) Repair, replacement, or refund

1. A. If, after affording opportunity for an informal hearing, the secretary determines that:

   (i) a device intended for human use that is introduced or delivered for introduction into interstate commerce for commercial distribution presents an unreasonable risk of substantial harm to the public health,

   (ii) there are reasonable grounds to believe that the device was not properly designed or manufactured with reference to the state of the art as it existed at the time of its design or manufacture,

   (iii) there are reasonable grounds to believe that the unreasonable risk was not caused by failure of a person other than a manufacturer, importer, distributor, or retailer of the device to exercise due care in the installation, maintenance, repair, or use of the device, and

   (iv) the notification authorized by subsection (a) of this section would not by itself be sufficient to eliminate the unreasonable risk and action described in paragraph (2) of this subsection is necessary to eliminate such risk, the Secretary may order the manufacturer, importer, or any distributor of such device, or any combination of such persons, to submit to him or her within a reasonable time a plan for taking one or more of the actions described in paragraph (2). An order issued under the preceding sentence that is directed to more than one person shall specify which person may decide which action shall be taken under such plan and the person specified shall be the person who the Secretary determines bears the principal, ultimate financial responsibility for action taken under the plan unless the Secretary cannot determine who bears such responsibility or the Secretary determines that the protection of the public health requires that such decision be made by a person (including a device user or health professional) other than the person he or she determines bears such responsibility.

B. The Secretary shall approve a plan submitted pursuant to an order issued under subparagraph (A) unless he or she determines (after affording opportunity for an informal hearing) that the action or actions to be taken under the plan or the manner in which such action or actions are to be taken under the plan will not assure that the unreasonable risk with respect to which such order was issued will be eliminated. If the Secretary disapproves a plan, he or she shall order a revised plan to be submitted to him or her within a reasonable time. If the Secretary determines (after affording opportunity for an informal hearing) that the revised plan is unsatisfactory or if no revised plan or no initial plan has been submitted to the Secretary within the prescribed time, the Secretary shall (i) prescribe a plan to be carried out by the person or persons to whom the order issued under subparagraph (A) was directed, or (ii) after affording an opportunity for an informal hearing, by order prescribe a plan to be carried out by a person who is a manufacturer, importer, distributor, or retailer of the device with respect to which the order was issued but to whom the order under subparagraph (A) was not directed.

2. The actions that may be taken under a plan submitted under an order issued under paragraph (1) are as follows:

   A. To repair the device so it does not present the unreasonable risk of substantial harm with respect to which the order under paragraph (1) was issued

   B. To replace the device with a like or equivalent device that is in conformity with all applicable requirements of this chapter

   C. To refund the purchase price of the device (less a reasonable allowance for use if such device has been in the possession of the device user for one year or more:

      (i) at the time of notification ordered under subsection (a) of this section, or

(ii) at the time the device user receives actual notice of the unreasonable risk with respect to which the order was issued under paragraph (1), whichever first occurs.

3. No charge shall be made to any person (other than a manufacturer, importer, distributor, or retailer) for availing himself or herself of any remedy, described in paragraph (2) and provided under an order issued under paragraph (1), and the person subject to the order shall reimburse each person (other than a manufacturer, importer, distributor, or retailer) who is entitled to such a remedy for any reasonable and foreseeable expenses actually incurred by such person in availing himself or herself of such remedy.

Thus, before issuing an order under section 518, the FDA must first determine whether:

- The device presents an unreasonable risk of substantial harm to the public health.
- There are reasonable grounds to believe that the device was not properly designed or manufactured when the state of the art as it existed at the time of its design or manufacture is considered.
- There are reasonable grounds to believe that the risk is due to the conduct of the manufacturer, importer, distributor, or retailer, and not due to improper installation, maintenance, repair, or use.
- Notification of the defect alone will not eliminate the risk, and that repair, replacement, or refund is necessary to eliminate the risk.

Congress intended 518(b) "to be in addition to and not as an alternative to the notification requirements."[74]

If the FDA decides that the defect is the type that requires it to invoke section 518(b), it can direct the manufacturer, importer, distributor, or a combination of them to submit a plan for the repair, replacement, or refund of the device. If the FDA requires action from more than one party, it will designate which party has the responsibility to make the appropriate decisions for the plan. Once that party is designated, he or she is the one who will bear the financial responsibility for developing and implementing it. However, the FDA does have the ability to revisit this assignment and make a new designation. The FDA also has the power to order a manufacturer, importer, distributor, or retailer of the device to reimburse any other manufacturer, importer, distributor, or retailer for expenses incurred in complying with the order. The only limitation is that the financial aspects of the order "shall not affect" any contractual agreements between the parties. [FD&C Act § 518(c), 21 USC § 360h(c)] The FDA must also provide "opportunity for an informal hearing" before issuing the order requiring the plan.

Whoever has been designated by the FDA to develop the plan must have "a reasonable time" to submit a plan that satisfies the order. If a plan is not submitted, the FDA will then fashion one. Depending on what the FDA orders, the plan must propose one of the following:

- Repair the device in a way that eliminates the specific risk
- Replace the device with a like or equivalent device that conforms to FDA requirements
- Refund the purchase price: either the full purchase price if the user has had the device for less than a year as of the time the user receives notice of the risk, or at a discounted purchase price if the user has had possession for one year or more

If the user repairs or replaces the device on his or her own as provided by the approved plan, the user can seek reimbursement of those reasonable and foreseeable expenses from whichever party is subject to the order.

The FDA must approve a submitted plan to ensure it eliminates the unreasonable risk. Before a plan is rejected, the FDA must provide an opportunity for an informal hearing to review why it has been rejected. Upon disapproval, the FDA "shall order a revised plan to be submitted." If the FDA considers the revised plan to be unsatisfactory following the opportunity for an informal hearing, the FDA shall prescribe one. Again, largely because of the number of findings required and the elaborate procedures, the FDA has yet to issue an order under section 518(b).

Recall Authority

Until the SMDA added section 518(e), the FDA did not have explicit authority to order recalls of medical devices. Because the FDA never used its authority under 518(b), the recall authority added by section 518(e) in 1990 provided a different kind of recall power. The FDA issued a final rule on mandatory recall procedures that became effective on May 17, 1997. As described on the FDA website: Recalls are actions taken by a firm to remove a product from the market. Recalls may be conducted on a firm's own initiative, by FDA request, or by FDA order under statutory authority. A Class I recall is a situation in which there is a reasonable probability that the use of or exposure to a violative product will cause serious adverse health consequences or death. A Class II recall is a situation in which use of or exposure to a violative product may cause temporary or medically reversible adverse health consequences or where the probability of serious adverse health consequences is remote. A Class III recall is a situation in which use of or exposure to a violative product is not likely to cause adverse health consequences.[75]

The act defines "serious, adverse health consequences" to include "any significant adverse experience attributable to a device, including those which may be either life threatening, or involve permanent or long-term injuries."[76] The statutory and regulatory scheme provides for two types of recalls: the mandatory recall as well as a voluntary recall. The effect of the legislation is to provide the FDA with administrative injunctive power before there is a hearing extended to the company.

Mandatory Recall Order

The applicable regulations for a mandatory recall are set forth in 21 CFR Part 810. Under the regulation, before there is a recall, the FDA must find there is a reasonable probability that a device would cause serious, adverse health consequences or death. In such a case it will issue an order to cease distribution of the device and to notify healthcare professionals about the risk. For the purposes of the statute, "reasonable probability" means "it is more likely than not that an event will occur."[77]

Before it initiates a recall, the FDA will conduct a health hazard evaluation.[78] A health hazard evaluation is an evaluation by an ad hoc FDA committee that evaluates the risk and assigns a recall classification. If the FDA decides that the device poses a risk, the order is directed to "the appropriate person," which may include manufacturers, importers, distributors, and retailers. The FDA then issues a two-part order to immediately cease distribution of the device and notify healthcare professionals as well as device user facilities. These groups are advised about the order and told to immediately stop using the device. The order will include the device's brand name; its common name; the model, catalog, or product code number; and other identifying information such as lot or serial numbers. It will also include a contact name at the agency.

As a matter of practice, the FDA will provide an opportunity to consult with the agency before it issues a cease distribution and notification order.[79] The order identifies the specific device that is the subject of the order, requirements of the order, and basis for the recall.[80] The FDA may also include a model notification letter, which it considers binding on manufacturers, as well as a schedule for the completion of the notification.[81]

Once the order has been initiated, the FDA may require the manufacturer to provide specific information about the device, which may include the number of devices that have been distributed, names and addresses of all distributors, as well as the proposed strategy for complying with the order. The company can request a hearing on the actions required by the order. The company can also ask for a hearing to determine whether it should be modified, vacated, or amended to require a mandatory recall. The FDA can deny the request for a hearing if it determines no genuine and substantial issue of fact is raised by the request.[82] It can also submit a written request that the order be modified, vacated, or amended.[83] Normally, there are three working days to request the hearing, but because of the seriousness of the action, the FDA may grant a shorter period. The hearing generally must be held between two to ten working days after the FDA receives the request.[84] Once the hearing has been completed, the FDA must provide a written notification of its final decision within 15 working days or within 15 working days of the receipt of a written request for review of the order.[85]

If there is a mandatory recall, the FDA will provide for notice to individuals who are subject to the device's risk. The FDA may seek to provide notice through the media if there are significant difficulties in identifying the group. The FDA also has the power to specify the scope of the recall (wholesale, retail, user), as well as a timetable for the recall. The FDA may require the manufacturer to use a model notification letter, to submit a proposed compliance strategy, and to give periodic progress reports.[86] The only limitation to a recall is that the agency cannot order a recall if the health risks of recalling the device are greater than those of not recalling it.[87]

The notification must be by verified written communication that is conspicuously marked. Telephone calls or other personal contacts may be made in addition to, but are not a substitute for, the verified written communication.[88] The notice may be provided through affected individuals' health professionals rather than directly to individuals if the FDA agrees this is appropriate and the most effective method of notification.[89]

Effectiveness checks for a recall are required, and a strategy must be submitted for approval.[90] The purpose of the effectiveness check is to ensure the recall is working as the plan intended. Follow-up communications must be sent to all who fail to respond to the initial communication.[91] The appropriate person can request termination of the order by certifying compliance and including a copy of the most current status report.[92]

The FDA may terminate the order after determining that the person named in the order has taken all reasonable notification efforts, and either removed or corrected the device.[93]

The FDA will publish new mandatory recalls in its weekly *FDA Enforcement Report* unless it determines that such notification will cause unnecessary and harmful anxiety in individuals, and that initial consultation between individuals and their health professionals is essential.

FD&C ACT CHAPTER VII: GENERAL AUTHORITY

Section 704—Inspection

Section 704 of the FD&C Act[94] establishes the regulatory basis for an inspection of a device company. The Office of Regulatory Affairs (ORA) is charged with enforcing the law. ORA is the lead office for all U.S. FDA field activities. Additional information about ORA is available on its website at https://www.fda.gov/about-fda/fda-organization/office-regulatory-affairs.

Information regarding inspections, compliance, enforcement, and criminal investigations is available at https://www.fda.gov/inspections-compliance-enforcement-and-criminal-investigations. This website provides information to FDA investigators and inspectors to assist them in their daily activities, including:

- *Field management directives.* The primary vehicle for distributing procedural information/policy on the management of ORA field activities.
- *Inspection guides.* Guidance documents written to assist FDA personnel in applying the FDA's regulations, policies, and procedures during specific types of inspection or for specific manufacturing processes.
- *Foreign inspections—Guide to International Inspections and Travel.* Guide for FDA personnel performing inspections including standard operational, inspectional, and investigational procedures.

Reasonableness of the Inspection. Investigators from the FDA are authorized to enter and to inspect facilities "at reasonable times and within reasonable limits and in a reasonable manner…"[95] Note that the only limitation is that the times and scope be "reasonable."

Frequency of Inspections. Establishments that manufacture restricted devices are subject to inspection pursuant to section 704 of the FD&C Act with a frequency of at least once in every successive two-year period, following a first inspection within two years of registration.[96]

Consents and Refusals. The authority to conduct an inspection is statutorily mandated by the FD&C Act, and refusals of inspection are subject to criminal prosecution. The FD&C Act requires that the inspector present his or her credentials to the top management official at the facility, which should be the owner, operator, or agent in charge, and a signed, completed Form 482 Notice of Inspection.[97] Consent to the inspection will be implied if there is no express communication to the inspector that the inspection is being refused, in total or in part.[98]

A refusal to permit an inspection is a prohibited act and, therefore, punishable as a misdemeanor unless the investigator has failed to follow the procedures set forth in section 704 (that is, presenting of credentials and issuance of written Notice of Inspection).[99]

Warrants. The Supreme Court held in the landmark 1978 case of *Marshall v. Barlow's, Inc.* that administrative agency searches of commercial premises without a warrant are unreasonable in violation of the Fourth Amendment. The court further held, however, that there is an exception for industries that are so "pervasively regulated" that warrantless search authority is permitted.[100] In 1981, the Eighth Circuit determined that the drug manufacturing industry is pervasively regulated and within the Colonnade-Biswell exception to the warrant requirement.[101] In reaching this conclusion, courts have considered that the public health interest ought to be protected and that establishments operating in closely regulated industries, such as drugs, voluntarily subject themselves to numerous government regulations and to the restrictions placed on such activity. As such, they have no reasonable expectation of privacy.[102]

In *Marshall v. Barlow's, Inc.*, the court stated that such warrantless searches are upheld because "when an entrepreneur embarks on such a business, he has chosen to subject himself to a full arsenal of governmental regulation"[103] and "in effect consents to the restrictions placed on him."[104] Further, in the face of a long history of government scrutiny, such a proprietor has no "reasonable expectation of privacy."[105]

The Eighth Circuit stated in *Jamieson-McKames Pharmaceuticals* that it believed "the drug manufacturing industry is properly within the Colonnade-Biswell exception to the warrant requirement. The drug manufacturing industry has a long history of supervision and inspection. The present FD&C Act has its origins in the Food and Drug Act of 1906, 34 Stat. 768. That act was an attempt by Congress 'to exclude from interstate commerce impure and adulterated food and drugs' and to prevent the transport of such articles 'from their place of manufacture.'"[106]

Likewise, giving Miranda warnings of constitutional rights to owners, operators, or agents in charge of establishments being inspected is not necessary. The issuance of Miranda warnings is not applicable when individuals are not in custody, which is the typical situation during FDA inspections.[107]

Importantly, the decision by the Eighth Circuit in *Jamieson-McKames Pharmaceuticals* as it relates to warrants applied to drug manufacturers, and it is not clear that it extends to other FDA-regulated products. Further, FDA's *Investigation Operations Manual* does not instruct investigators to proceed without a warrant when consent is denied.[108]

Reasons for FDA Administrative Inspection

An inspection may occur for a variety of reasons. For a Class III device manufacturer, the initial inspection would probably be the preapproval inspection. As a condition for approval of the device, the device manufacturing facility is required to undergo an FDA inspection to determine its ability to produce the product as claimed, as well as its ability to comply with GMPs. All marketed devices are subject to periodic FDA inspections and to directed inspections when it comes to the agency's attention that there may be violations of the FD&C Act. Other types of enforcement actions taken by the agency, such as a seizure or a warning letter, might also trigger unannounced inspections. Likewise, if there has been a recall, the FDA might inspect a company to determine the background for the recall as well as to see what steps the company is taking to correct the problem. With an increasingly aware healthcare community and public, the company might also expect to see inspections following adverse events.

A special enforcement initiative may be part of local or national initiatives and will focus on particular types of industries or products (for example, devices that present an increased safety risk).

The Nuts and Bolts for Conducting Inspections

The *Investigation Operations Manual* is the basis for all inspections[109] and serves as primary guidance for FDA personnel performing investigational activities supporting the FDA's public health mission. Adherence is considered essential to assuring quality, consistency, and efficiency in field operations.

Present Credentials and Notice of Inspection

An inspection begins when the FDA investigator presents his or her official credentials and a properly signed, completed original written notice of inspection (form FDA 482) to the owner, operator, or agent in charge of the facility.[110] A separate written notice of inspection is required for each inspection unless an investigator makes multiple entries during a single inspection continuing over a period of time.

Scope of Inspection

FDA investigators are authorized to enter any factory, warehouse, or establishment where devices are manufactured, processed, packed, or held before or after introduction into interstate commerce. Investigators are also authorized to enter any vehicle used to transport or hold these devices, or cosmetics, in interstate commerce.[111]

The FDA inspector can examine not only the premises but also all equipment, finished and unfinished materials, containers, and labeling within the establishment or vehicle in which the devices are manufactured, processed, packed, held, or transported. Copies of documents can also be made. The refusal to permit access or copying of required records is a prohibited act punishable as a misdemeanor.[112]

There are limits, however. The agency's authority under the FD&C Act does not extend to financial data, sales data (other than shipment data), pricing data, personnel data (other than data as to the qualifications of technical and professional personnel performing functions subject to the act), or research data (other than, for device facilities, data relating to devices and subject to reporting and inspection under regulations lawfully issued pursuant to sections 519 or 520(g)[113]).

FDA's Authority to Inspect Records of Interstate Shipment by Common Carriers and Recipients

Section 703 of the FD&C Act requires that, upon an inspector's request, carriers engaged in interstate commerce, as well as those who receive or hold devices, must permit access to and copying of all records showing the movement in interstate commerce of medical devices.

If requested in writing, it is unlawful for any carrier or person to fail to permit access to and copying of such records. Evidence obtained from a carrier or person receiving such articles pursuant to a written request is not to be used in a criminal prosecution of the person from whom such evidence was obtained. Common carriers are not subject to the other provisions of the FD&C Act merely by reason of their receipt, carriage, holding, or delivery of foods, drugs, devices, or cosmetics in the usual course of business as carriers.[114]

If during the inspection the investigator obtains any sample of an article ("official sample"), a receipt describing the samples must be provided before the inspector leaves the premises.[115] When an official sample is collected for analysis, the FDA must, upon request, provide a part of such official sample for examination or analysis to any person named on the label, to the owner, or to the owner's attorney or agent.[116]

Samples Taken During Inspection

Documentary Sample (DOC Sample). In addition to official samples, investigators may also collect DOC samples. DOC samples are collected in situations where an actual physical sample is not practical (for example, a large, permanently installed device), where a physical sample is no longer available, or where there is little need for laboratory examination. DOC samples might also include copies of labels and other documents subject to inspection, such as transportation records, dealer affidavits, and an inventory of product on hand that documents the condition or practices at the facility or establishes facts of a past act.

301(k) Sample. A 301(k) sample is one collected from a product lot that became adulterated or misbranded while being held for sale after shipment in interstate commerce. Under section 301(k) of the FD&C Act, it is a prohibited act to do anything to a product after shipment in interstate commerce that results in the product being adulterated or misbranded.[117]

Post-Seizure Sample. After the U.S. marshal has seized a product, either the claimant or the government may obtain a sample for analysis. The sample may be collected only pursuant to court order.[118]

Investigational Sample (INV Sample). These samples are generally collected to document observations, support regulatory actions, or provide other information. INV samples may be used as evidence in court and are sealed and handled by the FDA in a careful manner to protect their integrity. Examples of INV samples include:

- Raw materials in process or finished products, to demonstrate manufacturing conditions
- Filthy materials and other articles collected for exhibition purposes to demonstrate manufacturing or storage conditions
- Samples collected during reconditioning under a court decree to determine whether reconditioning was satisfactorily performed
- Survey samples to provide information about industry practices regarding a particular issue
- Complaint samples collected during investigation of an injury or illness

An induced sample is an official sample that is obtained by the FDA by mail or through some other response to some type of advertisement or promotional activity. The sample is induced, generally by mail or telephone, without disclosing any association of the requestor or the transaction with the FDA.

In-Plant Photographs

Taking photographs during an inspection is not specifically authorized by the FD&C Act. Investigators, however, are directed to assume they have authority to take photographs. The *Investigations Operations Manual* notes at section 5.3.4:

Photos taken during [establishment inspections] are not classified as INV samples. They are exhibits. No C/R is used for photos taken unless the photos are part of an official sample. See *IOM* 4.1.4 for information on Official Samples.

Since photographs are one of the most effective and useful forms of evidence, every photo should be taken with a purpose. Photographs should be related to insanitary conditions contributing or likely to contribute filth to the finished product, or to practices likely to render it injurious or otherwise violative.

Section 5.3.4.1 provides additional details, including:

Do not request permission from management to take photographs during an inspection. Take your camera into the firm and use it as necessary just as you use other inspectional equipment.

If management objects to taking photographs, explain that photos are an integral part of an inspection and present an accurate picture of firm conditions. Advise management the U.S. courts have held that photographs may lawfully be taken as part of an inspection.

If management continues to refuse, provide them with the following references:

1. *Dow Chemical v. United States,* 476 section 227 (1986). This Supreme Court decision dealt with aerial photographs by the EPA, but the court's language seems to address the right to take photographs by any regulatory agency. The decision reads in part, "... When Congress invests an agency with enforcement and investigatory authority, it is not necessary to identify explicitly each and every technique that may be used in the course of executing the statutory mission..."
2. *United States of America v. Acri Wholesale Grocery Company, A Corporation, and Joseph D. Acri and Anthony Acri, Individuals.* U.S. District Court for Southern District of Iowa. 409 F. Supp. 529. Decided February 24, 1976.

If management refuses, obtain name and contact information for the firm's legal counsel, and advise your district management immediately. If you have already taken some photos, do not surrender the film to management. Advise the firm it can obtain copies of the photos under the Freedom of Information Act. See *IOM* 5.3.4.5.

Affidavits and Interviews

The FDA may ask for an affidavit as a part of the inspection process. The purpose of an affidavit is to document shipment in interstate commerce of components or finished products. Affidavits may also be used to establish particular facts or individual responsibility that may later be used for enforcement purposes (seizure, injunction, and prosecution). There is no requirement in the FD&C Act, or elsewhere, for anyone to sign such an affidavit.

The FD&C Act does not expressly authorize investigators to interview a company's employees. However, discussions with company representatives may be useful or necessary during an inspection in order to provide an investigator with complete and accurate information in the event that the investigator may have questions or need an explanation of certain processes, procedures, or records. The facts and circumstances of a particular situation may influence the decision of whether to allow employee interviews.

The *Investigation Operations Manual* also recognizes that there may be some value to confidential interviews and establishes a protocol. The manual instructs investigators that when they are faced with a situation involving informants who want to remain anonymous, they should contact their supervisor and follow the manual's procedures and any additional procedures in their district. They are further advised to adhere to the procedures per *IOM* section 5.2.9.1:

Type of meeting—Try to schedule a personal interview with the person rather than a telephone interview. At a face-to-face interview you can assess the person's demeanor, body language, overall presentation, and truthfulness.

Meeting location—The place and time of the interview should be the choice of the person, unless there is a concern with personal safety. If the person's suggested location is unsuitable, the investigator should suggest the location. When you conduct the interview off FDA premises, notify your supervisor of your destination, purpose, and estimated time of return. When an off-site interview has been completed, check in with your supervisor.[119]

Establishment Inspection Report

The report, called an establishment inspection report (EIR), is a detailed, written narrative that discusses the inspection. The EIR contains information such as the investigator's findings, history of the firm, persons interviewed, responsibility, operations, complaints, and corrective actions. It becomes the basis for the FDA's determination of what future action, if any, will be taken by the FDA. The reports are available under the Freedom of Information Act[120] if no action is contemplated. Additionally, FDA procedures state that the district office or other office responsible for the inspection "should endeavor to provide a copy of the EIR... to the inspected establishment at the earliest time possible once the inspection is deemed closed by the Agency."[121]

After an Inspection

When an inspection is completed, the investigator is obligated to give to the owner, operator, or agent in charge a written report summarizing the findings of the inspection. This Inspectional Observations (form FDA 483) report identifies objectionable conditions or practices observed during the inspection that, in the inspector's judgment, indicate that a device in such establishment may: "(1) consist in whole or in part of any filthy, putrid, or decomposed substance, or (2) [have] been prepared, packed, or held under unsanitary conditions whereby it may have become contaminated with filth, or whereby it may have been rendered injurious to health."[122]

Before leaving the inspection, the investigator is required to meet with the company to discuss the results of the inspection. Section 5.2.7 of the manual notes:

During the discussion, be frank, courteous, and responsive with management. Point out the observations listed on the FDA 483 are your observations of objectionable conditions found during the inspection and explain the significance of each. Try to relate each listed condition to the applicable sections of the laws and regulations administered by the FDA.

If significant deviations are observed during the inspection, you should inform management during the closeout discussion, the conditions observed may, after further review by the agency, be considered to be violations of the FD&C Act or other statutes. Legal sanctions available to the FDA may include seizure, injunction, civil money penalties, and prosecution.[123]

Thus, the primary purpose of such discussion is to inform management of the conditions observed by the investigator. Another purpose is to give the investigator an opportunity to elicit responses and commitments from the responsible individual. When the inspector's report is prepared, there will be a discussion of the meeting.

Refusal to Permit Entry or Inspection or to Permit Access to or Copying of Records

If the owner, operator, or agent in charge refuses entry or inspection, the FDA's district office will approach either the Department of Justice and/or the local U.S. Attorney's office to request assistance in obtaining an administrative inspection warrant from a federal magistrate judge.

The U.S. Attorney's office and FDA district office will work together in preparing an application for the warrant and present it to the judge or magistrate judge, who reviews it. If the application is found to be adequate, the magistrate judge will issue an administrative inspection warrant authorizing the FDA investigator to return to the facility and conduct the inspection.

If the owner, operator, or agent in charge still refuses entry or inspection pursuant to the warrant, that refusal is punishable as contempt of court for that individual's failure to obey an order of a federal court. Such warrants of inspection would contain language that would allow the investigator broader inspectional authority (for example, the taking of photographs) than allowed under section 704.[124]

Accredited Persons Inspection Programs

The Medical Device User Fee and Modernization Act of 2002 (MDUFMA) was signed into law on October 26, 2002. MDUFMA authorizes APs to conduct medical device facility inspections. An inspection by an AP is an alternative to the traditional inspection by an FDA official. An AP can evaluate a manufacturer's compliance with the QSR (21 CFR Part 820) and other FDA regulations and submit the findings to the FDA for final determination.

An AP is a third party recognized by the FDA who meets requirements set forth at section 704(g)(3) of the act. Participation in the program is entirely voluntary. Eligible manufacturers may request to utilize an AP or continue to have the FDA perform inspections. A benefit of the AP program is that it allows eligible manufacturers greater control over the timing of their inspections. In addition, some of the APs accredited by the FDA are already recognized by other countries as persons authorized to conduct ISO 13485 audits of device establishments. A single AP inspection may meet the requirements of more than one regulatory authority, thereby reducing the need for multiple inspections of the same establishment.

To be eligible to employ an AP in lieu of an inspection by the FDA, establishments must meet the following basic criteria under section 704(g)(6)(A) of the act:

- The establishment's most recent inspection was classified by the FDA as "no action indicated" (NAI) or "voluntary action indicated" (VAI).
- The establishment submits a notice to the FDA requesting clearance (approval) to use an AP and identifying the AP it intends to use, and the FDA agrees to the use of the selected AP.
- The establishment markets a device in the United States and markets or intends to market a device in one or more foreign countries.

- The AP is certified, accredited, or otherwise recognized by one of the foreign countries in which the device is to be marketed.
- The establishment submits a statement that the laws of one of the countries in which the device is to be marketed recognize an inspection of the establishment by the FDA.

In general, an AP may not perform more than two consecutive inspections of a particular establishment unless the establishment petitions the FDA for and receives a waiver. This provision of MDUFMA is intended to ensure periodic inspections by the FDA.

Chapter 6

The EU Medical Device Regulation

INTRODUCTION

For a company to sell or distribute a medical device in the European Union (EU), implementing a quality management system (QMS) and certifying it to ISO 13485 (the internationally recognized medical device quality management system standard) is not sufficient to meet the legal requirements. The EU requires that medical devices be CE marked. The CE mark indicates that the device complies with one of the routes of conformance (regulatory compliance) based on its classification.

The EU Medical Device (EU MDR) "Regulation (EU) 2017/745 of the European Parliament and of the council of 5 April 2017 on medical devices" amends directive 2001/83/EC, Regulation (EC) No. 178/2002 and Regulation (EC) No. 1223/2009 and repeals the following Council Directives: Active Implantable Medical Device Directive 90/385/EEC and Medical Devices Directive 93/42/EEC. The original date of application of the new rules was May 26, 2020, but was extended to May 26, 2021.

The quality auditor and professional may best use this chapter in the following way:

1. Review the most significant changes from MDD to MDR.
2. Review the "Documents and Records for Demonstrating Compliance" in the various sections.
3. Understand Table 6.1: Mandatory Documents and Records by Category and EU MDR Article.

THE MDD TO MDR TRANSITION

The most significant changes in the regulation (from the previous MDD and AIMD) include:

1. *Product scope expansion:* The definition of medical devices and active implantable medical devices covered under the EU MDR has been significantly expanded to include devices that do not have a medical intended purpose (for example, colored contact lenses and cosmetic

implant and materials). Also included in the scope of the regulation are devices designed for the purpose of "prediction and prognosis" of a disease or other health condition (for example, software intended to monitor physiological processes).

2. *Device reclassification:* The EU MDR requires device manufacturers to review the updated classification rules and update their technical documentation accordingly. Class III and implantable devices will have higher clinical and biocompatibility requirements.
3. *Qualified person identification:* Device manufacturers will be required to identify, at a minimum, one person within the organization who is ultimately responsible for all aspects of compliance with the requirements of the new regulation. The organization must document the specific qualifications of this individual relative to the required tasks. Exceptions may be applied to small enterprises.
4. *Specifications:* The EU MDR allows the EU Commission or expert panels to publish common specifications. These common specifications shall exist in parallel to the harmonized standards and the state of the art.
5. *Unique device identification (UDI):* The EU MDR mandates the use of UDI mechanisms. This requirement is expected to increase the tracing of specific devices through the supply chain, and facilitate the prompt and efficient recall of medical devices. The European Databank on Medical Devices (Eudamed) is expected to be expanded to provide efficient access to information on approved medical devices.
6. *Safety and performance requirements (SPR):* SPRs have replaced the MDD essential requirements.
7. *Clinical evidence (Class III and implantable medical devices):* Manufacturers must conduct clinical investigations if there is insufficient clinical evidence to support the product claims on both safety and performance of the device. Manufacturers are required to collect and retain post-market clinical data as part of the ongoing assessment of potential safety risks.
8. *Clinical evidence (Class IIa and IIb medical devices):* Manufacturers must rewrite the clinical evaluation with consideration on when an equivalence approach is acceptable and under which circumstances it is possible to justify not conducting a clinical investigation.
9. *Post-market oversight:* The EU MDR increases post-market surveillance requirements and oversight by the notified body. Unannounced audits, along with product sample checks and product testing, will increase oversight and help reduce risks from unsafe devices. Annual safety and performance reporting by device manufacturers is required.

Manufacturers should also be aware that other EU directives and regulations have amended the EU MDR, added to or amended the original regulation requirements, or can be used during the transition.

1. Human tissues and cells (Directive 2004/23/EC)
2. Animal by-products and derived products (Regulation No. 1069/2009)
3. Reclassification of breast implants (Directive 2003/12/EC)
4. Reclassification of hip, knee, and shoulder joint implants (Directive 2005/50/EC)

There are also EU directives that may be applicable, partially or in whole, to medical devices and may be required for CE marking and market access:

1. Cosmetic products (Regulation No. 1223/2009)
2. Medicinal products for human and veterinary use (Regulation No. 726/2004)
3. Personal protective equipment (Regulation No. 2016/425)
4. Telecommunication equipment (Directive 2014/53/EU)
5. Waste electrical and electronic equipment (WEEE) (Directive 2012/19/EU)
6. Restriction on certain hazardous substances in electrical and electronic equipment (RoHS) (Directive 2011/65/EU)
7. Pressure equipment (Directive 2014/68/EU)
8. Machinery (Directive 2006/42/EC)
9. Electrical equipment designed for use within certain voltage limits (low voltage) (Directive 2014/55/EC)

   Note: This is not an all-encompassing list. Refer to EUR-LEX.europa.eu for the current in-force documents.

In addition, there are standards and guidelines to use as references:

1. MEDDEV Guidelines on Medical Devices
2. Biological Evaluation Standard (ISO 10993)
3. Medical Electrical Equipment Standards (EN 60601)
4. Medical Device Quality Management System Standard (ISO 13485)
5. Medical Device Risk Management Standard (ISO 14971)

SCOPE AND PURPOSE OF THE MEDICAL DEVICE REGULATION

The purpose of the EU MDR is to harmonize the regulations and administrative provisions among the member states of the EEA and ensure the safety, health, protection, and performance characteristics of medical devices and in vitro diagnostic devices.

The format of the regulation consists of 10 chapters containing 123 articles and 17 annexes. These cover such key items as scope, definitions, manufacturers, notified bodies, authorized representative, importers, distributors, compliance and conformity, UDI, clinical evaluation and investigations, post-market surveillance and safety updates, and vigilance. The chapters are followed by 17 annexes, which include coverage of the general safety, technical documentation, post-market surveillance, conformity, UDI, notified bodies, classification rules, custom-made devices, clinical evaluation and investigation, and products without a medical purpose.

Before a manufacturer can place the CE marking on a medical device and legally sell to or within the EEA, it must be in compliance with all the requirements of the applicable regulation and directives.

REQUIREMENTS FOR COMPLIANCE

The following items should be considered in preparing for and demonstrating compliance with the regulation:

1. Determination of whether the product has to comply with the EU MDR, and one or more of the EU directives that may be appropriate
2. Classification of the device under the EU MDR
3. Conformity assessment routes (route to demonstrating compliance with the MDR, applying to and utilizing a notified body in conformity assessment, if appropriate)
4. Compliance with the safety and performance requirements
5. Awareness and utilization of appropriate harmonized standards
6. Risk analysis and assessment
7. Clinical evaluation, including premarket clinical data evaluation and post-market clinical follow-up plans
8. Preparation of technical file/design dossier
9. For non-EU manufacturers, the appointment of an authorized representative within the EU
10. UDI system
11. Identification of economic operators, defined as a manufacturer, an authorized representative, an importer, a distributor
12. Implementation of appropriate post-market surveillance systems, including proactive systems and reactive systems (reactive systems include complaints and device incident reporting/the vigilance system)
13. Declaration of conformity

14. CE marking: The EU Declaration of Conformity is a formal document that officially certifies the product fulfills the essential requirements needed to meet the applicable CE directives. This allows the manufacturer to obtain a CE mark for the medical device.

DETERMINING WHETHER THE PRODUCT MUST COMPLY WITH THE REGULATION

The intended use and classification must be considered. The manufacturer decides on the intended use and determines if the device fulfills the definition of a medical device in Article 2 (1) "Definitions." If it does meet the definition of a medical device, then the classification is determined in accordance with Article 51 "Classification of devices" and the rules contained in Annex VIII "Classification Rules."

Accessories to a device are treated under the regulation and the same applicable directive as the device. The only exception is accessories to IVD products that are used for patient-contacting, invasive sampling; these are treated as a medical device.

Note that this definition also applies to devices offered to EU citizens via the internet (Article 6 "Distant Sales")

Documents and records for demonstrating compliance:

1. The rationale for deciding the product is a medical device
2. The statement of the intended purpose and users of the device
3. The device classification rationale
4. The rationale for lifetime of the device, generally considered the shelf life plus the use or therapeutic duration of the device

TYPES OF MEDICAL DEVICES

Active implantable medical devices include cardiac pacemakers, defibrillators, infusion pumps, and neurostimulators. "Active" implies that the function of these devices is dependent on a source of energy other than gravity or human power. In almost all cases, this is electrical power but could be radioactivity or other energy sources.

Accessories specifically intended to be used only with active implantable medical devices are also covered by the MDR. Accessories and software, such as external pacemaker programming devices, are governed by the MDR even though they are not directly implanted.

Non-active implantable products such as heart valves and orthopedic implants, surgically invasive devices such as catheters and surgical instruments, noninvasive devices such as disposables, wound care devices, contact lenses, and disinfectants, and active (powered) devices such as ventilators, patient monitors, and therapeutic and electrosurgical equipment, are governed by the MDR.

In addition, the MDR covers accessories and software that are used with a medical device. Examples include the software used to control or program radiation treatment. The software, if provided separately, has the same classification as the device with which it is intended to be used.

If an IVD sample collection device is invasive to patients, such as a blood lancet or invasive swab, then that device is covered under the MDR.

CLASSIFICATION OF MEDICAL DEVICES

Note: The following classifications have been summarized from information provided in EU MDR ANNEX VIII "Classification Rules." Please review the EU MDR for further details, special rules, and exemptions.

Class I:

1. All noninvasive devices, unless one of the rules for other classes applies
2. All noninvasive devices that come into contact with injured skin or mucous membrane if they are intended to be used as a mechanical barrier, for compression, or for absorption of exudates
3. All invasive devices with respect to body orifices, other than surgically invasive devices, that are not intended for connection to an active device or that are intended for connection to a Class I active device, if they are intended for transient use
4. All invasive devices with respect to body orifices, other than surgically invasive devices, that are not intended for connection to an active device or that are intended for connection to a Class I active device, if they are intended for short-term use and if they are used in the oral cavity as far as the pharynx, in an ear canal up to the ear drum, or in the nasal cavity
5. All surgically invasive devices intended for transient use that are reusable surgical instruments
6. Software that is not intended to provide information that is used to make decisions or is intended to monitor physiological processes

Class IIa:

1. All noninvasive devices intended for channeling or storing blood, body liquid, cells or tissues, liquids or gases for the purpose of eventual infusion, administration, or introduction in the body
2. All noninvasive devices intended for modifying the biological or chemical composition of human tissues or cells, blood, other body liquids, or other liquids intended for implantation or administration into the body
3. Blood bags
4. All noninvasive devices that come into contact with injured skin or mucous membrane if they are principally intended to manage the microenvironment of injured skin or mucous membrane

5. All noninvasive devices that come into contact with injured skin or mucous membrane if they are intended to be used in all other cases not listed in IIa or IIb
6. All invasive devices with respect to body orifices, other than surgically invasive devices, that are not intended for connection to an active device or that are intended for connection to a Class I active device, if they are intended for short-term use, except if they are used in the oral cavity as far as the pharynx, in an ear canal up to the ear drum, or in the nasal cavity
7. All invasive devices with respect to body orifices, other than surgically invasive devices, that are not intended for connection to an active device or that are intended for connection to a Class I active device, if they are intended for long-term use and are used in the oral cavity as far as the pharynx, in an ear canal up to the ear drum, or in the nasal cavity and are not liable to be absorbed by the mucous membrane
8. All invasive devices with respect to body orifices, other than surgically invasive devices, intended for connection to a Class IIa, Class IIb, or Class III active device
9. All surgically invasive devices intended for transient use or short term unless listed in other classes
10. Implantable intended to be placed in teeth
11. All active therapeutic devices intended to administer or exchange energy unless listed in another class
12. Active devices intended for diagnosis and monitoring if they are intended to supply energy that will be absorbed by the human body
13. Software intended to provide information, which is used to take decisions, unless listed in another class.
14. Software intended to monitor physiological processes, except for those listed in other classes
15. All active devices intended to administer and/or remove medicinal products, body liquids, or other substances unless listed in IIb

Class IIb:

1. All noninvasive devices that come into contact with injured skin or mucous membrane if they are intended to be used principally for injuries to skin that have breached the dermis or mucous membrane and can only heal by secondary intent
2. All invasive devices with respect to body orifices, other than surgically invasive devices, that are not intended for connection to an active device or that are intended for connection to a Class I active device, if they are intended for long-term use, except if they are used in the

oral cavity as far as the pharynx, in an ear canal up to the ear drum, or in the nasal cavity and are not liable to be absorbed by the mucous membrane

3. All surgically invasive devices intended for transient use and intended to supply energy in the form of ionizing radiation, have a biological effect, or mainly absorbed, or are intended to administer medicinal products by means of a delivery system, if such administration of a medicinal product is done in a manner that is potentially hazardous taking account of the mode of application
4. Implantable devices and long-term surgical devices unless listed in another class
5. All active therapeutic devices intended to administer or exchange energy if their characteristics are such that they may administer energy to or exchange energy with the human body in a potentially hazardous way, intended to control or monitor the performance of active therapeutic devices, emit ionizing radiation purposes, or intended to directly influence the performance of such devices
6. Active devices intended to emit ionizing radiation and intended for diagnostic or therapeutic radiology, including interventional radiology devices
7. Software intended to monitor vital physiological processes where the variation could result in immediate danger to the patient
8. Software intended to provide information to make decisions that may cause a serious deterioration of a person's state or a surgical intervention
9. All active devices intended to administer and/or remove medicinal products, body liquids, or other substances if done in a manner that is potentially hazardous

Class III:

1. All noninvasive devices consisting of a substance or a mixture of substances intended to be used in vitro in direct contact with human cells, tissue, or organs taken from the human body or used in vitro with human embryos before their implantation or administration into the body
2. All surgically invasive devices intended for transient use or short-term use that are intended specifically to control, diagnose, monitor, or correct a defect of the heart or of the central circulatory system through direct contact with those parts of the body; are intended specifically for use in direct contact with the heart or central circulatory system or the central nervous system
3. Implantable devices and long-term surgical devices that come in direct contact with the heart, central circulatory system, or central nervous

system, have a biological effect, are absorbed, undergo chemical change in the body, are intended to administer medicinal products, are active implantable breast implants, joint, or spinal replacement (with the exception of ancillary components such as screws), or come into contact with the spinal column

4. All active devices that are intended for controlling, monitoring, or directly influencing the performance of active implantable devices
5. Software intended to provide information to make decisions that may cause death or an irreversible deterioration of a person's state of health or surgical intervention

QUALITY MANAGEMENT SYSTEMS, PROCESSES, AND RESOURCES FOR MEDICAL DEVICES

In addition to product requirements, the company or companies developing, producing, commercializing, and distributing the medical device shall also have design, engineering, manufacturing, risk management, quality management, medical, and regulatory systems and processes in place per international standards (ISO).

Documents and records for demonstrating compliance:

1. A strategy for complying with regulations
2. The design and manufacturing processes (Article 10 (1)), such as product realization process
3. The risk management process (Article 10 (2))
4. The clinical evaluation process (Article 10 (3))
5. Safety and performance (Article 5(2))
6. Development and maintenance of technical documentation, UDI, and the EU declaration of conformity processes (Article 10(4-8))
7. The quality management system (Article 10(9)) including management responsibility
8. The post-market surveillance planning process (Article 10 (10))
9. The labeling development process, including producing language translations (Article 10 (11)
10. The corrective action and recall process (Article 10 (12))
11. The regulatory authority interaction process (Article 10(14))—communication with authorities
12. The legal liability and damage compensation process (Article 10(16))
13. One or more persons overseeing the regulatory compliance (Article (15))
14. Access to technical, safety(risk), clinical, quality, and regulatory expertise (copies of CVs and contracts)

SAFETY AND PERFORMANCE REQUIREMENTS

All devices, regardless of the classification, are required in Article 5(2) to fulfill the general safety and performance requirements of EU MDR Annex 1. The key elements listed are general requirements, design and manufacture requirements, and information supplied with the device as summarized below:

General requirements

- Devices shall be designed and manufactured such that during normal conditions of use are suitable for the intended purpose, safe, and effective.
- Risk is reduced as far as possible, and a benefit-risk ratio is documented.
- Residual risk shall be assessed.

Design and manufacture requirements

- Devices shall be designed and manufactured to ensure the characteristics and performance requirements, including chemical, physical, and biological properties, are fulfilled.
- Device design and manufacturing shall eliminate or reduce as far as possible the risk of infection and adverse interaction with their environment or in combination with other devices, medicine, or equipment.
- Devices shall not be adversely affected during transport and storage, including contaminants and residues to patients.
- Devices shall be designed and manufactured in such a way as to reduce as far as possible the risks posed by substances or particles, including wear debris, degradation products, and processing residues that may be released from the device.

Information requirements

- Each device shall be accompanied by the information needed to identify the device and its manufacturer, and by any safety and performance information relevant to the user, or any other person, as appropriate.
- The claims made on labelling, instructions for use, and advertising shall comply with Article 7, Annex I (Chapter 3, 23) and Annex II.

Activities begin with risk management activities (Annex I, Chapter 1). Applicable requirements for the device are listed in Annex I, Chapter 2. Note that risk management during development does not finish with a positive benefit-risk report (Annex 1 (3)). The claims made on labelling, instructions for use, and advertising shall comply with Article 7. The final step is the preparation of the post-market surveillance plan (Article 84 and Annex III (1.1)). A list of product requirements, identification of harmonized standards and EU common specification, and other EU directives is recommended. For example, special requirements could be environmental (for example, for batteries) or health and safety (for example, for hazardous substances). The company needs to produce a device performance summary for each medical device. Devices must achieve the performance for their intended use and be manufactured in a way that, during normal conditions of use, they are suitable for their intended purpose. Medical devices must be safe and effective, and they shall not compromise the clinical condition or safety of patients, nor the safety and health of users or other persons. However, any residual risks that may be associated with their use must be assessed and weighed against the benefits to the patient. The risk-benefit analysis may be part of the risk management file and the clinical evaluation report. The post-market surveillance plan, periodic safety update report (PSUR), and post-market surveillance report (Articles 84, 85, 86, and Annex III (1.1)) shall include such items as product requirements, identification of harmonized standards and EU common specification (if applicable), nonserious and serious incidents, post-market clinical follow-up, trend reporting, relevant literature and databases, feedback and complaints, publicly available information on similar devices, processes and methods for collecting data, risk management, complaint investigations, competent authority communication, and corrective actions.

Each medical device shall have a documented safety and performance summary. The documentation shall contain information for the demonstration of conformity with the general safety and performance requirements set out in Annex I that are applicable to the device taking into account its intended purpose, and shall include a justification, validation, and verification of the solutions adopted to meet those requirements. The demonstration of conformity shall include: (a) the general safety and performance requirements that apply to the device and an explanation as to why others do not apply; (b) the method or methods used to demonstrate conformity with each applicable general safety and performance requirement; (c) the harmonized standards, CS, or other solutions applied; and (d) the precise identity of the controlled documents offering evidence of conformity with each harmonized standard, CS, or other method applied to demonstrate conformity with the general safety and performance requirements. The information referred to under this point shall incorporate a cross-reference to the location of such evidence within the full technical documentation and, if applicable, the summary technical documentation.

Documents and records for demonstrating compliance:

1. The risk management file and process to maintain it per Article 10(2)
2. A general requirements checklist or a trace matrix of planned testing
3. Labeling and instructions for use
4. Safety and performance summary
5. The post-market surveillance plan

RISK MANAGEMENT

Risk management shall be done for each medical device and appropriately documented to demonstrate the manufacturer's ability to assess and control the risks that are posed by the medical device throughout the life cycle of the product. The probability of occurrence must be considered for hazardous situations that can lead to potential failures, so controls to mitigate these potential effects can be implemented. The purpose of the risk management process is to describe a process of identification, evaluation, and addressing the risks that arise from design, use, and production processes for the medical device. The intent of the risk assessment process is to verify that the right materials are being used, to conform to customer specifications, and to ensure government regulations are being met, before finalizing the product design. The overall goal is to identify any potential failure that could be caused by the manufacturing processes, assembly processes, machines, fixtures, and production methods. The risk management plan includes all the information required to assess the risk of a medical device and includes the identification, description, life-cycle stages, risk assessment methodology, acceptance criteria, residual risk evaluation plan, verification activities, and post-production plan. The risk management file details the risk management activity for each medical device and includes risk acceptance, controls, and benefit-risk analysis. The risk management report compiles and summarizes the risk management activities.

Documents and records for demonstrating compliance:

1. Risk management plan
2. Risk management file
3. Risk management report

CLINICAL EVALUATION

All devices, regardless of the classification, are required by Article 5(3) to fulfill the clinical requirements of Article 61 and Part A of Annex XIV. Clinical evaluation begins with a clinical evaluation plan (CEP) per Annex XIV, part A. Whether the clinical evaluation will have to include a clinical trial or investigation will depend on the classification of the device, how novel the device is, and the amount of clinical data on equivalent devices in published literature. If a clinical investigation is necessary, it must be planned, approved, conducted, and reported per Articles 62-81 and Annex XV. The clinical investigation is the systematic evaluation of studies using human subjects to determine the safety and performance of a medical device. This critical step contains several required clinical investigation documents including informed consent, application form, investigator brochure, clinical investigation plan, safety and performance statement, proof of insurance, arrangement description, and clinical investigation report. The clinical evaluation process continues with post-market clinical follow-up and the post-market clinical follow-up plan (Annex XIV, Part B). Post-market surveillance shall be done for all medical devices distributed to the EU. The post-market surveillance system allows for a manufacturer to know what has happened to the medical device once it has been distributed.

Documents and records for demonstrating compliance:

1. The clinical evaluation plan (CEP) and report (CER)
2. Clinical investigation documentation (if applicable)
3. The post-market clinical follow-up (PMCF) plan
4. The post-market surveillance plan

TECHNICAL DOCUMENTATION

All devices, regardless of the classification, are required to fulfill the technical documentation requirements of Annexes II and III. Most documentation will have been generated for the safety and performance, biocompatibility (biological evaluation), and clinical evaluation requirements. If the device is a Class III device, an additional summary of safety and performance will be uploaded to the European registration database (Article 32). However, there are additional items, such as the UDI, to be placed in the technical documentation folders. The UDI is a barcode system that enables devices to be tracked wherever they are distributed in the EU (Article 27 and Annex VI, part C). A company shall maintain a list of all the UDIs manufactured or distributed.

Documents and records for demonstrating compliance:

1. The technical documentation (a list is helpful to demonstrate that the documentation is presented in a clear, organized, readily searchable, and unambiguous manner)
2. A list of all UDIs

Technical files must be updated under the following situations:

- Change in raw material supplier
- Change in dimensions or other characteristics of the medical device
- Change in address of the manufacturer
- Change in relevant standards
- Update in certificates or accreditation of suppliers and/or testing laboratories
- When new risks are discovered during post-market surveillance

DISTRIBUTION

Distribution of a medical device depends on several economic operators, defined as a manufacturer, an authorized representative, an importer, a distributor, or the person referred to in Article 22(1) and 22(3). Each economic operator has a responsibility for the medical device that is distributed within the EU. Distributors have obligations such as checking that the devices distributed comply with EU MDR, and reporting complaints and suspected serious incidents. An agreement between the distributor and the manufacturer shall include communication for reporting complaints and serious incidents. If the manufacturer does not reside in the EU, a legal representative ("Authorized Representative") within the EU must be appointed and the scope and mandate agreed upon (Article 11). Importers of product into the EU have specific obligations and also must register with the authorities (Article 13).

Documents and records for demonstrating compliance:

1. The agreements with an authorized representative, importer(s), and/or distributor (each economic operator)

DEVICE AND MANUFACTURER REGISTRATION

Economic operators (manufacturers, authorized representative, and importers) are required to register to obtain a single registration number (SRN) (Article 31). Manufacturers are required to upload information about each device, including its UDI information (Article 29).

Documents and records for demonstrating compliance:

1. The single registration number
2. The UDI data uploaded to EUDAMED
3. The EU Declaration of Conformity

CONFORMITY ASSESSMENT

Manufacturers may choose any notified body to perform the conformity assessment, as long as the notified body has the necessary capabilities for the type of device being considered. Manufacturers also have some flexibility in the conformity assessment route they follow, depending on the class of the device (Article 52). Conformity assessment information can be found in Annex IX, X, XI, and XIII. The EU Declaration of Conformity is a formal document that officially certifies the product fulfills the essential requirements needed to meet the applicable CE directives. This allows the manufacturer to obtain a CE mark for the medical device.

Documents and records for demonstrating compliance (one of the following):

1. An "EU quality management system certificate" for the manufacturer and an "EU technical documentation assessment certificate" for the device, or
2. An "EU type-examination certificate" for the device and either an "EU quality assurance certificate" for the routine production process or an "EU product verification certificate" for customer-specific production, or
3. In the case of a custom-made device, the documentation described in Annex XIII.

CE MARKING

The manufacturer is obliged to place the CE marking on the device. To commercialize the product in the EU, a CE mark certificate is needed. This certification verifies that a device meets all regulatory requirements for medical devices.

The CE marking must be either on the device or its primary package, the shipping/sales package, and the instructions for use. Reusable devices must have the CE marking on the device. The CE marking must appear as defined in the annexes listed previously. It must be at least 5mm high.

MARKET LAUNCH

Once the notified body certificates are received, the manufacturer is able to finalize the EU Declaration of Conformity (Annex IV) and the device registration (Annex VI). Manufacturers outside of the EU must provide their authorized representative with the technical documentation, the notified body certificates, and confirmation of the manufacturer's registration. The authorized representative shall register per Article 11. Manufacturers provide their importer with the EU Declaration of Conformity, confirmation of the registration, and the device labelling, and the importer registers per Article 13.

Distributors in the supply chain require their national language versions of the EU Declaration of Conformity and the packaging and instructions, including the importer's name and address, if applicable, and the UDI number (Article 14).

If the manufacturer has a website, the national language versions of the packaging and instructions shall be published on the website (Annex I, 23.1.).

The device can now be imported, marketed, distributed, supplied for use, and used within the EU.

Document and records for demonstrating compliance:

1. The final EU Declaration of Conformity, including versions in the language(s) of the countries where the device will be distributed
2. The final registration by the manufacturer
3. The registrations by the authorized representative and importer (if applicable)
4. The national language versions of the packaging and instructions available for distributors
5. The national language versions of the packaging and instructions published on the manufacturer's website

POST-MARKET LAUNCH AND MAINTENANCE

Device manufacturers have ongoing obligations once the device is on the market and being used. The obligations are summarized below:

1. Evidence of the benefit-risk determination being reviewed
   - Maintain the risk management system described in Annex 1 (3) per Article 10(2).

2. Evidence of the post-market clinical follow-up activities being performed and the clinical evaluation being updated
   - Execute the planned post-market clinical follow-up activities as described in Annex XIV Part B per Article 10(3).
3. Update the technical documentation, including the authorized representative's copy and history of changes
   - Keep the technical documentation described in Annexes II and III per Article 10(4). Custom-made devices shall update the documentation described in Annex XIII per Article 10(5). Keep the technical documentation, including records of any changes in the documentation or certificates, available for the EU authorities for at least 10 or 15 years after the final placing of the device variant on the market. This includes keeping up to date any technical documentation retained by authorized representatives (Article 10 (8)).
4. Evidence that the quality management system covers all the required processes and is being reviewed and updated
   - Keep the quality management system updated to ensure the – manufactured product remains compliant, including any changes in standards and regulations, and the processes remain effective and compliant (Article 10(9)).
5. Evidence of the post-market surveillance (PMS) activities taking place with the required scope
   - Maintain the post-market surveillance system activities as described in Article 83, paying particular attention to the interfaces listed in paragraph 3 a-h (Article 10 (10)). In addition to a post-market surveillance report, a periodic safety update report (PSUR) is required for Class IIa, IIb, and III devices.
6. Evidence of deviations and complaints being investigated and corrective action being taken to address nonconformities with appropriate parties being informed
   - Immediately take corrective action for any nonconforming devices, informing any distributors, the authorized representative, and importer. Immediately inform the competent authorities and the notified body of any devices that pose a serious risk (Article 10 (12)).
7. Evidence of incidents being investigated and serious incidents being reported within the required time
   - Report any serious incidents to the authorities, at the latest within 15 days after becoming aware. Report any field safety corrective actions, ideally in advance of taking action, as well as changes in trends in other incidents, all as described in Articles 87 and 88 (Article 10 (13).
8. Evidence of the person responsible for regulatory compliance carrying out his or her duties (Article 15)

9. Evidence of traceability of supply
   - Maintain traceability records of any devices received from or supplied to any other economic operators (for example, importers or distributors) or supplied to any health institutions of healthcare professionals (Article 25 (2)).
10. Evidence of updating or confirming the registration data
    - Update the EUDAMED database within one week of any changes to the registration data and reconfirm the accuracy of the data registration every second year (Article 31).

SUMMARY

A summary of EU MDR required documents and records is shown in Table 6.1. While these are the documents and records that the EU MDR has identified as mandatory, it is important to note that for the proper function of the quality management system, refer to ISO 13485.

For Class I (self-certified), annual notified body audits are not required. However, CER, technical file, and PMS activities must be kept updated.

For all other classes, audits are conducted each year by a notified body to ensure ongoing compliance with the MDR. Failure to pass the audit will invalidate the CE marking certificate. Clinical evaluation, PMS, and PMCF activities must be performed to maintain CE certification.

Table 6.1 EU MDR documents and records.

Category	Mandatory Documents and Records	EU MDR Articles, Chapters, and Annexes
Device Class	Device description, including rationale for "lifetime" of the device	Annex VIII
General Requirements	Single registration number (SRN)	Article 31
	EU declaration of conformity	Article 4
	Quality management system	Article 10
	Regulatory interaction and compliance	Article 10,15
	Legal liability and damage compensation	Article 10
	Economic operators agreements	Articles 11, 13
	Summary of safety and clinical performance	Article 32
	National language packaging and instructions	Article 14
	Registrations	Articles 6, 11, 13
	List of all UDIs, UDI uploaded	Articles 27, 29

(continued)

Table 6.1 EU MDR documents and records. *(continued)*

Category	Mandatory Documents and Records	EU MDR Articles, Chapters, and Annexes
Risk Management	Risk management plan	Annex I (1)
	Risk management file	Article 10, Annex I (1)
	Risk management report	Annex I (1)
	Benefit-risk reviewed post market	Annex I
Safety and Performance	Safety and performance Documentation	Article 5, Annex I
Clinical Evaluation	Clinical evaluation plan (CEP)	Annex XIV (A)
	Clinical evaluation report (CER)	Chapter VI, Article 61 (12), Annex XIV (4)
Clinical Investigation	Clinical investigation documentation	Articles 62-81
	Informed consent	Article 63
	Application form	Annex XV (II (1))
	Investigation brochure	Annex XV (II (2))
	Clinical investigation plan	Article 72, Annex XV (II (3))
	Safety and performance statement	Annex XV (II (4))
	Proof of insurance	Annex XV (II (4))
	Arrangement description	Annex XV (II (4))
	Clinical investigation report	Annex XV (III (7))
Post-Market Surveillance	Post-market surveillance plan	Article 84, Annex III
	Post-market surveillance report	Article 85
	Periodic safety update report (PSUR)	Article 86
	Post-market clinical follow-up plan (PMCF)	Annex XIV, Part B(6)
Technical File Documentation	Device description and specification	Annex II (1)
	Labels and instruction for use	Annex II (2)
	Design information	Annex II (3)
	Manufacturing process and validations	Annex II (3)
	Site identification	Annex II (3)
	Results of different preclinical and clinical testing	Annex II (6)
Traceability	Traceability records	Article 25
Vigilance	Complaints	Article 10, 87, 89
	Corrective action reports	Article 87

Chapter 7

Other International Regulations

INTRODUCTION

Many countries have specific regulations that apply to medical device manufacturing in that country. When auditing in any country, the auditor must be aware of the specific regulations that apply to ensure the audit scope is appropriate and the auditor is aware of any specific requirements.

Regulatory authorities in Australia, Brazil, Canada, Japan, and the United States are leading the Medical Device Single Audit Program (MDSAP) that will allow recognized third-party auditors to perform a single audit of a medical device manufacturer to be accepted by multiple regulators. The World Health Organization (WHO) and the European Union (EU) are official observers, while Argentina and Korea are affiliate members. The MDSAP audit has been designed to meet the requirements of ISO 13485:2016 and is based on a three-year audit cycle comprising an initial certification audit, surveillance audits in each of the two years following initial certification, and a recertification audit in the third year following the initial certification audit.

MDSAP benefits to manufacturers are to include a single audit in lieu of multiple separate audits by participating regulatory authorities, improved predictability of audit outcomes, flexibility to select from all authorized auditing organizations to perform audits, and increased confidence in the reliability of third-party audits.

The MDSAP Pilot Program started January 1, 2014; countries participating in the pilot included Australia, Brazil, Canada, United States, and Japan. MDSAP entered the operational phase in January 2017.

Regulatory authorities in the United States and Canada have already taken action to adopt MDSAP. The United States has indicated its intention to recognize MDSAP audit reports in lieu of its own inspection reports. Health Canada replaced its Canadian Medical Devices Conformity Assessment System (CMDCAS) with MDSAP, thereby making MDSAP the only option to demonstrate compliance with quality management system requirements for Canada effective as of January 2019.

Several of the countries with specific regulations are discussed in this chapter, including Canada, Japan, and Australia. Please refer to Chapter 6 for information on the EU regulations.

CANADA

Canada has specific regulations relating to medical devices and in guidance documents published relative to those regulations. A summary of the contents is as follows.

Canadian Medical Devices Regulations, SOR/98-282

The Canadian Medical Devices Regulations (CMDR) is issued under the authority of the Food and Drugs Act regarding food, drugs, cosmetics, and therapeutic devices. The CMDR provides for the classification of medical devices and establishes manufacturer requirements including device safety and effectiveness, labeling, device and establishment licensure, quality management system certification, distribution records, complaint handling and mandatory problem reporting, recalls, and registration for implantable devices.

Classification of medical devices and in vitro diagnostic devices is accomplished using risk-based classification rules provided in the CMDR. Products are classified into Classes I to IV. Class I corresponds to devices representing the lowest risk, and Class IV the highest. If a device can be classified into more than one class, the higher classification applies. Canadian classification rules are similar to those established for the EU. However, the classification of a particular device may differ among regulatory jurisdictions and therefore needs to be considered in each jurisdiction where the device will be marketed. For example, many devices that are Class II in Canada are Class I devices in the United States.

Medical devices are classified by applying 16 classification rules provided in Schedule 1, Part 1 of the CMDR. Device classification rules 1-12 consider invasiveness of the device (for example, invasive, noninvasive) and whether the device is active, whereas rules 13-16 are considered special rules and apply to circumstances as specified. Similarly, in vitro diagnostic devices are classified as Classes I through IV using a set of nine rules provided in Schedule 1, Part 2 of the CMDR.

Device classification determines the type of license required for a device and quality management system requirements. Class I devices require a medical device establishment license (MDEL) to be held by the manufacturer or distributor. Class II, III, and IV products require a device-specific Canadian medical device license (MDL) and certification to the ISO 13485 standard. MDL applications for Class II devices are generally simpler than a U.S. 510(k) premarket application and comparable for Class III MDL applications. Applications for a Class IV MDL are comparable to a U.S. premarket approval (PMA) application.

Medical device manufacturers are required to design and manufacture devices that are safe and effective. Manufacturers must take reasonable measures to identify risks inherent in the device, eliminate risks that can be eliminated, and minimize the hazard from potential failures for the projected useful life of the device. If risks cannot be eliminated, the manufacturer shall reduce the risks to the extent possible, provide appropriate protection for those risks, and provide information relative to the remaining risks with the device. Additionally, for the projected useful life of a medical device, its characteristics and performance shall not deteriorate under normal use to a degree that the health or safety of a patient or other person is adversely affected.

The CMDR establishes minimum device labeling requirements to include: device name, manufacturer name and address, device identifier (including devices that are part of a system or medical device group), control number for Class III and IV devices, package contents if not readily apparent, "sterile" if appropriate, expiration date, intended use unless self-evident, performance specifications if necessary to proper use of the device, and any special storage condition requirements. Labeling for medical devices sold to the general public is to be in both English and French, whereas the labeling for prescription devices may be in either language.

Distribution records of medical devices are to be maintained by the manufacturer, importer, and distributor and contain sufficient information to permit rapid and complete withdrawal of the medical device from the market. Retailers and healthcare facilities distributing medical devices for use within their facility are exempt from distribution record requirements. Distribution records are to be retained for the projected useful life of the device or two years after device shipment, whichever is longer.

Manufacturers, importers, and distributors of medical devices are to maintain records of reported problems pertaining to device safety or performance characteristics, including any customer complaints. Records of actions taken in response to a reported problem shall also be maintained.

Manufacturers and importers are required to report any incident involving a device sold in Canada related to a device failure or deterioration in effectiveness or inadequacy in its labeling or directions for use that has led to the death or serious deterioration in the health of a patient, user, or other person, if it were to reoccur. Incidents meeting these criteria are to be reported whether the incident occurred inside or outside of Canada, unless the incident occurred outside of Canada and either the manufacturer has indicated to the regulatory authority of the country its intention to take corrective action or the regulatory authority of the country has required the manufacturer to take corrective action.

Either prior to or upon initiating a recall, the manufacturer or importer of a medical device shall inform the Canadian regulatory authority. Information to be provided includes device name and identifier, name and address of the manufacturer and importer, reason for recall, risk evaluation, quantity of affected devices, time period affected devices were distributed in Canada, person the affected devices were sold to and quantity sold, copies of recall-related communications, recall strategy, proposed action to prevent reoccurrence, and contact information for the manufacturer or importer representative. Following recall completion, the manufacturer or import shall report on the recall results and action taken to prevent reoccurrence of the problem.

Manufacturers of implantable devices are required to provide two implant registration cards with the device to include manufacturer name and address, name and address of person designated by the manufacturer to collect implant registration information, notice explaining the purpose of the implant registration card, and advisement for the patient to notify the manufacturer of any address change.

Canadian Guidance on the Medical Device Regulations, GD210

The GD210 guidance document is intended to provide registrars that have been recognized by Health Canada under section 32.1 of the Medical Devices Regulations guidance on how to perform ISO 13485:2016 quality management system audits. The Canadian Medical Devices Conformity Assessment System (CMDCAS) has effectively been replaced by the MDSAP system as of January 2019.

Canadian Guidance on Audit Reports, GD211

This guidance document, GD211: Guidance on the Content of Quality Management System Audit Reports, is based on the work of study group 4 of the Global Harmonization Task Force (GHTF), and in particular on the technical content of GHTF document SG4/N33R16:2007 *Guidelines for Regulatory Auditing of Quality Management Systems of Medical Device Manufacturers—Part 3: Regulatory Audit Reports.*

JAPAN

The Japanese Pharmaceutical Affairs Law (JPAL), first enforced in 1950, was established to ensure the safety and effectiveness of pharmaceuticals and medical devices by placing restrictions on the handling and approval/certification of all drugs and medical devices. JPAL was significantly revised in 2005 to address Japan's complex regulatory environment, which was considered a significant contributing factor to time lags observed in drug and device approvals. To market a medical device in Japan requires the manufacturer not located in Japan to obtain a market authorization holder (MAH), to obtain licenses (that is, market approval of product, register key manufacturing sites), and to fulfill quality management system requirements and post-market responsibilities.

Foreign manufacturers are required to have a MAH to be responsible in Japan. The MAH must be physically located in Japan, is legally responsible for the release of product on the Japanese market, and is responsible for the product and all processes related to quality and safety.

Requirements to obtain a medical device license depend on the product classification and applicable Japanese standards (if available), as summarized in Table 7.1. The route to market is a two-step process consisting of licensing for the manufacturer, followed by licensing for the MAH. The Pharmaceuticals and Medical Devices Agency (PMDA) is responsible for conducting scientific reviews of marketing authorization applications for medical devices and monitoring their post-market safety.

In addition to JPAL,. the Ministry of Health, Labor and Welfare (MHLW) issued three key ministerial ordinances detailing compliance requirements for medical device manufacturers and MAHs.

1. MHLW Ministerial Ordinance No. 169: *Ministerial Ordinance on Standards for Manufacturing Control and Quality Control for Medical Devices and In-vitro Diagnostic Agents* provides manufacturing control and quality requirements applicable to manufacturing sites of medical device manufacturers, Japanese importers of medical devices, medical devices containing materials of biological origin, and in-vitro diagnostic reagent manufacturers.

Table 7.1 Product classification, Japan.

Classification	Device Description	Site Requirements	Product Approval
Class III, IV	Specially controlled medical devices	Accreditation and QMS audit	PMDA
Class II	Controlled medical devices	Accreditation and QMS audit	PMDA
Class II with Japan standard	Controlled medical devices	Accreditation and QMS audit	PMDA or qualified third party
Class I	General medical devices	Accreditation (potential QMS audit)	PMDA (notification only)

2. MHLW Ministerial Ordinance No. 2: *Regulations for Buildings and Facilities of Pharmacies, etc.* provides requirements that must be met by medical device manufacturers to obtain accreditation by MHLW as a foreign manufacturer.
3. MHLW Ministerial Ordinance No. 136: *Ministerial Ordinance on Quality Assurance for Drugs, Quasi-drugs, Cosmetics and Medical Devices* describes good quality practices applicable to all MAHs.

MHLW Ordinance No. 169 was revised in 2014 to be aligned with ISO 13485:2003 and was updated to 13485:2016 with public comment in 2019 and a three-year transition.

Note: JPAL was replaced by the Act on Securing Quality, Efficacy and Safety of Pharmaceuticals, Medical Devices, Regenerative and Cellular Therapy Products, and Cosmetics (PMD Act) in November 2014. Under the PMD Act, select Class III medical devices can undergo third-party certification, medical software programs are regulated independently, manufacturers must be registered instead of licensed, and the quality management system of the MAH is inspected by product family rather than by individual products.

AUSTRALIA

The Therapeutic Goods Administration (TGA) is responsible for regulating therapeutic goods in Australia including medical devices in accordance with requirements established in the Therapeutic Goods Act 1989, Therapeutic Goods Regulations 1990, and Therapeutic Goods (Medical Devices) Regulations 2002. The TGA regulates therapeutic goods through premarket assessment, post-market monitoring, licensing of Australian manufacturers, and compliance verification of Australian and overseas manufacturers to the same standards. Fundamental principles underlying the regulatory framework for medical devices are based on principles similar to those of the EU.

The manufacturer and sponsor have different responsibilities. The manufacturer of a medical device is the person responsible for design, production, packaging, and labeling before the device is supplied under the person's name. A sponsor must be a resident or carrying on business in Australia and is legally responsible for supplying the device in Australia. The manufacturer may also be the sponsor provided the requirements for sponsor are met.

Manufacturers are responsible for determining device classification by applying classification rules based on intended use of the device; level of risk to patients, users, and other persons; degree of invasiveness; and duration of use. Classification levels for Australia historically are harmonized with EU classification of medical devices.

Higher classification devices must undergo more stringent conformity assessment procedures than lower classification devices. For medical devices (except Class I), a manufacturer must hold a TGA Conformity Assessment Certificate or equivalent certification issued by a European notified body.

The Australian Register of Therapeutic Goods (ARTG) is the register of information concerning therapeutic goods for human use that can be imported, supplied, or exported. With a few exceptions specified in the legislation, for example, investigational devices, all medical devices must be included in the ARTG prior to being supplied in Australia.

Manufacturers and sponsors have post-market obligations intended to monitor market experience of the device and facilitate systematic failure investigations to prevent reoccurrence of an adverse event. The sponsor is legally responsible for the receipt and handling of complaints and adverse events.

The Australian Regulatory Guidelines for Medical Device (ARGMD) is maintained by TGA as a reference for medical device regulatory requirements in Australia. The ARGMD is considered as guidance with all regulatory decisions made in accordance with established regulations.

The TGA has made efforts to conform with MDSAP by the designation of conformity assessment bodies (CABs) aligning regulations with the European MD and IVD regulations and aligning with the MDSAP criteria. They are continuing to issue conformity assessment certificates (CA) for some devices.

BRAZIL

Medical devices are regulated by ANVISA (Agência Nacional de Vigilância Sanitária) and require approval before being sold in Brazil. Medical devices are classified ranging from Class I (low risk) to Class IV (highest risk) based on 18 classification rules codified in Resolution RDC (Resolução Da Diretoria Colegiada) 185. Brazilian classification rules are similar to those of the EU, including rules for noninvasive medical products, invasive medical products, active medical products, and special rules.

ANVISA requires all medical device manufacturers to complete device registration via either the *Cadastro* process or the *Registro* process. The *Cadastro* registration is for lower-risk Class I and II devices, and has a simplified application compared to the *Registro*. The *Registro* process is for higher-risk Class III and IV devices. ANVISA conducts the technical review and issues the registration.

Manufacturing locations are transitioning to the MDSAP process with review of the reports and assurance that the reports conform with the RDC process. Non-Brazilian device manufacturers without a physical location within Brazil must appoint a Brazilian Registration Holder (BRH). The BRH is responsible for submitting registration applications to ANVISA and maintains control of device registrations and Brazil Good Manufacturing Practice (BGMP) certification, if applicable.

Electro-medical devices must successfully achieve National Institute of Metrology, Quality and Technology (INMETRO) IEC 60601 product certification through an INMETRO accredited certification body before applying for ANVISA registration. Devices must be tested to the relevant parts of IEC 60601 by an INMETRO-accredited organization and the manufacturing facility audited prior to issuance of an INMETRO certificate. Certification is issued for up to five years with mandatory annual audits.

CHINA

The National Medical Products Administration (NMPA) is responsible for administration and supervision of food, drugs, cosmetics, and medical devices. The General Administration of Quality Supervision, Inspection, and Quarantine (AQSIQ) is responsible for mandatory safety registration, certification, and inspection for certain devices. All medical devices require registration before they can be sold in China. The Center for Medical Device Evaluation (CMDE) conducts dossier review during the registration process.

Classification of medical devices follows the requirements of Order No. 15. Three device classifications are established based on risk potential with registration requirements varying by classification:

- Class I: Device safety and effectiveness can be ensured through routine administration.
- Class II: Further control is required to ensure the safety and effectiveness of the device.
- Class III: Devices implanted into the human body, those used for life support or sustenance, or those that pose potential risks to the human body must be strictly controlled with respect to safety and effectiveness.

Foreign manufacturers appoint an agent located in China to coordinate its registrations. Approval in the country of origin is required prior to registration and is often demonstrated by a certificate of free sale (CFS) or certificate to foreign government (CFG). Class II and III devices commonly require in-country product testing by a CFDA-authorized laboratory, whereas CFDA will accept foreign test data for Class I devices.

Class II and III registrations are required unless a device of the same type has an established clinical history without serious adverse events, unless product safety and effectiveness can be demonstrated through nonclinical evaluation, and unless data from clinical trial or clinical use of a similar device can prove product safety and efficacy.

Chapter 8

Requirements for In Vitro Diagnostic (IVD) Devices

INTRODUCTION

In vitro diagnostic (IVD) products, by FDA definition, are those reagents, instruments, and systems intended for use in diagnosis of disease or other conditions, including a determination of the state of health, in order to cure, mitigate, treat, or prevent disease or its sequelae. Such products are intended for use in the collection, preparation, and examination of specimens taken from the human body. In short, IVDs are those devices that are tests performed using a blood, saliva, or other patient materials to detect diseases, conditions, compatibility, and may also be used to detect opportunities for personalized medicine.

IVDs have a wide range of use models; some are highly complex and may be only used exclusively in a laboratory environment by highly specialized lab personnel, while others are simple and may be in the home environment.

IVDs are considered medical devices as defined in section 201(h) of the Federal Food, Drug, and Cosmetic Act (FD&C Act) and may also be biological products subject to section 351 of the Public Health Service Act. Like other medical devices, IVDs are subject to premarket and post-market controls. IVDs are generally also subject to categorization under the Clinical Laboratory Improvement Amendments (CLIA '88) of 1988, as certified by the Center of Medicare and Medicaid.

IVD products are regulated by the FDA as medical devices. The Office of Health Technology 7: Office of In Vitro Diagnostics and Radiological Health within CDRH's Office of Product Evaluation and Quality (OPEQ) is responsible for the in vitro diagnostic, radiological health, and mammography quality standards programs. IVD companies, as with other medical device organizations, are required to develop and maintain a quality system per 21 CFR Part 820.

Some IVD devices used to test blood donor suitability and blood donor and recipient compatibility are licensed as biological products under Section 351 of the Public Health Service Act and are subject to the applicable regulations in 21 CFR Parts 600-680. This guidance is written to address only IVD devices that are approved or cleared under the FD&C Act and Part 800 of the device regulations, regardless of which center reviews the submission.

A general purpose reagent (GPR) is "a chemical reagent that has general laboratory application, is used to collect, prepare, and examine specimens from the human body for diagnostic purposes, and is not labeled or otherwise intended for a specific diagnostic application ...[General purpose reagents] do not include laboratory machinery, automated or powered systems." Classification information for GPRs can be found in 21 CFR 864.4010(a).

Analyte specific reagents (ASRs) are "antibodies, both polyclonal and monoclonal, specific receptor proteins, ligands, nucleic acid sequences, and similar reagents which, through specific binding or chemical reaction with substances in a specimen, are intended for use in a diagnostic application for identification and quantification of an individual chemical substance or ligand in biological specimens." Classification information for ASRs can be found in 21 CFR 864. 4020(a).

IVDs are classified into one of three regulatory categories in the United States. IVDs are classified in the lowest, Class I, if they pose relatively little risk to patients and the public health if they are inaccurate (such as a cholesterol test). Moderate-risk tests, such as pregnancy tests, are categorized as Class II, while tests in the highest risk, Class III, are considered to pose the greatest potential risk if they are inaccurate (such as a genetic test used to select cancer therapies). These categories correspond with increasing levels of regulatory scrutiny, with most tests in Class I—and some in Class II—being exempt from premarket requirements, while most Class II and all Class III tests requiring some form of premarket review before they can be used with patients.

To be approved or cleared through premarket review, IVDs must demonstrate safety and effectiveness through analytical and clinical validation, which are key standards in determining a test's accuracy. Analytical validation is focused on ensuring a test is able to correctly and reliably measure a particular analyte, while clinical validation is the process for determining whether the test can accurately identify a particular clinical condition in a given patient.

IVD products have additional labeling requirements under 21 CFR 809, Subpart B, In Vitro Diagnostic Products for Human Use. Before a manufacturer obtains marketing authorization for an IVD product, they must label the product in accordance with labeling regulations. The major IVD labeling topics are:

- Label requirements for the immediate container
- Labeling requirements for inserts and outer packaging
- Exemptions from labeling requirements
- Labeling for general purpose reagents and equipment
- Specific labeling requirements for analyte specific reagents
- Restrictions on sale distribution and use of ASRs
- Specific labeling requirements for over-the-counter (OTC) test sample collection systems
- Restrictions on the sale, distribution, and use of OTC test sample collection systems

21 CFR 809

Label Requirements for the Immediate Container (21 CFR 809.10(a))

The label for IVDs must state the following information, except in cases where it is not applicable. In addition, all information must appear on the outside container or wrapper, or be easily legible through the outside container or wrapper.

If the presence of any label information will interfere with the test, the information may appear on the outside wrapper or container instead of the label.

If the immediate containers are too small, or otherwise unable to bear labels with sufficient space, then the required labeling as listed below annotated with an asterisk (*) may appear on the outer container labeling only.

Label requirements are as follows:

- The established and proprietary names of the product, for example, cholesterol meters
- *The intended use or uses, for example, pregnancy detection, diabetes screening, etc.
- A statement of warnings or precautions for users listed in 16 CFR part 1500 (hazardous substances) and any other warnings appropriate to user hazards, and a statement "For In Vitro Diagnostic Use"
- Name and place of business of the manufacturer, packer, or distributor
- Lot or control number traceable to the production history
  - Multiple unit products must have traceability of the individual units
  - Instrument lot numbers must allow for traceability of subassemblies
  - A multiple unit product that requires use of its components as a system should have the same lot number, or other suitable uniform identification, on all units
- *For Reagents
  - Established (common or usual) name
  - Quantity, proportion, or concentration of all active ingredients; for example, mg., weight per unit volume, mg./dl etc., and for reagents derived from biological materials the source and measure of its activity, for example, bovine, I.U., etc.
  - Storage instructions adequate to protect the stability of the product, that is, temperature, humidity, etc.
  - Instructions for manipulation of products requiring mixing or reconstitution, along with instructions for storage of products that have been reconstituted or mixed

- Means to assure that the product meets appropriate standards of purity, quality, etc., at the time of use, including one or more of the following:
    - i. expiration date (date beyond which the product is not to be used)
    - *ii. statement of any visual indication of alteration
    - *iii. Instructions for a simple check to assure product usefulness
- *The net quantity of contents

Labeling Requirements for Inserts and Outer Packaging (21 CFR 809.10(b))

Labeling must contain in one place the following information in the *format* and *order* listed below, except where information is not applicable, or as specified in a standard for a particular product class.

If the device is a reagent intended as a replacement in a diagnostic system, labeling may be limited to that information necessary to adequately identify the reagent and to describe its use in the system.

If the device is a multiple purpose instrument used for diagnostic purposes and not committed to specific diagnostic procedures or systems, labeling can be restricted to those points annotated by an asterisk (*):

- *The proprietary and established product name
- *The intended use of the product and whether it is a qualitative or quantitative type of procedure, for example, screening, physician's office, home use, etc.
- Summary and explanation of the test, including a short history containing methodology and the special merits and limitations of the test
- The chemical, physical, physiological, or biological principles of the procedure
- For reagents:
    - The common name, if any, and quantity, proportion, or concentration or each reactive ingredient; and for biological material, the source and measure of its activity
    - Appropriate cautions or warnings listed in 16 CFR Part 1500; the statement: "For In Vitro Diagnostic Use;" and any other limiting statements appropriate to the intended use of the product
    - Adequate directions for reconstitution, mixing, dilution, etc.
    - Appropriate storage instructions
    - A statement of purification or treatment required for use
    - Physical, biological, or chemical indications of instability or deterioration

- *For instruments:
  - Use or function
  - Installation procedures and requirements
  - Principles of operation
  - Performance characteristics and specifications
  - Operating instructions
  - Calibration procedures, including equipment and/or materials
  - Operational precautions and limitations
  - Hazards
  - Service and maintenance information
- Specimen collection and preparation for analysis, describing:
  - Special precautions/preparations
  - Additives necessary to maintain specimen integrity
  - Known interfering substances
  - Recommended specimen storage, handling, and shipping instructions
- A step-by-step outline of recommended procedures from the reception of the specimen to the obtaining of results. In addition to the following, this should include a list of any points that might improve precision or accuracy:
  - A list of materials provided and instruction for use, for example, reagents, equipment, etc.
  - A list of necessary materials that are not provided (include details such as sizes, numbers, types, and quality)
  - A description of the amounts of reagents necessary, and parameters such as time, temperature, etc.
  - A statement related to final reaction stability and any time restrictions on accurate measurements
  - Details of calibration, identifying and listing, and necessary preparation of the reference materials, samples, and blanks. Describe the calibration range including the highest and lowest values measured
  - Details of necessary quality control procedures and materials, for example, positive and negative controls, acceptable performance limits
- Explanation of the procedure for calculating the unknown, including the definition of each component of the formula, a sample calculation, and the number of significant figures appropriate for the answer
- Limitations of the procedure, for example, identify situations that will have an adverse impact on test results. If further testing, either more specific or more sensitive, is indicated, then the need for the additional test shall be stated

- Expected values, including how the range(s) was established and the populations on which it was established
- Specific performance characteristics as appropriate, including accuracy, specificity, precision, and sensitivity
- *Bibliography
- *Name and place of business of the manufacturer, packer, or distributor
- *Date of issuance of the last labeling revision by the firm

Exemptions from Labeling Requirements

Shipments or other deliveries of IVD devices are exempt from label and labeling requirements in the above headings and from standards listed under Part 861 provided the following conditions are met:

- A shipment or delivery for an investigation subject to Part 812, Investigational Device Exemption (IDE), if the device is in compliance with the subject IDE; or
- A shipment or delivery for an investigation that is not in compliance with Part 812 (most IVDs are exempt from the IDE because of the following labeling) if the following conditions are met:
  - A product in the laboratory research phase, not represented as an IVD, that is prominently labeled: "For Research Use Only. Not for use in diagnostic procedures;" and
  - A product that is being shipped or delivered for product testing prior to full commercial marketing that is prominently labeled: "For Investigational Use Only. The performance characteristics of this product have not been established."

Regulations allow for exceptions or alternatives to these labeling requirements in CFR 809.11. The appropriate FDA center director may grant an exception or alternative to any labeling provision listed in this section and not explicitly required by statute for specified lots, batches, or other units of an IVD product for human use, if the center director determines that compliance with such labeling requirement could adversely affect the safety, effectiveness, or availability of such products that are or will be included in the strategic national stockpile.

Labeling of General Purpose Reagents and Equipment

General purpose items include routine laboratory reagents such as hydrochloric acid and equipment such as glassware whose uses are generally known by persons trained in their use. They do not need to bear the directions for use listed under Label Requirements for the Immediate Container and Labeling Requirements for Inserts and Outer Packaging, if their labeling meets the requirements listed below. If the product packaging is too small to accommodate a label with sufficient space for the labeling, and if the product is packaged in an outer container that has all of the following on its labeling, then only those portions annotated with an asterisk (*) must be on the product label.

- Reagents:
  - *A declaration of the established name, if any, and quantity, proportion, or concentration of the reagent ingredient stated in a system generally recognized by the user
  - A statement of the purity and quality including a qualitative statement of any impurities. This can be satisfied by using a statement of conformity with a generally recognized and available standard
  - A statement of warnings or precautions for users as contained in the regulations in 16 CFR Part 1500 and any other appropriate warnings, and the statement: "For Laboratory Use"
  - Net quantity of contents in terms of weight or volume, or numerical count, or any combination thereof
  - Appropriate storage instructions
  - *Name and place of business of the manufacturer, packer, or distributor
  - *A lot or control number traceable to the manufacturing history of the product
  - A statement indicating the presence of and characterizing any catalytic or nonreactive ingredients, for example, buffers, preservatives, stabilizers.
  - For Class I exempt ASRs, the statement: "Analyte Specific Reagent. Analytical and performance characteristics are not established"
  - For Class II and III ASRs, the statement: "Analyte Specific Reagent. Except as a component of the approved/cleared test (name of approved/cleared test), analytical and performance characteristics of this ASR are not established."
- Equipment
  - Product labeling need include only a statement adequately describing the product, its composition, and physical characteristics, if necessary for its proper use.
  - The labeling for OTC test sample collection systems for drugs of abuse testing shall bear the following information in language appropriate for the intended users:
    (1) Adequate instructions for specimen collection and handling, and for preparation and mailing of the specimen to the laboratory for testing
    (2) An identification system to ensure that specimens are not mixed up or otherwise misidentified at the laboratory, and that user anonymity is maintained

(3) The intended use or uses of the product, including what drugs are to be identified in the specimen, a quantitative description of the performance characteristics for those drugs (for example, sensitivity and specificity) in terms understandable to lay users, and the detection period

(4) A statement that confirmatory testing will be conducted on all samples that initially test positive

(5) A statement of warnings or precautions for users as established in the regulations contained in 16 CFR part 1500 and any other warnings appropriate to the hazard presented by the product

(6) Adequate instructions on how to obtain test results from a person who can explain their meaning, including the probability of false positive and false negative results, as well as how to contact a trained health professional if additional information on interpretation of test results from the laboratory or follow-up counseling is desired

(7) Name and place of business of the manufacturer, packer, or distributor

Restrictions for the Sale, Use, and Distribution of Over-The-Counter (OTC) IVDs (§809.40)

OTC test sample collection systems for drugs of abuse testing, regulated by §864.3260, are restricted devices under section 520(e) of the FD&C Act subject to the following restrictions:

- Sample testing shall be performed in a laboratory using screening tests that have been approved, cleared, or otherwise recognized by the FDA as accurate and reliable for the testing of such specimens for identifying drugs of abuse or their metabolites.
- The laboratory performing the test(s) shall have, and shall be recognized as having, adequate capability to reliably perform the necessary screening and confirmatory tests, including adequate capability to perform integrity checks of the biological specimens for possible adulteration.
- All OTC test sample collection systems for drugs of abuse testing shall be labeled in accordance with 809.10(f) and shall provide an adequate system to communicate the proper interpretation of test results from the laboratory to the lay purchaser.

FDA-RECOGNIZED STANDARDS

Until recently, the FDA has not recognized standards for use by in vitro manufacturers other than the law enacted under the FD&C Act and its modification through later legislation. Recently, the FDA has provided an avenue for rapid clearance of IVD products if the manufacturer certifies conformance with an FDA-recognized standard. The recognized standards can be viewed on the CDRH website. Most standards related to IVDs originated from the NCCLS, now known as CLSI (Clinical Laboratory Standards Institute).

IVDR 2017/746

On May 27, 2017, the In Vitro Diagnostic Regulation (IVDR 2017/746) entered into force in the EU, replacing In Vitro Diagnostic Directive (IVDD 93/79/EC). The stricter oversight of a regulation was put in place to further protect patient safety.

The classification under the IVDR is risk-based in four categories, Class A-Class D. Class D devices are the highest risk; they present a personal and public health risk. Class C devices have a high personal health risk but lower public health risk, while Class B devices have a low to medium risk, and Class A devices are considered low risk. Questions on classification decision will be sent to the borderline decision group of the Medical Device Coordination Group (MDCG). IVD manufacturers may make judgements based on Annex VIII of the IVDR and provide a clear justification on their position with their notified body.

Safety and performance requirements are determined with harmonized standards and common specifications within the IVDR. Clarification of performance indicators are now provided, including scientific validity, analytical performance, and clinical performance, which will be part of a performance evaluation report (PER). Clinical evidence now requires more details to be collected and analyzed throughout the entire life cycle of an IVD. Evidence sources must be clarified, and clinical performance is required unless justified. Manufacturers now must establish and maintain a PER based on the clinical evidence. High-risk clinical performance studies are now defined, and requirements are now more detailed and extensive. The studies conducted must be authorized by authorities and the ethics committee.

The European Commission designates EU Reference Laboratories (EURLs) to help assess specific devices, a category or group of devices, or specific hazards related to a category or group of devices. With respect to IVDs, the role of EURLs is to verify the claimed performances of Class D devices with the applicable common specifications and carry out testing on samples of Class D IVDs. All IVD manufacturers are required to develop and maintain a quality system certified to ISO 13485. Manufacturers are now required to devise a post-market follow-up plan and continuously update the PER to promote better prevention or handling of adverse events and subsequently improve the quality and safety of IVDs.

Notified bodies are required for all Class A sterile, B, C, and D IVDs. IVDs that do not conform to the requirements in the IVDR will not be allowed to be on the market in the EU. Conformity assessments are a key part of getting an IVD in the market in the EU. Conformity assessments for IVDs in Classes B, C, and D require a notified body's intervention. The notified body assesses the conformity of the medical device and the manufacturer's quality management system (QMS) through the conformity assessment route that the manufacturer chooses. The manufacturer's QMS is examined, generally, to ensure it will lead to the manufacture of conforming product. The technical documentation is how the manufacturer proves the device conforms to the General Safety and Performance Requirements in Annex I of the IVDR.

The manufacturer's QMS is what must produce the conforming device, and how the device conforms is shown through the technical documentation, so the conformity assessment includes a review of both the QMS and the technical documentation. Manufacturers may generally choose between two conformity assessment routes depending on the structure of their QMS and company. The main difference between the two conformity assessments is the scope of the QMS assessed. Manufacturers of Class A IVDs may still self-certify their products. It is important that the manufacturer weigh the choice of conformity assessment carefully to determine its most efficient option.

Annex VIII: Assessment Based on a Quality Management System and on Assessment of the Technical Documentation

In this conformity assessment route, the notified body assesses the manufacturer's QMS and the device's technical documentation during audits. Class D devices must also undergo batch verification. During batch verification, the notified body may ask an EURL to verify the claimed performance and compliance of the IVD with the common specifications through laboratory testing. In addition, the technical documentation for IVDs for self-testing and near-patient testing in Classes B, C, and D must be assessed.

Annexes IX and X: Type Examination and Production Conformity Verification

The second conformity assessment route is Annexes IX and X together, meaning the notified body uses the procedures in both Annexes IX and X to assess the conformity of the manufacturer's QMS (Annex X) and technical documentation (Annex IX). Annex IX, type examination, is generally a review of the technical documentation for the device type. Operationally, these reviews function in a similar way to technical documentation reviews for Class D devices. Additionally, Annex IX includes testing for when an EURL is designated for a specific device undergoing review. In terms of the QMS assessment, Annex X includes a review of the manufacturer's QMS for manufacturing and final inspection of the IVDs it manufactures. Annex X also requires the manufacturer examine each manufactured batch of IVDs to confirm its conformity with the technical documentation.

IVDs are also subject to unique device identifier (UDI) requirements. While the primary requirement of UDI is to simplify post-market surveillance data to regulatory authorities and the IVD manufacturer, IVDR also provides for a UDI database to be established to validate, collate, process, and make the core data elements for UDIs accessible to the public. For more information on UDI, see Chapters 4 and 18.

Chapter 9

International Standards for Quality Systems

Selection of the appropriate quality management system standard varies based on the type of organization, such as a medical device manufacturer or testing laboratory.

ISO 9001

ISO 9001:2008 was revised and released as ISO 9001:2015 *Quality management systems—Requirements*. The 2015 version of the standard cancelled and replaced ISO 9001:2008. ISO 9001:2015 restructures the standard into 10 clauses for alignment with the high-level structure (HLS) described in Annex SL of ISO/IEC Directives Part 1; the HLS is intended to support organizations using multiple management systems by applying a consistent structure across management system standards. Changes in ISO 9001:2015 include an increased emphasis on risk-based thinking, leadership engagement, and performance monitoring. Additionally, specific requirements for quality manual, management representative, and preventive action have been removed in ISO 9001:2015.

ISO 9001:2015 *Quality management systems—Requirements* specifies generic requirements intended to be applicable to all organizations regardless of size or product/service provided. The standard is not specific to medical devices; however, it may be applied by organizations supplying products/services to medical device manufacturers as well as the medical device manufacturers themselves. ISO 9001 helps organizations organize processes, improve the efficiency of those processes, and continuously improve. ISO 9001 is intended to support organizational alignment with other management systems such as those specific to environmental management, occupational health and safety management, or risk management.

The ISO 9001:2015 standard consists of 10 clauses; the initial three clauses are primarily administrative. General requirements or context of the organization are provided in clause 4, including establishment of a quality management system and determining the scope of that system.

Clause 5 specifies leadership commitment requirements from top management to demonstrate that commitment by developing and applying the quality system, meeting customer requirements, establishing and maintaining a suitable quality policy, defining and communicating responsibility and authority, and conducting management reviews at planned intervals.

Requirements related to planning are specified in clause 6, including addressing risks and opportunities, conducting quality planning, developing measurable and quantitative quality objectives to support the quality policy required by clause 5, and planning quality system changes.

Clause 7 details the support for the quality system from implementation to application. This clause ensures the quality system has the appropriate resources to implement, maintain, and continually improve the quality system. Personnel must have appropriate competence, training, and awareness. This clause also ensures that appropriate communication methodologies are put in place, establishing consistency of any information or content. Finally, this clause describes the requirement for quality system documentation necessary to execute and maintain the quality system. Requirements are provided for document distribution, retention, access, usage, retrieval, preservation and storage, control, and disposition of such information. Controls must also be in place to prevent the unintentional use of obsolete information.

Clause 8 specifies requirements for product and services including operational planning; customer-related processes such as requirements ordering and fulfillment, and the records taken at each step; product and service design and development; purchasing and supplier selection; approval and maintenance, including outsourced processes, processes for production and provision of services, and controlling equipment used for monitoring or measurement and providing the infrastructure and work environment necessary to achieve product requirements. This clause also provides the requirements for releasing products and services, and controlling nonconforming outputs from any point in the delivery of a product or service.

The measurement, analysis, and improvement requirements in clause 9 allow the organization's personnel to step back after executing their product or service and see how the customer has reacted to these positive changes. The requirements include coverage for internal audit and management review.

Clause 10 focuses on driving continuous improvement of the company, based on results of the data analysis in clause 9. The requirements for handling nonconformities and corrective actions are detailed in this clause.

ISO 13485

The ISO 13485 standard was revised in 2016 as ISO 13485:2016 *Medical devices—Quality management systems—Requirements for regulatory purposes.* ISO 13485:2016 cancelled and replaced both ISO 13485:2003 and ISO/TR 14969:2004. Changes in ISO 13485:2016 include a greater emphasis on risk-based decision-making, controls for outsourced processes, appropriate infrastructure, and post-market activities. A comparison between the 2003 and 2016 versions of the standard is provided in information Annex A of ISO 13485:2016. ISO 13485:2016 does not apply the HLS utilized in ISO 9001:2015. In addition to the following information, see Chapter 12 for more details on ISO 13485.

ISO 13485:2016 *Medical devices—Quality Management systems—Requirements for regulatory purposes* specifies quality management system requirements for "the design and development, production, installation and servicing of medical devices and the design, development, and provision of related services." This version of the standard is based on ISO 9001:2015 and follows its formatting.

The first three clauses are administrative in nature, with clause 3 providing terms and definitions supplemental to ISO 9000:2000 *Quality management systems—Fundamentals and vocabulary*. The scope of the 2016 revision is to allow for global alignment of medical device quality systems, ultimately to support the Medical Device Single Audit Program (MDSAP).

Clause 4 specifies general requirements for a quality management system including those for roles and responsibilities, control of records required to meet regulatory requirements and change control, quality manual, medical device file, validating any software used to manage a part or entire quality system prior to use, and control of documents and records.

Management responsibility requirements, including management commitment, regulatory emphasis, quality policy, quality planning, management representative, and management review with added inputs and outputs are provided in clause 5.

Clause 6 specifies requirements for resource management including competence, awareness, and training for human resources, as well as requirements for infrastructure and work environment, including contamination control.

Clause 7 addresses product realization with requirements including planning product realization, customer-related processes, regulatory requirements, communication, design and development controls from planning to design inputs, design verification, validation and transfer, purchasing, controlling product and services provided including installation and servicing, process validation, identification and traceability, validation of sterile barriers and processes, and monitoring and measuring devices.

Requirements for measurement, analysis, and improvement are specified in clause 8, including feedback, internal audit, customer complaints and regulatory agency reporting, monitoring and measurement of processes and product, controlling nonconforming product, collecting and analyzing appropriate data to assess the quality management system, improving the quality management system, and corrective and preventive action (CAPA).

The *ISO Handbook: ISO 13485:2016—Medical Devices—A Practical Guide* was published by ISO in 2017, providing guidance for the application of ISO 13485. The guide was written by some of the same subject matter experts who were on ISO/TC 210 and gives practical advice to organizations seeking to develop, implement, and maintain their quality management system to the ISO 13485:2016 standard.

ISO/IEC 17025

ISO/IEC 17025:2017 *General requirements for the competence of testing and calibration laboratories* specifies general requirements for the competence to carry out testing and calibration conducted with standard methods, nonstandard methods, and laboratory-developed methods to ensure laboratories produce valid results.

This international standard applies to all organizations performing tests and/or calibrations regardless of the number of personnel or the scope of testing and/or calibration activities. The standard is applicable to first-, second-, and third-party laboratories as well as to laboratories where testing and/or calibration are elements of inspection and product certification. The standard also helps facilitate cooperation between laboratories and other bodies by generating wider acceptance of results between countries. Test reports and certificates can be accepted from one country to another without the need for further testing, which, in turn, improves international trade.

A laboratory may use ISO/IEC 17025 in developing its management system for quality, administrative, and technical operations. Only those accreditation bodies that include the scope of ISO/IEC 17025 may certify a laboratory to the standard. ISO/IEC 17025 is the standard to which most labs must hold accreditation to be deemed technically competent. In many cases, suppliers and regulatory authorities will not accept test or calibration results from a lab that is not accredited.

Compliance of testing and calibration laboratories with ISO/IEC 17025 implies the necessity of implementing a quality management system. Although not explicitly required, these laboratories will typically implement ISO 9001, as the requirements in ISO 9001 are similar to those mentioned in ISO/IEC 17025. For those testing and calibration laboratories that already have ISO 9001 in place, ISO/IEC 17025 provides technical competence requirements specific to these laboratories that are not addressed in ISO 9001, such as establishing monitoring and measuring requirements, determining measurement uncertainty, and utilizing a proficiency testing process.

Chapter 10

Quality System Regulation (QSR) Requirements

INTRODUCTION

The Quality System Regulation (QSR) published October 7, 1996, was a revision of the medical device good manufacturing practice (GMP) regulation. The following sections provide detail and guidance on each section of the regulation. The sections are intended to be brief overviews and not extensive evaluations of the regulation. Each section contains an overview, excerpts from the regulation itself, and a discussion. The reader should refer to the regulation (21 CFR 820) and the preamble as published in the *Federal Register* for a more complete understanding of the FDA's requirements.

The FDA is currently reviewing the adoption of ISO 13485:2016 as a replacement for the QSR. As the QSR is a U.S. regulation, it is published in the *Federal Register* and available to the public and manufacturers free of charge. ISO 13485:2016 is a copyright document and not freely available, nor can it be published in the *Federal Register.* Along with the adoption of ISO 13485:2016, the FDA has recognized that there are some differences that the FDA will compensate for with the adoption of ISO 13485:2016. The FDA has agreed to an additional time period for small manufacturers to comply with ISO 13485:2016. Additionally, the FDA's requirements for some areas, such as complaint handling, are more stringent, and these requirements will remain.

Even if the QSR is retired, the historical document will still provide information regarding FDA areas of emphasis and may be utilized as a reference to prepare for FDA inspections and to educate auditors regarding areas of importance.

PREAMBLE

The preamble was published in the *Federal Register* vol. 61, no. 195, October 7, 1996, and precedes *Part 820 Quality System Regulation for Medical Devices.* The preamble also includes changes to *21 CFR Part 808 Exemptions from Federal Preemption of State and Local Medical Device Requirements* and *21 CFR 812 Investigational Device Exemptions.* The FDA's rationale for the QSR, as it is presently written, is contained in the preamble. The information is a valuable resource for interpretation and provides insight into the position the FDA has taken in stating the requirements.

The preamble is organized in the following manner:

Supplementary Information:

- I Background
- II Decision to Make Working Draft Available for Comment
- III Open Public Meeting and GMP Advisory Committee
- IV Implementation of the Final Rule
- V Response to Comments and Rationale for Changes
- VI Summary of Changes from the July 1995 Working Draft to the Final Rule and Rationale
- VII Environmental Impact
- VIII Intergovernmental Partnership
- IX Economic Impact
- X Congressional Review
- XI References

Discussion

Section I discusses the background for the 1996 version of the QSR. This section identified the Safe Medical Device Act (SMDA), which provided the FDA the authority to amend the Federal Food, Drug, and Cosmetic Act (FD&C Act) section 510(f), adding preproduction design controls to the current good manufacturing practice (CGMP) regulation.

Sections II and III provide historical information as to how the FDA solicited feedback on the 1993 medical device CGMP regulations, proposed revisions, and request for comments. Subsequent publication of the 1995 working draft incorporated the FDA's response to the comments and allowed a final review period before issuing the final regulation on October 7, 1996.

Section IV provides rationale for the implementation of the final rule in two phases, where the FDA implemented a special one-year transition program allowing manufacturers a grace period to become fully compliant with the requirements of § 820.30, Design Controls. This section emphasizes that manufacturers were responsible to take reasonable steps to come into compliance with the requirements during the June 1, 1997, to June 1, 1998, period. The FDA stated that firms would be inspected against the design control requirements during the transition period, but a separate design control inspection strategy report would be issued in lieu of a form FDA 483 for observed noncompliance.

Of primary importance in understanding the content of the QSR is section V, Response to Comments and Rationale for Changes. The FDA's response to the working draft, as well as explanations for changes, is contained in 204 comments that cover the entire scope of the QSR, Subparts A through O. The FDA conveys its support for international harmonization of standards governing medical devices and provides rationale for not adopting ISO 9001:1994 *Quality systems—Model for quality assurance in design, development, production, installation, and servicing* verbatim. Complications with copyright issues were a first concern, and second, the FDA's position that ISO 9001:1994 as a quality system standard is insufficient to protect the public health. Throughout this section of the preamble, the FDA makes reference to the ISO 9001:1994 standard and the ISO committee draft (CD) revision of ISO/CD 13485 *Quality systems— Medical devices—Supplementary requirements to ISO 9001* and provides specific rationale for similarities or differences relevant to the subpart or requirement discussed.

Section VII, Environmental Impact, states that an environmental impact statement is not required, as the final rule does not have a significant impact on the human environment.

The economic impact discussed in section IX summarizes that changes to the CGMP regulation will require manufacturers engaged in design, manufacture, contract sterilization, and packaging of medical devices to expand their quality systems to include new areas such as preproduction quality assurance and purchasing controls. This section includes comments from the 1993 proposed changes to the CGMP regulation and the FDA's supporting rationale for changes to the regulation emphasizing close harmonization with ISO standards where possible.

Section X, Congressional Review, identifies the changes required to be considered a major rule and is followed by specific changes to the following sections: *Part 808—Exemptions from Federal Preemption of State and Local Medical Device Requirements; Part 812—Investigational Device Exemptions;* and a complete rewrite of *Part 820—Quality System Regulation for Medical Devices.*

GENERAL PROVISIONS

The purpose of the scope is to state the requirements in Part 820 that regulate the methods, facilities, and controls used for the design, manufacture, packaging, labeling, storage, installation, and servicing of all finished devices intended for human use. The regulation is intended to ensure that finished devices are safe and effective and otherwise in compliance with the FD&C Act. Part 820 establishes the fundamental requirements applicable to manufacturers of finished devices and clarifies that manufacturers that engage in only some operations of the part need only comply with those requirements applicable to their operations.

The regulation is broad in that it applies to a variety of medical devices, and the implementation of the requirements will vary based on the size of the organization, the complexity of the medical device, and the risks associated with the product.

The following sections will address the individual regulatory requirements referencing the applicable section of the QSR, applicable definitions, and important points following the section.

Regulatory Requirement 21 CFR § 820.1(a) Applicability

1. CGMP requirements are set forth in this QSR. The requirements in this part govern the methods used in, and the facilities and controls used for, the design, manufacture, packaging, labeling, storage, installation, and servicing of all finished devices intended for human

use. The requirements in this part are intended to ensure that finished devices will be safe and effective and otherwise in compliance with the FD&C Act. This part establishes basic requirements applicable to manufacturers of finished medical devices. If a manufacturer engages in only some operations subject to the requirements in this part, and not in others, that manufacturer need only comply with those requirements applicable to the operations in which it is engaged. With respect to Class I devices, design controls apply only to those devices listed in 21 CFR §820.30(a)(2). This regulation does not apply to manufacturers of components or parts of finished devices, but such manufacturers are encouraged to use appropriate provisions of this regulation as guidance. Manufacturers of human blood and blood components are not subject to this part but are subject to Part 606 of this chapter. Manufacturers of human cells, tissues, and cellular and tissue-based products (HCT/Ps), as defined in 1271.3(d) of this chapter, that are medical devices (subject to premarket review or notification, or exempt from notification, under an application submitted under the device provisions of the act or under a biological product license application under section 351 of the Public Health Service Act) are subject to this part and are also subject to the donor-eligibility procedures set forth in Part 1271 subpart C of this chapter and applicable current good tissue practice procedures in Part 1271 subpart D of this chapter. In the event of a conflict between applicable regulations in Part 1271 and in other parts of this chapter, the regulation specifically applicable to the device in question shall supersede the more general.

2. The provisions of this part shall be applicable to any finished device as defined in this part, intended for human use, that is manufactured, imported, or offered for import in any state or territory of the United States, the District of Columbia, or the Commonwealth of Puerto Rico.
3. In this regulation, the term "where appropriate" is used several times. When a requirement is qualified by "where appropriate," it is deemed to be "appropriate" unless the manufacturer can document justification otherwise. A requirement is "appropriate" if nonimplementation could reasonably be expected to result in the product not meeting its specified requirements or the manufacturer not being able to carry out any necessary corrective action.

Discussion

The regulations apply to manufacturers of finished medical devices that are intended for human use, which are manufactured, imported, or offered for import, in any state or territory of the United States, the District of Columbia, or the Commonwealth of Puerto Rico. 21 CFR Part 820 also applies to manufacturers of HCT/Ps that are regulated as medical devices. Manufacturers of blood and blood components are not subject to 21 CFR Part 820 but rather to 21 CFR Part

606. Component manufacturers are not subject to the requirements of this part but are encouraged to comply with the regulation as guidance. Finished device manufacturers are responsible under § 820.50, Purchasing Controls, to ensure that component manufacturers (namely suppliers) meet specified requirements as laid out in the design control process.

The term *manufacturer* is defined in § 820.3(o) and includes people who perform some or all of the functions identified in the QSR. It is important to recognize that while a firm may not be involved in all the functions from design to distribution, it may be considered a manufacturer under this regulation and be required to comply with the requirements applicable to its operation.

Several requirements are qualified with the term "where appropriate" throughout 21 CFR Part 820. When a requirement has been identified as "where appropriate," it is to be considered appropriate if nonimplementation may contribute to the product not meeting specified requirements, or if the manufacturer's ability to facilitate or carry out corrective action may be compromised as a result of not implementing the requirement. Objective evidence, including a firm's rationale, must be documented when a "where appropriate" requirement has not been implemented.

Regulatory Requirement 21 CFR § 820.1(b) Limitations

The QSR in this part supplements regulations in other parts of this chapter except where explicitly stated otherwise. If it is impossible to comply with all applicable regulations, both in this part and in other parts of this chapter, the regulations specifically applicable to the device in question shall supersede any other generally applicable requirements.

Discussion

The QSR applies to all medical devices unless stated otherwise. Certain Class I devices have been exempted from design control requirements, while the classification of other devices may identify certain products that are exempt from specific sections of this regulation. Exemption from GMP requirements as codified in the classification regulations 21 CFR Parts 862 to 892 will not exempt device manufacturers from the requirements of § 820.180 Records-General Requirements and § 820.198 Complaint Files, nor will the manufacturer be exempt from registration and listing.

Regulatory Requirement 21 CFR § 820.1(c) Authority

Part 820 is established and issued under authority of sections 501, 502, 510, 513, 514, 515, 518, 519, 520, 522, 701, 704, 801, and 803 of the act.[125] The failure to comply with any applicable provision in this part renders a device adulterated under section 501(h) of the act. Such devices, and any person responsible for the failure to comply, are subject to regulatory action.

Discussion

This section specifies the legal authority under which the QSR requirements are written and defines the consequences for noncompliance. Failure to comply with any requirement may render the product adulterated.

Regulatory Requirement 21 CFR § 820.1(d) Foreign Manufacturers

If a manufacturer that offers devices for import into the United States refuses to permit or allow the completion of an FDA inspection of the foreign facility for the purpose of determining compliance with this part, it shall appear for purposes of section 801(a) of the act, that the methods used in, and the facilities and controls used for, the design, manufacture, packaging, labeling, storage, installation, or servicing of any devices produced at such facility that are offered for import into the United States do not conform to the requirements of section 520(f) of the act and this part and that the devices manufactured at that facility are adulterated under section 501(h) of the act.

Discussion

While the FDA does not have authority outside the United States, foreign manufacturers if requested by the FDA are required to permit or allow the FDA to inspect their facilities to ensure compliance with the QSR. If a foreign manufacturer refuses an inspection by the FDA, its manufactured devices are considered adulterated under section 501(h) of the FD&C Act and subject to import detention and refusal of entry.

Regulatory Requirement 21 CFR § 820.1 (e) Exemptions or Variances

1. Any person who wishes to petition for an exemption or variance from any device quality system requirement is subject to the requirements of section 520(f)(2) of the act. Petitions for an exemption or variance shall be submitted according to the procedures set forth in 10.30 of this chapter, the FDA's administrative procedures. Guidance is available from the Center for Devices and Radiological Health, Division of Small Manufacturers Assistance (DSMICA). (Note: DSMICA was reorganized as the Division of Industry and Consumer Education (DICE) effective April 2014.)
2. The FDA may initiate and grant a variance from any device quality system requirement when the agency determines that such variance is in the best interest of the public health. Such variance will remain in effect only so long as there remains a public health need for the device and the device would not likely be made sufficiently available without the variance.

Discussion

Anyone may petition for an exemption or variance from all or part of the QSR. An exemption means that a manufacturer is not required to comply, while a variance is permission to substitute a method of control different from those specified in the regulation requirements. The regulation specifies where guidance is available and how FDA priority for public health is considered. Exemption from GMP requirements as codified in the classification regulations 21 CFR Parts 862 to 892 will not exempt finished device manufacturers from the requirements of § 820.180 Records-General Requirements and § 820.198 Complaint Files.

The QSR establishes the foundation of the quality system and is stated in broad terms to allow manufacturers the flexibility for implementing a quality system that is suitable and effective for their organization. The requirements in § 820.20 Management Responsibility are the basis for responsibility, authority, and accountability over the quality system. These requirements include establishing a quality policy, defining measurable objectives for quality, defining the organization structure, appointing the management representative, and conducting management reviews, quality planning, and quality system procedures.

The following sections will address the individual regulatory requirements of the applicable sections of the QSR, applicable definitions, and important points following each section.

Regulatory Requirement 21 CFR § 820.3 Definitions

Act means the Federal Food, Drug, and Cosmetic Act, as amended (secs. 201-903, 52 Stat. 1040 et seq., as amended (21 U.S.C. 321-394)). All definitions in section 201 of the act shall apply to the regulations in this part.

Complaint means any written, electronic, or oral communication that alleges deficiencies related to the identity, quality, durability, reliability, safety, effectiveness, or performance of a device after it is released for distribution.

Component means any raw material, substance, piece, part, software, firmware, labeling, or assembly that is intended to be included as part of the finished, packaged, and labeled device.

Control number means any distinctive symbols, such as a distinctive combination of letters or numbers, or both, from which the history of the manufacturing, packaging, labeling, and distribution of a unit, lot, or batch of finished devices can be determined.

Design history file (DHF) means a compilation of records that describes the design history of a finished device.

Design input means the physical and performance requirements of a device that are used as a basis for device design.

Design output means the results of a design effort at each design phase and at the end of the total design effort. The finished design output is the basis for the device master record. The total finished design output consists of the device, its packaging and labeling, and the device master record.

Design review means a documented, comprehensive, systematic examination of a design to evaluate the adequacy of the design requirements, to evaluate the capability of the design to meet these requirements, and to identify problems.

Device history record (DHR) means a compilation of records containing the production history of a finished device.

Device master record (DMR) means a compilation of records containing the procedures and specifications for a finished device.

Establish means define, document (in writing or electronically), and implement.

Finished device means any device or accessory to any device that is suitable for use or capable of functioning, regardless of whether it is packaged, labeled, or sterilized.

Lot or batch means one or more components or finished devices that consist of a single type, model, class, size, composition, or software version that are manufactured under essentially the same conditions and that are intended to have uniform characteristics and quality within specified limits.

Management with executive responsibility means those senior employees of a manufacturer who have the authority to establish or make changes to the manufacturer's quality policy and quality system.

Manufacturer means any person who designs, manufactures, fabricates, assembles, or processes a finished device. Manufacturer includes but is not limited to those who perform the functions of contract sterilization, installation, relabeling, remanufacturing, repacking, or specification development, and initial distributors of foreign entities performing these functions.

Manufacturing material means any material or substance used in or used to facilitate the manufacturing process, a concomitant constituent, or a byproduct constituent produced during the manufacturing process, which is present in or on the finished device as a residue or impurity not by design or intent of the manufacturer.

Nonconformity means the nonfulfillment of a specified requirement.

Product means components, manufacturing materials, in-process devices, finished devices, and returned devices.

Quality means the totality of features and characteristics that bear on the ability of a device to satisfy fitness-for-use, including safety and performance.

Quality audit means a systematic, independent examination of a manufacturer's quality system that is performed at defined intervals and at sufficient frequency to determine whether both quality system activities and the results of such activities comply with quality system procedures, that these procedures are implemented effectively, and that these procedures are suitable to achieve quality system objectives.

Quality policy means the overall intentions and direction of an organization with respect to quality, as established by management with executive responsibility.

Quality system means the organizational structure, responsibilities, procedures, processes, and resources for implementing quality management.

Remanufacturer means any person who processes, conditions, renovates, repackages, restores, or does any other act to a finished device that significantly changes the finished device's performance or safety specifications, or intended use.

Rework means action taken on a nonconforming product so it will fulfill the specified DMR requirements before it is released for distribution.

Specification means any requirement with which a product, process, service, or other activity must conform.

Validation means confirmation by examination and provision of objective evidence that the particular requirements for a specific intended use can be consistently fulfilled.

1. *Process validation* means establishing by objective evidence that a process consistently produces a result or product meeting its predetermined specifications.

2. *Design validation* means establishing by objective evidence that device specifications conform with user needs and intended use(s).

Verification means confirmation by examination and provision of objective evidence that specified requirements have been fulfilled.

Human cell, tissue, or cellular or tissue-based product (HCT/P) regulated as a device means an HCT/P as defined in 1271.3(d) of this chapter that does not meet the criteria in 1271.10(a) and that is also regulated as a device.

Unique device identifier (UDI) means an identifier that adequately identifies a device through its distribution and use by meeting the requirements of 830.20 of this chapter. A UDI is composed of:

1. *A device identifier*—a mandatory, fixed portion of a UDI that identifies the specific version or model of a device and the labeler of that device; and

2. *A production identifier*—a conditional, variable portion of a UDI that identifies one or more of the following when included on the label of the device:

   (i) The lot or batch within which a device was manufactured;

   (ii) The serial number of a specific device;

   (iii) The expiration date of a specific device;

   (iv) The date a specific device was manufactured.

   (v) For an HCT/P regulated as a device, the distinct identification code required by 1271.290(c) of this chapter.

Universal product code (UPC) means the product identifier used to identify an item sold at retail in the United States.

Regulatory Requirement 21 CFR § 820.5 Quality System

Each manufacturer shall establish and maintain a quality system that is appropriate for the specific medical device(s) designed or manufactured, and that meets the requirements of this part.

Discussion

The definition for *quality system* includes not only procedures and processes but also the organizational structure, responsibilities, and resources necessary to manage quality. It is also important to acknowledge the use of the term manufacturer and recognize that, by definition, all finished device manufacturers are required to comply with the requirements of this part.

The requirement to define, document, and implement a quality system is stated in broad terms to provide manufacturers the flexibility to design quality systems that will be appropriate and successfully implemented in their organization. What may be appropriate for one manufacturer may not be appropriate for another for the following reasons: size of the company, complexity of the product, sophistication of the manufacturing process, significance and risks associated with the product, and company culture. These are factors that should be considered when designing a quality system.

QUALITY SYSTEM REQUIREMENTS

Regulatory Requirement 21 CFR § 820.20(a) Quality Policy

Management with executive responsibility shall establish its policy and objectives for, and commitment to, quality. Management with executive responsibility shall ensure that the quality policy is understood, implemented, and maintained at all levels of the organization.

Discussion

The regulation clearly places responsibility on management with executive responsibility, the highest-ranking member of senior management, for establishing the policy and objectives for quality and ensuring the policy is understood, implemented, and maintained throughout the organization. The quality policy should reflect the overall intentions and direction of the organization with respect to quality.

Each manufacturer is different in size, culture, customers, and the product or service it provides. The quality policy should reflect the organization for which it is intended. Quality objectives should align with the quality policy and be stated in terms that can be measured. If quality objectives are not stated in measurable terms, it is not possible to monitor performance and commitment to achieving those objectives. The quality policy and objectives for quality are topics to be addressed at formal management reviews, where progress can be tracked and adjustments made where appropriate to ensure that the policy and objectives are understood, implemented, and maintained.

The definitions, along with the requirements, require the highest level of management in the organization communicate the commitment and direction for quality to all personnel. Senior management is responsible for ensuring that the quality policy is understood, implemented, and maintained at all levels of the organization. The regulation does not prescribe how to accomplish the communication of the quality policy. A variety of methods, including printing the quality policy on all employee badges, all-employee communication meetings, or posting the quality policy in strategic locations throughout the facility (for example, conference rooms, cafeterias, main reception area), will accomplish the requirement. Whichever method of communication is used, employees should be familiar with the quality policy, adhere to the direction the quality policy provides, and know where to locate it.

Regulatory Requirement 21 CFR § 820.20(b) Organization

Each manufacturer shall establish and maintain an adequate organizational structure to ensure that devices are designed and produced in accordance with the requirements of this part.

Responsibility and authority. Each manufacturer shall establish the appropriate responsibility, authority, and interrelation of all personnel who manage, perform, and assess work affecting quality, and provide the independence and authority necessary to perform these tasks.

Resources. Each manufacturer shall provide adequate resources, including the assignment of trained personnel for management, performance of work, and assessment activities including internal quality audits, to meet the requirements of this part.

Management representative. Management with executive responsibility shall appoint, and document such appointment of, a member of management who, irrespective of other responsibilities, shall have established authority over and responsibility for:

(i) Ensuring that quality system requirements are effectively established and effectively maintained in accordance with this part

(ii) Reporting on the performance of the quality system to management with executive responsibility for review.

Discussion

The FDA has identified three fundamental principles that are essential to understanding the requirements necessary to establish and maintain an appropriate organization structure. The structure is important to ensure compliance with the quality system requirements and must also ensure the manufacturer is capable of consistently producing safe and effective devices.

1. Responsibility and authority requires that the organizational structure demonstrate the independence and authority of the quality function. The quality system must not be compromised as a result of the structure of the organization and reporting relationships.
2. The requirement for sufficient resources is broad, again recognizing the variety of finished device manufacturers that must comply with these requirements. The manufacturer is responsible for determining what is "sufficient," where all requirements of the QSR are met. The term *resources* should be regarded in the broadest sense to include considerations such as personnel, supplies, sufficient funding, buildings, and equipment.

3. Management with executive responsibility is responsible for documenting the appointment of the management representative. Documenting the appointment can be accomplished by incorporating in a position description, by documenting in the quality manual, or by identifying on the organizational chart. The responsibilities of the management representative are to ensure the quality system is effectively implemented and maintained, and to report on the performance of the quality system to management with executive responsibility on a periodic or as-needed basis. While the individual appointed to this position may have other responsibilities within the organization, it is imperative that potential conflicts that may impact the quality system are considered when this individual is selected. Responsibility and authority for the quality system must not be compromised.

Regulatory Requirement 21 CFR § 820.20(c) Management Review

Management with executive responsibility shall review the suitability and effectiveness of the quality system at defined intervals and with sufficient frequency according to established procedures to ensure that the quality system satisfies the requirements of this part and the manufacturer's established quality policy and objectives. The dates and results of quality system reviews shall be documented.

Discussion

The purpose of the management review is to provide an objective review of the overall health of the quality system, ensure that the quality policy is implemented, and ensure that objectives for quality are being met. A written procedure is required to define how management with executive responsibility will evaluate the quality system and the frequency for such reviews. Management with executive responsibility must participate, and it is expected that they act on the information, making adjustments to the quality system where necessary and providing resources to ensure its continued suitability.

The method for conducting management reviews is not specified in the regulation, allowing manufacturers the flexibility to conduct management reviews in a manner that suits their organization. Management reviews can be accomplished through a formal report circulated to top management or through a formal meeting. Regardless of the chosen method for conducting management reviews, the written procedure needs to describe how they are conducted and documented. The FDA will not request copies of the documented results of a management review during a routine inspection, but it may request that the firm certify in writing that it has been conducted, the date the review was conducted, and the participants.

Section 820.100(a)(7) Corrective and Preventive Action, makes a specific reference to "Submit relevant information on identified quality problems, as well as corrective and preventive actions, for management review." This requirement addresses decisions concerning what corrective and preventive action (CAPA) data the manufacturer will consider to be relevant for the formal management review process. The target audience should be a factor when making this decision, as the management review process is not intended to be the forum for analyzing and reviewing all CAPA data. In addition, comment 53 in the preamble identifies additional elements of the quality system for incorporation into management review and includes the organization structure, adequacy of staffing and resources, the quality of the finished device in relation to the quality objectives, internal and external product and process performance feedback, supplier audit results, and internal audit results.

Regulatory Requirement 21 CFR § 820.20(d) Quality Planning

Each manufacturer shall establish a quality plan that defines the quality practices, resources, and activities relevant to devices that are designed and manufactured. The manufacturer shall establish how the requirements for quality will be met.

Discussion

The requirements for quality planning are specific to a product or family of products, stating how requirements for quality are met. A quality plan includes methods and resources during all stages of manufacturing, including design, procurement, production, acceptance activities, installation, and servicing (when applicable to the manufacturer) necessary to ensure that quality requirements are met.

Quality plans will tie product-specific requirements to existing quality system procedures. They do not require the development of a new set of procedures or instructions over and above those that already exist, although the development of quality plans may identify the need for additional procedures where additional controls may be necessary.

Regulatory Requirement 21 CFR § 820.20(e) Quality System Procedures

Each manufacturer shall establish quality system procedures and instructions. An outline of the structure of the documentation used in the quality system shall be established where appropriate.

Discussion

An outline of the structure of the documented quality system is necessary when the documentation methods are multitiered, utilizing, for example, a quality manual, standard operating procedures (SOPs), work instructions, and forms.

A smaller firm may have a less complex documentation system and may satisfy the requirements with a quality manual and a minimal number of written procedures, such as those required to support and demonstrate device compliance to the device master record and the elements of the regulation. This requirement is qualified as "where appropriate," as the FDA recognizes the documentation structure must be suitable to the organization's needs and the products manufactured. An outline of the documentation system should be considered appropriate when quality system documentation will require explanation to understand how related documents have been established to meet the requirements of the regulation.

Regulatory Requirement 21 CFR § 820.22 Quality Audit

Each manufacturer shall establish procedures for quality audits and conduct such audits to assure the quality system is in compliance with the established quality system requirements and to determine the effectiveness of the quality system. Quality audits shall be conducted by individuals who do not have direct responsibility for the matters being audited. Corrective action(s), including a reaudit of deficient matters, shall be taken when necessary. A report of the results of each quality audit, and reaudit(s) where taken, shall be made, and such reports shall be reviewed by management having responsibility for the matters audited. The dates and results of quality audits and reaudits shall be documented.

Discussion

The quality audit requirement is considered by the FDA to be crucial. The FDA says that without the feedback from quality audits, the manufacturer would be operating in an open-loop system with no assurance that the process used to design and produce medical devices is operating in a state of control.

The FDA emphasizes that individuals who conduct audits do not have direct responsibility for the matters being audited, and notes that small manufacturers may need to use outside auditors to ensure this independence but does not require that outside auditors be used. The dates of the quality audits must be documented, the results reviewed with the management responsible for the area audited, and the independence of the auditor confirmed. If the audit results indicate areas of concern regarding the effectiveness of the quality system, those areas need to be reaudited with the date of reaudit documented and the results.

It is important to note that at this time, the FDA does not review quality audit reports as part of a routine inspection. The FDA investigators do review the procedures used for audits and ask for confirmation that the audit has been conducted and corrective action completed if required, but they do not review the audit report.

Regulatory Requirement 21 CFR § 820.25 Personnel

a. *General.* Each manufacturer shall have sufficient personnel with the necessary education, background, training, and experience to assure that all activities required by this part are correctly performed.

b. *Training.* Each manufacturer shall establish procedures for identifying training needs and ensure that all personnel are trained to adequately perform their assigned responsibilities. Training shall be documented.

1. As part of their training, personnel shall be made aware of device defects that may occur from the improper performance of their specific jobs.
2. Personnel who perform verification and validation activities shall be made aware of defects and errors that may be encountered as part of their job functions.

Discussion

The FDA's expectation for personnel is clear in that it expects a manufacturer to have adequate and sufficient personnel and that the personnel are trained. The FDA expects job descriptions reflect the requirements for the positions and the hiring practices demonstrates that qualifications are met. Generally, the expectation is that there is a training program regarding specific skills for company positions and that the program identifies training requirements for each person and provides documented records of the training that can be reviewed.

The FDA also emphasizes that the personnel have specific information about device defects that may occur from improper performance, and that performance of verification and validation activities specifically requires documented training.

DESIGN CONTROLS

Design controls are the systems and procedures that provide the framework for the design and development process. The use of design controls clearly identifies the checkpoints and approval processes necessary to move the design to the next step. The use of design controls identifies discrepancies between specifications and final design results or outputs and ensures that testing processes effectively identify deficiencies in the process. Design control systems provide visibility of the design process to a company's upper management and effectively guarantees that users or customers are involved in the process of determining product specifications and ensuring that products meet those specifications.

The FDA divides the design process into the following areas:

- Design planning
- Design input
- Design output
- Design review
- Design verification
- Design validation
- Design transfer
- Design changes

Project Management

The design control process phases can be adapted to the organization's needs. Very few companies follow the same design process but adapt the process to the needs of the organization. A typical design project does not lend itself to literal and linear following of the design control sections. More typically, companies follow a design process that consists of some variation of the following processes:

- Concept
- Design and development
- Verification and validation testing
- Transfer to manufacturing

An effective design control system integrates the regulatory requirements with the company's project development philosophy.

The following sections discuss each regulatory area, individually referencing the applicable section of the QSR and providing a list of important points following that section reference. Many of the sections that follow apply to more than one of the design process elements listed previously.

Regulatory Requirement 21 CFR § 820.30(a) Design Controls

General. Each manufacturer of any Class III or Class II device, and the Class I devices listed in paragraph (a) (2) of this section, shall establish and maintain procedures to control the design of the device to ensure that specified design requirements are met.

Discussion

Design controls are applicable for all Class II and Class III types of devices, and most Class I devices are exempt from design control. Manufacturers should review the device classification for design control requirements. Class I devices currently subject to design controls include devices automated with computer software, tracheobronchial suction catheters (§ 868.6810), surgeon gloves (§ 878.4460), protective restraints (§ 880.6760), manual radionuclide applicator systems (§ 892.5650), and radionuclide teletherapy sources (§ 892.5740).

Regulatory Requirement 21 CFR § 820.30(b) Design and Development Planning

Each manufacturer shall establish and maintain plans that describe or reference the design and development activities and define responsibility for implementation. The plans shall identify and describe the interfaces with different groups or activities that provide, or result in, input to the design and development process. The plans shall be reviewed, updated, and approved as design and development evolves.

Discussion

The FDA expectation is that design planning is a documented process. While most companies regularly meet, discuss, and update designs as they evolve, the FDA is looking for plans that are approved and updated as required. Most manufacturer's use project planning software for this process, which allows for planning activities and creation of project timelines. The design plan is a formal document, and updates are reviewed and approved as required.

Regulatory Requirement 21 CFR § 820.30(c) Design Input

Each manufacturer shall establish and maintain procedures to ensure that the design requirements relating to a device are appropriate and address the intended use of the device, including the needs of the user and patient. The procedures shall include a mechanism for addressing incomplete, ambiguous, or conflicting requirements. The design input requirements shall be documented and shall be reviewed and approved by designated individual(s). The approval, including the date and signature of the individual(s) approving the requirements, shall be documented.

Discussion

Defining the design input or specifications for a product is the beginning of the design control process. The design input forms the basis for the product design and for the requirements for testing that design. Important concepts in establishing the initial design input are:

- An effective design starts with specifications developed by team members who are familiar with the intended use and the desired function of the product.
- The more time spent clearly identifying design input requirements, the less time will be spent later design changes.
- Design input requires a combination of resources to adequately establish it, including customer input, designer input, and input from sales and marketing.

At the final stages of design input, there needs to be a review to determine if the inputs meet the needs of the device as well as the ability to manufacture and test the device. It is important to make sure the intent of the regulation is met and any incomplete, ambiguous, or conflicting requirements are resolved.

Regulatory Requirement 21 CFR § 820.30(d) Design Output

Each manufacturer shall establish and maintain procedures for defining and documenting design output in terms that allow an adequate evaluation of conformance to design input requirements. Design output procedures shall contain or make reference to acceptance criteria and shall ensure that those design outputs that are essential for the proper functioning of the device are identified. Design output shall be documented, reviewed, and approved before release. The approval, including the date and signature of the individual(s) approving the output, shall be documented.

Discussion

Design output is identified as the results of the design effort. It is important that the design output be expressed in terms that identify the characteristics of the design that are crucial to the safety and proper functioning of the device but are also able to be compared with design input to ensure that input requirements are met in later phases. Every document produced need not be considered part of design output, but certainly top-level documents that specify components, processes, and systems should be referenced. The following records are typically considered to be design output:

- Work products
- Block diagrams, flowcharts, software code, system, or subsystem design specifications
- Product specifications
- Manufacturing procedures
- Packaging and labeling
- Quality assurance procedures

Design output is a formal process that must be written, reviewed, and approved before released. The design output should include all factors affecting the device--not only specifications, but including safety, production documentation, inspection of raw materials and components, in process and final inspection, and obsolescence. Attention should be paid to the outputs needed to confirm that the proper functioning of the device be confirmed based on the design inputs.

Regulatory Requirement 21 CFR § 820.30(e) Design Review

Each manufacturer shall establish and maintain procedures to ensure that formal documented reviews of the design results are planned and conducted at appropriate stages of the device's design development. The procedures shall ensure that participants at each design review include representatives of all functions concerned with the design stage being reviewed and an individual(s) who does not have direct responsibility for the design stage being reviewed, as well as any specialists needed. The results of a design review, including identification of the design, the date, and the individual(s) performing the review, shall be documented in the design history file (DHF).

Discussion

Design reviews are intended to:

- Provide a systematic assessment of design results, with attention to safety, performance, human factors, and compatibility with other devices especially electronic interfaces and software
- Provide feedback to designers on existing or emerging problems
- Assess project progress
- Provide confirmation that the project is ready to move on to the next stage of development
- Identify areas for further investigation and design
- Confirm by the presence of an individual with no direct responsibility for the design, the adequacy of the phase reviewed prior to moving to the next phase

Review types:

- Internal
- External
- Formal
- Phase related
- General design

Regulatory Requirement 21 CFR § 820.30(f) Design Verification

Each manufacturer shall establish and maintain procedures for verifying the device design. Design verification shall confirm that the design output meets the design input requirements. The results of the design verification, including identification of the design, method(s), the date, and the individual(s) performing the verification, shall be documented in the DHF.

Discussion

Design verification and design validation are associated concepts with very important differences. Medical device manufacturers are encouraged to use the terminology of the quality system requirements in their internal procedures. Generally, design verification is considered to be the process of verifying at each design stage that the design output conforms to defined design input requirements for that stage. Examples of this would be measuring critical dimensions of prototype components or testing the output of an electronic component. This verification process could include specific tests or evaluations and is generally performed in the laboratory or a design setting. This qualification should include component testing as well as any required software testing and validation. It is best to use a traceability matrix to confirm and be able to verify that all the design inputs have been tested and the outputs have met the requirements of the design requirements. In this phase, the risk management files, including failure mode and effects analyses (FMEAs) and fault tree analyses (FTAs), should be updated, and the need for animal testing may be initiated.

Any conflicting requirements must be resolved and if there are problems with the design, they must be addressed in this stage.

Regulatory Requirement 21 CFR § 820.30(g) Design Validation

Each manufacturer shall establish and maintain procedures for validating the device design. Design validation shall be performed under defined operating conditions on initial production units, lots, or batches or their equivalents. Design validation shall ensure that devices conform to defined user needs and intended uses and shall include testing of production units under actual or simulated use conditions. Design validation shall include software validation and risk analysis, where appropriate. The results of the design validation, including identification of the design, method(s), the date, and the individual(s) performing the validation, shall be documented in the DHF.

Discussion

While design verification verifies that design output meets design input requirements, design validation is the act of assuring that the design will conform to user needs and intended use(s). Design validation is a formal process and involves the manufacture of products under manufacturing conditions or simulating manufacturing conditions with red-lined manufacturing documents or near-final manufacturing documents. Products are tested thoroughly using finished product specifications and simulated use conditions, and testing should include in-process and final inspection criteria. The software testing should be completed on the products and any programing validated under use conditions. The risk management file and risk documentation such as process FMEAs and FTAs should be complete. The sources of potential patient harm to users and patients is documented, and the severity of harms is understood and documented. Any harms should be reduced to safe levels during this phase or well documented and understood and accepted by all levels of the organization.

Design validation should include the validation master plan activities, and these should be completed as part of this phase. Inspection release criteria should be documented for the products, which will be sampled based on validation activities with the processes that will be 100 percent inspected identified.

Design validation may consist of clinical studies. Most often, products are tested using simulated use conditions, and the products are evaluated in the laboratory using developed inspection criteria. Design validation is an essential element of design control. It requires use/evaluation of the product in a setting that either simulates use or constitutes real use (clinical studies).

Regulatory Requirement 21 CFR § 820.30(h) Design Transfer

Each manufacturer shall establish and maintain procedures to ensure that the device design is correctly translated into production specifications.

Discussion

To produce any product, a set of production specifications/procedures is used to specify the production methods to enable the product to be consistently manufactured. Design transfer is the phase releasing the production specifications after review and approval that are critical to device quality. The set of documentation specific to design transfer is called the device master record (DMR), which includes tests and specifications that are related to ensuring the device as built meets the requirements for the device. It may be necessary to set up pilot manufacturing to formally evaluate the procedure that will be used to routinely manufacture the device.

Regulatory Requirement 21 CFR § 820.30(i) Design Changes

Each manufacturer shall establish and maintain procedures for the identification, documentation, validation, or, where appropriate, verification, review, and approval of design changes before their implementation.

Discussion

There are two methods to control design changes:

- *Document control*—Use of existing control of documents, including tracking their status and revision history including final release
- *Design change control*—Identification and control of changes within the design control process, and tracking their resolution prior to design transfer within the design control files

The main objectives of design changes are ensuring that:

- There is evaluation of changes to determine if they are significant to the design.
- Changes are implemented in such a manner that the original problem is resolved and the degree of testing and documentation proportional to the significance of the change.
- If new concerns or problems are identified, they are tracked to resolution.
- Design documentation is updated to accurately reflect the revised design and any additional design review of activities documented.

Regulatory Requirement 21 CFR § 820.30(j) Design History File

Each manufacturer shall establish and maintain a DHF for each type of device. The DHF shall contain or reference the records necessary to demonstrate that the design was developed in accordance with the approved design plan and the requirements of this part.

Discussion

The manufacturer is required to create a design history file (DHF). Many required documents have been described in the previous paragraphs; the compilation of these records is the DHF.

The purpose of the DHF is to record the evolution of the design process ending with the final design release criteria. The content of the DHF should be specified in the SOP and refer to the location of the documents.

The DHF should include all the files needed to demonstrate that the device conforms to the design specifications. Once the design specifications are released, they may be controlled by the document control system. However, should significant changes be made to materials, processes, or documentation, they should be evaluated for conformance to the original released design specifications.

DOCUMENT CONTROLS

Under the general requirements of this section, which state, "Each manufacturer shall establish and maintain procedures to control all documents that are required by this part," manufacturers are expected to develop written procedures to describe how all product, process, and quality system documentation required by the regulation will be reviewed and approved and subsequent changes to those documents controlled. The requirements stated in § 820.40 Document Control address two basic issues:

- Document approval and distribution § 820.40(a)
- Document changes § 820.40(b)

The following section will address the individual regulatory requirements referencing the applicable section of the QSR, applicable definitions, and important points following each section.

Discussion

Throughout the regulation, there are references to preparing and approving documents in accordance with the requirements of § 820.40. These references include:

- § 820.50 Purchasing Controls
- § 820.70(b) Production and Process Changes
- § 820.181 Device Master Record (DMR)
- § 820.186 Quality System Record

It is important to recognize that where the regulation makes this specific reference, the initial release of documents and any subsequent changes to those documents must be controlled under the procedures developed to meet the following requirements. Documents must be controlled to prevent accidental use of a previous revision. This can be accomplished by documenting the process of removing and replacing obsolete documents. As many document control systems are now electronic, the FDA requires that if electronic signatures are used to approve and release documents, a method of assurance is present that confirms that the signature is in fact the approver's signature.

Regulatory Requirement 21 CFR § 820.40(a) Document Approval and Distribution

Each manufacturer shall designate an individual(s) to review for adequacy and approve prior to issuance all documents established to meet the requirements of this part. The approval, including the date and signature of the individual(s) approving the document, shall be documented. Documents established to meet the requirements of this part shall be available at all locations for which they are designated, used, or otherwise necessary, and all obsolete documents shall be promptly removed from all points of use or otherwise prevented from unintended use.

Discussion

21 CFR § 820.40(a) addresses the initial release of a document and the establishment of a document control unit. Written procedures are required to identify an individual or group of individuals who are responsible for the review and approval of documents. The responsibilities of those individuals who review and approve documents should be clearly defined in the procedure to ensure accuracy of the document and that the document meets the requirements of the regulation. The date and signatures of the individuals approving the document must be recorded. The requirement is flexible in terms of capturing the signatures in written form or as an electronic signature, recognizing that the manufacturer is obligated to meet and comply with the requirements of 21 CFR Part 11 Electronic Signatures and Records Rule, and the requirements of § 820.70(i).

Written procedures should describe how documents are distributed to ensure only approved documents are available at all locations where they are used, ensuring controls are in place to either remove or otherwise prevent unintended use of superseded documents or those that have become obsolete.

Regulatory Requirement § 820.40(b) Document Changes

Changes to documents shall be reviewed and approved by an individual(s) in the same function or organization that performed the original review and approval, unless specifically designated otherwise. Approved changes shall be communicated to the appropriate personnel in a timely manner. Each manufacturer shall maintain records of changes to documents. Change records shall include a description of the change, identification of the affected documents, the signature of the approving individual(s), the approval date, and when the change becomes effective.

Discussion

The regulation requires that individuals in the same function or organization who performed the original review and approval also review and approve changes to any documents. The intent of this requirement recognizes that those individuals (same function or organization) who performed the original review and approval are typically those who possess the greatest knowledge and insight and are best suited to determine the impact of the change. The requirement is flexible, allowing the manufacturer the ability to specifically designate an individual(s) who did not perform the original review; however, the intent of the requirement should be achieved.

Formal documented change records provide the reviewers and approvers sufficiently detailed information to adequately determine the impact of the change. This review is very important, as a poor review can negatively affect product quality.

Changes to specifications, methods, processes, or procedures specific to the product should consider, as appropriate, design verification or validation, process validation, training, and regulatory submissions, as well as potential impact to distributed product. The record of change must include a description of the change being made, identify all documents affected, the date, and the signatures of the approvers. The procedure must also address how the manufacturer defines "when a change becomes effective." The regulation does not prescribe how this is accomplished and leaves that decision to the manufacturer. Some manufactures use the term "effective date," which identifies the date a new document may be used. Others assign a specific lot number or batch number identifying when a new document may be used. Both methods will meet the requirement as long as it is described in the written procedure.

Manufacturers are responsible for implementing methods to communicate approved changes in a timely manner to ensure affected personnel are aware of the change. Document changes are often corrections and process or product improvements that require implementation within a specified time frame. To ensure timely communication and implementation of the change, the process should recognize the significance of a change and convey the appropriate sense of urgency based on the nature and details of the change.

PURCHASING CONTROLS

The scope of the requirements for purchasing controls includes suppliers, subcontractors, and consultants—in essence all products and services that affect, directly or indirectly, the finished device or the quality system. The FDA does not regulate suppliers of components that are not classified as a finished device and distributed to a finished device manufacturer; the finished device manufacturer is held accountable to ensure that the products and services it purchases conform to specified requirements. The intent of the requirement is to select only those suppliers, contractors, and consultants who demonstrate the capability to provide quality products and services that meet the manufacturer's requirements and establish necessary controls to ensure that the product or service conforms to specified requirements.

There are two sections to the requirements for purchasing controls. One addresses the evaluation, selection, and manufacturer controls, based on the evaluation results. The second section concerns the control of purchasing data, the specified requirements for the product or service provided, and the associated purchasing documents used for procurement.

The following section will address the individual regulatory requirement referencing the section of the QSR, applicable definitions, and important points following each section.

Regulatory Requirement 21 CFR § 820.50 Purchasing Controls

Each manufacturer shall establish and maintain procedures to ensure that all purchased or otherwise received product and services conform to specified requirements.

Discussion

The requirement applies to all purchased or otherwise received product and services. The goal of purchasing control is to ensure that out-of-specification components, materials, or services do not result in any nonconforming finished devices to be released and placed into the market.

To understand the extent to which purchasing control requirements apply, it is important to understand the definitions of product, component, and manufacturing material. *Product,* as defined, incorporates the term *component* and can include raw materials, piece parts, packaging, labels or labeling, subassemblies, and manufacturing materials. *Manufacturing materials* are those materials used during the manufacturing process but not intended to be part of the finished product. While subpart § 820.3 of the regulation does not include a definition for the term *service,* it is discussed in the preamble under comment 102, which states, "As used in the regulation, 'service' means parts of the manufacturing or quality system that are contracted to others." Services can include activities such as sterilization, calibration, testing, pest control, waste disposal, cleaning, environmental monitoring, and installation.

Regulatory Requirement 21 CFR § 820.50(a) Evaluation of Suppliers, Contractors, and Consultants

Each manufacturer shall establish and maintain the requirements, including quality requirements that must be met by suppliers, contractors, and consultants. Each manufacturer shall:

1. Evaluate and select potential suppliers, contractors, and consultants based on their ability to meet specified requirements, including quality requirements. The evaluation shall be documented.
2. Define the type and extent of control to be exercised over the product, services, suppliers, contractors, and consultants, based on the evaluation results.
3. Establish and maintain records of acceptable suppliers, contractors, and consultants.

Discussion

The procedures for suppliers, contractors, and consultants must require documented evaluation criteria that ensure the products and services delivered meet the firm's specifications and requirements.

The evaluation of suppliers, contractors, and consultants is presented in three basic requirements:

1. *Evaluation and selection.* Potential suppliers, contractors, and consultants must be evaluated to determine whether they are capable of meeting the manufacturer's specified requirements, including quality requirements. While the regulation does not contain a specific requirement to establish evaluation criteria, written procedures need to describe how a supplier, contractor, or consultant is evaluated, and the results of the evaluation must be documented.

   The documented method of evaluation should be appropriate and based on the significance of the product or service in relation to the finished device. The more significant the product or service is, the more comprehensive the evaluation method should be. Methods of evaluation may include supplier audits, historical data review, or surveys.

   If the supplier is new, the assessment should be performed prior to delivery of the first product or creation of the service.

2. *Control based on evaluation results.* Manufacturers are required to define and document the type and extent of control over the suppliers, contractors, and services that are needed to assure the products and services meet the requirements necessary for the finished product. The level of control a manufacturer puts into practice is based on the results of the evaluation of the supplier and the goods and services. The intent is to maintain an appropriate balance of supplier and manufacturer controls to ensure that the product or service provided will meet requirements.

3. For example, the manufacturer may need additional receiving acceptance controls if a supplier does not have a specific capability or is implementing corrective action as a result of nonconformity found during the evaluation process This appropriate mix of assessment

of suppliers and receiving acceptance activity must be defined and documented to assure the specifications of the finished product can be met.

4. *Maintain records of acceptable suppliers.* Records of acceptable suppliers, contractors, and consultants must be maintained. The written procedure must address how records are maintained to ensure that only suppliers, contractors, and consultants who have demonstrated they are capable to meet requirements are used.

Regulatory Requirement 21 CFR § 820.50(b) Purchasing Data

Each manufacturer shall establish and maintain data that clearly describe or reference the specified requirements, including quality requirements, for purchased or otherwise received product and services. Purchasing documents shall include, where possible, an agreement in which the suppliers, contractors, and consultants agree to notify the manufacturer of changes in the product or service so manufacturers may determine whether the changes may affect the quality of a finished device. Purchasing data shall be approved in accordance with § 820.40.

Discussion

The requirement applies to the approval of purchasing data (written or electronic), including the purchasing document(s) used to procure the product or service. The specified requirements must be clear and unambiguous and approved before the data are released. Quality requirements must also be clear and unambiguous and specify the quality control and quality assurance procedures, standards, or other applicable requirements necessary to ensure the product or service is adequate for its intended use and produces a safe and effective device.

Purchasing requirements should document, where possible, an agreement that suppliers, contractors, and consultants will notify the manufacturer of changes in the product or service provided. The regulation does not specify how this agreement is conveyed. It can be stated on the purchase order, included in a signed supplier agreement, or included as part of a supplier contract. The manufacturer is ultimately responsible for the finished device and is required to review the change for potential impact on the quality of the finished device. The FDA qualifies this requirement as "where possible," recognizing that some suppliers are not willing to provide this information. However, the FDA will hold the manufacturer accountable for the quality of the finished device, and expects that appropriate manufacturer controls are implemented to detect possible changes should the manufacturer consider this type of supplier acceptable.

The reference to § 820.40 Document Controls applies to all purchasing data. The DMR includes product-specific materials component specifications, manufacturing materials, and packaging and labeling specifications and is governed by the requirements of § 820.40 and § 820.181 Device Master Record. The specified requirements, including requirements for quality for contractors and consultants, must also be controlled under the requirements of § 820.40.

IDENTIFICATION AND TRACEABILITY

Product identification and traceability requires a manufacturer to properly identify product that is manufactured and requires systems that allow traceability of the product from receipt of the raw materials and components to its finished device. The level of detail and other specific requirements vary depending on the product type.

Regulatory Requirement 21 CFR § 820.60 Identification

Each manufacturer shall establish and maintain procedures for identifying product during all stages of receipt, production, distribution, and installation to prevent mix-ups.

Discussion

The requirement defined for identification is intentionally broad to allow the manufacturer the flexibility to use the systems for identifying its product that works best for its business. The main point is that the manufacturer provides a method to identify its materials, components, and products at all points in the process up to and including the user, and that such method(s) are formally established. As part of this process, it is important to prevent inadvertent use or release of nonconforming product to manufacturing.

Regulatory Requirement 21 CFR § 820.65 Traceability

Each manufacturer of a device that is intended for surgical implant into the body or to support or sustain life, and whose failure to perform when properly used in accordance with instructions for use provided in the labeling can be reasonably expected to result in a significant injury to the user, shall establish and maintain procedures for identifying with a control number each unit, lot, or batch of finished devices and where appropriate components. The procedures shall facilitate corrective action. Such identification shall be documented in the DHR.

Discussion

The requirement for traceability applies to those devices that fall into the category of what was formerly defined as "critical devices or critical components." As currently stated in the regulation, it is only required by law that any device "intended for surgical implant into the body or to support or sustain life and whose failure to perform when properly used in accordance with instructions for use provided in the labeling can be reasonably expected to result in a significant injury" must have a control number for each unit, lot, or batch. This requirement is not to be confused with the device-tracking requirements as defined in Part 821, which require that specific medical devices be tracked to the end user by a unique control number or serial number. Although traceability is only required on implants and life-supporting or life-sustaining devices (as defined in § 820.65), it may be appropriate to apply traceability procedures to a broader population of medical devices. While it may demand that the manufacturer incur additional costs, traceability can be very beneficial when conducting a failure investigation to help isolate an incident to only those units that were affected by a certain quality problem. It may be appropriate to perform a risk analysis on the finished device and the component to determine which devices or components are best suited to be traceable through commercialization. While the applications of this requirement have some flexibility, the manufacturer must establish procedures to assure that the approach is deployed consistently and proficiently so as to facilitate corrective action. Thus, it may be beneficial to track the batch numbers to eliminate the depth of degree of a possible recall in the future.

PRODUCTION AND PROCESS CONTROLS

Production and process controls are those techniques, procedures, and methods that are used to ensure that all processes perform as intended and designed devices conform to specifications. Examples of production and process controls are procedures that document the process, any methods for monitoring processes such as statistical process control, or recording of process output measurements, and workmanship standards. This section of the regulation also requires that production changes are controlled and that systems for calibration and control of measurement equipment are in place. This section is important, as it ties into the requirements from the design and development process to make certain that the device conforms to specifications.

Regulatory Requirement 21 CFR § 820.70 Production and Process Controls

a. *General.* Each manufacturer shall develop, conduct, control, and monitor production processes to ensure that a device conforms to its specifications. Where deviations from device specifications could occur as a result of the manufacturing process, the manufacturer shall establish and maintain process control procedures that describe any process controls necessary to ensure conformance to specifications. Where process controls are needed, they shall include:

1. Documented instructions, SOPs, and methods that define and control the manner of production
2. Monitoring and control of process parameters and component and device characteristics during production
3. Compliance with specified reference standards or codes
4. The approval of processes and process equipment
5. Criteria for workmanship, which shall be expressed in documented standards or by means of identified and approved representative samples

b. *Production and process changes.* Each manufacturer shall establish and maintain procedures for changes to a specification, method, process, or procedure. Such changes shall be verified or where appropriate validated according to 820.75, before implementation and these activities shall be documented. Changes shall be approved in accordance with 820.40.

c. *Environmental control.* Where environmental conditions could reasonably be expected to have an adverse effect on product quality, the manufacturer shall establish and maintain procedures to adequately control these environmental conditions. Environmental control system(s) shall be periodically inspected to verify that the system, including necessary equipment, is adequate and functioning properly. These activities shall be documented and reviewed.

d. *Personnel.* Each manufacturer shall establish and maintain requirements for the health, cleanliness, personal practices, and clothing of personnel if contact between such personnel and product or environment could reasonably be expected to have an adverse effect on product quality. The manufacturer shall ensure that maintenance and other personnel who are required to work temporarily under special environmental conditions are appropriately trained or supervised by a trained individual.

e. *Contamination control.* Each manufacturer shall establish and maintain procedures to prevent contamination of equipment or product by substances that could reasonably be expected to have an adverse effect on product quality.

f. *Buildings.* Buildings shall be of suitable design and contain sufficient space to perform necessary operations, prevent mix-ups, and assure orderly handling.

g. *Equipment.* Each manufacturer shall ensure that all equipment used in the manufacturing process meets specified requirements and is appropriately designed, constructed, placed, and installed to facilitate maintenance, adjustment, cleaning, and use.

   1. *Maintenance schedule.* Each manufacturer shall establish and maintain schedules for the adjustment, cleaning, and other maintenance of equipment to ensure manufacturing specifications are met. Maintenance activities, including the date and individual(s) performing the maintenance activities, shall be documented.
   2. *Inspection.* Each manufacturer shall conduct periodic inspections in accordance with established procedures to ensure adherence to applicable equipment maintenance schedules. The inspections, including the date and individual(s) conducting the inspections, shall be documented.
   3. *Adjustment.* Each manufacturer shall ensure that any inherent limitations or allowable tolerances are visibly posted on or near equipment requiring periodic adjustments or are readily available to personnel performing these adjustments.

h. *Manufacturing material.* Where a manufacturing material could reasonably be expected to have an adverse effect on product quality, the manufacturer shall establish and maintain procedures for the use and removal of such manufacturing material to ensure that it is removed or limited to an amount that does not adversely affect the device's quality. The removal or reduction of such manufacturing material shall be documented.

i. *Automated processes.* When computers or automated data processing systems are used as part of production or the quality system, the manufacturer shall validate computer software for its intended use according to an established protocol. All software changes shall be validated before approval and issuance. These validation activities and results shall be documented.

Discussion

Production and process controls include all elements for producing a product to ensure the product meets the criteria that have been established during the design process. Some of the elements are fairly straightforward. For example, procedures describing how the product is to be made and the associated steps must be documented adequately. Procedure formats can vary, but the regulations require that they are reviewed and approved. The procedures could include instructions for assembly, methods for processing, or inspection guidelines/instructions. Also, a device history record (work order), or other system for tracking and defining the order of the processes and, if required, the processor, is needed. All manufacturing processes must be monitored. A validated process must be monitored in specific ways as described in the process validation section, and it is important to track the individual producing the product step and the training. However, some techniques for monitoring the result of each process either on an individual component basis or periodically must be included.

All documentation of production processes and the processes themselves must be under change control. Any changes to the processes once they have been established must be documented and evaluated for either process validation or as design changes.

In the event the environment can affect the product, special controls must be implemented to ensure that the environment is controlled as required. Some products require clean rooms for control of particulate, or control of bioburden or pyrogens, to assure the product can be effectively sterilized. Any environmental controls must be documented and validated, and subsequently monitored, or verified regularly.

Buildings and associated production areas must be adequate for the purpose intended. This can take many forms, from simple assurance that product mix-ups do not take place to specific area controls for environmental requirements.

Equipment used in the manufacturing process can be classified as equipment requiring qualification, as defined in the process validation section, or as simpler equipment such as measuring equipment, fixtures, and manufacturing aids. All equipment must be defined in such a way that it can be controlled and duplicated if required. Any equipment requiring periodic maintenance needs a system for assuring that the maintenance is conducted as required and does not affect the quality of the product.

Personnel performing manufacturing operations must be properly trained and must be instructed on how the operation(s) being performed can affect the quality of the product. Additionally, any specific health issues must be considered. Manufacturing operations may use material other than that specifically described in the device master record for the product. Such material is typically called manufacturing material and can consist of lubricants, process aids, joining materials, and other similar products. The use of manufacturing material must be documented, and additional control may be required.

In the event that software is used with automated processing equipment to perform a function such as assembly or testing of the product, the software must be validated. Refer to § 820.70(i) for more information. Software must be validated to assure the process performs as intended. If the software code cannot be obtained, then "black box" testing to the degree necessary to understand and control the software to confirm the intended use is met should be performed.

If inspection, measuring, and/or test equipment are used to manufacture product, then calibration and qualification of the equipment may be required. If a process can cause a deviation from the device specification, then the process must be controlled. Additionally, processes that are not fully verified must be validated. Control methods include a variety of techniques and vary from simple procedures describing the process to complex software-based systems for collecting data and providing information that can be used to adjust the process.

Regulatory Requirement 21 CFR § 820.72 Inspection, Measuring, and Test Equipment

a. *Control of inspection, measuring, and test equipment.* Each manufacturer shall ensure that all inspection, measuring, and test equipment, including mechanical, automated, or electronic inspection and test equipment, is suitable for its intended purposes and is capable of producing valid results. Each manufacturer shall establish and maintain procedures to ensure that equipment is routinely calibrated, inspected, checked, and maintained. The procedures shall include provisions for handling, preservation, and storage of equipment, so that its accuracy and fitness for use are maintained. These activities shall be documented.

b. *Calibration.* Calibration procedures shall include specific directions and limits for accuracy and precision. When accuracy and precision limits are not met, there shall be provisions for remedial action to reestablish the limits and to evaluate whether there was any adverse effect on the device's quality. These activities shall be documented.

   1. *Calibration standards.* Calibration standards used for inspection, measuring, and test equipment shall be traceable to national or international standards. If national or international standards are

not practical or available, the manufacturer shall use an independent reproducible standard. If no applicable standard exists, the manufacturer shall establish and maintain an in-house standard.

2. *Calibration records.* The equipment identification, calibration dates, the individual performing each calibration, and the next calibration date shall be documented. These records shall be displayed on or near each piece of equipment or shall be readily available to the personnel using such equipment and to the individuals responsible for calibrating the equipment.

Discussion

Calibration is essential to the proper manufacture of medical devices. An effective calibration program includes a system for identifying equipment requiring calibration and ensuring that recalibration takes place as required. The calibration program must also include methods for remedial action and to evaluate the adverse effect on the quality of the device if the measurement equipment is found out of its calibration limits. If the measurement equipment is capable of adjustments that could cause an error in the results, the equipment should be protected.

Calibration of equipment requires documented procedures that specify the method of calibration and the standards used. Standards should be traceable to a national standards organization such as the National Institute for Standards and Technology (NIST) or an equivalent. When calibration according to a standard practice is not possible, an alternative is acceptable, provided that the alternative remains stable. If measurement equipment requires specific storage and use conditions, such as temperature and humidity, for proper results, those must be specified.

Regulatory Requirement 21 CFR § 820.75 Process Validation

a. Where the results of a process cannot be fully verified by subsequent inspection and test, the process shall be validated with a high degree of assurance and approved according to established procedures. The validation activities and results, including the date and signature of the individual(s) approving the validation and, where appropriate, the major equipment validated, shall be documented.

b. Each manufacturer shall establish and maintain procedures for monitoring and control of process parameters for validated processes to ensure that the specified requirements continue to be met.

1. Each manufacturer shall ensure that validated processes are performed by qualified individual(s).
2. For validated processes, the monitoring and control methods and data, the date performed, and, where appropriate, the individual(s) performing the process or the major equipment used shall be documented.

c. When changes or process deviations occur, the manufacturer shall review and evaluate the process and perform revalidation where appropriate. These activities shall be documented.

Discussion

Process validation has long been an FDA requirement. Prior to the preceding additions to the CGMP, the 1987 FDA guidance document *General Principles of Process Validation* was intended to apply to all FDA-regulated industries. Process validation based on the 1987 guidance did not consider the "fully verified" principle that was introduced in the 1996 CGMP. The 1987 guidance was replaced by the *Guidance for Industry; Process Validation: General Principles and Practices* issued by the FDA in January 2011.[126]

A documented procedure should be generated to specify the phases of qualifying a process to be used in product manufacturing. The level of detail of this procedure is based on the needs of the manufacturer and the processes to be evaluated. The procedure should specify the requirements to review the effects of process changes on validation, of maintenance and equipment modification, and of moving the equipment to another location. Any required processing documents or subsequent evaluation documents should be specified in the procedure.

Any process qualification must begin with an evaluation of the process itself. This is best accomplished using process flow diagrams or other equivalent descriptions of the process. The use of techniques including process FMEA or other types of risk assessment is also crucial to understanding the process and determining the emphasis of the process qualification program.

Once the process has been described and analyzed, the next step is to identify the verification steps in the process and any equipment and software used in the process. If the verification steps can be shown to fully verify the process (generally meaning 100 percent of the process outcome is verifiable), then no full validation or performance qualification would be required. The process will be 100 percent inspected as part of the production process. However, a manufacturer may make a business decision to validate the process, bypassing the step to fully verify the process in manufacturing. In this case, the process may be sampled.

After the equipment has been identified, the installation and operational qualification requirements can be established. Generally, qualification comprises an installation qualification ensuring that the equipment is installed correctly and operational qualification ensuring that the equipment performs the process required. Installation and operational qualification may be combined if it is desirable. All qualification protocols should follow a format that is predetermined and documented. All protocols should be approved in advance and executed, and then the results should be approved when the results of the protocol are met.

While operational qualification typically includes worst-case or challenge studies, it is not essential that worst-case studies be done. Process characterization studies to determine the operating parameters of the process precede any worst-case studies. *Worst case* is defined as those conditions that are within the typical operating parameters of the process. So, in general, the process characterization determines the bounds of the process, and the worst-case values are those that are expected to be used in normal processing.

Following equipment qualification, a performance qualification protocol is written and executed should the process be required to be fully validated. The performance qualification is evidence that the process performs as designed and can statistically produce the product within specification. Therefore, all performance qualifications should take place according to procedures that will be used in normal processing. Performance qualifications must include a large enough sample to be representative of the production process and duration. If the process covers multiple shifts, any effects should be covered in the process qualification.

At this point, if the process has gone through the steps of installation qualification, operational qualification, and process qualification, the process can be said to be validated. However, the process must be monitored to confirm specifications and regulatory requirements are met. Monitoring frequency can be based on the results of the various characterization and worst-case studies, and can use the relative process risk determined by the risk management file or in the process FMEA.

ACCEPTANCE ACTIVITIES

Regulatory Requirement 21 CFR § 820.80 Receiving, In-Process, and Finished Device Acceptance

a. *General.* Each manufacturer shall establish and maintain procedures for acceptance activities. Acceptance activities include inspections, tests, or other verification activities.

b. *Receiving acceptance activities.* Each manufacturer shall establish and maintain procedures for acceptance of incoming product. Incoming product shall be inspected, tested, or otherwise verified as conforming to specified requirements. Acceptance or rejection shall be documented.

c. *In-process acceptance activities.* Each manufacturer shall establish and maintain acceptance procedures, where appropriate, to ensure that specified requirements for in-process product are met. Such procedures shall ensure that in-process product is controlled until the required inspection and tests or other verification activities have been completed, and all or necessary approvals are received and are documented.

d. *Final acceptance activities.* Each manufacturer shall establish and maintain procedures for finished device acceptance to ensure that each production run, lot, or batch of finished devices meets the acceptance criteria. Finished devices shall be held in quarantine or otherwise adequately controlled until released. Finished devices shall not be released for distribution until: (1) the activities required in the DMR are completed; (2) the associated data and documentation is reviewed; (3) the release is authorized by the signature of a designated individual(s); and (4) the authorization is dated.

e. *Acceptance records.* Each manufacturer shall document acceptance activities required by this part. These records shall include: (1) the acceptance activities performed; (2) the dates acceptance activities are performed; (3) the results; (4) the signature of the individual(s) conducting the acceptance activities; and (5) where appropriate the equipment used. These records shall be part of the DHR.

Discussion

The FDA provides very specific requirements for acceptance activities. Procedures are required for all acceptance activities, including incoming inspection, in-process acceptance activities, and final acceptance activities. These procedures require specific instructions for how to inspect and test product.

They also emphasize that a finished device is not released for distribution until all required activities in the device master record are completed, reviewed, and released by a designated individual.

The FDA is aware that companies supplying product to the manufacturer may perform the activities noted. That does not change the record-keeping requirements but places an additional focus on purchasing controls and control of suppliers. The FDA does allow "urgent use" of incoming raw materials, but these are recorded as a deviation. This practice should be limited and, if frequently used, may indicate a problem with the supplier delivery or ordering process. Under no circumstances should final release of the product occur until the specified incoming inspection criteria have been met.

Regulatory Requirement 21 CFR § 820.86 Acceptance Status

Each manufacturer shall identify by suitable means the acceptance status of product, to indicate the conformance or nonconformance of product with acceptance criteria. The identification of acceptance status shall be maintained throughout manufacturing, packaging, labeling, installation, and servicing of the product to ensure that only product that has passed the required acceptance activities is distributed, used, or installed.

Discussion

Acceptance status requirements are clear in the QSR. The FDA expects the status of product is clearly indicated so as to ensure that product is not mixed up and is released only after all the requirements for production and release have been obtained. Status can be identified by several means, including clear labeling and other methods.

With components upon receipt, the initial status may be a quarantine sticker applied to the product, and, post inspection, this sticker is removed or covered with a release or acceptance sticker. During each following stage for product acceptance, the in-process acceptance may be indicated by acceptance signatures on the paperwork or device history record. At final inspection, the paperwork is signed off, indicating that the product has met all the requirements for final release.

NONCONFORMING PRODUCT

Manufacturers must be able to identify and disposition product that is found to be nonconforming. Disposition may vary depending on the nonconformance and type of product problem.

Regulatory Requirement 21 CFR § 820.90 Nonconforming Product

a. Control of nonconforming product. Each manufacturer shall establish and maintain procedures to control product that does not conform to specified requirements. The procedures shall address the identification, documentation, evaluation, segregation, and disposition of nonconforming product. The evaluation of nonconformance shall include a determination of the need for an investigation and notification of the persons or organizations responsible for the nonconformance. The evaluation and any investigation shall be documented.

b. Nonconformity review and disposition

   1. Each manufacturer shall establish and maintain procedures that define the responsibility for review and the authority for the disposition of nonconforming product. The procedures shall set forth the review and disposition process. Disposition of nonconforming product shall be documented. Documentation shall include the justification for use of nonconforming product and the signature of the individual(s) authorizing the use.
   2. Each manufacturer shall establish and maintain procedures for rework, to include retesting and reevaluation of the nonconforming product after rework, to ensure the product meets its current approved specifications. Rework and reevaluation activities, including a determination of any adverse effect from the rework upon the product, shall be documented in the DHR.

Discussion

Manufacturers are required to establish a procedure that provides a system for the identification, control, and disposition of nonconforming product:

- Identification: Means of identifying the status of the product
- Documentation: Means to record product that is nonconforming
- Evaluation: Review of the extent and severity of the defect
- Segregation: Place to physically store or otherwise assure restricted access
- Disposition: Cross-functional team to complete the investigation and make a decision on the nonconformity (that is, use as-is, rework, return, or scrap the product)

This process should clearly define the roles and responsibilities of the team members related to the activities to process the nonconforming product. The requirement to investigate the root cause of the defect, and the link of this process into the corrective and preventive action system, should be specified. Any investigation, as well as the disposition, correction, and any need for corrective action, should be documented. The nonconformances identified should be included in the trend analysis program. It is critical that the quality data collected from this system are trended. There should then be a regular review associated with defect trends in order to prevent and correct product quality problems.

An important process in the disposition of nonconforming product is to correct the defect with the product and bring the product into conformance. Most often, bringing the product back into conformance will require rework of the product. To rework the product will require a systematic approach. The method of rework needs to be identified and any testing required must be specified. The rework process needs to be formally documented. This includes the documentation of the rework process and creation of records to confirm that steps required by the rework have been completed. The process needs to be checked against the design requirements of the product to confirm that these requirements continue to be met. Once the rework has been completed, the product must be tested to make certain that the product requirements have been met and there are no effects on the product's intended use or regulatory requirements. This should all be documented in the rework release paperwork.

CORRECTIVE AND PREVENTIVE ACTION

According to the FDA's *Guide to Inspections of Quality Systems* (August 1999), "the purpose of the corrective and preventive action subsystem is to collect information, analyze information, identify and investigate product and quality issues, and take appropriate and effective corrective and/or preventive action to prevent their recurrence. Verifying or validating corrective and preventive actions, communicating corrective and preventive action activities to responsible people, providing relevant information for management review, and documenting these activities are essential in dealing effectively with product and quality issues, preventing their recurrence, and preventing or minimizing device failures."

Regulatory Requirement 21 CFR § 820.100 Corrective and Preventive Action

a. Each manufacturer shall establish and maintain procedures for implementing corrective and preventive action. The procedures shall include requirements for:

   1. Analyzing processes, work operations, concessions, quality audit reports, quality records, service records, complaints, returned product, and other sources of quality data to identify existing and potential causes of nonconforming product or other quality problems. Appropriate statistical methodology shall be employed where necessary to detect recurring quality problems.

2. Investigating the cause of nonconformities relating to product, processes, and the quality system.
3. Identifying the action(s) needed to correct and prevent recurrence of nonconforming product and other quality problems.
4. Verifying or validating the corrective and preventive action to ensure that such action is effective and does not adversely affect the finished device.
5. Implementing and recording changes in methods and procedures needed to correct and prevent identified quality problems.
6. Ensuring that information related to quality problems or nonconforming product is disseminated to those directly responsible for assuring the quality of such product or the prevention of such problems.
7. Submitting relevant information on identified quality problems, as well as corrective and preventive actions, for management review.

b. All activities required under this section, and their results, shall be documented.

Discussion

Section 820.100 refers to analysis of data sources to identify existing and potential causes of nonconforming product and other quality problems. A corrective and preventive action (CAPA) system is not specific to product nonconformances; it also includes process and quality system nonconformities.

Manufacturers are responsible for establishing documented procedures that address the regulatory requirements for CAPA. The documented system must establish responsibility for CAPA, identify CAPA data sources, address how CAPA actions are carried out (which includes emphasis on obtaining the root cause of the problem), identify how CAPA effectiveness and adequacy are verified, and disseminate the information to responsible parties.

The only difference in processing a corrective action (actual) versus a preventive action (potential) is the method of identifying the data source or nonconformance. It is not necessary to have two individual systems. Corrective actions occur when an identified product or quality data source detects an actual problem. Such data sources may include:

- Acceptance activity data (component, in-process, final test)
- Product nonconformance reports
- Process performance data
- Equipment maintenance records
- Audits (internal, supplier, third-party)
- Management review outputs
- Complaints

- Medical device reports
- Servicing
- Recalls
- Legal claims

Preventive actions result when analysis of the data sources (often the same as those listed previously) detects the potential or an unfavorable trend that has not previously occurred. Statistical methods should be used for the analysis, as appropriate. Examples include statistical process control charts, Pareto analysis, regression analysis, design of experiments, histograms, and scatter plots.

A CAPA program developed by medical device manufacturers must include evaluation of customer complaints and returned product, nonconforming material reports (NCMRs), servicing, post-market surveillance, medical device reporting, vigilance reporting, advisory notices, and removals and corrections. In addition, all quality system activities that can potentially identify a nonconformance (provide an input) need to interact with the CAPA program. Such systems include:

- Management responsibility
- Quality audit
- Design controls
- Purchasing controls
- Production and process control
- Process validation
- Acceptance activities
- Nonconforming product
- Installation
- Servicing

An effective, compliant, and "closed-loop" CAPA program will ascertain that methods are established to confirm management commitment to quality. Specific CAPA requirements for procedures are as follows:

First, management is able to demonstrate responsibility for implementing the CAPA system. Although CAPA procedures can delegate responsibility for the implementation and maintenance of the CAPA system to one or several functions (often quality assurance or regulatory affairs), the FDA emphasizes that it is management's responsibility to ensure that all nonconformity issues are handled according to regulatory requirements. Management can show commitment to and ownership of the CAPA system by providing the necessary organizational freedom for handling nonconformity issues, ensuring appropriate systems are in place, and making certain that appropriate resources have been allocated.

Identification of CAPA Inputs. These inputs must include product, process, and quality data sources. Reference the examples provided previously.

Documentation of CAPA Activities. Requirements for documenting the CAPA activities required should be clearly documented in a written procedure or corresponding form(s). Such documentation includes identification of the actual or potential nonconformance, a record of the investigation, the CAPA action plan, implementation and follow-up activities, and conclusions. The degree of the action taken to minimize the actual or potential nonconformities must be in line with the magnitude of the problem and commensurate with the risk.

Analysis of Data and Investigation of the Problem. Where possible, the analysis and investigation should be taken to the level necessary to determine the root cause. A system can be established to ensure that actions taken are consistent with the nonconformity type and that the degree of actions taken is proportionate to the significance of the nonconformity and the potential impacts and risks. The FDA expects procedures for assessing the risk, the actions that need to be taken for different levels of risk, and how to correct or prevent the problem from reoccurring, depending on that risk assessment. It is also important to note that analysis and investigation may lead to more than one solution. The rationale for choosing one solution over another should be documented.

Generation of an Action Plan. As appropriate, the CAPA action plan should consider both short- and long-term corrective actions. The action plan identifies who is responsible for implementing the action and within what time frame. When a CAPA is in response to a product nonconformity, the system must provide for control and action to be taken on the suspect devices.

Implementation of the Proposed Action. The FDA expects CAPAs to be implemented in a timely fashion. An escalation process should be developed to address CAPAs that are not implemented accordingly.

Verification or Validation of Action Taken. All CAPAs require checks to ensure that actions taken were appropriate, adequate, and effective in eliminating the cause(s) of the nonconformance. These checks must also ensure that the action had no adverse effects on the product and/or system. If a CAPA is found to be inadequate or ineffective, the system should require the CAPA process to be reopened, as the root cause was not identified.

Communication of Action Taken. The system must allow for communication mechanisms to disseminate information to those directly responsible, including suppliers. Relevant CAPA information must also be included as an input to the management review process. Procedures should define criteria to determine what information is considered relevant for management review.

Root Cause Investigation. To investigate the causes of failures, they must first be identified. Product, process, and quality system failures and nonconformities are identifiable in several subsections of the QSR, including nonconforming product,[127] corrective and preventive action,[128] and complaint files.[129] All three of these quality system elements include a requirement for evaluation and investigation; therefore, procedures for conducting failure investigation and root cause investigation are necessary. Procedures should address the following:

- *Responsibilities and ownership of the process.*
- *Systems for ensuring that the investigation is commensurate with the significance and risk of the nonconformity.* The extent of an investigation depends on the product, process, or system involved, its degree of complexity, and the risk and impact of the failure, nonconformance, or problem.
- *Provisions for how investigations are conducted, what records are maintained, and format requirements.*
- *Methods for identifying the failure modes and determining the significance of the failure modes (using tools such as risk analysis).*
- *Rationale for determining if a failure analysis should be conducted as part of an investigation.* Duplicate investigations are not necessary if it can be demonstrated that the same type of failure, problem, or nonconformity has already been investigated. In addition, if the cause of failure is obvious, a formal investigation may not be needed. If an investigation is not performed, and there is a regulatory or company requirement to do so, the reason must be documented and signed by the individual making the decision not to investigate.
- *Depth of the failure analysis.* The depth of the analysis must be sufficient to determine the root cause, so corrective action necessary to correct the problem can be taken.

An effective root cause investigation will include the following activities:

- *Identify.* The problem, failure, or nonconformity must be clearly identified, defined, and documented.
- *Investigate.* The cause(s) of the failure must be analyzed. All failures have a single similar property: failures adhere to the principles of cause and effect. The problem must be investigated and documented, including results of the analyses, identification of the failure mode(s), and conclusions regarding root cause(s). Failure analysis should be conducted by appropriately trained and experienced personnel and the persons conducting the failure analysis identified.
- *Act.* A thorough failure investigation should include information and other data that can be useful in developing a plan to act on the failure. Once the cause(s) have been analyzed, a firm can determine those over which it has control.
- *Document.* A record is required of the investigation, follow-up, and conclusions.

LABELING AND PACKAGING CONTROL

One of the primary sources of recalls and problems in the medical device industry lies in the control of packaging and labeling operations. Mix-ups that occur may result in product that is damaged in shipment or packaged with wrong information, thus not indicating what is in the package. If these mislabeling issues occur, they can cause significant problems.

Regulatory Requirement 21 CFR § 820.120 Device Labeling

Each manufacturer shall establish and maintain procedures to control labeling activities.

a. *Label integrity.* Labels shall be printed and applied so as to remain legible and affixed during the customary conditions of processing, storage, handling, distribution, and, where appropriate, use.

b. *Labeling inspection.* Labeling shall not be released for storage or use until a designated individual(s) has examined the labeling for accuracy including, where applicable, the correct unique device identifier (UDI) or universal product code (UPC), expiration date, control number, storage instructions, handling instructions, and any additional processing instructions. The release, including the date and signature of the individual(s) performing the examination, shall be documented in the DHR.

c. *Labeling storage.* Each manufacturer shall store labeling in a manner that provides proper identification and is designed to prevent mix-ups.

d. *Labeling operations.* Each manufacturer shall control labeling and packaging operations to prevent labeling mix-ups. The label and labeling used for each production unit, lot, or batch shall be documented in the DHR.

e. *Control number.* Where a control number is required by 820.65, that control number shall be on or shall accompany the device through distribution.

Discussion

The FDA requires manufacturers to establish control of device labeling activities to ensure that labeling remains affixed and legible throughout the distribution cycle and device shelf life. It is required that labeling contains accurate information, that storage and operations (for example, line clearance) prevent labeling mix-ups, and that a control number is applied when required by regulation.

The term *labeling* is defined broadly and includes all labels and written, printed, or graphic matter on the device, on its packaging, or accompanying the device, such as the instructions for use or separately supplied literature that is used by marketing to promote the device.

If an electronic reading device is used to proof labels, this does not eliminate the role of the designated individual, who stills needs to inspect and review the labels.

Regulatory Requirement 21 CFR § 820.130 Device Packaging

Each manufacturer shall ensure that device packaging and shipping containers are designed and constructed to protect the device from alteration or damage during the customary conditions of processing, storage, handling, and distribution.

Discussion

The FDA expects the manufacturer to ensure that packaging and shipping containers are appropriately designed to protect the device from damage. To ensure this, the manufacturer is generally expected to conduct shipping and shelf-life tests during product design that are intended to provide confidence that shipping and storage do not harm the product. It is important to consider physical effects from the shipping process in addition to temperature and other environmental considerations used to store the devices prior to use.

HANDLING, STORAGE, DISTRIBUTION, AND INSTALLATION

Product handling, storage, distribution, and installation are key areas of product manufacture where the manufacturer must ensure that the product is handled correctly, stored correctly prior to and after distribution (with storage conditions documented in the labeling) and, where appropriate, installed correctly.

Regulatory Requirement 21 CFR § 820.140 Handling

Each manufacturer shall establish and maintain procedures to ensure that mix-ups, damage, deterioration, contamination, or other adverse effects to product do not occur during handling.

Regulatory Requirement 21 CFR § 820.150 Storage

a. Each manufacturer shall establish and maintain procedures for the control of storage areas and stock rooms for product to prevent mix-ups, damage, deterioration, contamination, or other adverse effects pending use or distribution and to ensure that no obsolete, rejected, or deteriorated product is used or distributed. When the quality of product deteriorates over time, it shall be stored in a manner to facilitate proper stock rotation, and its condition shall be assessed as appropriate.

b. Each manufacturer shall establish and maintain procedures that describe the methods for authorizing receipt from and dispatch to storage areas and stock rooms.

Discussion

Consideration should be given during the design phase when determining the needs of a product relative to handling and storage practices. Handling of product should be minimized relative to human contact in order to reduce any opportunity for damage, contamination, and mix-ups.

Storage areas should be designed to avoid negative impact on product and maintained as such by formally established procedures. Employees who are assigned to handle product should be trained to assure they are able to detect a quality defect and then be aware of what action to take if a defect is found. Where special environmental considerations are important for the product, those requirements must be accounted for in the design, construction, maintenance, and monitoring of the storage facilities. Similar regard should be given to the design of the containers and shelving for the product. Formally documented specifications should be established that define the storage requirements for each product. Evidence of this should be available in the quality system records for the facility.

Many times, manufacturers do not allow for handling and storage requirements beyond their own premises. It is necessary for the product to be designed to withstand all environmental conditions with which it can come into contact. Special test methods must be selected and employed to assure that the product is designed, packaged, and labeled to withstand the storage and transit conditions to which it will be exposed. Where special storage and/or handling is required beyond the manufacturer premises, those requirements should be clearly labeled on the outside of the product container for easy access by the distribution chain and end user.

Regulatory Requirement 21 CFR § 820.160 Distribution

a. Each manufacturer shall establish and maintain procedures for control and distribution of finished devices to ensure that only those devices approved for release are distributed and that purchase orders are reviewed to ensure that ambiguities and errors are resolved before devices are released for distribution. Where a device's fitness for use or quality deteriorates over time, the procedures shall ensure that expired devices or devices deteriorated beyond acceptable fitness for use are not distributed.

b. Each manufacturer shall maintain distribution records that include or refer to the location of:

   1. The name and address of the initial consignee;
   2. The identification and quantity of devices shipped;
   3. The date shipped; and
   4. Any control number(s) used.

Discussion

Manufacturers/distributors typically have a procedure(s) that defines the requirements of how to "pick and ship" medical devices per a customer order. Those procedures must allow for method(s) of reviewing both the product and the customer order. The product selected should be reviewed to assure that it matches the product number on the customer order, that it is within the prescribed shelf life, that the product is not damaged, and that the picked quantity matches the order quantity. Where a control number is required for traceability, the procedure must also specify that requirement for recording the control number in the distribution record.

In the event that a product is found to be nonconforming, there must be a method for handling and dispositioning the product in question. Every employee must have training records that reflect his or her ability to perform the operations as defined in the applicable procedures.

The systems employed at the point of shipment must assure that an accurate distribution record is generated for each customer. It should be possible to easily perform a product recall at the point of distribution, assuring that the records are complete and accurate. It may be useful to perform a "mock" recall as part of an internal audit program. This practice would give an indication of whether, in the event of a recall, all affected products (that is, internal and external) can be located and retrieved as quickly as possible to minimize any risk to the user and/or patient.

Distribution records should be readily accessible in the event of either a quality investigation or a compliance audit. The retention, storage, and retrieval of those records should be part of the records management program for the manufacturer.

Regulatory Requirement § 820.170 Installation

a. Each manufacturer of a device requiring installation shall establish and maintain adequate installation and inspection instructions, and, where appropriate, test procedures. Instructions and procedures shall include directions for ensuring proper installation so that the device will perform as intended after installation. The manufacturer shall distribute the instructions and procedures with the device or otherwise make them available to the person(s) installing the device.

b. The person installing the device shall ensure that the installation, inspection, and any required testing are performed in accordance with the manufacturer's instructions and procedures and shall document the inspection and any test results to demonstrate proper installation.

Discussion

Installation typically applies to any device that requires special instructions by the manufacturer (or a contractor thereof) to assure that it is in working order upon delivery. This typically means that the device requires some level of assembly or testing when it arrives at a user facility. Installation should be treated as a quality system requirement, as this is the final assembly and testing of the device prior to use on the patient and should have a specific procedure.

Where installation applies, the manufacturer is required to assure that installation is considered during the design of the device. This also implies the need to consider human factors not only for use but also for installation. The installation and associated test requirements must be formally documented as part of the DMR and provided upon delivery of the device. After the device is installed and tested, those records become part of the DHR. Where an installed device fails the final test post-installation, that failure should be treated within the formal quality systems the same way any device failure is handled at final test. Any failures, investigations, rework, and subsequent retest are also part of the DHR. Where rework must be employed, such rework procedures should be validated.

RECORDS

This section applies to all records and documents, both device-specific and quality system related, that are required by the QSR. Systems are necessary to explain the record management practice, identify records maintained and their location, and specify record retention periods.

There is no requirement for where records are maintained or how they are stored, as long as the location is known and accessible. All records must be retrievable; they should be easily located, legible, and in acceptable condition.

Regulatory Requirement 21 CFR § 820.180 General Requirements

All records required by this part shall be maintained at the manufacturing establishment or other location that is reasonably accessible to responsible officials of the manufacturer and to employees of the FDA designated to perform inspections. Such records, including those not stored at the inspected establishment, shall be made readily available for review and copying by FDA employee(s). Such records shall be legible and shall be stored to minimize deterioration and to prevent loss. Those records stored in automated data processing systems shall be backed up.

a. *Confidentiality.* Records deemed confidential by the manufacturer may be marked to aid the FDA in determining whether information may be disclosed under the public information regulation in Part 20 of this chapter.

b. *Record retention period.* All records required by this part shall be retained for a period of time equivalent to the design and expected life of the device, but in no case less than two years from the date of release for commercial distribution by the manufacturer.

c. *Exceptions.* This section does not apply to the reports required by § 820.20(c) Management review, § 820.22 Quality audits, and supplier audit reports used to meet the requirements of § 820.50(a) Evaluation of suppliers, contractors, and consultants, but it does apply to procedures established under these provisions. Upon request of a designated employee of the FDA, an employee in management with executive responsibility shall certify in writing that the management reviews and quality audits required under this part, and supplier audits where applicable, have been performed and documented, the dates on which they were performed, and that any required corrective action has been undertaken.

Discussion

All records required by the QSR must be stored at a location that is reasonably accessible to both the manufacturer and FDA investigators. Although records can be maintained at remote locations, the FDA expects such records to be readily available during an FDA inspection. If a foreign manufacturer maintains records at a remote site, the FDA expects those documents to be produced within a day or two.

Reproductions of required records are acceptable only if they are true and accurate copies of the original. Records may be maintained electronically as long as the records remain protected, change controlled, and accessible. Systems are necessary to ensure electronic records are adequately backed up. Similar to other automated processes, electronic record systems must be validated.

Records may also be maintained as microfilm or microfiche reductions. Any equipment necessary for viewing and copying these records must be available.

Records deemed confidential by a manufacturer should be appropriately identified to assist the FDA in determining whether specific information may be disclosed under the Freedom of Information Act. Best practice is to mark as confidential only those records that are trade secret or proprietary information rather than routinely marking all documents provided to the FDA.

Section 820.180(b) requires that all records, including quality records, be maintained for the shelf life of the product but not less than two years. This date starts upon release for commercial distribution by the manufacturer. It is up to the manufacturer to determine the shelf life and/or usable life of the device.

Meetings or reports of management review, internal quality audit reports, and supplier audit reports are not subject to FDA review. The FDA will not request to review or copy audit reports during a routine inspection. The FDA may, however, request copies of these reports in litigation under applicable procedural rules or by inspection warrant.

Regulatory Requirement 21 CFR § 820.181 Device Master Record

Each manufacturer shall maintain device master records (DMRs). Each manufacturer shall ensure that each DMR is prepared and approved in accordance with § 820.40. The DMR for each type of device shall include, or refer to the location of, the following information:

a. Device specifications including appropriate drawings, composition, formulation, component specifications, and software specifications;

b. Production process specifications including the appropriate equipment specifications, production methods, production procedures, and production environment specifications;

c. Quality assurance procedures and specifications, including acceptance criteria and the quality assurance equipment to be used;

d. Packaging and labeling specifications, including methods and processes used; and

e. Installation, maintenance, and servicing procedures and methods

Discussion

The DMR is intended to describe the "what" and the "how" of producing a finished device. The DMR contains the documentation for the device specifications and all other documents required for the procurement, manufacture (for example, fabricate, assemble, mix), labeling, packaging, testing, and release of a device or family of devices. The DMR will also contain, if applicable, documents describing the sterilization, installation, and servicing of a device.

The procedures that the manufacturer places in the DMR must clearly define the requirements the manufacturer is following and when particular activities are appropriate. The DMR can be maintained as a single-source document, one or more files of the actual records, an index of these documents (noting their location), or any combination of these. Because a DMR typically contains many documents, manufacturers often use an index or bill of materials.

The contents of the DMR must be technically correct and include the most recent revisions of the documents. The DMR should also be directed toward the intended user. Evidence must exist to show that the documents have been checked for adequacy and approved for use. Changes to the DMR must be done in accordance with § 820.30 and § 820.40.

The listing of typical DMR documents in § 820.181 is relatively self-explanatory. Manufacturers may support the documentation by using production aids (for example, photographs, sample assemblies, and limit samples). Production aids must be identified and must be current, correct, and approved for the intended operation.

Regulatory Requirement 21 CFR § 820.184 Device History Record

Each manufacturer shall maintain device history records (DHRs). Each manufacturer shall establish and maintain procedures to ensure that DHRs for each batch, lot, or unit are maintained to demonstrate that the device is manufactured in accordance with the DMR and the requirements of this part. The DHR shall include, or refer to the location of, the following information:

a. The dates of manufacture;

b. The quantity manufactured;

c. The quantity released for distribution;

d. The acceptance records that demonstrate the device is manufactured in accordance with the DMR;

e. The primary identification label and labeling used for each production unit; and

f. Any unique device identifier (UDI) or universal product code (UPC), and any other device identification(s) and control number(s) used.

Discussion

A DHR provides a manufacturer with traceability to all raw material and manufacturing operations. The intent of the DHR is to provide evidence that the device lot or batch was manufactured in accordance with the DMR. Although minimum requirements for a DHR are identified in § 820.184, it is not uncommon for a DHR to contain or reference the following information (as applicable to the product manufactured):

- Finished device batch number, lot number, control number, or serial number
- Materials used and any necessary identifiers (part number, control number)
- Manufacturing dates
- Quantity started and completed
- Quantity released
- Test and inspection records
- Primary labeling
- Identification of individuals performing the operations
- Documents utilized
- References to appropriate nonconforming material reports and/or corrective and preventive actions
- Final batch release quantity

Unique records required for distribution under § 820.160 may also be maintained with the DHR (for example, name and address of the initial consignee, quantity of devices shipped, and date shipped).

Regulatory Requirement 21 CFR § 820.186 Quality System Record

Each manufacturer shall maintain a quality system record. The quality system record shall include, or refer to the location of, procedures and the documentation of activities required by this part that are not specific to a particular type of device(s), including, but not limited to, the records required by § 820.20. Each manufacturer shall ensure that the quality system record is prepared and approved in accordance with § 820.40.

Discussion

The quality system record comprises general procedures and documentation of activities not directly related to a specific product or process. For many manufacturers, the quality system record comprises the quality manual, lower-level SOPs, and the records documenting those activities.

Regulatory Requirement 21 CFR § 820.198 Complaint Files

a. Each manufacturer shall maintain complaint files. Each manufacturer shall establish and maintain procedures for receiving, reviewing, and evaluating complaints by a formally designated unit. Such procedures shall ensure:

   1. All complaints are processed in a uniform and timely manner;
   2. Oral complaints are documented upon receipt; and
   3. Complaints are evaluated to determine whether the complaint represents an event that is required to be reported to the FDA under part 803 or 804 of this chapter, Medical Device Reporting.

b. Each manufacturer shall review and evaluate all complaints to determine whether an investigation is necessary. When no investigation is made, the manufacturer shall maintain a record that includes the reason no investigation was made and the name of the individual responsible for the decision not to investigate.

c. Any complaint involving the possible failure of a device, labeling, or packaging to meet any of its specifications shall be reviewed, evaluated, and investigated, unless such investigation has already been performed for a similar complaint and another investigation is not necessary.

d. Any complaint that represents an event that must be reported to the FDA under part 803 or 804 of this chapter shall be promptly reviewed, evaluated, and investigated by a designated individual(s) and shall be maintained in a separate portion of the complaint files or otherwise clearly identified. In addition to the information required by 820.198(e), records of investigation under this paragraph shall include a determination of:

   1. Whether the device failed to meet specifications;
   2. Whether the device was being used for treatment or diagnosis; and
   3. The relationship, if any, of the device to the reported incident or adverse event.

e. When an investigation is made under this section, a record of the investigation shall be maintained by the formally designated unit identified in paragraph (a) of this section. The record of investigation shall include:

   1. The name of the device;

2. The date the complaint was received;
3. Any unique device identifier (UDI) or universal product code (UPC), and any other device identification(s) and control number(s) used;
4. The name, address, and phone number of the complainant;
5. The nature and details of the complaint;
6. The dates and results of the investigation;
7. Any corrective action taken; and
8. Any reply to the complainant.

f. When the manufacturer's formally designated complaint unit is located at a site separate from the manufacturing establishment, the investigated complaint(s) and the record(s) of investigation shall be reasonably accessible to the manufacturing establishment.

g. If a manufacturer's formally designated complaint unit is located outside of the United States, records required by this section shall be reasonably accessible in the United States at either:

1. A location in the United States where the manufacturer's records are regularly kept; or
2. The location of the initial distributor.

Discussion

Any communication received by a manufacturer noting alleged deficiencies of a distributed product falls within the complaint handling system. The complaint handling system is not a stand-alone quality component. It is a part of a systematic approach to quality and is intricately linked with corrective and preventive action, servicing, and adverse event reporting.

To maintain consistency within the complaint handling process, § 820.198(a) requires that a manufacturer formally designate a complaint handling group, unit, or individual. This section also requires a manufacturer to maintain complaint files and establish and maintain a documented procedure. The documented complaint handling procedure should address:

- Methods for receiving, reviewing, evaluating, and investigating complaints (written, electronic, or oral)
- Assignment of responsibilities for operating the system
- Corrective actions
- Maintenance of records
- Statistical analysis requirements

Manufacturers are required under § 820.198(b) to review and evaluate all complaints received. It is during this initial review and evaluation that the manufacturer determines if the complaint is valid and whether to investigate the complaint. If the decision is not to investigate, the justification must be documented.

An investigation is required if the complaint involves the alleged failure of a device (or its labeling or packaging) to meet specification or if the complaint meets the medical device reporting (MDR) criteria.[130] Duplicative investigations are not required if it can be shown that the same nonconformity has already been investigated. A reference to the original investigation is an acceptable justification for not conducting a second investigation.

Those complaints meeting MDR reporting criteria must be clearly identified and segregated for purposes of prioritization. Investigation records for these complaints must address the specific requirements outlined under § 820.198(d)(1) through (d)(3). There are mandatory reporting times set forth by the FDA for filing electronic reports, so it is important to prioritize the investigation of these complaints.

Written records of all investigations must be maintained. Complaint files and investigations should contain sufficient information to show that the report was properly reviewed and, if required, investigated. Section 820.198(e) identifies the basic information that is required for all complaint investigations, including:

- Name of the device
- Date the complaint was received
- Reference to any control numbers, lot numbers, or serial numbers
- Complainant contact information including name, address, and phone number
- Nature of the complaint
- Results of investigation (corrective action taken, justification if no action taken, dates of investigation, name of investigator, reply, if any, to the complainant)

In most cases, manufacturers record the majority of this information [(e)(1)–(e)(5)] for all complaints received. The FDA expects manufacturers to make a "good faith" effort to obtain any missing complaint data. As a result, attempted communications with the complainant to obtain missing information should be documented regardless of whether the complainant responds or provides the requested information. Traditionally, three attempts to obtain missing information are recommended. At least one of these attempts must be in writing.

21 CFR § 820.198(f) requires that if the manufacturing facility is different from the formally designated complaint handling unit, the manufacturing facility receives or has access to complaint and investigation information. Firms with complaint handling units located abroad must have access to complaint files at a location within the United States.[131] In both situations, duplicate records are not required as long as there is reasonable access to the complaints and records of the investigation. The manufacturer's procedures must ensure that the manufacturing site (domestic or abroad) is notified of any applicable complaints.

SERVICING

Products that can wear out in the field may require servicing and/or repair. Servicing can consist of routine maintenance or repair of defective devices.

Regulatory Requirement 21 CFR § 820.200 Servicing

a. Where servicing is a specified requirement, each manufacturer shall establish and maintain instructions and procedures for performing and verifying that the servicing meets the specified requirements.

b. Each manufacturer shall analyze service reports with appropriate statistical methodology in accordance with 820.100.

c. Each manufacturer that receives a service report that represents an event that must be reported to the FDA under part 803 of this chapter shall automatically consider the report a complaint and shall process it in accordance with the requirements of 820.198.

d. Service reports shall be documented and shall include:

1. The name of the device serviced;
2. Any unique device identifier (UDI) or universal product code (UPC), and any other device identification(s) and control number(s) used;
3. The date of service;
4. The individual(s) servicing the device;
5. The service performed; and
6. The test and inspection data.

Discussion

Servicing is typically required for reusable equipment (for example, MRI units, respirators, and wheelchairs). Where the manufacturer defines a device as reusable, the manufacturer is required to develop user manuals (for example, use, service, and maintenance) as part of the finished product and as part of the DMR. Similar to the installation instructions, servicing should be considered and developed during the design phase of product development. Use and service instructions and maintenance instructions may be found in separate manuals, but both need to be established. In addition, a list of spare parts should be provided as part of these manuals.

Service may be handled in several ways. Users may be qualified to perform the service and maintenance on their own, they may employ qualified staff, or they may contract this service out to a contractor or back to the original manufacturer. In any case, whenever service (preventive or corrective) is made to a medical device, there should be a documented record of that service. The records should be reviewed for statistical trends and for complaints and MDRs. Where a trend of servicing is identified that had not been previously identified and accounted for in the maintenance programs, the maintenance programs should be reviewed and upgraded as necessary.

Service events that are not performed per planned maintenance should be considered a customer complaint. Where an incident occurs that may relate to patient hazard or it has been identified that a patient was involved, an evaluation for MDR reportability should be performed and reported as required. In addition to trending and complaint review, service records are considered part of the DHR.

STATISTICAL TECHNIQUES

In typical medical device manufacturing, a variety of statistical techniques are used. Commonly, a sampling plan is used for validation activities, acceptance, receiving, in-process, and final inspection. That sampling plan must be based on a well-established standard and should be appropriate to the process. Statistics are used throughout the organization. Each type of statistic and the method used should be identified and documented.

Regulatory Requirement 21 CFR § 820.250 Statistical Techniques

a. Where appropriate, each manufacturer shall establish and maintain procedures for identifying valid statistical techniques required for establishing, controlling, and verifying the acceptability of process capability and product characteristics.

b. Sampling plans, when used, shall be written and based on a valid statistical rationale. Each manufacturer shall establish and maintain procedures to ensure that sampling methods are adequate for their intended use and to ensure that when changes occur, the sampling plans are reviewed. These activities shall be documented.

Discussion

The requirement for statistical techniques is one of the least difficult requirements. It can be met by documenting the techniques used. However, it is more difficult to identify and use an appropriate technique. Sampling techniques typically have been based on military standards or the ANSI/ASQ Z1.4 standard, *Sampling Procedures and Tables for Inspection by Attributes* or other programs, such as that described in *Zero Acceptance Sampling Plans* by Nicholas L. Squeglia. The zero acceptance plan has gained in use with the emphasis on risk management, as defective units are not allowed. The chosen sampling method should have a specific basis for its choice and use. That rationale can be based on the studies done previously during process and product development. Other statistical techniques that are used, including statistical process control and design of experiments, should be developed in a similar manner. Statistical techniques are regularly applied in conducting process validations, and the specific technique chosen must be documented and justified based on risk.

Chapter 11

Post-market Surveillance

U.S. SECTION 522 POST-MARKET SURVEILLANCE STUDIES

The U.S. FDA is authorized by section 522 of the Federal Food, Drug and Cosmetic Act (FD&C Act) to require a manufacturer to conduct post-market surveillance for a duration of up to 36 months for a Class II or III medical device meeting any of specified criteria. Such criteria are if device failure would be reasonably likely to have serious adverse health consequences, if the device is expected to have significant use in pediatric patients, if the device is intended to be implanted for more than one year, or if the device is intended to be life-sustaining or life-supporting and will be used outside a device user facility. A post-market surveillance order may be issued at the time of device clearance/approval or anytime thereafter. Once an order is issued, the manufacturer must submit a post-market surveillance plan within 30 days and commence post-market surveillance not later than 15 months after the date of order issuance. Failure to comply with a section 522 order is a prohibited act rendering the device misbranded.

Manufacturers must submit an interim post-market surveillance report every six months for the first two years of post-market surveillance and then annually until the surveillance is completed. Changes to an approved post-market surveillance plan require FDA approval before being implemented.

U.S. PRODUCT RECALLS

Recalls are a method for companies to remove product from the market where the product has been shown to not meet its specified requirements, presents a risk to health, and/or violates FDA regulations. Recalls can consist of notification to users, corrections in the field (for example, inspection, relabeling), or actual return to the manufacturer of product; see Chapter 5 for Corrections and Removals under 21 CFR Part 806.

The FDA has specific requirements for recalls that are described in the following sections.

FDA Policy

Even when the statutory provisions under the FD&C Act § 518 are not met, the FDA can request that a device be recalled, or a firm can recall a device on its own initiative. The FDA often uses its powers to order a recall under § 518(e) as leverage in achieving voluntary recalls. The mechanics of a voluntary recall are set forth in 21 CFR Part 7 *Enforcement Policy* (which applies to all FDA-regulated products).

The FDA defines *recall* broadly as "a firm's removal or correction of a marketed product that the FDA considers to be in violation of the laws it administers and against which the agency would initiate legal action, for example, a seizure."[132]

Recalls do not include market withdrawals or stock recoveries. However, should you classify your product return in this manner, you should make certain that your withdrawal or recovery is justified and that your action is not a violation of the FD&C Act. An example of a return that is justifiable is a normal stock rotation practice or removal of a product due to a product enhancement, such as making the product easier to use but not affecting the use of the product.

The FDA's policies with respect to recalls emphasize a collaborative effort between the agency and the company. Although the FDA has authority under the FD&C Act to order a mandatory device recall, it has rarely exercised this authority. Most recalls of products regulated by the FDA are carried out voluntarily by the manufacturers or distributors of the product. In some instances, a company discovers that one of its products is defective and recalls it entirely on its own. In others, the FDA informs a company of findings that one of its products is defective and suggests or requests a recall. Usually, the company will comply; if it does not, then the FDA can seek a court order authorizing the federal government to seize the product.

This cooperation between the FDA and its regulated industries has proven over the years to be the quickest and most reliable method to remove potentially dangerous products from the market. This method has been successful because it is in the interest of the FDA, as well as industry, to remove unsafe and defective products from the field as quickly as possible.

The FDA has guidelines for companies to follow in recalling defective products that fall under the agency's jurisdiction. These guidelines make clear that the FDA expects these firms to take full responsibility for product recalls, including follow-up checks to assure recalls are successful. Under the guidelines, companies are expected to notify the FDA when recalls are started, to make progress reports to the FDA on recalls, and to advise the FDA when the manufacturer has determined the recall can be closed.

The guidelines also call on manufacturers and distributors to develop contingency plans for product recalls that can be put into effect if and when they are needed. The FDA's role under the guidelines is to monitor company recalls and assess the adequacy of a firm's actions. After a recall is completed, the FDA makes sure the product is destroyed by arranging with the manufacturer to witness destruction or reviewing the manufacturer's action to suitably recondition. The FDA investigates why the product was defective and may issue a Form 483 during this visit.

Voluntary Recalls

A voluntary recall is a firm-initiated recall; in other words, it is the alternative to an FDA mandatory recall or other legal action. While the FDA has mandatory recall authority for devices, it has rarely exercised this authority. The FDA, however, may request a firm to initiate a recall.

There are several incentives for a company to recall a product, including the moral duty to protect its customers from harm and the desire to avoid private lawsuits if injuries occur. The alternatives to recall are seizures, injunctions, or criminal actions. These are often accompanied by adverse publicity, which can damage a firm's reputation.

Mandatory Recalls

The FDA was granted mandatory recall authority by the Safe Medical Devices Act (SMDA) of 1990.[133] If an entity does not conduct a voluntary recall and, after providing that entity with an opportunity to consult with the FDA, the agency determines that there is "a reasonable probability that a device intended for human use would cause serious, adverse health consequences, or death," the FDA may issue an order requiring a recall. Such order would require that the entity/person named in the order "(1) cease distribution of the device; (2) notify health professionals and device user facilities of the order; and (3) instruct these professionals and device user facilities to cease use of the device."[134]

The FDA also would provide the entity named in the order with an opportunity to request a regulatory hearing or submit a written request that the order be modified, vacated, or amended.[135]

As noted previously, the FDA has rarely exercised its mandatory recall authority for devices.

Mechanics and Classification of a Recall

A manufacturer of any FDA-regulated product may voluntarily initiate a recall to "...carry out [its] responsibility to protect the public health and well-being from products that present a risk of injury or gross deception or are otherwise defective."[136] 21 CFR § 7.41 through § 7.59 provide guidance for the elements of a voluntary recall.

The FDA classifies recalls as either Class I, II, or III based on the relative degree of health hazard presented by the product being recalled. Following are descriptions of each class:

- Class I: "A situation in which there is a reasonable probability that the use of, or exposure to, a violative product will cause serious adverse health consequences or death."
- Class II: "A situation in which use of, or exposure to, a violative product may cause temporary or medically reversible adverse health consequences or where the probability of serious adverse health consequences is remote."
- Class III: "A situation in which use of, or exposure to, a violative product is not likely to cause adverse health consequences."[137]

The FDA will determine the class based on an evaluation of the health hazard presented by the product being recalled. Factors that will be considered include: (1) whether any disease or injuries have already occurred from use of the product; (2) whether any existing conditions could contribute to a clinical situation that could expose humans or animals to a health hazard; (3) assessment of the hazard to various segments of the population (for example, the elderly, children); (4) assessment of the degree of seriousness of the health hazard; (5) assessment of the likelihood of occurrence of the hazard; and (6) assessment of the immediate or long-range consequences of occurrence of the hazard.[138]

If the FDA becomes aware of this violation, it will engage in the same evaluation through an ad hoc committee of FDA scientists.[139] Factors that the committee and the firm should take into account when evaluating the nature of the risk and classification of the potential recall include:

1. Whether any disease or injuries have already occurred from the use of the product.
2. Whether any existing conditions could contribute to a clinical situation that could expose humans or animals to a health hazard. Any conclusion shall be supported as completely as possible by scientific documentation and/or statements that the conclusion is the opinion of the individual(s) making the health hazard determination.
3. Assessment of hazard to various segments of the population, for example, children, surgical patients, pets, livestock, etc., who are expected to be exposed to the product being considered, with particular attention paid to the hazard to those individuals who may be at greatest risk.
4. Assessment of the degree of seriousness of the health hazard to which the populations at risk would be exposed.
5. Assessment of the likelihood of occurrence of the hazard.
6. Assessment of the consequences (immediate or long-range) of occurrence of the hazard.[140]

If a risk is found that warrants a recall, the firm either on its own or in conjunction with the FDA will create a recall strategy. Recalls are considered more appropriate than seizure when "many lots of product have been widely distributed." Even though the FDA only has the power to order a recall for medical devices, it is not without alternatives if a company does not respond to its request:

> Seizure, multiple seizure, or other court action is indicated when a firm refuses to undertake a recall requested by the Food and Drug Administration, or where the agency has reason to believe that a recall would not be effective, determines that a recall is ineffective, or discovers that a violation is continuing.[141]

Alternatively, the FDA has the ability to request a recall if "a product that has been distributed presents a risk of illness or injury or gross consumer deception," if the firm has not initiated a recall, or if the FDA has determined that "agency action is necessary to protect the public health and welfare."[142]

If the FDA does request a recall, it will take these steps:

1. It will notify the firm of the determination and the need to begin a recall.
2. The notification must be made by letter or telegram, but this can be preceded by an oral communication or visit by an authorized representative, followed by written confirmation.
3. The notification in whatever form must specify the violation, the classification of the health hazard, the recall strategy, and other "appropriate instructions."

If the firm agrees with the FDA evaluation, it can follow up with its input on the need for the recall or how it should be conducted. A firm may decide on its own to initiate a recall prior to any contact with the FDA. Such recalls are governed by § 7.46 (firm-initiated recalls).[143]

If the reason for the removal or correction is not apparent, the firm should consult with the appropriate FDA district office. In the words of the regulation, such consultation should occur when "the reason for the removal or correction is not obvious or clearly understood but where it is apparent, e.g., because of complaints or adverse reactions regarding the product, that the product is deficient in some respect."[144]

The firm can initiate the recall if it "believes the product to be violative." If it does so, it must notify the appropriate district office. "Such removal or correction will be considered a recall only if the Food and Drug Administration regards the product as involving a violation that is subject to legal action, e.g., seizure."[145] Once a decision to recall is made, the firm will be requested to provide the FDA with the following information:

1. Identity of the product involved
2. Reason for the removal or correction and the date and circumstances under which the product deficiency or possible deficiency was discovered
3. Evaluation of the risk associated with the deficiency or possible deficiency
4. Total amount of such products produced and/or the time span of the production
5. Total amount of such products estimated to be in distribution channels
6. Distribution information, including the number of direct accounts and, where necessary, the identity of the direct accounts
7. A copy of the firm's recall communication if any has been issued, or a proposed communication if none has been issued
8. Proposed strategy for conducting the recall

9. Name and telephone number of the firm official who should be contacted concerning the recall[146]

Once the recall has been initiated, the FDA reviews the materials and conducts its own investigation to decide on the classification of the recall and on modifications to the suggested strategy. The FDA also advises the firm that the recall will be placed in the weekly FDA enforcement report. If there is a firm-initiated recall, the FDA remains involved.

These sections also recognize that recall is an alternative to an FDA–initiated court action for removing or correcting violative, distributed products by setting forth specific recall procedures for the FDA to monitor recalls and assess the adequacy of a firm's efforts in recall.

Elements of a Model Recall

Anticipatory risk planning:

- Develop a written procedure for the conduct of recalls that identifies who is responsible for directing recalls, implementing communications, and covering all other aspects of the recall. Review it regularly to determine whether updating is necessary and ensure that all relevant employees are trained on the latest version of the procedure.
- Form an internal recall task force chaired by a top executive. It should be composed of quality control/quality assurance, sales, medical, legal, and regulatory.
- Develop a chain of reporting.
- Integrate product compliance and quality control systems.
- Develop a system to track and manage customer lists.
- Conduct a mock recall.
- If there is the possibility of a recall, develop a recall team.

Elements of a successful recall include:

- Notify the FDA, as appropriate, and identify all other applicable agencies in the other markets in which the device is sold.
- Identify all customers/consignees of the affected product, which may include support from stocking distributors for their distribution list, should the firm wish to conduct the recall on their behalf or if the distribution contract mandates the manufacturer undertake responsibility for all recalls.
- Establish customer hot lines and develop a system to track the progress of the recall.
- Draft notices to physicians, distributors, and/or patients, as appropriate.
- Develop a team to determine the cause of the problem.

- Create a chronology as part of the investigation.
- Collect all adverse event reports related to the event(s) triggering the recall.
- Implement a plan for the return/correction of the product and a location for storage of the returned devices.
- Prepare for the FDA investigations and inspections, as well as foreign regulatory agency requests and responses.
- Identify all reporting requirements, for example, pharmacovigilance reports in the European community as well as other country reporting requirements.

Establish priorities:

- Make the safety of the patient number one.
- Immediately identify what caused the problem and then contain it.
- Identify and bracket the problem lot(s) for recall.
- Get the expertise you need (for example, legal, toxicology, public relations, security).
- After notifying the FDA, keep the recall coordinator advised.
- Develop a strategy for any public communications (for example, via the media).
- Develop an international strategy.
- Keep your insurance carriers advised—you may have a claim under your policy.

Overview of a Recall Strategy

A firm initiating a recall must develop a strategy for conducting the recall. In developing a strategy, firms often conduct their own health hazard evaluation. The strategy should take into account the health hazard evaluation, the degree to which the product's defect or deficiency is obvious, the extent to which the product remains in the marketplace, and the availability of essential products.[147] The recall strategy should address the depth of the recall, the need for public warnings, and effectiveness checks to verify that the consignees intended to be notified in fact received notification about the recall.[148]

The *recall strategy* is defined by the regulations to be "a planned specific course of action to be taken in conducting a specific recall, which addresses the depth of recall, need for public warnings, and extent of effectiveness checks for the recall."[149] The recall strategy is shaped by these factors:

1. Results of health hazard evaluation
2. Ease in identifying the product

3. Degree to which the product's deficiency is obvious to the consumer or user
4. Degree to which the product remains unused in the marketplace
5. Continued availability of essential products[150]

Although the FDA will review the adequacy of a strategy, the firm is encouraged not to delay its recall while waiting for the FDA.[151]

Elements of a Recall Strategy

The regulations provide the following elements of a recall strategy.

Depth of recall. The individuals and entities to which a recall should be directed are dependent on two factors: the seriousness of the risk and the scope of the distribution chain. The levels that must be addressed include:

1. Consumer or user level, which may vary with product, including any intermediate wholesale or retail level
2. Retail level, including any intermediate wholesale level
3. Wholesale level[152]

The regulations are also very clear as to the obligations for and content of communications with those who are being asked to return the product; all of it is dependent on the seriousness of the hazard involved. The purpose of the communication, whatever its form, should be:

1. That the product...is subject to a recall.
2. That further distribution or use of any remaining product should cease immediately.
3. Where appropriate, that the direct account should in turn notify its customers who received the product about the recall.
4. Instructions regarding what to do with the product.[153]
5. It is advisable to return all product on hand at the external distributors immediately to prevent any accidental shipment of recall product. This is in addition to making certain that the distributor will contact all consignees immediately to return any unused product as directed by the manufacturer.

The communication can be sent by telegram, mailgram, or first-class letter. The document should be "conspicuously marked, preferably in bold red type, on the letter and the envelope" that the matter involves a recall. "The letter and the envelope should be also marked: 'urgent' for Class I and Class II recalls and, when appropriate, for Class III recalls. Telephone calls or other personal contacts should ordinarily be confirmed by one of the aforementioned methods and/or documented in an appropriate manner."[154]

The regulations also provide the contents of the communication should:

1. Be brief and to the point
2. Identify clearly the product, size, lot number(s), code(s) or serial number(s), and any other pertinent descriptive information to enable accurate and immediate identification of the product
3. Explain concisely the reason for the recall and the hazard involved, if any
4. Provide specific instructions on what should be done with respect to the recalled products

Provide a ready means for the recipient of the communication to report to the recalling firm whether it has any of the product, for example, by sending a postage-paid, self-addressed postcard or by allowing the recipient to place a collect call to the recalling firm.[155]

They also detail what should not be included, that is, the recall communication should not contain irrelevant qualifications, promotional materials, or any other statement that may detract from the message.[156] The firm should also develop a follow-up strategy for those who do not respond.

Public warning. The second component of the recall strategy is to address the issue of if and how the public is to be alerted about the recall. It is limited to "urgent situations where other means for preventing use of the recalled product appear inadequate."

The regulations make clear that the preference is for the FDA to work with the firm and to have the agency issue the recall advisory. If the firm decides to issue its own warning, the FDA suggests that it give the agency the opportunity to comment on its content. The regulations continue:

The recall strategy will specify whether a public warning is needed and whether it will issue as:

(i) General public warning through the general news media, either national or local as appropriate; or

(ii) Public warning through specialized news media, for example, professional or trade press, or to specific segments of the population such as physicians, hospitals, etc.[157]

Section 7.50 emphasizes that the FDA will advise the public of the recall in its weekly enforcement report.[158]

Effectiveness checks. A recall is only as good as its effectiveness in getting a return of the device. As noted by the regulations, "The purpose of effectiveness checks is to verify that all consignees at the recall depth specified by the strategy have received notification about the recall and have taken appropriate action."

The regulations emphasize that the recalling entity can utilize a variety of methods that include "personal visits, telephone calls, letters, or a combination thereof." The regulations also emphasize that while the firm is ultimately responsible for conducting the checks, the FDA will assist "where necessary and appropriate."

Depending on the classification of the risk, the recall strategy must also include the percentage of individuals to be contacted for effectiveness verification:

(i) Level A: 100 percent of the total number of consignees to be contacted

(ii) Level B: Some percentage of the total number of consignees to be contacted, which percentage is to be determined on a case-by-case basis but is greater than 10 percent and less than 100 percent of the total number of consignees

(iii) Level C: 10 percent of the total number of consignees to be contacted

(iv) Level D: 2 percent of the total number of consignees to be contacted

(v) Level E: No effectiveness checks[159]

Status reports. As a part of the recall process, the firm must develop a plan to submit periodic status reports to the appropriate district office to assist the agency in evaluating the progress of the recall.[160] The FDA will decide the frequency of the reports, depending on the urgency of the recall, which generally will range from two to four weeks. The reports should include the following:

1. Number of consignees notified of the recall, and date and method of notification
2. Number of consignees responding to the recall communication, and quantity of products on hand at the time it was received
3. Number of consignees who did not respond
4. Number of products returned or corrected by each consignee contacted, and the quantity of products accounted for
5. Number and results of effectiveness checks that were made
6. Estimated time frames for completion of the recall[161]

Status reports are discontinued when the recall is terminated.[162]

Termination of the Recall

Once the FDA decides that "all reasonable efforts have been made to remove or correct the product in accordance with the recall strategy, and when it is reasonable to assume that the product subject to the recall has been removed and proper disposition or correction has been made commensurate with the degree of hazard of the recalled product," it will give written notification to the firm. Likewise, the firm can request in writing with its current status report that the recall be terminated for the same reasons.[163]

Court-Ordered Recalls: Initiated by the FDA Seeking Injunctive Relief

The courts were initially hesitant to become involved with recalls but are now more willing to do so to balance the extent of danger to the public as opposed to the harm to the manufacturer if there is a recall. An example is *United States v. K-N Enterprises*, 461 F. Supp. 988 (N.D. Ill 1978), which ordered a recall on the basis that the damage possibly sustained by the defendants because of an improper recall was outweighed by the potential harm to the public in consuming unapproved drugs.

Websites About Recalls

Helpful websites include:

- Recalls, market withdrawals, and safety alerts:
  https://www.fda.gov/safety/recalls-market-withdrawals-safety-alerts
- Enforcement reports:
  https://www.fda.gov/safety/recalls-market-withdrawals-safety-alerts/enforcement-reports

  A weekly publication that contains information on actions taken in connection with agency regulatory activities, such as recalls and field corrections, medical device notification, injunctions, seizures, prosecutions, and indictments.
- Medical product safety information
  https://www.fda.gov/safety/medwatch-fda-safety-information-and-adverse-event-reporting-program/medical-product-safety-information

  Provides links to medical device reporting data files, adverse drug reaction reporting data files, labeling changes related to drug safety, annual adverse drug experience report, "dear health professional" letters, and other safety notifications.
- Medical device safety communications
  https://www.fda.gov/medical-devices/medical-device-safety/safety-communications
- Biologics recalls
  https://www.fda.gov/vaccines-blood-biologics/safety-availability-biologics/recalls-biologics

EUROPEAN UNION (EU) DEVICE INCIDENT REPORTING (VIGILANCE)

Regulatory Requirement

Within the full and self-declaration conformity assessment annexes of the directives, there is a requirement for the manufacturer to institute and keep up to date a systematic procedure to review experience gained from devices in the post-production phase, including the provisions for post-market clinical follow-up where appropriate, and to implement appropriate means to apply any necessary corrective action. This undertaking must include an obligation for the manufacturer to notify the competent authorities of the following incidents immediately on learning of them:

(i) any malfunction or deterioration in the characteristics and/or performance of a device, as well as any inadequacy in the instructions for use that might lead to or might have led to the death of a patient or user or to a serious deterioration in his state of health;

(ii) any technical or medical reason connected with the characteristics or performance of a device leading for the reasons referred to in subparagraph (i) to systematic recall of devices of the same type by the manufacturer.

In addition to the requirements defined in the aforementioned annexes of each directive, guidance on reporting incidents is provided in the vigilance guidance document. This document is MEDDEV 2.12/1 *Guidelines on a Medical Devices Vigilance System.*

Discussion

The manufacturer must institute and keep up to date a systematic procedure for reviewing experience gained from devices in the post-production phase and implementing appropriate means to apply any necessary corrective actions and report device incidents.

This post-market surveillance activity includes both active and reactive activity—active post-market surveillance involves the manufacturer determining appropriate levels of activity to positively confirm that the clinical and risk assessment that were conducted premarket, and the reactive activity includes compliance and incident reporting requirements.

Incidents are events that have led to a death or to a serious deterioration in the state of health of a patient, user, or other person. Near-incidents are events that might lead to a death or a serious deterioration in health. In assessing the link between the device and the incident or near-incident, the manufacturer should consider:

- The opinion of healthcare professionals, based on valid evidence
- The results of the manufacturer's own preliminary assessment of the incident
- Evidence from previous, similar incidents
- Other evidence held by the manufacturer

Incidents must be reported immediately to the relevant European authorities; MEDDEV 2.12/1 provides guidance to manufacturers on discharging incident reporting responsibilities as well as the issuance of field safety notices (recalls). This MEDDEV can be downloaded from the European Commission website. This guideline is updated periodically to advise manufactures on the current accepted notification practices, and it is provided after intensive consultation with competent authorities, commission services, industries, and interested parties.

A Field Safety Corrective Action (FSCA) is an action taken by the manufacturer to reduce the risk of death or serious deterioration of health that would be associated with the use of the medical device. This process is a synonym for recall. The FSCA may include:

- Return of the medical device to the supplier
- Device modification
- Device exchange
- Device destruction
- Device retrofit of modification
- Advice on use or follow-up regarding patients

This is reported and notified to the users on a field safety notice (FSN). The manufacturer competes the FSN according to MEDDEV 2.12-1. The FSN is a communication from the manufacturer or its representative sent out to customers and/or end users.

The manufacturer or authorized representative is required to report to the national competent authority responsible for the manufacturer the technical and medical reason leading up to the FSN/recall. The format for this notification is included in MEDDEV 2.12-1. This notification should also be sent to all competent authorities of the countries where the device is sold as well as the notified body. With each notification, a copy of the FSN should be included. Normally, the manufacturer should allow the national competent authority 48 hours for receipt and comment to the FSN, unless there is high probability of a serious public health threat.

Once the FSN is issued, the guidelines for action, as well as follow-up, are given in the MEDDEV 2.12-1.

Part III

Technical Medical Device Knowledge

Chapter 12

Risk Management

Risk management is a system-level requirement and cannot be isolated to software, hardware, or operational procedures. The risk management program must encompass a system-wide perspective that addresses all engineering disciplines and operational requirements. A comprehensive approach to a risk management process is defined in ISO 14971:2019 *Medical devices—Application of risk management to medical devices* and IEC 62366-1:2015 *Medical devices—Application of usability engineering to medical devices.*

The usability engineering process described in IEC 62366 is intended to provide reasonable product usability by minimizing use errors and use-associated risks. Usability testing and evaluation is a key element of the risk management process.

> Note: ISO 14971:2019 was reviewed and confirmed on December 18, 2019. IEC 62366:2007 and IEC 62366:2007/Amended 1:2014 were revised to IEC 62366-1:2015 *Medical devices—Part 1: Application of usability engineering to medical devices,* which was released in December 2015. IEC/TR 62366-2 *Medical devices—Part 2: Guidance on the application of usability engineering to medical devices* was released on April 28, 2016. IEC 62366-1 Edition 1.0 *2020-06 Amendment 1 Medical Devices—Part 1: Application of usability engineering to medical devices* was released as AMD1:2020 and was published to correct identified inaccuracies.

ISO 14971

The ISO 14971 standard defines a risk management process for the manufacturer to identify hazards associated with its medical devices, estimate and assess associated risks, apply risk control measures, and monitor the effectiveness of applied measures. The standard is intended for the complete life cycle of a medical device. Also, many of the informative annexes in 14971 have now been transferred to the TR 24971 to permit easier annex amendment and continue to be valuable coaching tools.

Risk Analysis

Analysis of risks is a critical first step. The earlier in the design and development process risks are identified, the more comprehensive the design solutions are that can be provided to eliminate or reduce the risks. Although no single risk analysis method is optimum for all applications, the following list provides some of the more common and established techniques for risk analysis:

1. Identification of hazards applicable to the product.
2. Basic risk analysis: determining the severity and probability/likelihood for each identified hazard.
3. Failure mode and effects analysis (FMEA) to evaluate safety risk conditions. Design FMEAs primarily focus on hardware, material, and software failures, and lately cyber risks. Process FMEAs focus on risk-related issues in the manufacturing processes. Use/application FMEAs focus on risk-related issues in the use environment, whether with the operator/user or patient.
4. Fault tree analysis (FTA) examines hazards for causes of safety risk conditions as a result of intended use conditions, environmental conditions, operator error, software errors, and integration errors. FTAs begin with a listing of hazards, then continue with the listing of sequential causes (top to bottom), resulting in an upside-down tree-like diagram, helping design teams very early in the development process to understand and then to eliminate or reduce risk of the device or manufacturing process.
5. Review of complaints and recalls for similar devices to determine applicability to the current device design and operation.
6. Review of established standards and guidelines, including FDA guidelines, general requirements for medical device safety (IEC 60601-1 series standards), Essential Requirements of the Medical Device Directive 93/42/EEC (MDD), and now the EU Medical Device Regulation (2017:745).

Risk Estimation

Adequacies of risk controls are to be determined in accordance with a risk model. The purpose of the model is to quantify the severity and probability of occurrence of harm and to ensure that appropriate risk control requirements have been defined.

Severity

A severity rating is defined to provide a measure of the worst credible harm that could result should the hazard event occur. Severity is based on a qualitative measure of the potential consequence of a hazard and may be defined to be one of the categories shown in Table 12.1. This table is only an example severity rating table; different medical device designers and manufacturers have different rating scales.

Table 12.1 Severity rating scale—measure of the possible consequences of a hazard.

Rating	Definition
Catastrophic	Results in patient death
Critical	Results in permanent impairment or life-threatening injury
Serious	Results in injury or impairment requiring professional medical intervention
Minor	Results in temporary injury or impairment not requiring professional medical intervention
Negligible	Inconvenience or temporary discomfort

Probability of Occurrence

Probability of occurrence is defined as the likelihood of harm over the life of the system, taking into consideration the defined requirements. In determining probability of occurrence, the total user population, hours of operation, and system life may be taken into account. Example categories for the probability of occurrence, or probability of harm due to a safety risk, are defined in Table 12.2. Estimation will encompass the circumstances and entire sequence of events from occurrence of the initiating cause through to the occurrence of harm. Probabilities will vary from organization to organization, and possibly from product to product, due to product use or process complexities or risks. Probability of occurrence may also be called frequency, likelihood, or just occurrence.

Table 12.2 Probability of occurrence rating scale.

Description	Probability
Frequent	$\geq 10^{-3}$
Probable	$<10^{-3}$ and $\geq 10^{-4}$
Occasional	$<10^{-4}$ and $\geq 10^{-5}$
Remote	$<10^{-5}$ and $\geq 10^{-6}$
Improbable	$<10^{-6}$

Risk Control

Risk severity and probability of occurrence are used to evaluate the adequacy of risk control measures to ensure the residual risk is as low as possible. Ranking of risk severity and probability can help to identify which risks present the greatest overall risk and the necessity for additional risk control measures. The complete evaluation of individual risks is to be used to evaluate the overall risk of the device. An example of a diagram used to assess the acceptability of the overall device safety is provided in Figure 12.1. Figure 12.1 identifies combinations of severity and probability of occurrence ratings that are acceptable (called "broadly acceptable") and unacceptable (called "intolerable"). The middle region represents the "as far as possible" (AFAP) area, where risks are still acceptable although deserve special attention, as they may approach the intolerable region. The MDR's General Safety and Performance Requirements (see Chapters 6 and 16) state that to reduce risks as far as possible means the reduction of risks as far as possible without adversely affecting the benefit-risk ratio. Three-region risk charts are common and have various nomenclatures. In simplest form, risks can be identified as low, medium, or high. Low and medium risks would typically be categorized as acceptable as long as all available controls have been applied, while high risks would be unacceptable and require further risk reduction.

AFAP has been in place since EN ISO 14971:2012 was released, and as the 2019 version of ISO 14971 becomes fully implemented, organizations should note that the concept of "as low as reasonably practicable" (ALARP) is certainly no longer current. All risks should be reduced to AFAP.

All risks are to be tracked to system requirements, specifications, and corresponding tests or labeling to ensure the effectiveness of the defined safety requirements. System requirements are to be formally tested in accordance with applicable design validation procedures. Labeling requirements are to be verified as correctly implemented in manuals, instructions for use (IFU), training materials, or other labeling as required.

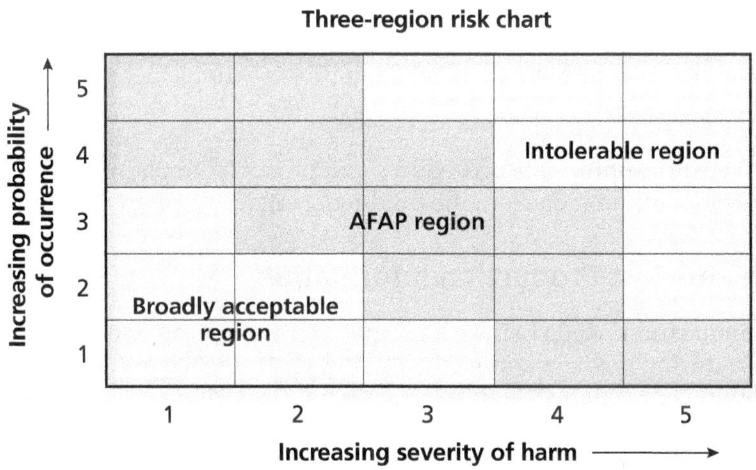

Figure 12.1 Evaluation of risk level.

Precedence of Actions for Risk Reduction

The commonly preferred approach to addressing risks generally is to include system design features that preclude the occurrence of the associated events that can lead to a risk event. Based on the level of risk posed, other approaches may also be appropriate. System risk control strategies in order of preference are as follows:

1. Design for minimal risk: From the outset of the development process, the system design should encompass principles to eliminate or minimize the potential for safety risks.

2. Develop protective measures: If a risk cannot be eliminated or adequately reduced through design techniques, the risk should be reduced through the use of protective design features or methods to detect the condition and to produce a warning signal to alert personnel, or to cause a safe shutdown of the device, or otherwise to protect the user, operator, or patient from the hazardous condition, and still (if possible) warn the user/patient of the shutdown. Use of audio and visual alarms should be examined to determine appropriateness to the operational environment.
3. Develop labeling and operational procedures and provide training: When the use of design techniques, devices, and warnings cannot adequately reduce the risk, labeling and training in the use of the product are to be applied. Tasks that have potential risk impacts require training and qualification of operations personnel.

Risk Management Review

Before releasing the medical device into distribution, the manufacturer must review the execution of the risk management plan. The results of the risk management process are to be provided in a risk management report. The report should provide documentation/verification of three major achievements:

1. The risk management plan has been properly implemented/executed.
2. The overall residual risk is acceptable.
3. There are appropriate procedures and processes in place to collect and review information from the production and post-production phases.

Production and Post-Production Information

Each manufacturer needs to have a program for evaluating issues related to risks that arise during device manufacturing and performance in the field, including information generated by the user, installation, device maintenance, the supply chain, publicly available information, and information related to generally acknowledged state of the art. The evaluation program should assess customer complaints and other reported events for possible safety relevance including:

1. Whether previously unrecognized hazards are identified
2. Whether the estimated risk from a previously identified safety hazard is no longer appropriate
3. Whether the original assessment is otherwise invalid

Summary

A comprehensive risk management program is essential for the development and maintenance of any medical device. Benefits from an effective program include not only more-effective design decisions but also reductions in maintenance costs, regulatory risk, and legal liability. Identification of risks can also support a more focused program for verification and validation activities.

IEC 62366

IEC 62366-1:2015 *Medical devices—Application of usability engineering to medical devices* specifies a usability engineering process for a device manufacturer to assess and mitigate risks caused by usability problems associated with normal use, that is, operation per the device instructions for use or in accordance with generally accepted clinical practice for devices not provided with instructions for use. Additionally, the standard differentiates between normal use (correct use or use error) and abnormal use. Usability is related to medical device safety and is therefore directly linked with risk management. However, risk management is a decision-making process to determine acceptable risk, whereas usability engineering is a design and development process for the device user interface that addresses usability-related risks. Annex A of IEC 62366-1 demonstrates the information flow between the risk management process per ISO 14971 and the usability engineering process per IEC 62366-1.

A key term in IEC 62366-1 is user interface, which is defined as the means by which the user and the medical device interact. User interface includes the traditional computer-related term of graphical user interface, or the screen. User interface also applies broadly to any way in which the user feels, sees, or hears the device and the information generated by the device. The usability engineering process specified in IEC 62366-1:2015 addresses user interactions through the medical device life cycle including: transport, storage, installation, operation, maintenance and repair, and disposal. The process may be used to identify abnormal use. Results of the usability engineering process are recorded in the usability engineering file and may include records located in the manufacturer's design history file or risk management file. Compliance to the standard is verified by inspection of the usability engineering file.

The standard allows for scalability of the usability engineering effort for design modifications based on the significance of the change as determined by risk analysis. According to the standard, tailoring of the usability effort may vary based on size and complexity of the user interface, potential severity of harm of the device, complexity of the use specification, applicability of user interface of unknown provenance (UOUP), and the extent of modification of the user interface.

UOUP refers to the user interface or part of the user interface of a medical device previously developed for which adequate records of the usability engineering process are not available. UOUP is described in Annex C of IEC 62366-1 and applies to devices that were commercialized prior to the publication of the standard. Rather than the full usability engineering process described in the following text, the UOUP provision relies on existing documentation such as use specification, review of post-production information, hazards and hazardous situations related to usability, risk control, and residual risk evaluation.

The main content of IEC 62366-1 describes a more complete usability engineering process that minimizes risk for brand new designs and for designs that have been modified to the point that the user interface has changed. Activities are specified for the full usability engineering process but may be completed in a convenient order due to the iterative nature of the process. The process includes:

- Prepare a use specification. The use specification describes the application of the medical device to include the device indication for use, intended patient population, intended anatomy or tissue type the device interacts with, user profile, intended conditions of use, and operating principle. These attributes are considered fundamental design inputs to identify known and foreseeable hazards and hazardous situations relating to the user interface. The use specification is developed during the design and development process in conjunction with other concurrent design activities. Typically, the use specification will evolve during this process. Formative testing of the evolving use specification may occur.

  Note that many design processes are considered "agile" where the design evolves in steps during the design process. In the same way, the use specification will be updated as required.

- Identify user interface characteristics related to safety and potential use errors. Risk analysis related to safety according to ISO 14971 can be used for this step. The tables included in the standard and other methods may also be helpful. The result of this process is identification of the use errors.
- Identify known or foreseeable hazards and hazardous situations. Identifying hazards and hazardous situations related to usability is also in accordance with ISO 14971. Usability-focused device characteristics related to safety are identified. Known or foreseeable hazards to patients, users, and other persons are identified. Reasonably foreseeable events that involve the user interface and may result in a hazardous situation are also to be identified. Consider the use specification, hazards and hazardous situations of similar devices, and identified use errors in this process.
- Identify and describe hazard-related use scenarios. Reasonably foreseeable hazard-related use scenarios associated with the hazards and hazardous situations should include all tasks and their sequences associated with the severity determined in the risk analysis process.
- Select the hazard-related use scenarios to be included in the summative evaluation. Selection of the use scenarios can either include all hazard-related use scenarios or a subset based on severity. Use scenarios that include normal and fault-related situations should be considered.
- Establish the user interface specification. The user interface specification should consider the use specification, the identified use errors, and the hazard-related use scenarios. Requirements shall include testable technical requirements including any associated with risk controls. All device-related functions including controls, displays, instructions, and other related design features are considered.

- Establish a user interface evaluation plan. Prepare and maintain a user interface evaluation plan specifying the test methods of usability of the primary operating functions, success criteria based on the usability specification, and involvement of representative intended users. The user interface evaluation plan addresses the frequent-use scenarios and reasonably foreseeable worst-case use scenarios identified in the use specification. Use appropriate usability engineering methods and techniques to design and implement the user interface per the use specification, and validated tests to ensure acceptable user interface.
- Plan and execute formative and summative evaluations of the hazard-related use scenarios and document in the usability engineering file. Formative evaluation is executed iteratively throughout the design control process to inform design decisions, prior to summative evaluation. In formative evaluation planning, the user interface evaluation plan can include the evaluation methods being used during the design process, what part of the user interface is being tested, when those tests are conducted, and particularly how those tests are repeated as the design evolves.

  Summative evaluation is executed on the final device design, at the end of user interface development. It is typically performed on representative devices that have completed the design process. Summative evaluation will specify the evaluation method being used and the objective evidence that the evaluation was conducted. It includes what part of the interface is being tested, confirms the safety-related issues, and simulates representative use.

Annex B of IEC 62366-1 contains examples of possible hazardous situations related to usability, as well as potential risk control measures. When considering the appropriateness of risk control measures, the ISO 14971 priority order should be followed:

1. Inherently safe design and manufacture

   Example—easy-to-use hospital guardrail mechanism, conspicuous indication of not being engaged, two-step mechanism to unlock guardrail.

2. Protective measures in the medical device itself or in the manufacturing process

   Example—availability of needle disposal cups to prevent needle sticks after catheter insertion

3. Information for safety and, where appropriate, training to users

   Examples—Diagrams in instructions for use that clearly demonstrate proper technique, and certification of users/installers to verify training effectiveness

When considering risk, Annex D of IEC 62366-1 lists various types of use errors that should be considered and prevented with the aforementioned types of controls. Use error may be categorized as:

1. Perception error

   Example—Failure to see or hear information

2. Cognition error

   Example—Inability to remember or understand

3. Action error

   Example—Inappropriate force applied to a component, or inability to activate a control

ISO 13485

In ISO 13485:2016 *Medical devices—Quality management systems—Requirements for regulatory purposes,* the addition of risk-based controls was a central intended purpose of the revision of the standard. Specifically, ISO 14971:2007 is mentioned in clauses 3.9 (Life Cycle) [3.8 in 14971:2019], 3.17 (Risk) [3.18 in 14971:2019], and 3.18 (Risk Management) [3.24 in 14971:2019]. Primarily as part of the quality management system the organization in section 4.1.2 (b) is required to "apply a risk-based approach to the control of the appropriate processes needed for the quality management system." Within the context of the standard, risk pertains to safety or performance requirements of the medical device or meeting applicable regulatory requirements.

According to and interpreting ISO 13485, the following areas require risk control measures:

- Software—Validation and revalidation shall be proportionate to the risk associated with the use of the software.
- Human resources—The methodology used to check effectiveness of training is proportionate to the risk associated with the work for which the training or other action is being provided.
- Work environment and contamination control—Personnel and the work environment could affect medical device safety and performance.
- Product requirements—User training and product use could affect medical device safety and performance.
- Design and development—The review of design and development changes shall include evaluation of the effect of the changes on constituent parts and product in process or already delivered, inputs or outputs of risk management, and product realization processes. Risk management processes, including hazard analysis and risk control, are integral to the design processes.

- Purchasing—Criteria shall be established for the evaluation and selection of suppliers. The criteria shall be proportionate to the risk associated with the medical device. Therefore, supplier evaluation, selection, and management are all areas in which controls are implemented and proportionate to the risk.
- Production and service—Controls placed on manufacturing processes, inspection of components, and finished devices ensure medical device safety (thus reducing risk).
- Monitoring and measurement—The input gathered in the feedback process shall serve as potential input into risk management for monitoring and maintaining the product requirements, as well as the product realization or improvement process.

There are many potential approaches to implementing a risk-based control of appropriate processes. For one, a FMEA could be used in which quality system processes and their potential failure modes are rated in terms of severity and probability of occurrence. Per ISO 13485, severity ratings would be based on the effect of the failure on either: (1) safety or performance requirements of the medical device, or (2) meeting applicable regulatory requirements. It is recommended to consider both (1) and (2) in the quality system risk analysis to ensure accounting for the most serious consequence. Once severity and probability of occurrence of each quality system failure mode are estimated and rated, risks can be categorized as low, medium, and high, and controls can be implemented commensurate with the risk similar to typical ISO 14971 practices that are applied to medical devices.

One final thought: Remember that since the 2007/2012 version of ISO 14971, risks must be reduced "as far as possible" (AFAP). This can be accomplished when all available controls to reduce risk for a specific risk element for a product (or process) have been applied. Since there are a finite number of controls applicable to any device, and especially to any potential risk, once all fitting risk-reducing controls have been applied, it can truly be said that the risks have been reduced as far as possible.

Chapter 13

Human Factors and Usability Engineering

HUMAN FACTORS REFERENCES

The FDA's Human Factors and Medical Devices section (https://www.fda.gov/medical-devices/device-advice-comprehensive-regulatory-assistance/human-factors-and-medical-devices) describes human factors/usability engineering as focusing on the interactions between people and devices. Figure 13.1 describes the inputs and outputs that exist through the user interface. The user interface includes all the ways users interact with the device, including traditional elements such as a graphical user interface and extending to all visual, auditory, and tactile perceptions. User interface is considered via testing throughout all phases of a device's use.

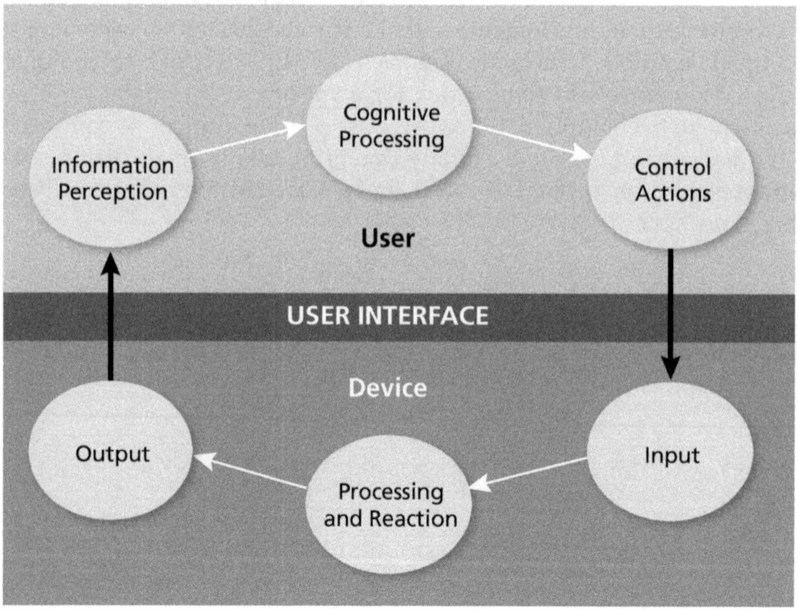

Figure 13.1 Device-user interface in operational context.[164]

In Human Factors Considerations (https://www.fda.gov/medical-devices/human-factors-and-medical-devices/human-factors-considerations), human factors engineering is described as an understanding of how people interact with technology and the study of user interface design. The reader should also refer to Chapter 12 content on IEC 62366-1:2015 for additional information on the application of usability engineering to medical devices. IEC 62366 contains a great deal of information on human factors engineering as it relates to usability engineering.

Another important reference is ANSI/AAMI HE75:2009/(R)2018, *Human Factors engineering—Design of medical devices.* HE75 is very comprehensive at several hundred pages and considers the following:

- Users
- Managing risk
- Basic human skills and abilities
- Anthropometry and biomechanics
- Environmental considerations
- Usability testing
- Signs, symbols, and markings
- User documentation
- Packaging design
- Design for post-market issues
- Cross-cultural/cross-national design
- Alarm design
- Accessibility consideration
- Design elements
  - Controls
  - Displays
  - Automation
  - Software user interfaces
- Integrated solutions
  - Hand tools
  - Workstations
  - Design of mobile medical devices
  - Home healthcare

FDA QUALITY SYSTEM REGULATION (QSR)

The QSR can be considered to specifically apply to human factors and usability engineering in a number of different areas. Refer to Chapters 4 and 10 for more information on each section:

Design input—The manufacturer establishes and maintains procedures to ensure the design requirements include human factors. Design input includes the range of decisions related to the device including controls, displays, functions, and others.

Design verification—The manufacturer performs tests to ensure the design input meets the design output. In general, design verification is early-stage confirmation of each of the design elements.

> Formative studies may be conducted at any time during design control, including around design verification, to collect feedback, identify potential problems, and "inform" the design. Formative studies are iterative and consider all design and user information available at the time of the study. As the design develops toward the final device, formative studies may be a test run of the summative study.

Design validation—The manufacturer ensures that the devices conform to user needs by demonstrating that the potential for use error has been minimized and users can appropriately interface with a device in a realistic use environment, potentially including clinical studies.

> Summative testing includes design validation of the user interface and human factors considerations. The final design is comprehensively tested, including all aspects of the user interface. Not only is the physical device tested but also any instructions for use, labeling, and training. If design changes are made after successful summative testing, then the summative testing must be repeated on the new design.

Human factors engineering impacts and includes three major components of the device-user system: device users, device use environments, and device user interfaces.

Users

Device users must be able to use a medical device without making use errors that would impact care or device safety. Users might be limited to certain groups based on training and need, and must also include those who install, maintain, repair, and regularly test the devices. Users can range from lay people to trained medical professionals. For example, an automatic external defibrillator is intended to be used by lay individuals responding to a potential heart attack.

Usability testing is an integral part of the risk management process, as indicated in Chapter 12. Testing is important to determine whether risks identified in the risk analyses need to be reduced or eliminated. Generally, summative testing of the finished device is focused on those areas with the greatest risk.

Managing the risk to users includes identifying use errors and use-related hazards. Prioritization, elimination, and reduction of use-related hazards is critical and is followed by implementation of an appropriate level of risk controls.

Use Environments

Use environment must include the range or variety of conditions that could define a user interface design. Environments for consideration could include lighting level, noise level, a room with multiple models of the same device, other equipment in the room, a moving vehicle, ambient temperature, and other weather conditions.

User Interfaces

The device user interface includes all the points of interaction between the user and the device and would include not just use of the device but also setup, calibration, maintenance, and repair. Some considerations of the user interface include:

- Size and shape of the device
- Elements providing information to the user including lights and displays
- Graphical user interfaces
- Overall user-system interfaces
- Components that are connected
- Hardware components that control the device
- Patient connected components
- Packaging and labeling

USABILITY TEST PLANNING

Use Scenarios

Use scenarios are a key part of the human factors engineering process. Use scenarios include the various factors that were presented in the previous paragraphs. They generally include both typical and nontypical conditions of use and a variety of situations covering both environmental and operator variability.

One method commonly used in human factors engineering is called "assurance or safety cases." Assurance cases use input from the risk management process and the usability process to design and document the factors impacting human factors using a systems approach. An assurance or safety case starts with the defined hazards of the device and determines safety through the integration of hazards, defined arguments, test data, analysis results, user studies, human factors, and other appropriate inputs.

When considering the process through which the user interacts with the device, critical tasks are identified. Critical tasks are those that would create the highest-risk situations if executed incorrectly or incompletely. Human factors validation should ensure that critical tasks are clearly understood and can be performed without errors.

The usability test process typically includes obtaining informed consent, introduction to the test facility, recording the users' first impressions of the device, and executing specific tasks that are performed by the user according to defined protocols and plans. After testing, the user is interviewed to provide impressions of the device and an analysis of the use errors that may have occurred. The usability test during the formative or early design stage may be less formal, while the summative/design validation tests would be formal and carefully documented. Test data during the summative evaluation should be considered as formal design output.

Sample Subjects and Sizes for Testing

The users selected for validation should be representative of the people who will be using the device, which may include different populations of patients (for example, pediatric, adult, elderly, male/female) and different medical professionals (for example, nurses, doctors, various languages). The use of employees should be avoided to prevent bias or conflict of interest. According to HE75, which provides a detailed statistical rationale, the minimum number of users should be 5-8 for formative testing and 15 for summative testing. The recommended number of users applies to each distinct user population separately, without grouping them together. Training that is representative of the actual planned training should be given prior to validation studies.

POST-MARKET STUDIES

Finally, post-market studies and data are integral to understanding the device's human factors issues. Complaint data and other post-market information depending on the device's specific regulatory requirements are critical to an understanding of how the device is being used. An effective process for evaluating post-market data relating to hazards resulting from use errors is important. Use errors may or may not have been identified during the risk management process. For previously identified hazards, it is important to the frequency of the use-related events so that information can be fed back into potential design improvements. New use errors may also be identified and would feed into the risk management and design control processes.

Chapter 14

Biological Evaluation

Biological evaluation of medical devices is called biocompatibility testing and is performed to determine the potential toxicity resulting from contact of the component materials of the device with the body. The testing is aimed at proving that the materials will not cause any adverse local or systemic effects, will not be carcinogenic, and will not cause any reproductive or developmental effects.

ISO 10993

The international series of biocompatibility testing standards for medical devices is the ISO 10993 series, which consists of several standards addressing various aspects of such testing. ISO 10993-1 *Biological evaluation of medical devices—Part 1: Evaluation and testing in the risk management process* is the framework for choosing the necessary tests based on the nature, degree, frequency, and duration of exposure of the device to the body. Primary among the updates to 10993-1:2018 is the focus on risk management and its use to determine the required testing. The standard was also revised to minimize the use of animal testing. Absolute adherence to the suggested test matrix in the standard is not essential because of such factors as the design of the device and a successful history of the materials in similar devices. If a device is made of materials with a long history of safe use that have been well characterized in the published literature, it may not be necessary to conduct all the tests suggested in the standard. The revised standard also now includes material characterization and other new categories as identified in the following text.

The revised standard begins with the assessment of available information and comparison of that information to the data needed to assess the biological safety of the device. These data are used to make an overall risk assessment of the biological endpoint of the device.

Selection of testing and the choice of test procedures are based on the following:

- The nature, degree, duration, frequency, and conditions of exposure
- The chemical and physical nature of the device
- The exclusion of tests based on leachable chemicals or known profiles
- Ration of device surface area to body size and mass

- Existing information in literature
- Sensitivity and specificity of the test
- The minimization of pain, suffering, and distress to animals

The structure used in ISO 10993, Table A-1 for the selection of tests is based on the following scheme for surface medical devices, externally communicating medical devices, and implant medical devices.

I. Nature of body contact. Devices that contact the body fall into one of three categories:
   A. Surface contacting, in which case the device may contact:
      1. Intact skin only
      2. Mucosal membranes
      3. Breached or compromised surfaces (ulcers or burns)
   B. External communicating, in which case the device may contact:
      1. Blood path indirectly, such as in the case of solution administration sets
      2. Tissue/bone/dentin
      3. Circulating blood
   C. Implanted devices, which may be in contact with:
      1. Tissue (pacemakers or breast implants)
      2. Bone (orthopedic implants)
      3. Blood (heart valves or pacemaker leads)

II. Duration of contact. The time the device is in contact with the body:
      1. Limited (less than 24 hours)
      2. Prolonged (24 hours to 30 days)
      3. Permanent (more than 30 days)

Certain devices may have limited exposure with brief contact with the body, and many of those may not need to be tested. Other devices may have multiple contact durations, and then the more rigorous testing applies.

After the device has been properly categorized using the aforementioned scheme, the recommended tests are chosen from the tables of initial and supplementary tests for consideration within the ISO 10993-1 standard. The standard lists the suggested tests with a short description of each in Section 6.3. Note that physical and/or chemical information is required for all medical devices. All others are at the discretion of the assessment experts. Summaries of those tests follow; please refer to the standard for detailed information:

- Physical and chemical testing: This is required for all devices and includes review of all materials, chemicals, and processes. Data for each may already exist.
- Cytotoxicity: Cell culture tests to determine cell death or inhibition of growth

- Sensitization: Tests that estimate the potential for contact sensitization
- Irritation: Tests that estimate the irritation potential of devices, materials, or their extracts
- Haemocompatibility: Tests to evaluate the effects of blood-contacting devices
- Material-mediated pyrogenicity: Tests to detect material-medicated pyrogenic reactions
- Acute systemic toxicity: Tests to estimate the effects of toxic leachable materials
- Subacute or subchronic toxicity: Tests not less than 24 hours but not for the device lifetime to determine the effects of single or multiple exposures of the device
- Chronic toxicity: Tests for the duration of the device lifetime to determine the effects of single or multiple exposures
- Implantation effects: Tests to determine local pathological effects on living tissue
- Genotoxicity: Tests to assess for gene mutations of changes
- Carcinogenicity: Tests to evaluate the carcinogenetic effects of the device
- Reproductive and developmental toxicity: Tests to evaluate the effect of the device on reproductive function
- Degradation: Tests to evaluate material left in human tissue
- Toxicokinetic studies: Tests to evaluate the absorption, distribution, metabolism, and elimination of leachable and degradation products

Ethylene oxide residuals are not listed within the initial or supplementary evaluation test matrices in ISO 10993-1. However, those tests will apply depending on the product. Residual testing demonstrating a product has an acceptable level of ethylene oxide residuals is appropriate for devices sterilized with ethylene oxide.

Note also that pyrogenic reactions may be endotoxin-mediated or material-mediated. No single test can differentiate between endotoxin-mediated and material-mediated pyrogenic reactions. Endotoxin-mediated pyrogenicity originates from biologically active endotoxin from the outer membrane of gram-negative bacteria and fungi; the limulus amebocyte lysate (LAL) test is typically performed to measure the amount of endotoxin. The rabbit pyrogen test, described in the pharmacopeia of several countries including U.S. Pharmacopeia Chapter <151> Pyrogen Test, is currently recommended for testing material-mediated pyrogenicity.

Additional tests not specified in the ISO 10993-1 standard may be required depending on the possibility of specific target organ toxicity. The rationale for the tests chosen, or not chosen, should be documented in a comprehensive materials test plan.

Interpretation of the data, the strategy for the testing, criteria of the material acceptability, and any rationale for selection or waiving of tests should be determined by assessors with expert adequate knowledge and experience.

FDA GUIDANCE—USE OF INTERNATIONAL STANDARD ISO 10993-1, BIOLOGICAL EVALUATION OF MEDICAL DEVICES—PART 1: EVALUATION AND TESTING WITHIN A RISK MANAGEMENT PROCESS[165]

The flexibility inherent in the ISO 10993 standard resulted originally in the FDA publishing Blue Book Memorandum #G95-1 Use of International Standard ISO 10993, 'Biological Evaluation of Medical Devices Part 1: Evaluation and Testing,' in which a modified matrix is presented that includes optional tests to be considered. The FDA has replaced G95-1 with the guidance referenced previously, and it includes some of the additional testing from G95-1. Therefore, not only is it important to review the FDA guidance document prior to selecting a testing plan, but it is also advisable to consult with the appropriate FDA review division in the Office of Device Evaluation, CDRH, prior to initiating tests of any new device materials. Failure to do so can result in unnecessary, expensive, and time-consuming tests.

Biocompatibility testing is part of the overall medical device quality management plan and, as such, may require that materials be retested based on changes in the product design, source of materials, or device indications.

Chapter 15
Packaging

INTRODUCTION

Packaging of sterile products is important to ensure that a safe product arrives intact at its end user and that the product remains sterile throughout its specified shelf life and storage conditions. When a product is recalled because of a sterility issue, it is usually because the packaging has been compromised, not the sterilization process. Like sterilization, packaging operations are validated in a manner consistent with the requirements for process controls. The packaging materials and design are also validated to ensure the integrity of the unit before distribution (for example, Is the packaging appropriate for the sterilization method used?) and during transit and storage. The permeability of the package to the sterilant, suitability of closures, and variability associated with material finish, thickness, and composition are design factors to be considered. The sterilization cycle may compromise the effectiveness of the packaging design.

Packaging design depends on the sterility claim: either the product is entirely sterile or only the fluid path is sterile. In the first case, the packaging consists of: (1) a primary package (which may have two layers) containing the product; (2) a secondary package containing one or more primary packages to facilitate storage and internal transport by the user; and (3) a transport package to protect the product(s) during external transit from the manufacturer or distributor to the user. In the second case, where the claim is for fluid path sterility only, the secondary and transport packages are sufficient, given that there are closures and fittings—to keep the inside of products sterile—that have been validated at least to the standards of the primary package.

The design of packaging that protects the product may be contradictory to ease of product sterilization. Compromises may need to be made in materials and packaging design, possibly involving further packaging operations after sterilization. For example, packaging for ethylene oxide (EO) sterilization must be permeable to the sterilant gas, but it must also be able to "breathe" at a rate fast enough to prevent seal or film failure during the vacuum steps at the beginning and end of the cycle. Yet, the material must not be so permeable that it fails to protect against contamination. A compromise design may involve an impermeable plastic film primary package with an air filter "port" that allows easy flow of air in and out of the package without risk of product contamination.

ISO 11607

As with the sterilization process, packaging is validated according to a documented study protocol to establish that the packaging process will consistently yield product that meets the specifications. ISO 11607-1:2019 *Packaging for terminally sterilized medical devices—Part 1: Requirements for materials, sterile barrier systems and packaging systems* details the requirements to be met when validating a product/ package combination.

The updates to ISO 11607-1:2019 include the following:

- Definitions aligned with ISO 11139-2018
- Evaluation of usability for aseptic presentation
- Inspecting sterile barrier system integrity
- Revalidation
- Standard test methods in Annex B
- Environmental aspects in Annex D
- Guidance on ways to differentiate a sterile barrier from protective packaging

The validation study begins with the packaging materials, which are evaluated for such properties as microbial barrier, toxicity, physical and chemical properties, compatibility with the sterilization process to be used, forming and sealing characteristics, and shelf-life limitations. Characteristics of the chosen materials are specified according to standard requirements, as listed in ISO 11607-1, and requirements specific to the product and the packaging and sterilization process. General material requirements include such characteristics as "free of holes, cracks, or tears," "nonleaching and nontoxic," and such physical properties as tensile strength, thickness variation, tear resistance, burst strength, and chemical properties such as pH and chloride and sulfate content. Additional requirements may apply to adhesive-coated materials, formed packages, and reusable containers. ISO/TS 16775 *Packaging for terminally sterilized medical devices— Guidance on the application of ISO 11607-1 and ISO 11607-2* provides guidance in the choice of materials and in the use of standardized test methods to satisfy the ISO 11607-1 requirements. For example, ASTM F1608 *Standard Test Method for Microbial Ranking of Porous Packaging Methods* (Exposure Chamber Method) is a suggested method for testing microbial barrier properties. Tests suggested include methods for accelerated aging, gas transmission, oxygen transmission, tensile strength, tear resistance, odor, pH, wet strength, porosity seal strength, and burst strength.

After the packaging materials have been chosen, the packaging is validated for compatibility with the sterilization process and product. Variability in the packaging materials during routine supply is a consideration. Likewise, product mass, sharp edges, and chemical interactions between product and packaging are considerations. Labeling is part of the packaging and therefore should be considered in the packaging validation study. Labeling, including adhesives and inks, should not be affected by the sterilization process or subsequent transport and storage. Microbial barrier properties of porous and impermeable materials are characterized. Finally, the transport and storage conditions of the packaging are validated, usually by a combination of real-time and accelerated shelf-life studies. The accelerated aging protocol can be developed using guidance contained in AAMI TIR 17:2008 *Compatibility of materials subject to sterilization*. Validation of transport conditions may involve testing the packaging at the maximum and minimum transport temperatures, low atmospheric pressure (high altitude), high relative humidity, controlled drop, and extended periods of vibration (sometimes referred to as "shake, rattle, and roll" testing).

Package forming and sealing is also part of the packaging validation study. The equipment used in forming and/or sealing is validated to document the effectiveness in meeting operating limits and tolerances consistently. The equipment qualification includes the ability to monitor key parameters, calibration and maintenance procedures, inspection of tooling, cleaning procedures, software validation (if applicable), and operator training.

The process development proceeds with studies to establish the upper and lower processing limits, including such parameters as temperature, pressure/vacuum, dwell time, energy levels (radio frequency), and torque limits. The process limits are challenged during a process verification study in which packages are produced at the upper and lower parameter limits that result in packages meeting specifications. In other words, the upper and lower limits of the forming parameters are used to produce packages that are inspected to determine whether the packages meet dimensional requirements such that the product fits into the package and the package fits into the sealing machine and the secondary package. For the sealing process, packaging is inspected for seal width, punctures or tears, channels or open seals, and material delamination or separation. Finally, a process performance qualification study is used to document the effectiveness and reproducibility of the process in multiple production runs. Established procedures for machine setup, sealing and forming process parameters, test methods for seal width, continuity and integrity, and process start-up are used during the study. Essential process parameters are monitored during the study. Results of the study are summarized and used as the process certification package. Any change in equipment, product, packaging materials, or process that may change the original validation and affect the sterility, safety, or efficacy of the product will result in the need to revalidate the affected processes.

After the packaging process has been validated, routine package inspection is used to determine whether specifications are being met on a lot-to-lot basis. A sampling scheme is developed, and methods for visual inspection, seal/closure evaluation (tensile seal strength test, burst/creep pressure test), and physical testing (internal pressure test, dye penetration test, vacuum leak test) are implemented. Testing is usually performed after sterilization to ensure compatibility between the packaging and the sterilization process.

An ongoing program of packaging evaluation is implemented to monitor package integrity during handling, distribution, and storage. Analysis of test data from this program will determine whether further limits are necessary on the handling, distribution, and storage of the product.

A review of ISO 11607-1 and AAMI TIR22 Guidance for ANSI/AAMI/ISO 11607, *Packaging for terminally sterilized medical devices—Part 1 and Part 2:2006* is essential prior to auditing a sterile medical product packaging operation. AAMI TIR22 provides a wealth of background information to be used in the implementation of ISO 11607. The TIR is also a good source for a description of the various test methods, such as the dye penetration test.

ASTM D4169

ASTM D4169-16 *Standard Practice for Performance Testing of Shipping Containers and Systems* provides a uniform basis for evaluating, in a laboratory, the ability of shipping units to withstand the distribution environment. This is accomplished by subjecting them to a test plan consisting of a sequence of anticipated hazard elements encountered in various distribution cycles. This practice is not intended to supplant material specifications or existing preshipment test procedures.

ASTM F1980

ASTM F1980-16 *Standard Guide for Accelerated Aging of Sterile Barrier Systems for Medical Devices* provides guidance and direction for conservative accelerated aging factors and ensures that medical devices have adequate information for establishing shelf-life data. The standard also emphasizes that real-time aging programs are the best data and are required.

DEVICE SHELF LIFE

According to FDA guidance *Shelf Life of Medical Devices, April 1991,* device shelf life is defined as the term or period during which a commodity remains suitable for the intended use, with an expiration date that represents the termination or end of the shelf life. For most devices, deciding whether there should be defined shelf-life parameters includes analysis to determine whether the product degrades in a way that would lead to failure. Risk analysis using tools such as hazard analysis and fault tree analysis would also be considered to determine if a shelf life is required, as would usability analysis and human factors data and studies.

Certain stability criteria must be considered in determining the product's shelf life. The U.S. Pharmacopoeia (2019 USP42-NF37) defines stability as "the extent to which a product retains, within specified limits throughout its period of storage and use the same properties and characteristics that it possessed at the time of manufacture." Stability concerns include the following:

- Chemical: Does the material degrade due to interactions with other materials or on its own?
- Physical: Do physical characteristics vary with time—appearance, viscosity, others?
- Microbiological: Do sterile devices remain sterile?
- Therapeutic: Do the therapeutic properties or diagnostic functions vary with time?

- Toxicological: Do degradation byproducts produce adverse effects?
- Biocompatibility: Does the biocompatibility of the product change during storage?

Device specifications are the major criteria used in determining the predicted shelf life and in determining the tests to be used to establish and confirm the shelf life. Establishing the target shelf life is done during the design process and can be based on a number of factors including those listed previously, as well as literature reviews, compilation of information and data from similar products, and technological analysis. Specifications may be generally grouped into internal or external categories. Examples include:

- Internal (for example, components)—Are there component interactions or degradation due to the specific nature of the component that could cause operating characteristics to change? An example of this is a battery in a battery-powered device. Batteries of various types have self-discharge properties that change the battery capacity with time.
- External (for example, shipping)—Can the shipping or storage conditions of the device cause a breakage in the device or a failure of the sterile package barrier? Using the same battery example, a battery stored at high temperatures may fail quicker than if stored at a lower temperature.

There are a range of testing procedures and areas to be considered in shelf-life determination.

- Sampling plan for finished devices. How many devices are going to be needed for initial testing and how many for continued testing as products are manufactured?
- Raw materials. Are raw materials subject to their own special considerations as they are used and built into the finished device?
- Storage of samples. How and where are samples intended for testing going to be stored, under what environmental conditions, and what labeling is required to avoid mix-ups?
- Accelerated aging. In early testing, accelerated aging is typically used with elevated temperature as the acceleration parameter. Evidence must be available that indicates the impact of the increased temperature or whatever acceleration parameter was used. Real-time aging is also used to support shelf-life determinations required to provide assurance of shelf-life determination.
- Simulation of stresses. Shipping and handling stress plans including vibration and simulated or real shipping tests may be used. Plans may also include studies to determine the effect of potential mishandling.

The FDA regulates medical devices by identifying required characteristics in various areas of the Code of Federal Regulations. The specific sections for in vitro diagnostics products are in 21 CFR 809. Manufacturing and storage conditions must be controlled. Specifications and testing of sterile devices include some specific requirements such as:

- The sterilization method
- The method used to validate the sterilization method
- The sterility assurance level of the device
- The device packaging
- Sterilization residual determination
- Pyrogen testing, if required

A review of applicable standards and guidances should be performed during the design and manufacturing processes.

Chapter 16

General Safety and Performance Requirements

All devices, regardless of the classification, are required in EU MDR 2017/745 Article 5(2) to fulfill the general safety and performance requirements (GSPR) of EU MDR and the EU MDR annexes. Annex I contains the GSPR. The items below are examples of the key elements of these requirements, although it is recommended to completely review the GSPR as written in the MDR.

GENERAL REQUIREMENTS

- Devices shall achieve the performance intended by the manufacturer and shall be designed and manufactured in such a way that, during normal conditions of use, they are suitable for their intended purpose. They shall be safe and effective and shall not compromise the clinical condition or the safety of patients, or the safety and health of users or, where applicable, other persons, provided that any risks that may be associated with their use constitute acceptable risks when weighed against the benefits to the patient and are compatible with a high level of protection of health and safety, taking into account the generally acknowledged state of the art.
- The requirement to reduce risks as far as possible means the reduction of risks as far as possible without adversely affecting the benefit-risk ratio, and this is done through safe design and manufacture. Risk management activities (Annex I, Chapter 1) shall be established, implemented, and documented. Applicable requirements for the device are listed in Annex I, Chapter 2. Devices shall conform to safety principles, taking account the generally acknowledged state of the art.
- Medical devices must be safe and effective and shall not compromise the clinical condition or safety of patients, or the safety and health of users or other persons. However, any residual risks that may be associated with their use must be assessed and weighed against the benefits to the patient. The benefit-risk analysis may be part of the Risk Management File (Annex I) and the Clinical Evaluation Report ((Annex XV).

REQUIREMENTS REGARDING DESIGN AND MANUFACTURE

- Devices shall be designed and manufactured in such a way as to ensure the characteristics and performance requirements are fulfilled, including chemical, physical, and biological properties. For example, biological (biocompatibility) evaluation testing and reports shall be performed per EN ISO 10993:2018.
- Devices and their manufacturing processes shall be designed in such a way as to eliminate or reduce as far as possible the risk of infection to patients, users, and, where applicable, other persons.
- If the device is intended for use in combination with other devices or equipment, the whole combination, including the connection system, shall be safe and shall not impair the specified performance of the devices. Devices shall be designed, manufactured, and packaged in such a way that their characteristics and performance during their intended use are not adversely affected during transport and storage, including contaminants and residues to patients.
- Devices shall be designed and manufactured in such a way as to reduce as far as possible the risks posed by substances or particles, including wear debris, degradation products, and processing residues, that may be released from the device.
  - Refer to Annex I, Chapter 1 for the listing of safety and performance requirements for specific substances, particles, and contamination.
- Other considerations:
  - Refer to Annex I, Chapter 1 for the listing of safety and performance requirements for specific types of devices and incorporation of materials of biologic origin, medicine, diagnostic, radiation, programmable, active devices, mechanical or thermal risk, supplying energy, and lay users.
  - All devices, regardless of the classification, are required to fulfill the technical documentation requirements of Annexes II and III. Most documentation will have been generated for the safety and performance, biocompatibility (biological evaluation), and clinical evaluation requirements. However, there are additional items such as the unique device identifier (UDI) to be placed in the technical documentation folders (Article 29).

REQUIREMENTS REGARDING THE INFORMATION SUPPLIED WITH THE DEVICE

- Each device shall be accompanied by the information needed to identify the device and its manufacturer, and by any safety and performance information relevant to the user, or any other person, as appropriate. Such information may appear on the device itself, on the packaging, or in the instructions for use, and shall, if the manufacturer has a website, be made available and kept up to date on the website.

- The claims made on labelling, instructions for use, and advertising shall comply with Article 7, Annex I (Chapters 3, 23) and Annex II. Where devices, parts thereof or materials used therein as referred to in Annex I, Section 10.4.1., contain substances referred to in points (a) or (b) of Annex I Section 10.4.1. in a concentration above 0.1 percent weight by weight (w/w), the presence of those substances shall be labelled on the device itself and/or on the packaging for each unit or, where appropriate, on the sales packaging, with the list of such substances. If the intended use of such devices includes treatment of children, treatment of pregnant or breastfeeding women, or treatment of other patient groups considered particularly vulnerable to such substances and/or materials, information on residual risks for those patient groups and, if applicable, on appropriate precautionary measures shall be given in the instructions for use.

ADDITIONAL CONSIDERATIONS FOR SAFETY AND PERFORMANCE

- A device performance summary for each medical device such as a safety and performance statement shall be documented. EU devices must achieve the performance for their intended use and must be manufactured in a way that, during normal conditions of use, they are suitable for their intended purpose.
- The post-market surveillance plan, periodic safety update report (PSUR), and post-market surveillance report (Articles 84, 85, 86, and Annex III (1.1)) shall include such items as product requirements, identification of harmonized standards and EU common specification (if applicable), nonserious and serious incidents, post-market clinical follow-up, trend reporting, relevant literature and databases, feedback and complaints, publicly available information on similar devices, processes and methods for collecting data, risk management, complaint investigations, competent authority communication, and corrective actions.

Chapter 17

Software Development and Maintenance for Products

REGULATIONS

The two primary documents governing medical device software are ANSI/AAMI/IEC 62304:2006 *Medical device software—Software life cycle processes* and the FDA guidance *General Principles of Software Validation.* ANSI/AAMI/IEC 62304 is considered an FDA-recognized consensus standard; therefore, complying with it provides a presumption of conformity with FDA requirements.

A useful categorization of software affected by FDA regulation is found in FDA guidance *General Principles of Software Validation,* which applies to:

1. Software used as a component, part, or accessory of a medical device
2. Software that is itself a medical device (for example, blood establishment software)
3. Software used in the production of a device (for example, programmable logic controllers in manufacturing equipment)
4. Software used in implementation of the device manufacturer's quality system (for example, software that records and maintains the device history record).

This chapter primarily addresses software as a medical device or as a component of a medical device. Software in processes and in documentation should be addressed as part of Chapter 10 (QSR), Chapter 4 (21 CFR, Part 11), and Chapter 12 (ISO 13485).

Unless specifically exempted in a classification regulation, any medical device software product developed after June 1, 1997, regardless of its device classification, is subject to applicable design control provisions (21 CFR 820.30). Specific requirements to validate device software are found in 21 CFR 820.30(g) as follows:

> Each manufacturer shall establish and maintain procedures for validating the device design. Design validation shall be performed under defined operating conditions on initial production units, lots, or batches, or their equivalents. Design validation shall ensure that devices conform to defined user needs and intended uses and shall include testing of production units under actual or simulated use conditions. Design validation shall include software validation and

> risk analysis, where appropriate. The results of the design validation, including identification of the design, method(s), the date, and the individual(s) performing the validation, shall be documented in the DHF.

Section 3060(a) of the 21st Century Cures Act, enacted on December 13, 2016, amended the FD&C Act to exclude certain software functions from the definition of device under section 201(h) of the act.

IEC 62304 utilizes the philosophy of primary life-cycle processes and supporting processes. It is assumed that medical device software is developed and maintained within a quality management system. The software development process, as well as the risk management process, would both be primary life-cycle processes. The risk management process is already addressed by ISO 14971, so by making ISO 14971 a normative reference, only minor additional risk management requirements are needed for software. Some minor risk management activities in a supporting process ensure that hazard causes and the software items in which they arise are identified and documented. As risks related to cybersecurity have emerged, risk management should also include cybersecurity considerations. However, the software is categorized into one of three safety classifications to determine which activities and tasks are applicable to the software throughout the processes, activities, and tasks.

IEC 62304 does not prescribe a specific life-cycle model. Although the FDA uses a waterfall model in explanatory design control information, any life cycle may be used. The users of the standard are responsible for selecting an appropriate life-cycle model for the software project and for mapping the processes, activities, and tasks of the standard onto that life-cycle model. This is similar to the FDA's approach in *General Principles of Software Validation,* "The guidance does not recommend the use of any specific software life cycle model. Software developers should establish a software life cycle model that is appropriate for their product and organization." However, mapping the software life-cycle model to both IEC 62304 and the QSR's design controls is strongly suggested.

The general requirements of IEC 62304 include a quality system, usually ISO 13485, although the FDA's QSR (21 CFR 820) may be used instead. The general requirements also include a risk management system using ISO 14971 that incorporates the supporting software risk management process and requires participation in risk management by one or more persons active in the software development.

The manufacturer must also assign each software item into a software safety class of A, B, or C based on possible effects on the patient, operator, or others resulting from a hazard. Where software items are combined into the overall software, the safety class for each is the highest safety class of the software items. The classes and the definitions are:

Class A: No injury may occur

Class B: Nonserious injury may occur

Class C: Death or serious injury may occur

The FDA defines a similar approach in *General Principles of Software Validation.* Validation coverage should be based on the software's complexity and safety risk—not on a firm's size or resource constraints. The selection of validation activities, tasks, and work items should be commensurate with the complexity of the software design and the risk associated with the use of the software for the specified intended use. For lower-risk devices, only baseline validation activities may be conducted. As the risk increases, additional validation activities should be added to cover the additional risk. Validation documentation should be sufficient to demonstrate that all software validation plans and procedures have been completed successfully.

A specific type of software to consider is software of unknown provenance (SOUP) or commercial off-the-shelf software (COTS). This is software that is not developed by the device manufacturer but is used as part of or as the software medical device. This includes libraries incorporated into device software and external packages incorporated as operating systems or communications systems. The FDA recommends that software test, verification, and validation plans identify the exact OTS software (title and version) that is to be used *(Off-The-Shelf Software Use in Medical Devices, FDA, September 27, 2019[166]).* When the software is tested it should be integrated and tested using the specific OTS software that will be delivered to the user.

SOFTWARE DEVELOPMENT PLANNING AND PROCESS

Software is often a component of a medical device. Virtually all such software containing medical device systems are considered programmable electrical medical systems (PEMS) by IEC 60601-1. Requirements for software are a subset of the requirements for a programmable electrical medical system (PEMS), as medical devices containing software are termed in IEC 60601-1. Because PEMS includes elements that are not software, all the requirements of IEC 60601-1 for PEMS are not addressed in IEC 62304, specifically validation (design validation), which is done at the system level. IEC 60601-1 refers to software in a PEMS as PESS, programmable electrical sub-system. Thus, when the software is a medical device in its own right rather than part of a physical product, validation is completed at the end of the software development life cycle (SDLC) instead of at the end of the system development.

The software development effort needs to be planned. The SDLC must be defined, the software safety class must be established, and the outputs from the process must be commensurate with the software safety class, at a minimum. The software development environment (SDE) is defined, and the means for managing SOUP or COTS software are established. The plan also establishes the approach to software verification and validation.

ANSI/AAMI/IEC 62304:2006 and ISO 14971 define the expected level and content of documentation associated with the risk level of the software.

Neither IEC 62304 nor FDA's *General Principles of Software Validation* recommend the use of any specific software life-cycle model. Software developers should establish a software life-cycle model that is appropriate for their product and organization. The software life-cycle model that is selected should cover the software from its birth to its retirement.

Figure 17.1 Relationship between IEC 62304 and other standards.

Activities in a typical software life-cycle model include the following:

- Quality planning
- System requirements definition
- Detailed software requirements specification
- Software design specification
- Construction or coding
- Testing
- Installation
- Operation and support
- Maintenance
- Retirement

Software validation is accomplished through a series of activities and tasks that are planned and executed at various stages of the SDLC. These tasks may be one-time occurrences or may be iterated many times, depending on the life-cycle model used and the scope of changes made as the software project progresses.

Verification, testing, and other tasks that support software validation occur during each of these activities. A life-cycle model organizes these software development activities in various ways and provides a framework for monitoring and controlling the software development project. Several software life-cycle models (for example, waterfall, spiral, rapid prototyping, incremental development, etc.) are defined in the FDA's *Glossary of Computerized System and Software Development Terminology (8/95).*

REQUIREMENTS DEFINITION

The purpose of the requirements definition phase is to define and analyze the functionality, interfaces, and other constraints applicable to the system. This is the most important phase of the software development process because it not only defines what the software is to do, but it also defines the basis for how the software is to be tested (the requirements are used as the basis for defining the test procedures used for verification and validation).

A documented software requirements specification provides a baseline for both validation and verification. The software validation process cannot be completed without an established software requirements specification (Ref: 21 CFR 820.3(z) and (aa) and 820.30(f) and (g)).

The following are analyzed during this phase:

1. Definition of the requirements—including usability, security, capacity, and timing—in a manner to support ease of understanding and presentation to the customer
2. Identification of potential safety risks and security risks through the conduct of a risk analysis
3. Definition of interface requirements for interfacing hardware and/or software components, including required inputs, outputs, and constraints

A requirements specification and a risk analysis are developed for the system during this phase. A review including the customer should be conducted to verify the correctness of these documents. Note that risk controls (mitigations) implemented in software are considered requirements and must be verified as part of the overall verification and validation planning.

A risk unique to software is cybersecurity. Medical devices, like other computer systems, can be vulnerable to security breaches, potentially impacting the safety and effectiveness of the device. By carefully considering possible cybersecurity risks while designing medical devices, and having a plan to manage emerging cybersecurity risks, manufacturers can reduce cybersecurity risks posed to devices and patients.

CYBERSECURITY

The FDA notes in the *Draft Guidance: Content of Premarket Submissions for Management of Cybersecurity in Medical Devices*[167] that medical devices are increasingly connected to the Internet, hospital networks, and other medical devices to provide features that improve healthcare and increase the ability of healthcare providers to treat patients. These same features also increase the risk of potential cybersecurity threats. Medical devices, like other computer systems, can be vulnerable to security breaches, potentially impacting the safety and effectiveness of the device.

Software applications designed to protect information systems, including software devices, from harmful or malicious code ("viruses," "worms," etc.) are becoming more commonplace as devices become increasingly interconnected and therefore exposed to the external information environment.

Because a risk management process that narrowly focuses on the ISO 14971 definition of "harm" may limit the scope of software risk management, AAMI TIR57:2016 incorporates considerations that risks include effects outside the traditional scope of physical harm and may include "reduction of effectiveness" and "breach of data and systems security." AAMI's document includes definitions that facilitate understanding cybersecurity.

> ***Data and systems security.*** Operational state of a medical device in which information assets (data and systems) are reasonably protected from degradation of confidentiality, integrity, and availability
>
> > Note 1 to entry: Security, when mentioned in this document, should be taken to include data and systems security.
> >
> > [Source: ANSI/AAMI/IEC 80001-1:2010, 2.5, modified—"MEDICAL IT-NETWORK" has been replaced with "medical device" and Note 2 was redacted.]
>
> ***Harm.*** Physical injury or damage to the health of people, or damage to property or the environment, or reduction in effectiveness, or breach of data and systems security
>
> > [Source: IEC 80001-1:2010, definition 2.8]
>
> ***Threat.*** Any circumstance or event with the potential to adversely impact organizational operations (including mission, functions, image, or reputation), organizational assets, individuals, or other organizations through an information system via unauthorized access, destruction, disclosure, modification of information, and/or denial of service
>
> > Note 1 to entry: Identical to NIST definition (SP 800-53) with the phrase "or the Nation" redacted.
> >
> > [Source: SP 800-53; SP 800-53A; SP 800-27; SP 800-60; SP 800-37; CNSSI-4009]
>
> ***Vulnerability (a type of hazard).*** Weakness in an information system, system security procedures, internal controls, or implementation that could be exploited or triggered by a threat source
>
> > [Source: SP 800-53; SP 800-53A; SP 800-37; SP 800-60; SP 800-115; FIPS 200]

It is important to note that a cybersecurity risk may not be a safety risk, so having a separate software risk management process for cybersecurity is generally preferred.

Threats and vulnerabilities cannot be eliminated; therefore, reducing cybersecurity risks is especially challenging. The healthcare environment is complex, and manufacturers, hospitals, and facilities must work together to manage cybersecurity risks. By carefully considering possible cybersecurity risks while designing medical devices, and having a plan to manage emerging cybersecurity risks, manufacturers can reduce cybersecurity risks posed to devices and patients.

In addition to premarket guidance, the FDA has also published post-market guidance (*Post-market Management of Cybersecurity in Medical Devices, Food and Drug Administration December 28, 2016*[168]) that further offers recommendations for comprehensive management of medical device cybersecurity risks and continuous improvement throughout the total product life cycle, and incentivizes changing marketed and distributed medical devices to reduce risk.

On the premarket side, manufacturers should establish design inputs for their device related to cybersecurity, and establish a cybersecurity vulnerability and management approach as part of the software validation and risk analysis that is required by 21 CFR 820.30(g). The approach should appropriately address the following elements:

- Identification of assets, threats, and vulnerabilities
- Assessment of the impact of threats and vulnerabilities on device functionality and end users/patients
- Assessment of the likelihood of a threat and of a vulnerability being exploited
- Determination of risk levels and suitable mitigation strategies
- Assessment of residual risk and risk acceptance criteria

In a premarket submission, manufacturers should provide the following information related to the cybersecurity of their medical device:

1. Hazard analysis, mitigations, and design considerations pertaining to intentional and unintentional cybersecurity risks associated with the device, including:
   - A specific list of all cybersecurity risks that were considered in the design of the device
   - A specific list and justification for all cybersecurity controls that were established for the device
2. A traceability matrix that links the actual cybersecurity controls to the cybersecurity risks that were considered.
3. A summary describing the plan for providing validated software updates and patches as needed throughout the life cycle of the medical device to continue to assure its safety and effectiveness. The FDA typically will not need to review or approve medical device software changes made solely to strengthen cybersecurity.
4. A summary describing controls that are in place to assure that the medical device software will maintain its integrity (for example, remain free of malware) from the point of origin to the point at which that device leaves the control of the manufacturer.
5. Device instructions for use and product specifications related to recommended cybersecurity controls appropriate for the intended use environment (for example, antivirus software, use of firewall).

For devices in the marketplace, a proactive and risk-based approach to the post-market phase for medical devices, through engaging in cybersecurity information sharing and monitoring, promoting "good cyber hygiene" through routine device cyber maintenance, assessing post-market information, employing a risk-based approach to characterizing vulnerabilities, and timely implementation of necessary actions can further mitigate emerging cybersecurity risks and reduce the impact to patients.

To manage post-market cybersecurity risks for medical devices, a company should have a structured and systematic approach to risk management and quality management systems consistent with 21 CFR part 820. For example, such a program should include:

- Methods to identify, characterize, and assess a cybersecurity vulnerability
- Methods to analyze, detect, and assess threat sources; for example:
  - A cybersecurity vulnerability might impact all the medical devices in a manufacturer's portfolio based on how its products are developed; or
  - A cybersecurity vulnerability could exist vertically (that is, within the components of a device), which can be introduced at any point in the supply chain for a medical device manufacturing process.

It is recommended as part of a manufacturer's cybersecurity risk management program that the manufacturer incorporate elements consistent with the NIST Framework for Improving Critical Infrastructure Cybersecurity (that is, identify, protect, detect, respond, and recover).[169]

The FDA recognizes that medical devices and the surrounding network infrastructure cannot be completely secured. Design, architecture, technology, and software development environment choices may result in the inadvertent incorporation of vulnerabilities. The presence of a vulnerability does not necessarily trigger patient harm concerns. Rather, it is the impact of the vulnerability on the safety and essential performance of the device that may present a risk of patient harm. Vulnerabilities that do not appear to currently present a risk of patient harm should be assessed by the manufacturer for future impact.

SYSTEM AND SOFTWARE SPECIFICATION

Often, software is a subset of a (medical device) system. As such, there is typically a parent specification driving the software specifications. In such cases, the software requirements need to be reviewed to ensure they completely elaborate the system specifications allocated to hardware and are consistent with the parent specifications.

SOFTWARE DESIGN

Design typically follows a hierarchical approach: architecture, high-level design, and (if necessary) low-level design. The purpose of the architecture phase is to identify an optimum architecture for implementation of the requirements. During this phase, the following activities occur:

1. Alternative design approaches are analyzed, and trade-off studies are performed to select the optimum design architecture. The design architecture should be depicted using a graphical notation.
2. Requirements are partitioned to isolate safety-critical aspects (where necessary).

A typical output of the architecture phase is an architecture block diagram. The high-level design phase elaborates the architecture:

1. Establish classes and high-level design structure.
2. Specify implementation algorithms and interface formats for hardware and software components.
3. Establish software-to-software interfaces and software-to-hardware interfaces. This creates a "contract" between the interface endpoints, thus ensuring the "sides" can be implemented independently.

Other outputs of the architecture phase are state diagrams, class diagrams, and interface specifications.

Finally, if low-level design is necessary (typically only if the software is safety-critical), typical low-level design artifacts include database design or schema and screen mockups. Low-level design can also be used to establish the structure of the software units.

Design descriptions are developed to describe the design. Supplemental design studies and supporting implementation history information are documented, as applicable. Peer reviews of the design artifacts are conducted to verify the quality of the design and implementation strategy. The design is reviewed to ensure complete coverage of and compliance to the parent specifications.

Software source code should be placed in the configuration control system during the initial design phases.

IMPLEMENTATION AND TEST

During implementation, each software unit is coded and verified as correctly implemented. Prototypes may be prepared to demonstrate effective system operation. During this phase, the following activities occur:

1. Software program units are coded in accordance with established programming guidelines.
2. Unit testing is performed, as necessary, to verify correctness.

3. Unit testing for program units that satisfy safety requirements is formally documented, when required.

4. Code reviews are performed as indicated in the development plan.

5. Integration testing is conducted per the development plan.

It should be noted that state-of-the-art software development practices, including "agile" methods, are iterative in nature; that is, design a little, build a little, iterate. The SDLC and/or software development plan can outline the method(s) used and when artifacts are baselined (placed under change control).

VERIFICATION AND VALIDATION

The verification and validation of software is consistent with the verification and validation of medical devices. Software requirements are verified for correct implementation. The purpose of software verification is to demonstrate that specified requirements are satisfied. System validation test procedures are to be maintained and used for retesting as required throughout the maintenance phase. During this phase, the following activities occur:

1. Testing is conducted in accordance with the approved test procedures to verify satisfaction of requirements. Control of the test environment and procedures is maintained to provide a baseline for future testing.

2. Tests are conducted to demonstrate that identified safety risks have been successfully eliminated or mitigated. Stress testing is conducted to verify safe program operation and performance under maximum loading and worst-case scenarios.

3. If the software runs on a medical device (equipment), testing is to be done on production-equivalent units under defined operating conditions, as applicable. Use of simulated environments is permissible when it can be justified that the simulated environment has no bearing on the results.

4. Testing is conducted under actual or simulated use conditions, as applicable.

5. Discrepancy or anomaly reports are generated for any defects that arise during verification testing.

6. Regression testing is performed as changes are made to ensure that the integrity of the baselined system is not affected.

7. A test summary report is often generated to document or summarize the results of the test activities, including any anomalies that were observed (including test failures) during testing.

8. A traceability matrix is created to demonstrate the completeness of the test program and to ensure that all specified requirements are tested.

Validation for software parallels device regulations. The intent is to confirm that the system meets user needs and intended uses. But validation for software also means that the software is under control as defined by the SDLC. From the FDA guidance on software validation:

> Software validation is highly dependent upon comprehensive software testing and other verification tasks previously completed at each stage of the software development life cycle. Planning, verification, traceability, configuration management, and many other aspects of good software engineering are important activities that together help to support a conclusion that software is validated.

It is evident the guidance expects validation to be more than testing, but testing is an important part. Generally, testing will focus on:

1. User interface testing. Does the user interface conform to user needs in the intended use environment? Factors to consider include colors used, font selection, and font size.
2. Usability. Assess whether the software conforms to the types of users for whom use is intended. For example, nontechnical users may not readily comprehend what is taken for granted by "techies." Usability assessment should also include a user assessment of any instructions for use.
3. If the software runs on a medical device (equipment), testing is to be done on production-equivalent units under defined operating conditions, as applicable. Use of simulated environments is permissible when it can be justified that the simulated environment has no bearing on the results.
4. Testing is to be conducted under actual or simulated use conditions, as applicable.
5. Discrepancy reports are generated for any defects that arise during verification testing.
6. Operations and support documentation are reviewed to ensure they are accurate and adequately address operation and support requirements.

SOUP AND COTS SOFTWARE

SOUP or COTS software incorporated in a software system needs to be validated for its intended use (in the software). To do so implies that the intended use is established. Further, when validating SOUP or COTS software, efforts need to be taken to identify and assess any known errors or issues and determine the impact on the software system. For the lowest level of concern for the software, the FDA expects a hazard analysis and basic documentation. The highest level of concern would require that as well as describing and justifying residual risk and having special documentation.

DESIGN TRANSFER

While "design transfer" is more aligned with mechanical assemblies and process controls, there is an aspect of design transfer for software. The software development environment needs to be well defined and controlled to ensure repeatability in the build/release process. The configuration management system needs to establish a means to identify, down to the unit level, the exact configuration of the system. This also includes commercial (SOUP/COTS) software used. The manufacturer should ensure the integrity of all software releases. This is typically accomplished through means such as checksums. A complete description of the released software baseline should be documented. This would include the software configuration, the software development environment, a list of known issues and their effects on the system, and a list of all associated documentation.

DESIGN CHANGES

Following the initial baseline, continuing engineering and programming support is to be provided for operational programs. These activities comprise the previously defined engineering phases (from requirements analysis through system verification and validation testing) that are to be performed as a system is modified.

Delivered software is to be maintained under version control. Every product change typically involves updates to documentation as well as the software. The specific documents that require updating are determined by the extent of the changes made and regulatory requirements. As a minimum, a history record shall be maintained to track changes made, the reason for the change, version numbers, and documentation updates. Use of an automated configuration management tool to track program change history is recommended.

The number and type of reviews to be conducted for maintenance changes is determined by the extent of the modification. Reviews shall be conducted to ensure that the changes have been successfully implemented and that the appropriate documentation has been updated. For safety-related changes, it is typical that safety-related test procedures are executed. For all changes, some level of verification is required. Depending on the risk, this can include software code (change) reviews, functional testing, regression testing, and possibly some level of revalidation.

All changes need to be traceable to the change "authorization vehicle." This can be requirements specifications (including updates) or specific issue reports. Verification of the change needs to confirm that only the authorized changes were implemented.

GUIDELINES FOR A SUCCESSFUL SOFTWARE DEVELOPMENT PROGRAM

The FDA guidelines for implementation of software may seem overwhelming at first, but they do provide for a great deal of flexibility. These guidelines are based on proven techniques that emphasize design engineering early in the development process. These techniques have been demonstrated to result in increased reliability and productivity due to less time spent in program testing and debugging. The FDA's stated objectives of product safety and effectiveness are also consistent with good business practices. The following is a list of the factors that lead to the greatest likelihood for success of software implementations:

1. Define internal procedures for conduct of a software development process, including standards for writing specifications, guidelines for how to validate process software, and forms for identifying and tracking safety risks.
2. Foster a team development environment, including frequent communication between programmers, quality assurance/testers, and target customers.
3. Manage requirements to ensure a clear understanding up front of customer needs and to prevent unwanted "requirements creep" during the development process.
4. Recognize the intent of the FDA definition of levels of concern, and define a validation program that focuses additional resources on critical areas.
5. Ensure that the development process allows for early and frequent reviews and quality testing of the developed software. Process audits are also helpful in identifying potential problems early in development phases.
6. Use automated tools where possible to facilitate the development process, including documentation tools, tools to help locate hard-to-find software errors, and automated test tools.
7. Establish a documentation strategy that minimizes effort by emphasizing quality over quantity through adherence to defined guidelines and effective review techniques.
8. Update software development procedures based on lessons learned from previous efforts through the definition of documentation templates, measurement tools, and checklists to increase effectiveness.
9. Provide procedure compliance and "best practices" training to all personnel associated with the development process, including developers, testers, and project managers.
10. Establish process measures to evaluate progress, and monitor quality of software code and associated documents during the development process.

These guidelines can help increase the effectiveness of a software development program. Whatever the maturity of the current software process, measures of effectiveness, and emphasis on continuous improvement can yield significant benefits in increased quality and productivity.

Chapter 18

Labeling

LABELS VERSUS LABELING

The U.S. FDA develops and administers regulations for labeling. The regulations pertaining specifically to medical devices are found in the following parts of Title 21 of the Code of Federal Regulations (CFR).

In section 201(k), a label is defined as: "display of written, printed, or graphic matter upon the immediate container of any article..." Note that the term "immediate container" does not include package liners. Any word, statement, or other information appearing on the immediate container must also appear "on the outside container or wrapper, if there is one, or on the retail package of such article, or is easily legible through the outside container of wrapper."

In section 201(m), labeling is defined as:

> "all labels and other written, printed, or graphic matter
>
> (1) upon any article or any of its containers or wrappers, or
>
> (2) accompanying such article at any time while a device is held for sale after shipment or delivery for shipment in interstate commerce."

The term "accompanying" is interpreted liberally to mean more than physical association with the product. It extends to posters, tags, pamphlets, circulars, booklets, brochures, instruction books, direction sheets, fillers, etc. Accompanying also includes labeling that is brought together with the device after shipment or delivery for shipment in interstate commerce. It is also important to note that all advertising is considered "labeling" by the FDA.

Other specific FDA labeling requirements are in the following regulations:

- General Device Labeling (21 CFR 801)
- In-Vitro Diagnostic Products (21 CFR 809)
- Investigational Device Exemptions (21 CFR 812)
- Unique Device Identification (21 CFR 830)
- Quality System Regulation (21 CFR 820)
- General Electronic Products (21 CFR 1010)

USE OF SYMBOLS

ISO 15223-1:2016 identifies requirements for symbols used in medical device labelling that convey information on the safe and effective use of medical devices. It also lists symbols that satisfy the requirements of this document. ISO 15223-1:2016 is applicable to symbols used in a broad spectrum of medical devices, which are marketed globally and therefore need to meet different regulatory requirements. These symbols may be used on the medical device itself, on its packaging, or in the associated documentation. The requirements of this document are not intended to apply to symbols specified in other standards.

Examples of the symbols identified in ISO 15223-1:2016 are:

Name Address 2015-06

This symbol is the official international symbol for "manufacturer." It is to be followed by the name and address of the manufacturing company, along with the date of manufacture, in some instances.

This symbol represents "caution," indicating the product user should proceed with caution, further examining the packaging for directions.

This symbol represents "biological risk," indicating there are potential biological risks that can emerge while using the product.

This symbol indicates the presence of natural rubber or dry natural rubber latex as a material of construction within the medical device or the packaging of a medical device.

UNIQUE DEVICE IDENTIFICATION (UDI)

The FDA established a UDI system to identify products from manufacturing through distribution to patient use. According to the FDA, the UDI is both in human- and machine-readable form and is intended to improve patient safety, modernize post-market surveillance, and facilitate medical device innovation.

Provisions for UDI are extensive and listed in 21 CFR 830. See Chapter 4 for additional information.

GLOBAL TRADE ITEM NUMBER (GTIN)

GS1 is an accredited issuing agency for the U.S. FDA for the UDI rule in the United States since 2013. Currently, most medical devices are identified with a GS1 identifier, and GS1 member organizations across the world are supporting their users in the implementation. UDI enables the globally unique identification of medical devices and improves patient safety and healthcare business processes. A single, global system of standards is fundamental to enable an efficient and effective implementation of UDI by all healthcare stakeholders worldwide. The

EU regulation on medical devices (EU MDR) and the EU regulation on in-vitro diagnostic devices (EU IVDR) provide the legal requirements for the European UDI system within Europe. GS1 is also designated as an issuing entity for the UDI in the EU.

Table 18.1 Unique device identification in GS1 terms.

UDI Regulatory Requirements	GS1 Standards
Basic UDI-DI *"New" level of identification in the EU*	GMN (global model number) *No application identifier (AI) for regulated medical devices*
UDI-DI * *Device identifier (DI)*	GTIN* *Global trade item number*
UDI-PI * *Production Identifier (PI) (if applicable)*	AI* Application Identifier (AI) • *Expiration date AI(17)—e.g., 141120* • *Batch—lot AI(10) - e.g., 1234AB* • *Serial number AI(21)—e.g., 12345XYZ* • *Manufacture date AI(11)—e.g., 250717*
Production identifier data will vary by medical device type and manufacturer current practice.	
UDI-DI + UDI-PI = UDI	GTIN or GTIN + AI(s) = UDI

*The HRI format shall follow the rules of the UDI issuing entity.

To calculate the GMN check characters, see www.gs1.org/services/gmn-generator.

Chapter 19

Controlled Environments and Utility Systems

Controlled environments may be required in the manufacture of medical devices depending on the application of the device. Controlled environments are typically used to ensure that the product being produced is not contaminated by environmental conditions. Those conditions can include particulate matter that is not viable or living but adheres to the device, particulates that are viable (for example, bacteria), and other contaminates that may be chemical or process related.

Controlled environments may also be required if processing conditions necessitate that the environment be maintained within certain ranges. Those ranges can include temperature and humidity and may also include other conditions.

It is most important to note that the controlled environment is product dependent. The product characteristics must be taken into account in any establishment of conditions for the environment. The environment can then be tested and validated to ensure it meets the requirements.

CONTROLLED ENVIRONMENTS

Work environments are required to be controlled when excursions of environmental conditions could be expected to have an adverse effect on product quality. There are two series of international standards that apply to cleanrooms: ISO 14644 and ISO 14698. The ISO 14644 standard series provides guidance for the design, classification, testing, and monitoring of cleanrooms and associated controlled environments. Cleanrooms are classified per international standard ISO 14644-1:2015 *Cleanrooms and associated controlled environments—Part 1: Classification of air cleanliness by particle concentration*. The ISO 14698 standard series provides guidance for the biocontamination control of cleanrooms and associated controlled environments.

The ISO 14644-1 standard was originally based on U.S. Federal Standard 209 E (FS 209E) issued in 1988. This federal standard used the reference size of 0.5 μm to present particle concentrations. Despite having been rescinded in 2001, references to FS 209E continue to persist. Table 19.1 compares airborne particulate cleanliness classifications per ISO 14644-1 and the obsolete FS 209E.

Table 19.1 Comparison of airborne particulate cleanliness class, 14644-1:2015 and U.S. Federal Standard 209 E.

ISO Classification Number (N)	Maximum concentration limits (particles/m^3 of air)						FS 209E (0.5 µm reference)
	0.1 µm	0.2 µm	0.3 µm	0.5 µm	1 µm	5 µm	
ISO Class 1	10	2	—	—	—	—	—
ISO Class 2	100	24	10	4	—	—	—
ISO Class 3	1,000	237	102	35	8	—	1
ISO Class 4	10,000	2,370	1,020	352	83	—	10
ISO Class 5	100,000	23,700	10,200	3,520	832	29	100
ISO Class 6	1,000,000	237,000	102,000	35,200	8,320	293	1,000
ISO Class 7	—	—	—	352,000	83,200	2,930	10,000
ISO Class 8	—	—	—	3,520,000	832,000	29,300	100,000
ISO Class 9	—	—	—	35,200,000	8,320,000	293,000	—

Cleanrooms can be classified according to the amount of particulate matter present. Particles counted can be liquid or solid. Cleanrooms can be classified in a range from ISO Class 1 to ISO Class 9. The ISO classification number is defined by the maximum concentration of airborne particles of various sizes. For example, an ISO Class 5 cleanroom cannot exceed a concentration level of more than 100,000 airborne particles of 0.1 micron per cubic meter of air and 29 particles sized 5 microns or greater per cubic meter of air.

For medical device purposes, the controlled environment is a combination of requirements. The particulate cleanliness is usually stated as described in the previous paragraph, but the other conditions also must be stated. To establish the environmental conditions, an initial qualification study is done prior to using the controlled environment. The initial study generally considers the following conditions:

- Pressure differential between the room and outside areas
- Airflow velocity
- Temperature/humidity
- Airflow visualization (for example, smoke study)
- Efficiency of filtering media
- Volume of air flowing into the space
- Air changes per period of time in the space
- Aerobic and anaerobic effects

Following the initial study, the room is also studied under typical use conditions to ensure it continues to meet requirements. Periodic monitoring and maintenance of the control equipment is essential to ensuring the controlled environment meets its requirements. The parameters must be monitored on a regular basis to ensure they continue to meet requirements, such as particle count/size, temperature, pressure differential, and humidity and should be defined in a documented plan.

Controls for entering and exiting the cleanroom should be defined for employees and visitors, including gowning procedures. Product and equipment entering the room should also be considered for controls to ensure that contamination is not introduced into the environment. Any employees working in the controlled environment should be properly trained on gowning procedures, requirements for attire, and behavior. If employees have health issues that may affect the cleanliness of the room or the product, they should not be permitted into the room until they have recovered.

In addition to requirements for particulate sizes and quantities, cleanrooms may be required to be monitored for biocontamination, per ISO 14698: ISO 14698-1:2003 *Cleanrooms and associated controlled environments—Biocontamination control—Part 1: General principles and methods provides guidance on monitoring of cleanrooms.* Typically, sampling of airborne and surface viable particles is performed using sampling plates. The plates are evaluated for viable contamination, including bacterial and fungal. The results are reported as colony forming units (CFU). The layout of the cleanroom and where work is conducted will direct where sampling should take place. The locations and frequency of sampling should be defined in a documented plan.

As applicable, the product manufactured in the controlled environment should also be monitored on a regular basis (for example, quarterly) to ensure that bioburden levels do not significantly change. Product is sent out for bioburden testing, with the results being reported as CFU. Product should also be tested for bacterial endotoxins (LAL testing).

The controlled environment should be maintained by defined housekeeping, disinfection, sanitization, and maintenance processes. These procedures should define the chemicals to be used and the frequency. Considerations for determining which chemicals to use should include the types of contamination in the room (fungal/bacterial as identified during initial qualification and periodic monitoring) and if there are any adverse effects on the materials in the room (for example, metal equipment, acrylic pass-throughs). All surface areas, including ceilings, walls, floors, work surfaces, and equipment in the room, should be considered for regular cleaning and disinfection. Procedures should include daily, weekly, monthly, quarterly, and annual schedules. Maintenance procedures would apply to changing of filters (HEPA) for the air system and any other related equipment maintenance.

UTILITY SYSTEMS

Each controlled environment or other manufacturing area may also contain a number of utilities used to control or run equipment and the environment. Typical utilities include:

- Heating, ventilating, and air conditioning (HVAC)
- Electrical power

- Emergency electrical power
- Water systems
- Compressed air
- Oil and particulate-controlled compressed air

Each of these utilities must be specified and tested in a manner similar to the controlled environment, including validation and ongoing monitoring.

FACILITY QUALIFICATION

To ensure each controlled environment and its related utilities meet the defined requirements, a facility qualification (validation) is performed. That qualification begins with the development of a master plan that describes the activities and specifications. The master plan will describe a combination of protocols that are executed to determine if each system functions as intended. The protocols can consist of installation qualification, operational qualification, and performance qualification. The validation protocols should consider various impacts to cleanroom operation, such as maximum number of occupants, power outages, loss of pressure, and processes/equipment used in the room.

Chapter 20

Sterile Medical Devices

Sterility assurance for sterile medical devices is of ultimate importance to the manufacturer, consumer, and regulatory agencies. Devices intended to be sterile but have been compromised and are nonsterile as a result of a sterilization process or packaging failure have been responsible for some of the largest recalls of medical devices. The assurance of sterility may be elusive, however, due to the variables associated with a sterilization process. Process deviations during sterilization are especially significant, since they have a direct and crucial impact on the safety of finished products. Therefore, regulatory agencies have required manufacturers to have a comprehensive quality assurance program that controls every aspect of the sterilization process. Such a program includes adequate validation, environmental controls, trained personnel, maintenance and calibration of equipment, record keeping, process controls and monitoring, packaging and labeling controls, and other measures applicable to the specific medical device manufacturer and sterilization method.

When a population of microorganisms is killed, the probability of a survivor can be calculated and may be expressed as the sterility assurance level (SAL) of the product. Most medical device sterilization processes are specified to a SAL of 10^{-6}, meaning that one in a million products might be nonsterile. For products used topically on intact skin, the SAL may be 10^{-3}.

VALIDATION STUDIES

Every sterilization process must be validated, since it is impossible to test each product for sterility without destroying the product (such testing would be called process verification). The requirement for process validation comes from process control requirements and appears in §820.70 Production and Process Controls: "Each manufacturer shall develop, conduct, control, and monitor production processes to ensure that a device conforms to its specifications." The regulation continues with specific requirements for process controls where they are needed. The remainder of Subpart G of 21 CFR §820 lists requirements for control of the production environment,[170] personnel,[171] contamination of equipment or product,[172] buildings,[173] equipment,[174] manufacturing material,[175] and automated processes,[176] as well as inspection, measuring, and test equipment.[177] Process controls apply to sterile products at every step of the manufacturing process, but in particular at the sterilization step. The FDA's *Guide to Inspections of Quality Systems* (QSIT) devotes a section to the auditing of sterilization process controls. In addition, there are numerous international standards devoted to aspects of the sterilization of healthcare devices (see Sterilization Methods section below). Validation of the sterilization process indicates the resultant SAL; the sterilization process controls should guarantee maintenance of the validated SAL.

A validation study procedure is the beginning of the process control documentation, and it should be specific to the sterilization process being studied rather than to a general procedure. The study demonstrates that the process consistently results in a product meeting specifications, which in this case includes the identified SAL (that is, 10^{-6}) and possibly sterilant residue and endotoxin levels. The basic elements of the study include demonstrated equipment installation performance, demonstrated process performance, and study documentation, review, and approval. The study report includes the product bioburden, sterilization cycle parameters and tolerances, criteria for acceptance of a successful study, process challenge studies (half-cycle runs for ethylene oxide, verification dose studies for radiation, or media fills for aseptic processing), and results of process control, monitoring, and acceptance activities (control charts, biological indicators, dosimeters). The study report provides the objective evidence that the process will consistently result in the product meeting its predetermined specifications and attributes, such as the desired SAL.

Part of the validation study includes the effect of the process on the product and its packaging. Records of post-sterilization product performance testing and packaging tests should indicate that the process, and any resterilization process, does not adversely affect product characteristics such as joint strength, impact resistance, color, and tensile strength and packaging integrity, permeability, and impact resistance. Labeling resistance to moisture and temperature is also part of the study. Any materials used in the sterilization process (for example, ethylene chlorohydrin) must be reduced to specified levels and documented in the validation study. Also included in the validation testing is the sterility assurance and package integrity for the defined shelf life (that is, five years). The shelf life is defined on the package labeling and identifies how long the device will remain sterile prior to use. Packaging should be validated per ISO 11607-1:2019 *Packaging for Terminally Sterilized Medical Devices—Part 1: Requirements for Materials, Sterile Barrier Systems and Packaging Systems* and ISO 11607-2:2019 *Packaging for Terminally Sterilized Medical Devices—Part 2: Validation Requirements for Forming, Sealing and Assembly Processes.*

Validation studies of traditional sterilization methods are done according to recognized standards specific to the sterilization process (see references in the Methods section). If a standard is used, the requirements of the standard must be met. If a standard is not used in the validation study, there must be valid scientific rationale documented in the protocol to support the method used in the process validation and subsequent product sterilization.

After the validation study has been completed and approved and the sterilization cycle is in use for devices intended for commercialization, process controls and cycle acceptance are documented in the device history record (DHR). Each cycle is approved based on current revision procedures and cycle specifications that are part of the device master record (DMR). If the sterilization cycle is outside the tolerances for operating or performance parameters, there are procedures for handling such nonconformances and for corrective action to eliminate reoccurrence of the nonconformity. If resterilization is indicated due to a process nonconformity, the effect of resterilization on the product and packaging should have been determined in the validation study to allow such reprocessing. If validation testing was not conducted on resterilization, the devices cannot be resterilized. Nonconformities may include positive biological indicators, high ethylene oxide residuals, high levels of bioburden, out-of-specification endotoxin (pyrogen) results, or packaging failures. Packaging failures after sterilization indicate a failure to properly validate the packaging and process combination during the original sterilization process validation. Periodic cycle revalidations are defined in the manufacturer's procedures and are necessary to assure the continued adequacy of the process based on possible changes in bioburden levels, bioburden resistance, product or package changes, or equipment modifications. Purchasing and receiving of such items as sterilant, sterilization indicators, contract sterilization services, and laboratory test services are controlled by current standard procedures.

Sterilization process controls extend to the validation of the software used to control the sterilization process. If the process is automated, software validation includes the software requirements document, software validation protocol, software validation activities, software change controls, and software validation results to confirm that the software will meet the sterilization process requirements and its intended use. If the software is developed by a subcontractor, a purchasing specification and a validation report confirming that the specified software requirements were met form the minimal documentation of such a contracted software development project.

If the sterilization process is not software controlled, operating and monitoring personnel are qualified and trained to ensure a consistently successful sterilization process. Both equipment operators and quality control personnel, including those working different shifts, are trained to recognize problems that can be caused by operational errors and by not following standard procedures. Formal on-the-job training is normally required for all personnel who perform the following sterilization operations, including:

1. Arranging sterilizer loads
2. Placing biological indicators or dosimeters
3. Managing pre- and post-sterilization packaging and warehousing
4. Calibrating and maintaining sterilization and environmental control equipment systems
5. Making decisions on acceptance and rejection or need for resterilization of products

Environmental controls may also play a part in the sterilization process depending on whether the product is or has been adequately cleaned prior to packaging. If the product cannot be cleaned, the primary production areas normally need to be environmentally controlled to minimize microbiological and particulate contamination. The number of bacteria on the product prior to sterilization (that is, product bioburden) is influenced by the production environment, handling of the product during manufacturing and cleaning processes, and hygiene of employees. The type and quantity of bacteria present on the product also influence the outcome of pyrogen testing. Some gram-positive bacteria, mycobacteria, fungi, and viruses can produce pyrogenic substances; however, pyrogens produced by gram-negative bacteria, that is, endotoxins, are of the most significance to medical devices. Bacterial endotoxins located in the outer membrane of gram-negative bacteria are lipopolysaccharides (LPS). LPS is released from bacteria after death and lysis of the cell during sterilization. The remains of the bacteria can produce a fever (that is, pyrogenic response) in patients under certain conditions.

If the product is labeled "pyrogen free," it is important to minimize bacterial contamination prior to sterilization and to monitor finished product for pyrogens after sterilization. The end use of the product will determine whether a pyrogen-free claim is appropriate and necessary. There are different methods of determining the presence of pyrogens, so the method used to make the determination (for example, limulus amebocyte lysate [LAL]) must be detailed in the monitoring procedures. Products intended to be sold in the United States are to be monitored for endotoxins by conducting LAL testing on a regular basis per AAMI ST72:2019 *Bacterial Endotoxins—Test methods, routine monitoring, and alternatives to batch testing.* Refer to Chapter 17 for Bacterial Endotoxin testing references. Procedures for control and monitoring of the manufacturing environment include employee gowning and hygiene, workstation cleaning and disinfection, microbiological monitoring, air filtration system maintenance, and trending of monitoring results. Any environmental monitoring program includes alert levels and action levels. Refer to Chapter 19 for more information on controlled environments.

Measurement and test equipment used in the sterilization process is calibrated and maintained according to specified procedures and schedules. Preventive maintenance procedures and schedules for the sterilization equipment ensure that the sterilization process parameters can be met consistently. Maintenance and calibration items to consider include the sterilizer instrumentation, such as gauges, recorder and test equipment, package sealing equipment, and cleaning of appropriate processing equipment.

Manufacturing materials required in the manufacture of sterile products may include ethylene oxide (EO), biological indicators, incubation media, and deionized water. Each is inspected and tested for identity, viability, integrity, and purity as applicable to ensure the material meet specifications. For example, when EO is used, the manufacturer either receives certification that the gas conforms to specifications of purity and blend, or conducts tests to ensure the gas meets specifications. If biological indicators are used, performance of the indicators is verified by testing or certificate of analysis.

Manufacturers frequently use contract sterilization, but the responsibility for product sterility rests with the manufacturer, not the contract sterilizer. The manufacturer must therefore be able to produce the same documentation that would be necessary if the sterilization were being done in-house. Such documentation includes the validation study—done according to guidance from a consensus standard—process specifications, product and packaging studies, procedures for cycle review and acceptance, monitoring procedures, and sterilization residual control.

Prior to release for distribution, standard procedures for testing, data, and document review, and release by a designated individual, are used to ensure that the finished products (lot, batch, serial number) meet acceptance criteria. The acceptance activities, including the dates of the activities, results, equipment used, and signature of the individuals conducting the activities, all form part of the product documentation (DHR) required by § 820.184. ISO 13485:2016 includes the requirement in Section 7.5.5 Particular requirements for sterile medical devices for the manufacturer to include records for the parameters for the sterilization process for each batch or lot of sterile product. This information should be documented in the DHR and reviewed prior to release. The product is held in quarantine or at a controlled warehouse until it has been released for distribution. The DHR also includes the dates of manufacture, quantity manufactured, quantity released for distribution, primary identification label and labeling for each unit, and any identification and control numbers used.

The DMR of sterile products includes the specifications for the sterilizer/sterilization process and sterilization cycle, including values for humidity, temperature, pressure, gas concentration, dwell time, and conveyor speed, as applicable to the sterilization method used. Specifications and procedures include those for facility cleaning, employee dress and practices, environment, packaging, labeling, and quarantine. There are instructions for performing the sterilization process, including arrangement of the sterilizer load, placement of biological indicators, identification of sterile and nonsterile product, packaging, and quarantine. Specifications for materials such as EO and other gaseous materials, monitoring equipment such as dosimeters, media, and biological indicators are also part of the DMR. Instructions for equipment calibration, checking of charts and logs, sterility assay procedures, inspection and testing of package integrity, and finished product analysis are also required to be in the DMR per § 820.181.

Examples of sterilization deficiencies indicating that the process may not be effective include the following:

1. Abnormal percentage of lots rejected as a result of failed sterility or pyrogen tests
2. History of cycle failures, operating problems, and frequent equipment breakdowns
3. Failure to properly maintain and calibrate instruments and to record such activities
4. Lack of records or incomplete records of the sterilization process and/or sterility tests
5. Failure to control the identification, segregation, and storage of finished sterile products and/or failure to control products awaiting sterility test results
6. Lack of adequate knowledge of process controls and measurement requirements by employees who operate equipment
7. Failure of the manufacturer to follow its own procedures for sterilizing products
8. Lack of specifications for the sterilization process.

STERILIZATION METHODS

The FDA has published a guidance document for the methods used to sterilize medical devices. This guidance document, *Submission and Review of Sterility Information in Premarket Notification (510(k)) Submissions for Devices Labeled as Sterile; Guidance for Industry and Food and Drug Administration Staff*[178] issued January 21, 2016, uses three different categories: established sterilization methods (Category A and Category B), and novel sterilization methods. Established Category A methods are sterilization methods that have a long history of use that has been demonstrated to be safe and effective. This history is well documented and has FDA-recognized standards for the process validation and controls. Established Category B methods are sterilization methods that do not have FDA-recognized standards, but there is published information available for the process validation and controls. Novel sterilization methods are newly developed methods for which there is limited published information and no FDA-recognized standards.

Details of each of these categories and the references for validation and controls are provided below.

Established Methods of Sterilization—Category A

Dry heat sterilization. This method is used to sterilize heat-stable items such as glassware and tools. This method is not widely used in medical device manufacturing because of the high temperatures involved. It may be used in aseptic production for sterilization and depyrogenation of glassware, such as vials, prior to filling. Requirements for this method may be found in ISO 11138- 3:2017 *Sterilization of health care products—Biological indicators—Part 3: Biological indicators for moist heat sterilization processes.*

Ethylene oxide (EO) wherein product is sterilized in a fixed chamber. This method is a widely used process for sterilizing medical devices. Although EO gas is toxic, flammable, and explosive, and the process leaves EO residuals that must be removed from the product by controlled aeration, the process has several appealing traits. The equipment used is relatively affordable, and the installation and operational validation process is well documented and straightforward.[179] The process involves multiple variables, including EO gas concentration, temperature, relative humidity, and exposure time, all of which must be controlled to within the limits specified during the process validation. The process usually has little detrimental effect on the materials or product being sterilized. The negative aspect of the process is the gas itself and the effect it can have on sterilizer operators and product handlers.

Process validation for EO. Sterilization validation using EO is conducted per ISO 11135:2014 *Sterilization of health-care products—Ethylene Oxide—Requirements for the development, validation and routine control of a sterilization process for medical devices.* This standard defines the requirements for installation qualification (IQ), operational qualification (OQ), and performance qualification (PQ), including microbiological performance qualification. There are two methods defined in the standard. Annex A defines the biological indicator/bioburden approach, and Annex B defines the overkill approach. The validation protocol should define the method used. The residual EO and ethylene chlorohydrin are also to be evaluated using such recognized standards as ISO 10993-7:2008 *Biological evaluation of medical devices—Part 7: Ethylene oxide sterilization residuals.* Control of the outgassing area used to aerate products and the liability associated with employee exposure to EO has resulted in numerous contractors who specialize in EO sterilization of large quantities of medical products (see AAMI TIR 14 Contract sterilization using ethylene oxide). Be aware that changing EO sterilization contractors will require a revalidation of the cycle to assure that microbial lethality is not affected by differences between the two facilities. Revalidation should be assessed. AAMI TIR28:2009/(R)2013 *Product Adoption and Process Equivalence for Ethylene Oxide Sterilization* defines the requirements for a manufacturer to adopt into an existing validation or to assess revalidation requirements. The scope includes adopting a new device/product, changes to devices/products, relocating a validated process, and how to determine equivalency of a sterilization process.

Process controls and monitoring for EO. A review of pertinent standards related to EO sterilization will help one become familiar with detailed requirements for control of the process. For example, when establishing a sterilization facility, AAMI TIR 15 *Physical aspects of ethylene oxide sterilization* is helpful in specifying the equipment to be purchased and in calculating such important parameters as percent relative humidity and EO gas concentration. As mentioned in the aforementioned EO validation section, ISO 11135:2014 *Sterilization of health-care products—Ethylene Oxide—Requirements for the development, validation and routine control of a sterilization process for medical devices* also defines process controls and monitoring to be implemented. Product bioburden determination and monitoring methods can be found in ISO 11737-1:2018 *Sterilization of Health Care Products—Microbiological methods—Part 1: Determination of a population of microorganisms on products.* Also, ISO 11737-2:2019 *Sterilization of Health Care Products—Microbiological methods—Part 2: Tests of sterility performed in the definition, validation and maintenance of a sterilization process* provides essential information for required sterility testing. Biological indicators, used in the validation and subsequent process control of EO sterilization, are subject to the requirements in ISO 11138-1:2017 *Sterilization of health care products— Biological indicators—Part 1: General requirements. The FDA Guide to Inspections of Quality Systems* (that is, QSIT) has sections devoted to sterilization process control, thereby providing a systematic approach to auditing sterile medical products, especially ones sterilized by EO.

Steam. Steam is the preferred method for sterilizing heat-stable implants such as orthopedic implants and mechanical heart valves, and the instruments used for surgical procedures. The process involves the control of two basic parameters: time and temperature. The relationship between the two variables and their lethal effect on microorganisms is expressed by such terms as *D value, F value, z value,* and F_0 *value.* Requirements for validation and control of moist heat sterilization, which includes saturated steam and air-steam mixtures, are found in such standards as AAMI TIR 13 *Principles of industrial moist heat sterilization* and ISO 17665-1:2006 *Sterilization of health care products—Moist heat—Part 1: Requirements for the development, validation and routine control of a sterilization process for medical devices.* Other regulatory and technical requirements may also apply to the steam sterilization of pharmaceuticals. A review of the standards will detail the information expected of manufacturers that sterilize products using moist heat.

Radiation (gamma or electron beam). This is a method of sterilizing products, by batch or continuous processors, using radiation from cobalt-60 or cesium-137 or using a beam from an electron or x-ray generator. Once medical product manufacturers became aware of the disadvantages of EO sterilization, such as the toxic effects of EO on operations personnel, attention was focused on radiation sterilization as an alternative to EO. Radiation has the advantage of only one process variable, time of exposure to the radiation source. However, the materials used in product and packaging design are crucial. Radiation has a deleterious effect on certain materials, such as Teflon, and can discolor materials that do not otherwise degrade. Changes in material impact strength, hardness, color, elasticity, and other performance characteristics may occur immediately or over time after radiation. Selection of radiation-stable materials is based on years of experience and testing that have been distilled into published guidance documents, including AAMI TIR 17:2017 *Compatibility of materials subject to sterilization.* After the selection of radiation-stable materials, a program involving the testing of products for all essential properties throughout their expected shelf life follows a determination of the maximum radiation dose expected.

Process validation for radiation. ISO 11137-1:2006 *Sterilization of health care products—Radiation—Part 1: Requirements for development, validation and routine control of a sterilization process for medical devices* is an excellent guidance document to the requirements for validation and control of radiation sterilization processes. This standard defines the requirements for IQ, OQ, and PQ, including dose mapping. Part of the validation includes establishing the maximum acceptable dose and the sterilization dose. One of two defined methods may be used to determine the dose. The first uses the number of bioburden and the resistance to radiation (if known). The second uses a set dose of either 25kGy or 15kGy that is substantiated during testing. This is referred to as either the VD_{max}^{25} or the VD_{max}^{15} method. Additional information for the use of these methods is found in ISO 11137-2:2013 *Sterilization of Health Care Products—Radiation—Part 2: Establishing the Sterilization Dose.* Radiation sterilization is dependent on the product bioburden, which is characterized during the validation study. Environmental controls and product bioburden monitoring receive more emphasis when the calculation of the radiation dose is directly related to the average product bioburden and the expected SAL. This is the method used to set the sterilization dose in method 1 of ISO 11137-1. The standard includes two additional methods of dose setting, as well as somewhat complicated calculations used in each method. Application of ISO 11137-1 should be left to knowledgeable and experienced individuals to assure proper interpretation of the standard and the nuances involved in this method of sterilization.

Process controls and monitoring for radiation. The real advantage of radiation sterilization is the one process variable—absorbed dose. Monitoring of a validated process involves the use of dosimeters to determine absorbed dose at various points in the product load. This information is provided by the contract sterilizer (if outsourced) and is maintained as part of the DHR. It is important that the loading configuration be consistent and dosimeters be placed as specified in the load. After using dosimeters to determine the absorbed dose meets cycle specification, the product may be released for distribution without delay. Additional ongoing monitoring for product sterilized with radiation includes the use of a dose audit and determination of product bioburden (typically performed quarterly). The results from the dose audit and the product bioburden are reviewed and trended to ensure the sterilization method is continuing to ensure the defined SAL.

Established Methods of Sterilization—Category B

Sterilization methods considered nontraditional by the FDA include:

1. Flexible bag systems (for example, ethylene oxide, in which EO is injected into a porous polymer bag ("bag method," "diffusion method," "sterilization pouch," "injection method")). AAMI TIR56:2013 *Guidance for the development, validation and routine control of an ethylene oxide sterilization process using flexible bag systems for the sterilization of medical devices* provides guidance of using this type of EO sterilization.
2. Hydrogen peroxide (H_2O_2). Hydrogen peroxide can be used to sterilize either in a liquid or a vaporized gas state. The gas vapor is hazardous but has a much shorter cycle time than other gases, such as EO.
3. Ozone (O_3). Ozone is a gas that has historically been used for disinfecting water and food. It has recently been used to sterilize medical devices that are made from heat-sensitive materials. It is a toxic and unstable gas and must be produced on-site but can destroy a wide range of pathogens.

Novel Sterilization Methods

Sterilization methods considered novel by the FDA include:

1. Vaporized peracetic acid
2. High-intensity light or pulse light
3. Microwave radiation
4. Sound waves
5. Ultraviolet light

There are several recognized standards that can be applicable to gas or liquid chemical sterilants for process validation and controls. Examples include ISO 14937:2009 *Sterilization of health care products—General requirements for characterization of a sterilizing agent and the development, validation and routine control of a sterilization process for medical devices* and ISO 14160:2011 *Sterilization of health care products—Liquid chemical sterilizing agents for single-use medical devices utilizing animal tissues and their derivatives—Requirements for characterization, development, validation and routine control of a sterilization process for medical devices,* but it is specific to medical devices incorporating materials of animal origin. Users of the aforementioned nontraditional methods should realize they are using methods that are outside the scope of specific FDA/CDRH-recognized standards and should be prepared with a thorough and well-documented process validation study. The study does not necessarily need to be submitted to the FDA in the 510(k) application, but the FDA may decide that inspection of the sterilization facility is a priority.

Chapter 21

Laboratory Testing and Failure Analysis

The quality laboratory is responsible for establishing specifications, sampling plans, and test procedures for raw materials, components, equipment, in-process materials, and finished products in the developmental and production environments. These plans and procedures must be executed, and the resultant data must be evaluated for conformance to the acceptance criteria defined in the plans, procedures, and specifications. Each of these activities must be identified in a procedure, and those procedures must be followed. When an auditor reviews the laboratory operation, he or she should observe and inquire about what the laboratory does.

Product testing and laboratory functions can be found in several departmental functions within the medical device firm. The medical device quality control laboratory may be any laboratory that performs physical/mechanical, chemical, and microbiological tests or performs inspections or tests of components. In-process and finished products are included as part of the laboratory testing function. Laboratories within research and development are not immune from the requirements of the quality system regulation (QSR) or current good manufacturing practice (CGMP).

The implementation of appropriate required procedures and the consistent execution of the procedures accomplish compliance with the regulation. Since 21 CFR Part 820 does not address laboratory operations, laboratory operations in the devices arena are often evaluated against the pertinent sections of 21 CFR Part 211 *Current Good Manufacturing Practice for Finished Pharmaceuticals.* 21 CFR § 820.70 *Production and Process Controls* and 21 CFR § 820.72 *Inspection, Measuring, and Test Equipment* also include many of the functions carried out in the quality laboratory.

The laboratory is the center for testing and analyses for the acceptance or rejection of raw materials, components, equipment, in-process materials, and finished products. The biological laboratory normally is responsible for monitoring the production environment and finished devices for the control of contamination and is often the responsible group for sterilization process validation. Laboratory personnel are required to have the education, training, and experience, or any combination thereof, to enable each person to perform his or her assigned functions.

APPROVED PROCEDURES

The auditor makes a judgment by determining whether there are approved procedures for each activity, that the procedures are adequate, that the procedures are being followed, and whether what the laboratory does is adequate. Laboratory procedures should include the following elements:

- Definition of the purpose and scope of the procedure
- List of responsibilities of those performing the procedure
- List of materials and equipment necessary to perform the procedure
- Detailed description of the steps to be performed
- Indication of where and how required data are to be recorded
- Evaluation of data against established specifications/acceptance criteria
- Directions for actions to be taken when a problem is identified with performance of the procedure

The quality control testing laboratory should have the necessary procedures to describe all testing and operational activities. The procedures generally fall into the following general categories:

- Quality management systems
- Testing and operating procedures
- Data accountability and integrity (including electronic data)
- Methods validation
- Personnel training
- Equipment
- Facilities

Quality Management Systems

The regulations require accountability for quality management. In the laboratory, for example, the manager or supervisors are held accountable for the review of analytical raw data, and for the work performed and the review of the analysts' data. The management system shall provide for the notification of the manager or supervisor when out of specification (OOS) test results are found. Procedures for the management system should include the following:

- Handling of OOS test results
- Notification of management of OOS results
- Investigation of OOS results and deviations
- Treatment of outlier results
- Procedures for the auditing and approval of contract testing laboratories

Testing and Operating Procedures

Operating procedures that describe good laboratory practices support that testing is performed accurately and according to approved test methods. The operating procedures identify controls, describe sampling and sampling plans, and provide methods for accountability of articles tested in the laboratory. Operating procedures should describe control of the following:

- Personnel attire
- Purchase, receipt, storage, labeling, and control of test samples:
  - Name of material
  - Lot/batch number
  - Container from which the sample was taken
  - Date/time of sampling
  - Name of sampler
- Purchase, receipt, storage, labeling, and control of chemicals, culture media, and reagents
- Purchase, receipt, storage, labeling, calibration, and control of laboratory reference standards, gauges, and analytical chromatography columns
- Expiration dating of standards and reagents
- Laboratory and glassware cleaning

Testing and inspection procedures describe critical equipment, materials, and steps to be used to determine conformance to specifications of the articles and systems being tested. Testing and inspection procedures should provide control of the following:

- Receiving inspection
- Quality inspection plans and accept/reject specifications for components and materials
- Inspection techniques and measurement equipment/instruments

Data Accountability

In the arena of raw data, GMP requires a complete record of all data secured in the course of each test, including all graphs, charts, and spectra from laboratory instrumentation, and a record of all calculations performed in connection with the test, including units of measure, conversion factors, and equivalency factors. Procedures in the laboratory should include at least the following:

- Handling of raw laboratory data
- Identification of instrument printouts
- Averaging results, rounding, and significant figures

- Second-party review of laboratory data
- Entry of data into laboratory information management system (LIMS) (if applicable)
- Changing data in LIMS (if applicable)

Methods Validation

Validation of biological and chemical analytical test methods is an essential element of the laboratory management system. It is critical that test methods be validated to determine the appropriateness and validity of the analyses being performed. The validation of test methods is coupled with the validation of critical equipment used to perform the test.

GMPs require that methods be validated. Validation of analytical methods basically means that documentation exists to prove that a method used is accurate, sensitive, and specific, and will reproducibly yield reliable results. Validation is required for noncompendial methods (those not codified in the U.S. Pharmacopeia (USP) or other internationally accepted standard methods). The following elements of analytical methods validation are addressed in the USP:

- Accuracy
- Precision
- Linearity
- Specificity
- Range
- Limit of detection
- Limit of quantitation
- Ruggedness and robustness

Personnel Training

The most critical element in the laboratory is an effective training program. Analysts are to be trained in the specific methods each performs, and that training is to be conducted and documented by qualified individuals. Training is to occur continuously or on an ongoing basis. A key indicator of GMP compliance in the laboratory is the training process used when new procedures are introduced or existing procedures are revised.

Equipment

Each piece of critical equipment in the laboratory is to have a unique identification. Procedures that are established for the operation and maintenance of the equipment are to be written and approved.

In the laboratory, each piece of critical equipment requires validation or qualification. Procedures or protocols are to be written and approved that list the criteria by which validation and qualification are performed. The procedures or protocols should include installation qualification (IQ), operational qualification (OQ), and performance qualification (PQ). Such procedures or protocols are applicable to any instrument that measures a condition of a test, including test and calibration instrumentation, inspection tools (apparatus and gauges), incubators/ovens, refrigerators, and autoclaves.

Each piece of critical equipment also requires calibration. Each item requiring calibration is to be covered by a procedure and to be recalibrated at a time period described in the calibration program. One of the key items to evaluate in a laboratory regarding calibration is the status of each instrument. Elements of the calibration program include:

- A procedure describing the calibration steps
- Established intervals and tolerance limits
- Standards that are identified and traceable
- Documentation of each calibration
- Procedures to follow when instruments fail calibration

Facilities

The laboratory facilities, like the facilities of the manufacturing areas, are to be in a state of control. This is applicable to HVAC systems, water sources, and equipment as well. Procedures are to be in place to demonstrate control. Procedures governing the laboratory consist of the following:

- Safety and handling of hazardous materials, including the decontamination of biological wastes
- Cleaning and sanitization of work surfaces and laboratory equipment
- Proper identification of labeling, equipment, and instrumentation

Documentation

GMP requires that laboratory procedures adequate to describe the activity shall be written, and all operations must conform to these procedures. In most laboratories, several types of procedures exist. Each document must be controlled. That is, a mechanism must exist through which all documents are approved before they become official, and a controlled means for making document changes must exist. Without proper controls, one can never be sure the method and procedures in use are correct. Procedures for documentation in the laboratory should address the following topics:

- Good documentation practices
- Use of laboratory notebooks and data sheets

- Control of laboratory notebooks and data sheets
- Control of forms
- Handling deviations from sampling and test procedures
- Documenting and handling of out-of-specification (OOS) results
- Preparation of protocols and reports

BIOLOGICAL TESTING

The microbiology laboratory is normally the group that performs environmental monitoring programs of critical systems. The standards and procedures used for environmental monitoring program activities are described in Chapter 19. The lab will, in most cases, perform product release or sterilization validation biological indicator testing if ethylene oxide (EO), steam, or dry heat processes are used for sterilization. The standards and procedures used for sterilization validation activities are described in Chapter 20:

- Challenge of microbiological test media (growth promotion)
- Preparation, storage, and control of microbiological test media
- Bacterial endotoxin test procedures
- Bioburden testing (products and packaging)
- Environmental monitoring programs of facilities systems (production environments, HVAC, water systems, compressed air systems)
- Biological indicator, biological indicator sterility testing
- Product sterility testing associated with radiation sterilization validations and dose audits

Sterility Testing

In the case of medical devices, product sterility tests are performed primarily in association with the validation of the sterilization process and are not performed as a test for product release. The sterility tests of biological indicators, those that are used to monitor the sterilization process, are used for product/process release. The validation of sterility tests is described in the U.S. Pharmacopeia-National Formulary (USP-NF) and the specific sterilization standard utilized for process validation.

Bioburden Testing

A sterile product item is one that is free of viable microorganisms. The international standards for sterilization of healthcare products require—when it is necessary to supply a sterile product item—that adventitious microbiological contamination of a healthcare product from all sources is minimized by all practical means.

Products that are produced under standard manufacturing conditions may have microorganisms on them, although in low numbers. Such items are nonsterile, and the purpose of the sterilization process is to inactivate the microbiological contaminants and thereby transform the nonsterile items into sterile ones.

The validation of procedures for the estimation of microbiological populations is outlined in ISO 11737-1:2018 *Sterilization of health care products—Microbiological methods—Part 1: Determination of a population of microorganisms on products.* The critical element is that a recovery factor be established for the methods utilized.

Bacterial Endotoxin Testing

Medical devices that are required to be pyrogen-free are tested by an assay for bacterial endotoxins. The test is the limulus amebocyte lysate (LAL) test, which may utilize gel clot, photometric, and kinetic test methods. Compendial procedures are outlined in the USP. The FDA's current thinking and recommendations for testing and acceptance criteria are provided in the 2012 Guidance Document *Pyrogens and Endotoxins Testing: Questions and Answers,* and refers to USP and ANSI/AAMI ST72:2019 *Bacterial Endotoxins—Test Methods, routine monitoring and alternatives to batch testing.* Based on this guidance document, medical device companies should define a sampling plan for in-process and finished products.

Environmental Testing

Monitoring of the manufacturing environments is an activity normally performed by the biological laboratory. The critical element of environmental and facilities/utilities monitoring (HVAC/water systems) is that specifications (alerts, action levels, limits) be established, and these specifications be established based on a statistical application. Water system specifications can be found in the USP. Environmental monitoring and control are addressed in Chapter 19.

ANALYTICAL TESTING

In medical device products, chemical analyses are not routinely utilized and may be limited to ultraviolet-visible (UV-VIS) spectroscopy and Fourier transform infrared spectroscopy (FTIR) analysis for the identification of raw materials or component materials. For in vitro diagnostics, more involved chemical analyses are often the case. Testing procedures should provide control of the following:

- Preparation of standards
- Expiration dating of standards
- Preparation, storage, and control of chromatographic mobile phases
- Procedures that contain specifications or acceptable limits

FAILURE ANALYSIS

An OOS test result is to be investigated to determine the root cause and to determine whether the result is a deviation of the measurement or manufacturing process. The initial phase of an investigation should assess laboratory data accuracy and, if possible, be conducted before the test preparation, for example, material extract is discarded. Analytical error should not be assumed. If the initial assessment does not demonstrate an error in the analytical method, the investigation should be expanded into a full-scale investigation. Each step of the investigation should be fully documented.

Laboratory errors should be relatively rare, and frequent errors indicate potential deficiencies in training, equipment calibration, or equipment maintenance. Laboratory management should determine the reliability of the OOS test result and its significance to the overall quality assurance program. Corrective action should be undertaken to prevent the reoccurrence of laboratory errors. Laboratory errors should be trended and reviewed by management to ensure problematic areas are identified and addressed appropriately.

Chapter 22
Validation

INTRODUCTION

"Validations are akin to scientific investigations in which the hypotheses are formulated, experiments are designed and conducted, data are collected and analyzed, and conclusions are reached. And like scientific discoveries, validations must be questioned and retested for the life of the process they cover."[180]

Medical device establishments are expected to comply with the FDA's Quality System Regulation (QSR) requirements. 21 CFR, Part 820.75 clearly states: "Where the results of a process cannot be fully verified by subsequent inspection and test, the process shall be validated with a high degree of assurance."

21 CFR Part 11 *Electronic Records; Electronic Signatures* requires the validation of computer systems and software that produce electronic records. These requirements also apply to electronic spreadsheets and databases such as Microsoft Excel and Access.

ISO 13485:2016 *Medical devices—Quality management systems—Requirements for regulatory purposes clause 7.5.6 Validation of processes for production and service provision* requires the organization to validate any processes for production and service provision where the resulting output cannot be or is not verified by subsequent monitoring or measurement and, as a consequence, deficiencies become apparent only after the product is in use or the service has been delivered.

GHTF/SG3/N99-10 *Quality Management Systems—Process Validation Guidance* is the "gold" standard regarding process validation. This guidance is intended to assist manufacturers in understanding quality management system requirements concerning process validation and has general applicability to manufacturing (including servicing and installation) processes for medical devices. The guidance provides general suggestions on ways manufacturers may prepare for and carry out process validations.

There are some definitions that must be presented prior to further discussing validation activities:

- Commissioning—The planned, documented, and managed engineering approach to the start-up and turnover of facilities, systems, and equipment.
- Qualification—The documented verification that all aspects of a facility, utility, or equipment that can affect product quality operate as intended throughout all anticipated ranges.

- Installation qualification (IQ)—Establishing by objective evidence that all key aspects of the process equipment and ancillary system installation adhere to the manufacturer's approved specification and that the recommendations of the supplier of the equipment are suitably considered.
- Operational qualification (OQ)—Establishing by objective evidence process control limits and action levels that result in product that meets all predetermined requirements.
- Performance qualification (PQ)—Establishing by objective evidence that the process, under anticipated conditions, consistently produces a product that meets all predetermined requirements.
- Process performance qualification (PPQ)—Establishing by objective evidence that the system, under anticipated conditions, consistently produces a product that meets all predetermined requirements.
- Prospective validation—Establishing documented evidence, prior to process implementation, that a system performs as is intended, based on preplanned protocols.
- Retrospective validation—Validating a system that has been operating for some time. There are various schools of thought on how to approach retrospective validation. Some may feel that a full-blown validation is required to assure the system is functioning properly.
- Concurrent validation—Used to establish documented evidence that a facility and process will perform as they are intended, based on information generated during actual use of the process.
- Revalidation—Repeating the original validation effort or any part of it that also includes investigating and reviewing existing performance data.
- Validation—Confirmation, through the provision of objective evidence, that the requirements for a specific intended use or application have been fulfilled. Validation answers the question, "Are we making the right thing?"
- Verification—Confirmation, through the provision of objective evidence, that specified requirements have been fulfilled. Verification answers the question, "Are we making the thing right?"

VALIDATION DETERMINATION

The first step in validation is determining the need. Figure 22.1 is an example process validation decision tree that can be used to determine and document the validation decision.[181] The validation decision should be documented as objective evidence and recorded in the validation master plan (VMP) or master validation plan (MVP).

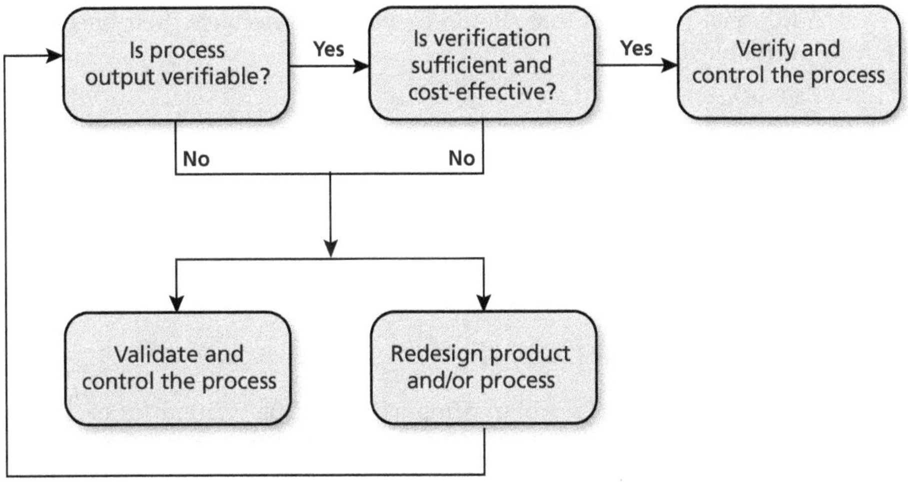

Figure 22.1 Process validation decision tree.

The following list from the GHTF Study Group 3 Quality Management Systems Process Validation Guidance (January 2004) provides examples of processes that should be validated, may be satisfactorily covered by verification, and may be verifiable, but, for business purposes, validation can be chosen:

1. Processes that should be validated:
   - Sterilization processes
   - Cleanroom ambient conditions
   - Aseptic filling processes
   - Sterile packaging sealing processes
   - Lyophilization process
   - Heat-treating processes
   - Plating processes
   - Plastic injection molding processes
2. Processes that may be satisfactorily covered by verification:
   - Manual cutting processes
   - Testing for color, turbidity, total pH for solutions
   - Visual inspection of printed circuit boards
   - Manufacturing and testing of wiring harnesses
3. Processes for which an evaluation is made to determine the need for validation:
   - Certain cleaning processes
   - Certain human assembly processes
   - Numerical control cutting processes
   - Certain filling processes.

Additional processes that should be validated because their outputs are not fully verifiable include:

- Casting
- Forging
- Welding
- Coating
- Passivation

VALIDATION DOCUMENTATION

A separate validation protocol and report should be written for each validated process. As a minimum, the protocol should delineate the requirements for the:

- Sample size (including rationale)
- Equipment being used
- Associated risk
- Test methods employed
- Predefined acceptance criteria
- Revalidation criteria
- Training requirements

Validation protocols are the most effective when cross-functional teams are utilized and should minimally include representatives from operations, quality, project management, regulatory affairs, engineering, and maintenance. When the protocol is executed, any deviations encountered should be documented, investigated, and closed prior to accepting the validation report.

Once a process has been successfully validated, it must be controlled and monitored to ensure that the process has not drifted and that specifications continue to be met. Monitoring of the process may be accomplished by one or more of the following but is not limited to these items:

- Periodic destructive testing
- Lot release testing
- The ongoing review of performance data collected during manufacturing operations including the use of control charts and process capability data
- Monitoring of NCRs, deviations, and complaint data

REWORK

FDA regulations and ISO standards speak about reworking nonconforming product. 21 CFR 820.90 *Nonconforming product* (2): Each manufacturer shall establish and maintain procedures for rework, to include retesting and reevaluation of the nonconforming product after rework, to ensure that the product meets its current approved specifications. Rework and reevaluation activities, including a determination of any adverse effect from the rework upon the product, shall be documented in the device history record (DHR).

ISO 13485:2016 clause 8.3.4 Rework: The organization shall perform rework in accordance with documented procedures that consider the potential adverse effect of the rework on the product. These procedures shall undergo the same review and approval as the original procedure.

After the completion of rework, product shall be verified to ensure that it meets applicable acceptance criteria and regulatory requirements.

There may be times that rework activities must be validated especially if the output of the rework process is not fully verifiable, as in the case of welding.

TEST METHOD VALIDATION AND MEASUREMENT SYSTEM ANALYSIS

Test method validation (TMV) and measurement system analysis (MSA), also known as gage repeatability and reproducibility (GR&R) studies, analyze the variation of measurements of a gage (repeatability) and the variation of measurements by operators (reproducibility). Every observation (measurement) of a process contains both actual process variation and measurement variation. GR&R studies can be performed on variable and attribute measurements. Figure 22.2 shows many of the characteristics of process variation, while Figures 22.3 and 22.4 demonstrate repeatability and reproducibility, respectively.

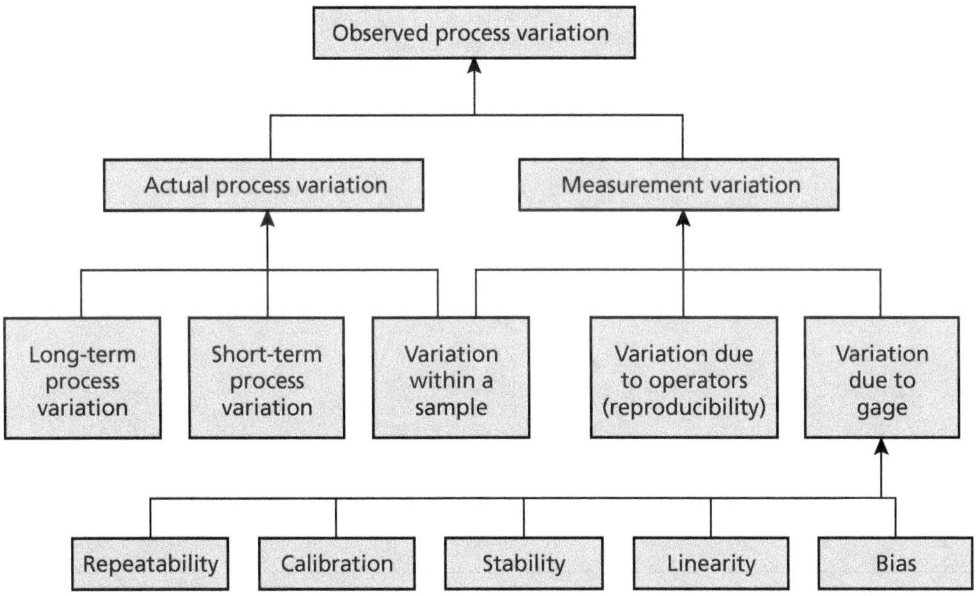

Figure 22.2 Possible sources of process variation.[182]

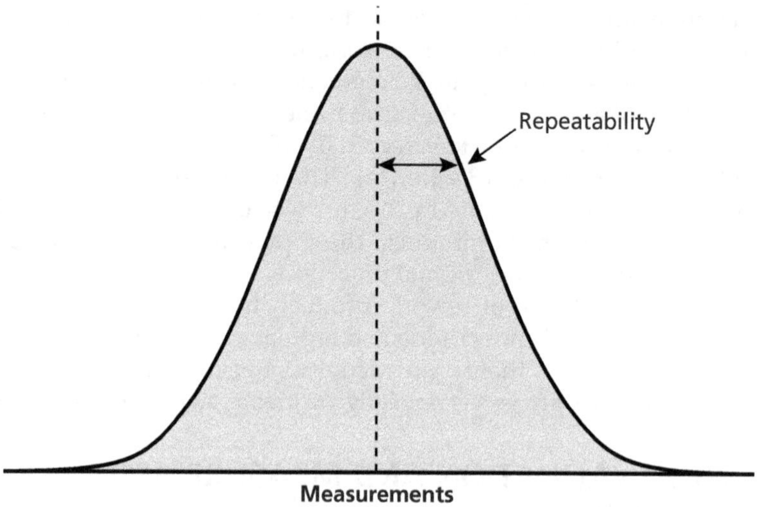

Figure 22.3 Repeatability.[183]

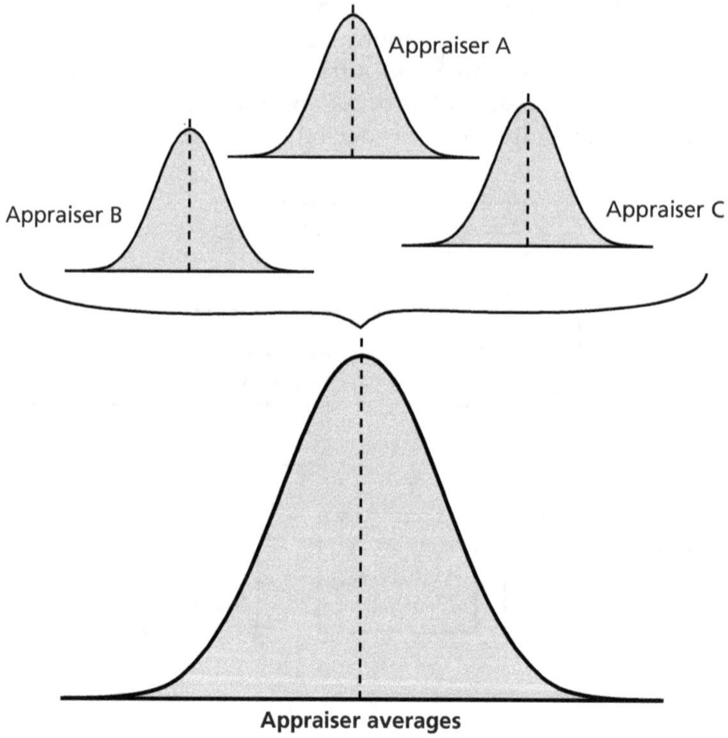

Figure 22.4 Reproducibility.[184]

Terminology related to TMV, MSA, and GR&R

- Linearity—The extent to which a measuring instrument's bias varies along its full operating range with the measured quantity. In a gage R&R study, linearity is the difference in the bias values throughout the expected operating range of the gage.
- Bias—The difference between a measured value and a known or accepted reference value.
- Calibration—The comparison of two instruments or measuring devices—one of which is a standard of known accuracy traceable to national standards—to detect, correlate, report, or eliminate by adjustment any inaccuracy of the instrument or measuring device, as compared to the standard.
- Repeatability—The variation in measurements obtained when one measurement device is used several times by the same person to measure the same characteristic on the same product.
- Reproducibility—The variation in measurements made by different people using the same measuring device to measure the same characteristic on the same product.
- Stability—(1) of a gage: it is the ability of a gage to retain its accuracy over time and usage; (2) of a process: a process is said to be stable if it shows no recognizable pattern of change.

Variable gage studies provide a tremendous amount of statistical data about the measurement system, including linearity, bias, stability, repeatability, and reproducibility. Both statistical and graphical methods are useful to determine the performance of the gage.

Performing attribute gage studies provides a unique set of challenges when compared to studies using variable data. With variables measurements, the degree of conformity or nonconformity can be qualified with a physical measurement.

Attribute assessments either accept or reject a part, without any indication of how good or bad the part actually is—only that it is good or bad. Because of pass/fail or good/bad (binary) data, there is less statistically known about the process/parts being inspected.

There are two basic approaches to conducting attribute gage studies. The first approach uses known reference parts that represent the full range of variation of what is considered good or bad. To fully challenge the robustness and the ability of the measurement system, it is important to select some parts that are marginally considered good and marginally considered bad.

The other approach uses multiple operators without a standard to determine whether a part is acceptable or unacceptable. As with the aforementioned approach that uses a standard or reference parts, the study should be conducted with parts that represent the full range of variation.

Chapter 23

Reprocessing/Reuse and Cleaning of Medical Devices

In recent years, medical devices have become increasingly complex, and that has led to the manufacture of devices that are more difficult to clean and disinfect or sterilize. Scientific advances in the knowledge and technology involved in reprocessing reusable medical devices have also been observed. Proper reprocessing of reusable medical devices is necessary to help assure these devices remain safe and effective over their intended lifetime of multiple reuses and can be appropriately prepared for their next clinical use.

FDA GUIDANCE

The U.S. Food and Drug Administration (FDA) released its *Final Guidance for Industry and Staff; Processing/Reprocessing Medical Devices in Health Care Settings: Validation Methods and Labeling* on March 17, 2015, with an update to Appendix E issued on June 9, 2017.[185] The primary purpose of the guidance is to ensure that reusable medical devices are appropriate and safe for their application when reprocessed and reused. Both the manufacturer and user of a reusable device have responsibilities to ensure the safe and effective reprocessing of reusable medical devices.

This guidance provides recommendations regarding labeling and validation of reprocessing instructions for reusable devices. The guidance document does not apply to processes used in industrial settings to manufacture single-use devices intended to be sold sterile or to the reprocessing of devices labeled for single-use. The guidance specifically applies to four device reprocessing situations:

- Reusable medical devices initially supplied as sterile and requiring the user to reprocess (that is, clean and disinfect or sterilize) the device after initial use prior to the subsequent patient use.
- Reusable medical devices initially supplied nonsterile and requiring the user to process (that is, clean, clean and disinfect, or clean and sterilize) the device for initial use, as well as to reprocess the device after each use.
- Reusable medical devices intended to be reused only by a single patient and intended to be reprocessed between each use.
- Single-use medical devices initially supplied as nonsterile to the user and requiring the user to process the device prior to its use.

PROCESS OVERVIEW

Three steps are identified in the reprocessing of reusable medical devices:

- Reprocessing starts at the point of clinical use with initial cleaning and to prevent drying of soil and contaminants in and on the device.
- The reusable device is thoroughly cleaned in a dedicated cleaning area.
- Depending on its intended use, the device is disinfected or sterilized and routed back into use.

GENERAL CONSIDERATIONS FOR REUSABLE MEDICAL DEVICES

The designs of the reusable medical devices should ensure they are easy to clean, disinfect, and/or sterilize. Consideration should be made for complex designs to provide ports for flushing out contaminants and/or being able to disassemble them for thorough cleaning. Manufacturers should also provide adequate labeling for reprocessing, including the identification of cleaning/sterilization/disinfectant supplies that are required. Users should ensure they have appropriate infrastructure, such as facilities, equipment, and identified supplies, to follow the manufacturer's instructions.

GENERAL CONSIDERATIONS FOR REPROCESSING INSTRUCTIONS IN DEVICE LABELING

To comply with the requirements for adequate directions for use per 21 CFR Part 801, a reusable device should include reprocessing instructions. Provision of adequate and effective reprocessing instructions requires development of the cleaning process and disinfection or sterilization method, and validation of the cleaning process, disinfection, or sterilization method to demonstrate the instructions are complete and understandable. There are some devices for which the FDA has provided specific labeling guidance. These FDA guidance documents, technical information reports (TIRs) from AAMI (such as AAMI TIR 12, *Designing, testing, and labeling reusable medical devices for reprocessing in health care settings: A guide for medical device manufacturers,* and AAMI TIR30, *A compendium of processes, materials, test methods, and acceptance criteria for cleaning reusable medical devices),* ISO standards (ISO 17664:2017, *Sterilization of Medical Devices—Information to be provided by the manufacturer for the processing of resterilizable medical devices),* and current clinical practice guidelines should be used as references when developing reprocessing instructions.

Human factors should be considered when developing reprocessing instructions. The instructions should include consistent terminology and formatting to help the user better understand the content and compliance. The instructions should include any known human factors issues related to reprocessing the specific type of device. Post-market data can be used to identify these known issues. There are several FDA guidance documents and international standards on human factors that should be referenced when developing reprocessing instructions.

Cleaning, disinfection, and sterilization are distinct processes and therefore should be validated separately. The FDA will review labeling of reusable devices containing reprocessing instructions. If a U.S. premarket submission is required for a device, these validations should be completed prior to making a submission and adequate reprocessing instructions provided in the labeling.

FDA'S CRITERIA FOR REPROCESSING INSTRUCTIONS

The FDA guidance provides six criteria for reprocessing instructions it considers appropriate to ensure users understand and correctly follow the reprocessing instructions. The criteria are:

1. Labeling should reflect the intended use of the device.
2. All reprocessing instructions for reusable devices should advise users to thoroughly clean the device.
3. The instructions should indicate the appropriate microbicidal process for the device.
4. Reprocessing recommendations should be technically feasible and include only device and accessories that are legally marketed.
5. The instructions should be comprehensive.
6. The instructions should be understandable.

EU MDR REPROCESSING FOR SINGLE-USE MEDICAL DEVICES

Article 17 of the European Medical Devices Regulation 2017/745 (MDR) covers reprocessing of single-use medical devices. It indicates that reprocessing of single-use devices is only permitted if specifically allowed by national law in a member state. It also sets down requirements when such reprocessing is permitted, unless the member state sets out stricter national requirements.

Organizations that reprocess single-use devices for further use are considered to be the manufacturer of the reprocessed device and assume the obligations of the manufacturer in Article 10 of the MDR.

VALIDATION OF REPROCESSING METHODS

Manufacturers are required to validate the design of reusable devices and the reprocessing methods associated with reuse, in accordance with 21 CFR Part 820, to ensure the device can be effectively reprocessed over its life. Devices subject to design controls under § 820.30 must consider labeling, including reprocessing instructions, during design validation to assure user needs and intended uses are met.

Any known post-market human-factors-related issues with the specific reusable device or a similar device should be addressed when developing reprocessing instructions. Such issues may be identifiable by reviewing complaint files, published literature, and reported adverse events. Reprocessing instructions should also be validated under design controls to ensure users will be able to understand and follow the instructions.

VALIDATION OF CLEANING PROCESS

The FDA recommends developed cleaning processes and instructions are validated to demonstrate that reprocessing methods are adequate to allow the device to undergo further processing and the reprocessing instructions effectively convey the reprocessing methods. Validation of the cleaning process should use soils that are clinically relevant to the device, specify predetermined acceptance criteria for cleaning endpoints, address the most inaccessible device locations (for example, mating surfaces, lumens), and include a statistically relevant number of replicate samples. Cleaning validations should use an artificial soil that creates the worst-case challenge to the cleaning process, inoculate the device in all locations that are likely to contact the patient or that are difficult to clean, and simulate use conditions. Cleaning validation protocols should be conducted under challenge conditions (for example, shortest contact time, lowest temperature, weakest dilution) to account for worst-case cleaning process conditions.

VALIDATION OF TERMINAL REPROCESSING

The guidance recommends disinfection processes are validated in accordance with product-specific FDA guidance documents and recognized consensus standards. Similarly, the FDA recommends sterilization validation is completed in accordance with applicable FDA guidance documents and recognized consensus standards. Where possible, validation of terminal reprocessing should be completed in FDA-cleared equipment, for example, medical washer-disinfector, sterilizer.

Chapter 24

Common Medical Device Directives and Standards

Many directives and standards apply to medical device manufacturing. Those directives and standards generally apply to a specific area or specific type of medical device. Prior to auditing any medical device manufacturer, auditors must review the product manufactured to ensure they are aware of any specific directives and standards. This chapter is not intended as an exhaustive review of all the possible directives and standards available. The following are some of the more common directives and standards, and each is simply summarized to provide the reader with general information on their application. Please verify the current version and refer to the actual standards for specific information.

DIRECTIVES

Directive refers to a legislative act issued by the European Commission that establishes a general rule that EU member countries must achieve. An EU member country transfers each directive into national law as it deems appropriate; therefore, implementing laws may differ by individual country. See Chapter 6 for EU directives specific to medical devices. Additional directives related to medical devices include:

1. *Directive 2011/65/EU of the European Parliament and of the Council of 8 June 2011 on the restriction of the use of certain hazardous substances in electrical and electronic equipment (RoHS); Annex II was amended by Directive 2015/863 for the list of restricted substances (adding four additional restricted substances to the previous list of six).*

   The Restriction on Hazardous Substances (RoHS) directive lays down rules on the restriction of the use of hazardous substances in electrical and electronic equipment (EEE) with a view to contributing to the protection of human health and the environment, including the environmentally sound recovery and disposal of waste EEE.

2. *Directive 2012/19/EC of the European Parliament and of the Council of 4 July 2012 on waste electrical and electronic equipment (WEEE)*

   The purpose of this directive is the prevention of waste electrical and electronic equipment (WEEE) and, in addition, the reuse, recycling, and other forms of recovery of such wastes to reduce the disposal of waste. It also seeks to improve the environmental performance of all operators involved in the life cycle of EEE, for example, producers, distributors, and consumers, and in particular, those operators directly involved in the treatment of WEEE.

REGULATIONS

Regulation is a type of EU legislation that is similar to a national law, except it is applicable to all EU member states. *Regulation (EC) No 1907/2006 of the European Parliament and of the Council of 18 December 2006 concerning the Registration, Evaluation, Authorization and Restriction of Chemicals* (REACH) regulation is intended to ensure a high level of protection of human health and the environment, including the promotion of alternative methods for assessment of hazards of substances, as well as the free circulation of substances on the internal market while enhancing competitiveness and innovation. See Chapters 6 and 8 for EU regulations specific to medical devices (for example, MDR and IVDR).

The regulation lays down provisions on substances and preparations that are defined in the regulation. These provisions apply to the manufacture, market placement, or use of those substances on their own, in preparations, or in articles, and to the market placement of preparations. The regulation is based on the principle that it is for manufacturers, importers, and downstream users to ensure they manufacture, place on the market, or use such substances that do not adversely affect human health or the environment. Multiple guidance documents have been issued to facilitate implementation of REACH.[186]

STANDARDS

A *standard* can be described as horizontal or vertical depending on its scope. A horizontal standard applies to a wide range of devices, whereas a vertical standard is specific to a certain type of device. ISO 5840 *Cardiovascular implants—Cardiac valve prostheses* is an example of a vertical standard. Examples of horizontal standards include:

1. ANSI/AAMI/IEC 62304:2006/AMD 1:2015 *Medical device software—Software life cycle processes*

   This standard establishes a risk-based classification for software and the management guidelines for each class. Compliance to ANSI/AAMI/IEC 62304 provides a presumption of conformity to U.S. FDA requirements for software development for medical devices.

2. IEC 60601-1 Ed. 3.2 EN:2020 *Medical electrical equipment—Part 1: General requirements for basic safety and essential performance*

   IEC 60601 is a series of standards concerning electrical safety and electromagnetic compatibility (EMC). The IEC 60601-1 international standard applies to the basic safety and essential performance of medical electrical equipment and medical electrical systems. The standard provides information on how to identify and test hazards of medical electrical equipment. Any medical device that includes electrical systems must meet the requirements of the standard. Testing to the standard is done by certified laboratories and includes review of design and testing to ensure electrical safety. The standard also requires the manufacturer to have a risk management system in place. There are many collateral standards for IEC 60601-1 that provide particular requirements for specific medical devices, device environments, or medical device components (for example, IEC 60601-1-8 Ed. 2.2 EN:2020 *Medical Electrical Equipment—Part 1-8: General Requirements for Basic Safety and Essential Performance—Collateral Standard: General Requirements, Tests and Guidance for Alarm Systems In Medical Electrical Equipment and Medical Electrical Systems).* Depending on the specific device specification, the applicable collateral standards should be reviewed.

3. ISO 13485:2016 *Medical devices—Quality management systems—Requirements for regulatory purposes*

   This international standard establishes the framework for quality management systems to be implemented by medical device manufacturers. Compliance (and registration through a notified body) will establish presumption of conformity to the EU MDD/MDR. See Chapters 9 and 12 for further discussion of this standard.

4. ISO 14971:2019 *Medical devices—Application of risk management to medical devices*

   This international standard establishes the basic principles for risk management. The standard outlines a standard process to follow and provides guidance on characterizing risk. See Chapter 12 for further discussion of this standard.

5. ISO/IEC 62366-1:2015 + A1:2020 *Medical devices—Application of usability engineering to medical devices and IEC/TR 62366-2:2016 Medical Devices—Part 2: Guidance on the Application of Usability Engineering to Medical Devices*

   These standards provide guidance on human interfaces to medical devices and cover the requirements of the EU MDD/MDR and IVDD/IVDR. See Chapter 12 for further discussion of these standards.

Chapter 25

Sources for New and Evolving Standards

Standards are established by several national and international organizations. The International Organization for Standardization (ISO), European Committee for Standardization (CEN), American National Standards Institute (ANSI), Association for the Advancement of Medical Instrumentation (AAMI), and ASTM International (known as the American Society for Testing and Materials until 2001) are among the most well-known standards development organizations. Other organizations, such as the International Medical Device Regulators Forum (IMDRF), European Commission, Notified Body Operations Group (NBOG), and Medical Device Coordination Group (MDCG), provide guidance documents that help form the basis for medical device industry norms.

FDA-RECOGNIZED CONSENSUS STANDARDS

The FDA Modernization Act of 1997 (FDAMA) amended section 514 of the FD&C Act to allow the FDA to recognize consensus standards developed by international (for example, ISO) and national (for example, AAMI, ASTM) organizations in the premarket review process and other requirements. FDA personnel often participate in the development of these standards. The standards management staff (SMS) within the FDA facilitates recognition of medical device consensus standards. A consensus standard is considered recognized by the FDA once it has published a notice in the *Federal Register*. The FDA maintains an online database[187] of recognized consensus standards, updated the Monday following publication of the list of recognized consensus standards in the *Federal Register*. Additionally, the FDA document, *Appropriate Use of Voluntary Consensus Standards In Premarket Submissions for Medical Devices—Guidance for Industry and Food and Drug Administration Staff*, issued September 14, 2018, provides guidance to CDRH and industry about recognizing and using consensus standards when evaluating premarket submissions.[188]

HIERARCHY OF STANDARDS IN THE EU

Since the medical device directives and the new medical device regulation lay down the requirements for safety and performance in very general terms, standards can be important guides to the manufacturer. Standards interpret the safety objectives and provide a technical route to demonstrate compliance. While compliance with the safety and performance requirements of the EU Medical Device Regulation (MDR) and In Vitro Diagnostic Regulation (IVDR) is mandatory, the use of harmonized standards is voluntary. However, the following order of standards is most likely to assure compliance. Refer to Chapter 6 for additional information on the MDR.

EU Harmonized Standards

The most direct route to compliance through standards is the use of harmonized standards. A manufacturer that uses harmonized standards in the design and production of devices is presumed in conformity with the relevant safety and performance requirements (generally identified in Annex Z of the European version of a standard).

Harmonized standards that have been developed specifically to address essential requirements of the medical device directives provide an assumption of conformity. In their absence, the manufacturer is entitled to comply with any appropriate specifications that may demonstrate conformity with the safety and performance requirements. However, the manufacturer must bear the burden of proving that the use of specifications or standards other than harmonized standards supports the product meeting the safety and performance requirements.

A manufacturer may decide not to use an existing harmonized standard, but the burden is on the manufacturer to show that the standards or specifications used fulfill the same requirements. This approach is not recommended unless there are mitigating circumstances.

International Standards

Where no harmonized standards exist, manufacturers may use standards that are issued by international standards developing organizations such as the ISO and IEC.

National Standards

The third-best choice is the use of European national standards, to be used when no harmonized standards or international standards exist. Also, other sources such as AAMI, ASTM, and FDA may be considered.

EU HARMONIZED STANDARDS LISTING

The European Commission defines a harmonized standard as a European standard developed by a recognized European standards organization, such as the European Committee for Standardization (CEN), European Committee for Electrotechnical Standardization (CENELEC), or European Telecommunications Standards Institute (ETSI). These standards are created following a request from the European Commission to one of these organizations, and manufacturers or conformity assessment bodies may use them to demonstrate that products, services, or processes comply with relevant EU legislation.

The EU regularly publishes a summary list of harmonized standards in the *Official Journal of the European Union (OJEU)*. This listing provides the European Standardization Organization (ESO), reference number and title of the standard, date of first publication in the *OJEU*, reference of superseded standard, and date the superseded standard ceases to have presumption of conformity. The list of harmonized standards is also maintained online.[189]

MEDICAL DEVICE GUIDANCE (MEDDEV)

The European Commission provides MEDDEVs as guidance to assist device manufacturers and notified bodies with conformity assessment processes. MEDDEVs are developed through consultation with interested parties and updated regularly. Although MEDDEVs are not legally binding, there is an expectation that manufacturers and notified bodies follow them. MEDDEV guidance documents are available online[190] and include:

- 2.1 Scope, field of application, definition
  - MEDDEV 2.1/1 Definitions of "medical devices," "accessory," and "manufacturer"
  - MEDDEV 2.1/2 Field of application of directive "active implantable medical devices"
  - MEDDEV 2.1/2.1 Treatment of computers used to program implantable pulse generators
  - MEDDEV 2.1/3 Borderline products, drug-delivery products, and medical devices incorporating, as integral part, and ancillary medicinal substance or an ancillary human blood derivative
  - MEDDEV 2.1/4 Interface with other directives—Medical devices/ directive 89/336/EEC relating to electromagnetic compatibility and directive 89/86/EEC relating to personal protective equipment
  - MEDDEV 2.1/5 Medical devices with a measuring function
  - MEDDEV 2.1/6 Qualification and classification of stand-alone software
- 2.2 Essential requirements
  - MEDDEV 2.2/1 Electromagnetic compatibility (EMC) requirements
  - MEDDEV 2.2/3 "Use by" date
  - MEDDEV 2.2/4 Conformity assessment of in vitro fertilization (IVF) and assisted reproduction technologies (ART) products
- 2.4 Classification
  - MEDDEV 2.4/1 Classification of medical devices
- 2.5 Conformity assessment
  - MEDDEV 2.5/3 Subcontracting quality systems related
  - MEDDEV 2.5/5 Translation procedure

  - MEDDEV 2.5/6 Homogenous batches (verification of manufacturers' products)
  - MEDDEV 2.5/7 Conformity assessment of breast implants
  - MEDDEV 2.5/9 Evaluation of medical devices incorporating products containing natural rubber latex
  - MEDDEV 2.5/10 Guideline for Authorized Representatives
- 2.7 Clinical investigation, clinical evaluation
  - MEDDEV 2.7/1 Clinical evaluation: Guide for manufacturers and notified bodies
  - MEDDEV 2.7/2 Guidelines for Competent Authorities for making a validation/assessment of a clinical investigation application under directives 90/385/EEC and 93/42/EC
  - MEDDEV 2.7/3 Clinical investigations: Serious adverse event reporting under directives 90/385/EEC and 93/42/EC
  - MEDDEV 2.7/4 Guidelines on clinical investigations: A guide for manufacturers and notified bodies
- 2.10 Notified bodies
  - MEDDEV 2.10/2 Designation and monitoring of notified bodies within the framework of EC Directives on medical devices
- 2.12 Market surveillance
  - MEDDEV 2.12/1 Guidelines on a medical devices vigilance system
  - MEDDEV 2.12/2 Post-market clinical follow-up (PMCF) studies
- 2.13 Transitional period
  - MEDDEV 2.13 Commission communication on the application of transitional provision of directive 93/42/EEC relating to medical devices (Official Journal 98/C242/05)
- 2.14 In-vitro diagnostic (IVD)
  - MEDDEV 2.14/1 Borderline and classification issues. A guide for manufacturers and notified bodies
  - MEDDEV 2.14/2 Research use only products
  - MEDDEV 2.14/3 Supply of instructions for use (IFU) and other information for IVD medical devices
  - MEDDEV 2.14/4 CE marking of blood based IVD medical devices for variant Creutzfeldt-Jakob Disease (vCJD) based on detection of abnormal PrP (host protein)
- 2.15 Other
  - MEDDEV 2.15 Committees/working groups contributing to the implementation of the medical device directives

Medical Device Coordination Group (MDCG)/Notified Body Operations Group (NBOG)

The MDR and the IVDR established the Medical Device Coordination Group (MDCG) to ensure harmonized implementation. The MDCG endorses the Notified Body Operations Group (NBOG) Best Practices Guides (BPG) that are related to the MDR and IVDR. There are several guidance documents that are found on the European Commission website, such as those for UDI, Eudamed (the database for product and manufacturer information), European Medical Device Nomenclature (EMDN), notified bodies, clinical investigation and evaluation, and new technologies.

International Medical Device Regulators Forum (IMDRF)

The International Medical Device Regulators Forum (IMDRF) is made up of volunteers from medical device regulatory bodies from around the world. They provide guidance documents to assist with international medical device regulatory harmonization. The IMDRF took over from the Global Harmonization Task Force (GHTF) and has built upon the foundations they initiated. There are many guidance documents available on their website (www.imdrf.org) and include cybersecurity, UDI, process validation, clinical evaluations, software, and post-market surveillance.

Part IV

Quality Tools and Techniques

Chapter 26

Quality Control and Problem-Solving Tools

Auditors may or may not use these basic tools during an audit, but they will need to understand and interpret them. These tools, in a large part, form the basis for the language of quality. Auditors must be able to recognize them, understand their purpose, interpret their results, and often determine whether the tool chosen is appropriate for the task and is properly applied.

Quality tools can help you identify causes, understand processes, collect and analyze data, generate ideas, keep projects on track, and make informed decisions for all your continuous improvement activities. Statistical methods such as process capability and sampling are additional tools for an auditor, especially when determining how many records should be reviewed during an audit. In this chapter, each tool will be introduced and explained, indicating how and why it is used.

PARETO CHARTS

A Pareto chart is used to graphically summarize and display the relative importance of the differences between groups of data. The Pareto principle states that 20 percent of causes determine 80 percent of problems. For example, 80 percent of the delays in a schedule arise from 20 percent of the possible causes of the delays. A Pareto chart quickly helps to identify issues through a visual depiction of the data from the highest impact to the lowest impact on quality. Figure 26.1 is an example of a Pareto chart.

CAUSE AND EFFECT

The cause and effect diagram, sometimes called an Ishikawa diagram or fishbone diagram, is used to associate multiple possible causes with a single effect. Thus, given a particular effect, the diagram is constructed to identify and organize possible causes for it. The primary branch represents the effect (the quality characteristic that is intended to be improved and controlled) and is typically labeled on the right side of the diagram. Each major branch of the diagram corresponds to a major cause (or class of causes) that directly relates to the effect. Minor branches correspond to more detailed causal factors. This type of diagram is useful in any analysis, as it illustrates the relationship between cause and effect in a rational manner. Causes can be derived from brainstorming sessions. These groups can then be labeled as categories of the fishbone. Causes can be traced back to root causes using this technique. Figure 26.2 is an example of a cause and effect diagram. The main categories are common but not an exhaustive list. Other categories may be chosen depending upon the problem being solved.

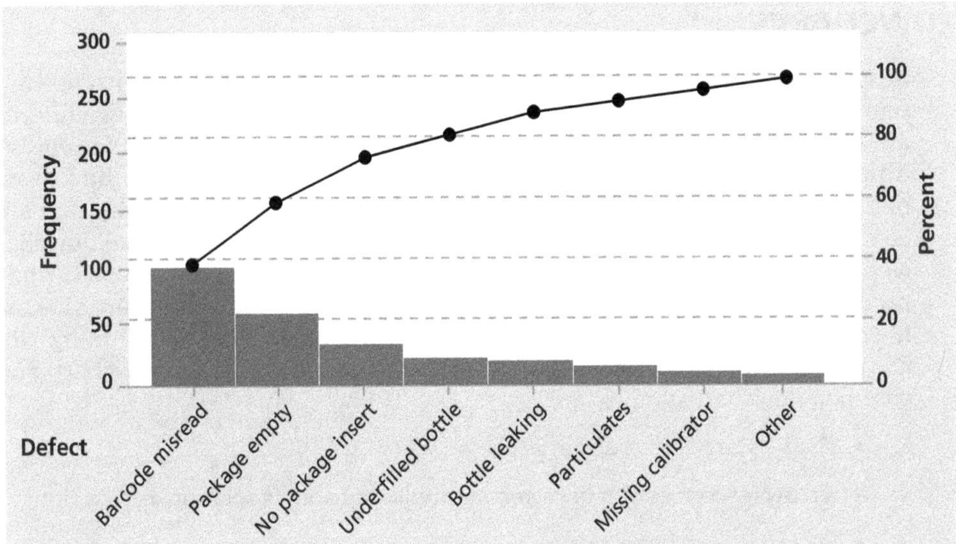

C2	104	56	34	21	19	12	10	9
Percent	39.2	21.1	12.8	7.9	7.2	4.5	3.8	3.4
Cum %	39.2	60.4	73.2	81.1	88.3	92.8	96.6	100.0

Figure 26.1 Pareto chart.

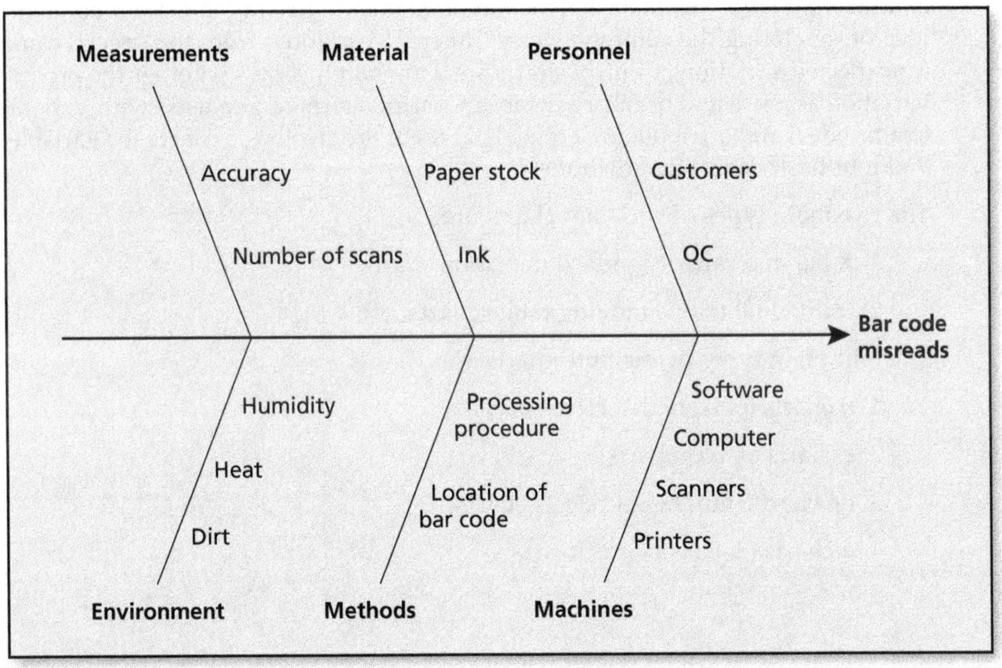

Figure 26.2 Cause and effect diagram.

FLOWCHARTS

A flowchart is a pictorial representation of a process. By breaking the process down into its constituent steps, flowcharts can be useful in identifying where errors are likely to be found in the system. Flowcharts use special shapes to represent different types of actions or steps in a process. Lines and arrows show the sequence of the steps and the relationships among them. Flowcharts are flexible and are a common tool for quality practitioners. Medical device companies use flowcharts as part of their risk management process to identify high-risk manufacturing or product-usage steps that could lead to potential harms. Flowcharts are also used in software development processes to map out scenarios for determining when alarms should be activated. Figure 26.3 shows an example of a flowchart. Some common flowchart symbols are:

- Oval—start or end of the process
- Arrows—connectors between symbols that shows relationship or flow
- Rectangle—process steps
- Diamond—decision points where potential risks or errors can occur

STATISTICAL PROCESS CONTROL

There are several methods used to trend data to highlight both the preventive and corrective nature of the system. Plotting data over time is a good visual method to identify trends. Statistical process control (SPC) techniques such as control charts provide an objective method to identify trends. SPC is based on the idea of separating the common cause (inherent variation) from the special cause (unexpected variation). Control charts are a method to assess whether the process variation is consistent or unpredictable. Control charts can be used with variable (continuous) and attribute (discrete) data; there are two basic charts for variables and four basic charts for attributes.

The two main types of variables charts are:

1. X-bar and range/standard deviation charts
2. Individual with a moving range charts

The four main types of attribute charts are:

1. p charts (percent defective charts)
2. c charts (defect charts)
3. np charts (number of rejects charts)
4. u charts (defects per unit charts)

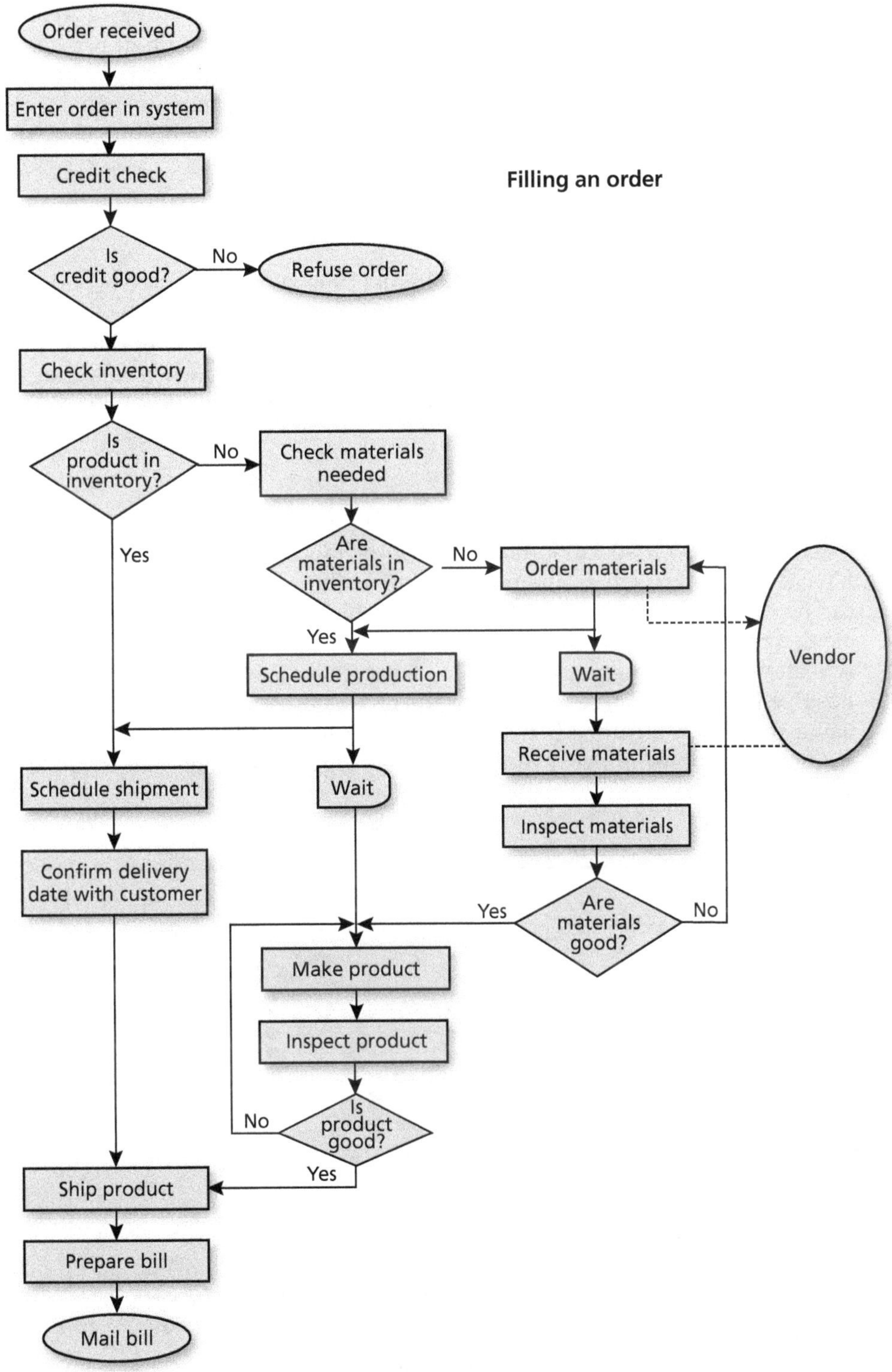

Figure 26.3 Process flowchart.

X-bar and range/standard deviation charts are used when subgroups of data are collected. An individual chart is used when a single data point is taken at a given time point. The p chart is used to estimate the percent defective. The c chart measures the number of defects in a sample when all subgroups are equal. The np chart is similar to the p chart with restriction of a constant subgroup size. The u chart measures the number of nonconformities per unit.

CHECK SHEETS

The check sheet is used to collect data in real time at the location where the data are generated. The data can be quantitative (numerical) or qualitative (descriptive). Check sheets are used when data can be observed and collected repeatedly by the same person or at the same location. They are primarily used when collecting data on the frequency or patterns of events, problems, defects, or defect location.

SCATTER DIAGRAM

Scatter diagrams are simple to construct and might be the best analysis when first looking at a new association between two or more variables. These are simply XY charts (graphs) where the output (dependent variable) is usually shown on the y-axis and the drivers (independent variable) on the x-axis. All dots grouped along a rough curve (or straight line) indicate further analysis could be valuable. A scatter plot can suggest correlations between variables. Correlations may be positive (rising), negative (falling), or uncorrelated. A formal statistical analysis using regression techniques with an equation for the line can be employed to study the relationship between the variables. Figure 26.4 shows an example of a scatter diagram.

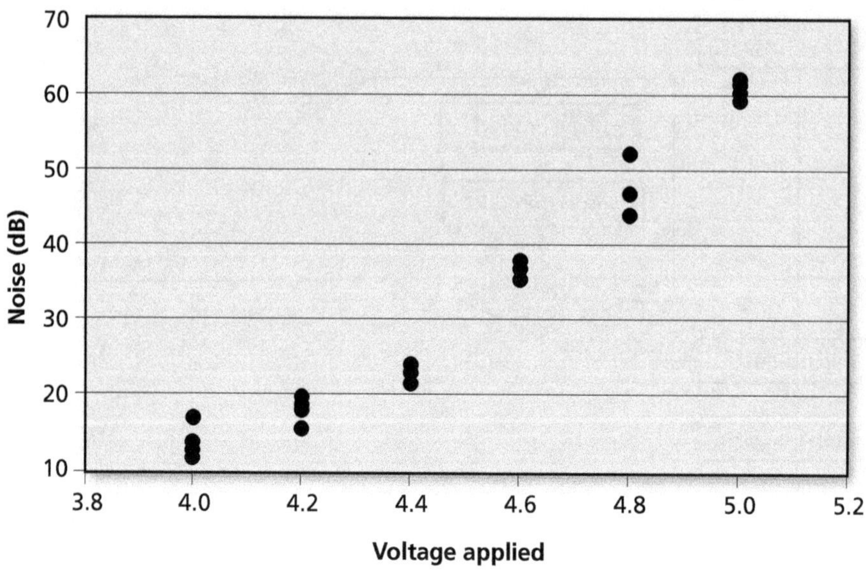

Figure 26.4 Scatter plot.

HISTOGRAMS

A histogram is used to assess the shape and spread of continuous sample data. Use a histogram prior to or in conjunction with an analysis to help confirm assumptions and guide further analysis. Histograms are sometimes confused with bar charts. A histogram is used for continuous data, where the bins represent ranges of data, while a bar chart is a plot of categorical variables. Figure 26.5 is an example of a histogram.

A histogram is a frequency distribution that shows how often each different value in a set of data occurs. A histogram is used when you:

- Are using data that are numerical
- Want to see the shape of the data's distribution, especially when determining whether the output of a process is distributed approximately normally
- Are analyzing whether a process can meet the customer's requirements
- Are analyzing the output from a supplier's process
- Are seeing whether a process change has occurred from one time period to another
- Are determining whether the outputs of two or more processes are different
- Wish to communicate the distribution of data quickly and easily to others

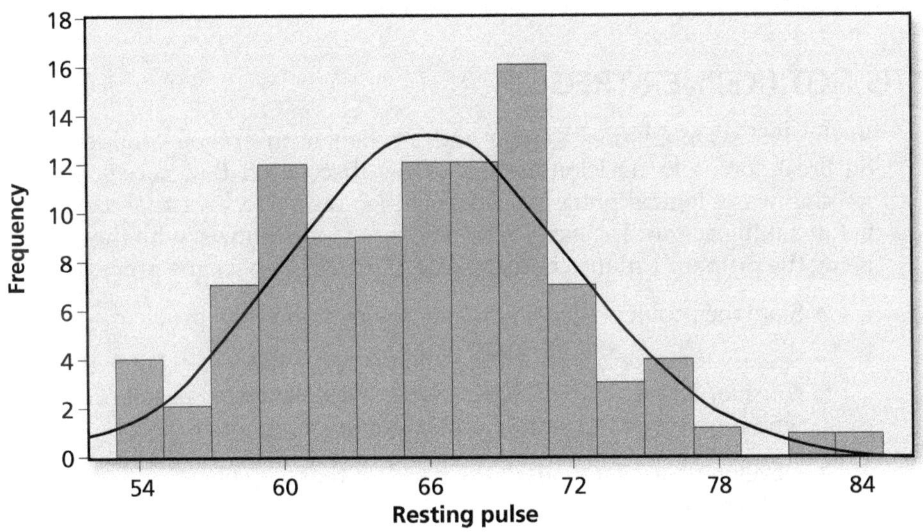

Figure 26.5 Histogram.

5 WHYS

The 5 Whys is an iterative technique used to explore the cause-and-effect relationships underlying a particular problem. By repeating the interrogatory question of "Why" the root cause of a defect or problem can be determined. The answer from a previous "Why" is the basis of the next "Why." The value of five is subjective based on anecdotal evidence on the number of iterations needed to resolve the problem. It is possible for more or less than five "Whys" to be needed to identify a root cause. Not all problems have a single root cause. This process is repeated with a different set of questions each time.

Unfortunately, this technique has no hard-and-fast guidelines about what questions to explore. The outcome depends on the knowledge and persistence of the people involved. The following is an example of how the 5 Whys can be used to identify the root cause of a failed pacemaker.

1. Why did the pacemaker stop working?
   a. The battery is dead.
2. Why is the battery dead?
   b. It has been 10 years since the pacemaker was implanted.
3. Why did the patient wait 10 years to replace the battery?
   c. The patient was never informed of battery life.
4. Why was the patient never informed of battery life?
   d. It was not part of the patient's discharge papers.
5. Root cause: Discharge papers include a battery check after five years.

IS/IS NOT (KEPNER-TREGOE)

In the 1950s, Dr. Charles Kepner and Dr. Benjamin Tregoe conducted research on breakdowns in decision-making. They discovered that successful decision-making was a logical process used to gather, organize, and analyze information before taking action. The basis of the approach is as follows, with the is/is not step being the primary unique characteristic of the Kepner-Tregoe process:

- State the problem (definition and description of the problem).
- Specify the problem by asking what is and what is not. For example, consider when and where the problem occurs and does not occur. Ask who is involved when the problem occurs, and who is not.
- Develop possible causes of the problem that are consistent with what is and what is not.
- Test and verify possible causes.
- Determine the most probable cause (root cause).
- Verify any assumptions.
- Try the best possible solution and monitor the situation after applying corrective actions.

ROOT CAUSE ANALYSIS

Root cause analysis (RCA) is a method for determining the cause of an ordered sequence of events that lead to an outcome or effect of interest. Commonly, root cause is used to describe the depth in the course of events where an intervention could reasonably be implemented to change performance and prevent an undesirable outcome. Quality tools such as the 5 Whys and cause and effect diagrams are useful to identify the root cause. RCA is a four-step process involving the following:

- Collecting data
- Identifying causal factor
- Identifying the root cause
- Generating a recommendation (that is, a solution) and implementation.[191]

As in any good closed-loop problem-solving process, verification of the effectiveness of the solution(s) should also be done.

PLAN-DO-CHECK-ACT

Plan-do-check-act (PDCA) is an iterative four-step process attributed to Dr. W. Edwards Deming. Plan addresses the what and why of the problem. The do is the experimental phase where you test your plan. Check involves comparing the output of the experiments with the expectations of the plan. Action is taken based on the output, either to implement a change or to revise the experiment or hypothesis.

SETTING ALERT AND ACTION LEVELS

Action and alert levels are internally set limits that are used to maintain process control. The determination of alert and action limits is usually based on historical data to avoid over-control of the process. Many organizations call this process guard banding, as the limits are narrower than the guidance or defined limits (specification limits). An alert limit allows the organization to increase vigilance without taking any action at this time. There may be an opportunity to evaluate if any deviations were taken from validated process conditions. Action limits are a signal of an apparent deviation that requires immediate action. No further processing should be performed until RCA is performed. Typically, alert limits are set as plus and minus two sigma, while the action limits are set as plus and minus three sigma. Alert and action items usually are part of an organization's SPC program.

Chapter 27

Process Improvement Techniques

Several techniques are available that would be considered quality tools. This chapter provides a brief explanation of several of these.

PROCESS CAPABILITY

Process capability compares the output of an in-control process to the specification limits by using capability indices. The comparison is made by forming the ratio of the spread between the process specifications (the specification "width") and the spread of the process values, as measured by six process standard deviation units (the process "width"). There are several common indices that are used to assess process capability. Some are used for short-term (C_p and C_{pk}) and others for long-term (P_p and P_{pk}) capability. C_p and P_p are estimates that determine if the process is capable if the process mean were to be centered between the specification limits. C_{pk} and P_{pk} are estimates that determine if the process is capable of producing, considering that the process mean may not be centered between the specification limits. All indices assume that the process output is approximately normally distributed.

$$C_p/P_p = \frac{USL - LSL}{6S}$$

$$C_{pk}/P_{pk} = min\left\{ \frac{USL - \overline{X}}{3S} ; \frac{\overline{X} - LSL}{3S} \right\}$$

where USL is the upper specification limit, LSL is the lower specification limit, $\overline{X}$ is the average, and S is the standard deviation. Note that S is different for P_p/P_{pk} calculations versus C_p/C_{pk} calculations. P_p and P_{pk} use the overall, or long-term, standard deviation. C_p and C_{pk} use the within-subgroup, or short-term, standard deviation.

As C_{pk} decreases, the probability of exhibiting an output that is outside its specification limits increases. The relationship between C_{pk} and parts per million (ppm) is defined using the standard normal distribution or Z-value. The total expected ppm is the sum of $Z(C_{pkL})$ and $Z(C_{pkU})$. Table 27.1 is an example of the calculation.

Table 27.1 Parts per million determination.

LSL	90
USL	110
$\overline{X}$	102
S	3
Lower specification C_{pk} (C_{pkL})	1.33
Upper specification C_{pk} (C_{pkU})	0.89
Parts per million lower specification (ppm_L)	32
Parts per million upper specification (ppm_U)	3830
Total parts per million (ppm)	3862

SIX SIGMA

Six Sigma is a business management strategy originally developed by Motorola USA in 1986. Six Sigma became well known after Jack Welch made it a central focus of his business strategy at General Electric in 1995, and today it is widely used in many sectors of industry.

Six Sigma seeks to improve the quality of process outputs by identifying and removing the causes of defects (errors) and minimizing variability in manufacturing and business processes. It uses a set of quality management methods, including statistical methods, and creates a special infrastructure of people within the organization (for example, Black Belts, Green Belts) who are experts in these methods. Each Six Sigma project carried out within an organization follows a defined sequence of steps (DMAIC) and has quantified financial targets (cost reduction and/or profit increase).

The term Six Sigma originated from terminology associated with manufacturing, specifically with statistical modeling of manufacturing processes. The maturity of a manufacturing process can be described by a sigma rating indicating its yield, or the percentage of defect-free products it creates. A six-sigma process is one in which 99.99966 percent of the products manufactured are statistically expected to be free of defects (3.4 defects per million). Motorola set a goal of six sigma for all of its manufacturing operations, and this goal became a byword for the management and engineering practices used to achieve it.

The DMAIC improvement model consists of five steps: define, measure, analyze, improve and control.

- *Define* refers to defining the goals of any given improvement effort. Top level improvement goals may include strategic efforts, such as increasing the ROI or market share. Closer to the operations level, an organization's goal may involve bettering the output of a given department. On the project level, the goals may involve decreasing defects and increasing production. Data mining methods are applied here for identifying prospective opportunities for enhancement.

- *Measure* refers to measuring the current process. Reliable and valid metrics need to be established so the different steps toward achieving the goal can be defined. This starts with the definition of the current baseline. Exploratory and descriptive data analyses are applied here for assisting with understanding the data.
- *Analyze* refers to the analysis of the system to recognize the disparity between the current system performance and the goal. Statistical tools are applied here for guiding the analysis.
- *Improve* refers to the improvements made to the system. Creativity must be employed in order to discover fresh ways of doing things cheaper, faster, and better. Project management and other management and planning tools are used here to facilitate the implementation of the new methodology. Statistical methods are also used to validate improvements that have been made.
- *Control* refers to controlling the new system. The enhanced system must be institutionalized through the modification of compensation and incentive programs, policies, material requirements planning, procedures, operating instructions, budgets, and other systems of management. ISO 9000 may be utilized to ensure accuracy of the documentation.

LEAN TOOLS

The term lean thinking refers to the use of ideas originally employed in lean manufacturing to improve functions in all departments of an enterprise. The National Institute of Standards and Technology (NIST), through its Manufacturing Extension Partnership, defines lean as "a systematic approach to identifying and eliminating waste (non-value-added activities) through continuous improvement by flowing the product at the pull of the customer in pursuit of perfection." ASQ defines non-value-added as "a term that describes a process step or function that is not required for the direct achievement of process output. This step or function is identified and examined for potential elimination."

Lean manufacturing seeks to eliminate or reduce these wastes by use of the following:

- Teamwork with well-informed, cross-trained employees who participate in the decisions that impact their function
- Clean, organized, and well-marked workspaces
- Flow systems instead of batch and queue systems (that is, reduce batch size toward its ultimate ideal, one)
- Pull systems instead of push systems (that is, replenish what the customer has consumed)
- Reduced lead times through more efficient processing, setups, and scheduling

The history of lean thinking may be traced to Eli Whitney, who is credited with spreading the concept of part interchangeability. Henry Ford, who went to great lengths to reduce cycle times, furthered the idea of lean thinking and later the Toyota Production System (TPS) packaged most of the tools and concepts now known as lean manufacturing.[192]

MEASUREMENT SYSTEMS ANALYSIS

Measurement systems analysis (MSA) is used to understand and quantify the variability associated with measurements and measurement systems. All processes, no matter how well they are designed and executed, possess the component of variability. It is only the degree of variability that varies from process to process.

The fourth edition of *Measurement Systems Analysis Reference Manual* (2010), from the Automotive Industry Action Group (AIAG), defines measurement as "the assignment of numbers [or values] to material things to represent the relations among them with respect to particular properties." Similarly, the manual defines a measurement system as "the collection of instruments or gauges, standards, operations, methods, fixtures, software, personnel, environment and assumptions used to quantify a unit of measure or fix assessment to the feature characteristic being measured; the complete process used to obtain measurements."

"MSA" is commonly used interchangeably with "gage repeatability and reproducibility" (gage R&R). MSA is a more comprehensive analysis quantifying variability components from gage stability, gage bias, gage linearity, gage repeatability, and reproducibility (that is, variability from operator measurements). Gage R&R is, in fact, a subset or component of MSA.[193]

For more information on MSA, including definitions of terms, please refer to Chapter 22, which describes MSA within the context of validation.

COST OF QUALITY

Cost of quality (COQ) or quality costs is the total cost associated with making, finding, repairing, or preventing defects. The following categories are associated with these costs: internal failure costs, external failure costs, appraisal costs, and prevention costs.

Internal failure costs include all the costs associated with the following: scrap, rework, retest, downtime, yield losses, and disposition of nonconforming material. External failure costs are those associated with defects detected after shipment to the customer. Appraisal costs are those associated with evaluation of product condition or status during a product's first passage through the manufacturing and assembly process. Prevention costs are those incurred to keep failure and appraisal costs to a minimum.

COQ is an important indicator of the effectiveness of a company's quality management system. It is important to relate the cost of quality to other operational data, for example, COQ as a percentage of sales or compared to profit.[194]

Chapter 28

Data Types and Sampling

QUALITATIVE AND QUANTITATIVE ANALYSIS

Qualitative Analysis

The aim of qualitative analysis is a complete, detailed description without quantification. No attempt is made to assign frequencies to the features that are identified in the data, although their relative relationship should be noted. Qualitative analysis allows for fine distinctions to be drawn because it is not necessary to put the data into a finite number of classifications. Findings of qualitative analysis are not tested to discover whether they are statistically significant or due to chance. One type of qualitative data would simply be presence or absence of a feature.

Quantitative Analysis

In quantitative analysis, features are counted, and more complex statistical models are constructed in an attempt to explain what is observed. Findings can be generalized to a larger population, and direct comparisons can be made between two populations as long as valid sampling and significance techniques have been used. Thus, quantitative analysis allows us to discover which phenomena are likely to be genuine reflections of the population and which are merely chance occurrences. The more basic task of just looking at a single variety allows one to get a precise picture of the frequency and rarity of particular phenomena and thus their relative normality or abnormality. However, the picture of the data that emerges from quantitative analysis is less rich than that obtained from qualitative analysis.

Quantitative data can be used to detect patterns and trends through the analysis of measurements conducted over time. Control charts, as described in Chapter 26, are a useful tool for quantitative analysis. Control charts or other time-based analysis can determine the difference between systemic problems and isolated problems.

- Systemic problems are due to a process not being inherently capable of meeting requirements. The system may be stable and in control, but the overall results are not acceptable. Systemic problems are due to common causes. A change to the system or structure is necessary to remediate.

- Isolated problems are unexpected and may occur occasionally in a system that is generally stable and in control. They are, however, an indication of instability and can be solved by addressing the root cause of the specific problem rather than changing the entire system. Isolated problems are due to special causes.

LEVELS OF MEASUREMENT

The measurements that lead to data and analysis can be classified further. Qualitative analysis refers to measurements that describe category or order. Quantitative analysis refers to measurements that describe numerical differences and ratios. Table 28.1 describes the four levels of measurement.

Table 28.1 Levels of measurement.

Measurement level	Qualitative or quantitative	Definition	Example
Nominal	Qualitative	Names, categories, or counts with no meaningful order.	The colors of M&M candies in a bag were: • Red 15 • Green 11 • Yellow 9 • Brown 8 • Blue 4
Ordinal	Qualitative	Order has some meaning, but differences between values are not meaningful.	The top three students had grade-point averages of: 1. 3.85 2. 3.72 3. 3.44 The differences are not meaningful to the ranks other than to set the order.
Interval	Quantitative	Order has meaning and differences between values can be determined. Ratios are not meaningful.	The average temperatures in winter, spring, and summer were 40 °F, 60 °F, and 80 °F, respectively. Differences are meaningful, but ratios are not. 80 °F is not twice as warm as 40 °F on a scientific scale.
Ratio	Quantitative	Both differences and ratios are meaningful. There is a valid starting point of zero.	The cost of a small bag of M&Ms is $1.50 and a large bag costs $3.00. The ratio is meaningful—the large bag costs twice as much.

ATTRIBUTES AND VARIABLES DATA

Basically, there are two types of data that may be collected as part of a problem-solving process: attribute data (or go/no-go information) and variable data (or measurement information). Variable data are preferred when available since fewer data points are required to make more reliable conclusions. However, collecting variable data is usually more expensive than collecting attribute data due to the nature of obtaining numerical measurements. On the other hand, attribute plans are nonparametric, meaning they do not assume a specific distribution and hence require more samples to obtain the same degree of confidence as variable plans. When comparing attribute and variable sampling plans, a cost/benefit analysis should be performed to weigh the value of the information and conclusions versus the overall cost.

Because the level of sensitivity of a measurement depends on the precision of the measuring device, there are times when variable data can be treated as attribute data. For example, suppose aluminum pins are produced that may be smaller than 1.065 inches in diameter but not larger. Rather than measuring each pin or even a sample of pins, options include:

- Create a plate that has a hole 1.065 inches in diameter bored through it (a go/no-go gauge).
- Insert each pin to be inspected into the hole.
- Classify any pin that passes through the hole as acceptable, treating others as rejects.

In this case, treating the variable as an attribute offers an efficient way to determine whether the pin will be effective. However, in general, treating variable data as attribute data will create a loss of information about the process capability, so they should be used with caution.

SAMPLING

Acceptance of incoming, in-process, or final product is often based on measuring a sample taken from a larger quantity of material. ISO 13485:2016 and the FDA's Quality System Regulation (QSR) both require that any time sampling plans are used, they must be based on a valid statistical rationale. Sampling is done to make inferences about an entire population without testing or inspecting every item in the population.

Auditors should be familiar with sampling plans for at least two reasons. First, an auditor will be evaluating quality systems that use statistical techniques such as sampling. An auditor should be able to converse intelligently with the auditee and be able to evaluate the suitability and effectiveness of sampling plans. Second, an auditor may utilize sampling principles first-hand during the course of an audit. For example, evaluating the compliance and effectiveness of a customer complaint-handling process may require reviewing a sample of customer complaints. If the sample of customer complaints was deemed compliant and acceptable, then the auditor could infer that the overall process is acceptable. Chapter 3 contains additional guidance on audit sampling.

Sampling plans utilize specific terms. Some of the most important are listed below.

- Acceptance quality limit or acceptable quality level (AQL)—The maximum defective rate or quality level having a "high" probability of being accepted, typically a 95 percent probability. AQL lots would therefore be routinely accepted by the sampling plan. AQL is associated with the Type I, or α, error.
- Producer's risk—The alpha (α) risk of rejecting a lot that is truly acceptable according to the desired quality level. This risk can lead to an error called alpha error or Type I error, which is the error of rejecting a good lot. The producer's risk is commonly set to 0.05.
- Confidence level—The probability of not making a Type I, or α, error. Confidence level is the probability of correctly rejecting a "bad" lot. Confidence is quantified as $1-\alpha$.
- Rejectable quality level (RQL) or lot tolerance percent defective (LTPD)—The maximum defective rate or quality level having a "low" probability of being accepted, typically a 10 percent probability. RQL lots would therefore be routinely rejected by the sampling plan. RQL is associated with the Type II, or β, error.
- Consumer's risk—The beta (β) risk of accepting a lot that is truly rejectable according to the desired quality level. This risk can lead to an error called beta error, or Type II error, which is the error of accepting a bad lot. The consumer's risk is commonly set to 0.10.
- Power of test—The probability of not making a Type II, or β, error. Power is the probability of correctly accepting a "good" lot. Power is quantified as $1-\beta$.

For additional definitions and explanations, the reader is referred to ISO 2859-1:1999 and A1:2011 *Sampling procedures for inspection by attributes—Part 1: Sampling schemes indexed by acceptance quality limit (AQL) for lot-by-lot inspection.* ISO 2859 also contains sampling strategies and tables.

The fundamental tool for selecting a sampling plan is the operating characteristic (OC) curve, shown in Figure 28.1. An OC curve has the defective rate on the horizontal axis and the probability of accepting a lot on the vertical axis. Figure 28.1 shows OC curves for accepting various numbers of defects (that is, 0, 3, 5, 10, and 15) in a sample size of 315. AQL and RQL lines are shown at 95 percent and 10 percent, respectively.

Risk management in conjunction with statistics can be a systematic process for the assessment, control, communication, and review of risks. Statistical tools support and facilitate quality risk management. Sample sizes for testing and inspection are derived from the risk management process, where the statistical risks are relative to the product risks. There is a relationship between the risk and sample size, as a greater number of samples should be tested for higher-risk situations. Desired confidence levels also vary depending on variation and risk. Table 28.2 is an example of higher risk levels being tested to lower AQLs and higher confidence levels.

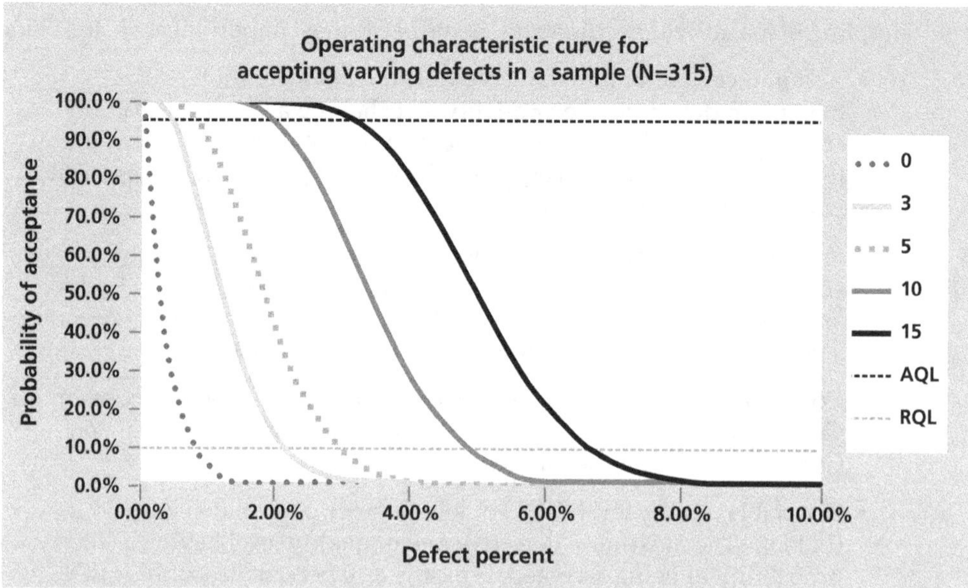

Figure 28.1 Operating characteristic curve.

Table 28.2 Linking risk to testing requirements.

Risk level from risk analysis	Defect class	AQL	Confidence level (alpha)
5 (highest risk)	Critical	0.015%	95% (5%)
4	Major	0.25%	95% (5%)
3	Minor	2.0%	90% (10%)
1-2 (lowest risk)	Cosmetic	10.0%	90% (10%)

Not all requirements are statistical. A valid sample might be a single test or unit, which is often called type testing. Type testing is used when one unit is representative of all units. Functional testing or testing of a final system is an example of such a test strategy. Nonstatistical tests, such as verification of the existence of a feature, can also be performed on a single unit of product. In all cases, there should be written criteria for when a test strategy is considered nonstatistical versus when the strategy is considered statistical. Further, for requirements that are statistical but for which recognized standards exist specifying a sample size and acceptance criteria, use of the recognized standard can be considered a valid justification.

When the distribution of measurements on products is Gaussian or normal (which may be visualized via a histogram), acceptance can be based on sampling plans using variables instead of attributes. Variable sampling plans are usually indexed using AQL just as attribute sampling plans are. As with attribute testing, larger sample sizes in variable testing provide greater confidence.

Part V
Appendices

Appendix A
Glossary of Terms

abnormal use—An intentional act or intentional omission of an act by the responsible organization or user of a medical device as a result of conduct that is beyond any further reasonable means of risk control by the manufacturer.

absorbed dose—The quantity of radiation energy imparted per unit mass of matter. The unit of absorbed dose is the gray (Gy), where one gray is equivalent to absorption of one joule per kilogram.

acceptance quality limit or acceptable quality level (AQL)—The maximum defective rate or quality level having a "high" probability of being accepted, typically a 95 percent probability. AQL lots would therefore be routinely accepted by the sampling plan. AQL is associated with the Type I, or α, error.

accessory—An article that, while not a device, is intended specifically by its manufacturer to be used together with a device in accordance with the use of the device intended by the manufacturer of the device.

accompanying document—A document accompanying a medical device and containing information for use by those accountable for the installation, use, and maintenance of the medical device, particularly regarding safety.

act—The Food, Drug, and Cosmetic Act (FD&C Act), 21 USC 321 et seq., as amended.

active implantable medical device—Any active medical device that is intended to be totally or partially introduced, surgically or medically, into the human body or by medical intervention into a natural orifice, and that is intended to remain after the procedure.

active medical device—Any medical device relying for its functioning on a source of electrical energy or any source of power other than that directly generated by the human body or gravity.

aeration—The removal of ethylene oxide and its reaction products (such as ethylene chlorohydrin) from a medical device using forced warm air ventilation.

ALCOA—When applied to data, means attributable, legible, contemporaneously recorded, original, and accurate.

analyte specific reagents (ASRs)—Antibodies, both polyclonal and monoclonal, specific receptor proteins, ligands, nucleic acid sequences, and similar reagents, which, through specific binding or chemical reaction with substances in a specimen, are intended for use in a diagnostic application for identification and quantification of an individual chemical substance or ligand in biological specimens.

aseptic—A condition resulting from a process in which sterile product is packaged in sterile containers in a manner that avoids contamination of the product, for example, the aseptic filling of sterile vials with sterile liquid.

audit—A systematic and independent examination to determine whether quality activities and related results comply with planned arrangements, and whether these arrangements are implemented effectively and are suitable to achieve objectives.

audit language—The language(s) routinely used for the communication or exchange of information between an auditee's personnel and auditors.

auditee—Any organization whose quality systems are to be audited for compliance with the relevant medical device regulatory requirements.

auditing organization—A body designated, based on specific regulations, to carry out audits according to assigned tasks.

auditor—A person with relevant qualifications and competence to perform audits or specified parts of such audits and who belongs to, or is authorized by, the auditing organization.

authorized representative (EU)—Any natural or legal person established in the community who, explicitly designated by the manufacturer, acts and may be addressed by authorities and bodies in the community instead of the manufacturer with regard to the latter's obligations under this directive.

bacteriostasis/fungistasis test—A test that utilizes selected microorganisms to demonstrate the presence of substances that may inhibit the multiplication of the microorganisms.

batch—A defined quantity of bulk, intermediate, or finished product that is intended or purported to be uniform in character and quality and that has been produced during a defined cycle of manufacture.

bias—The difference between a measured value and a known or accepted reference value.

bioburden—The population of living microorganisms, bacterial and fungal, on a raw material, component, finished product, or package.

biological indicator—A carrier inoculated with a known microorganism with a known resistance to the sterilization process under study.

calibration—The comparison of a measurement system or device of unknown accuracy to a measurement system or device of known accuracy to detect, correlate, report, or eliminate by adjustment any variation from the required performance limits of the unverified measurement system or device.

CCEA—When applied to data, an addition to ALCOA that means complete, consistent, enduring, and available.

checksum—A digit representing the sum of the correct digits in a piece of stored or transmitted digital data, against which later comparisons can be made to detect errors in the data.

commercial distribution (21 CFR § 807.3 (b))—Any distribution of a device intended for human use that is held or offered for sale but does not include the following: (1) internal or interplant transfer of a device between establishments within the same parent, subsidiary, and/or affiliate company; (2) any distribution of a device intended for human use that has in effect an approved exemption for investigational use under section 520(g) of the act and Part 812 of this chapter; (3) any distribution of a device, before the effective date of Part 812 of this chapter, that was not introduced or delivered for introduction into interstate commerce for commercial distribution before May 28, 1976, and that is classified into Class III under section 513(f) of the act, provided that the device is intended solely for investigational use, and under section 501(f)(2)(A) of the act the device is not required to have an approved premarket approval application as provided in section 515 of the act; or (4) for foreign establishments, the distribution of any device that is neither imported nor offered for import into the United States.

commissioning—The planned, documented, and managed engineering approach to the start-up and turnover of facilities, systems, and equipment. Developing the evidence that equipment has been provided and installed in accordance with its specification and that it functions within predetermined limits when operated in accordance with operational instructions.

complaint—Any written, electronic, or oral communication that alleges deficiencies related to the identity, quality, durability, reliability, safety, effectiveness, or performance of a device after it is released for distribution.

component—Any raw material, substance, piece, part, software, firmware, labeling, or assembly that is intended to be included as part of the finished, packaged, and labeled device.

concurrent validation—Used to establish documented evidence that a facility and process will perform as they are intended, based on information generated during actual use of the process.

confidence level—The probability of not making a Type I, or α, error. Confidence level is the probability of correctly rejecting a "bad" lot. Confidence is quantified as 1-α.

consumer's risk—The beta (β) risk of accepting a lot that is truly rejectable according to the desired quality level. This risk can lead to an error called beta error or Type II error, which is the error of accepting a bad lot. The consumer's risk is commonly set to 0.10 power of test

contract sterilizer—Any facility that offers to provide a contractual service intended to sterilize products that are manufactured by another establishment.

control number—Any distinctive symbols, such as a distinctive combination of letters or numbers or both, from which the history of the manufacturing, packaging, labeling, and distribution of a unit, lot, or batch of finished devices can be determined.

correction—An action taken to eliminate a detected nonconformity (for example, repair or rework). A correction can be taken in conjunction with a corrective action.

corrective action—An action taken to eliminate the cause of a detected nonconformity or other undesirable situation. Corrective action is taken to prevent reoccurrence of a nonconformity.

critical task—A user task that, if performed incorrectly or not performed at all, would or could cause serious harm to the patient or user.

D value—The exposure time to a sterilizing process that is required to produce a 1-logarithm or 90 percent reduction in the population of a microorganism, usually an indicator organism.

data integrity—The accuracy, completeness, and reliability of data throughout their life cycle.

design history file (DHF)—A compilation of records that describe the design history of a finished device.

design input—The physical and performance requirements of a device that are used as a basis for device design.

design output—The results of a design effort at each design phase and at the end of the total design effort. The finished design output is the basis for the device master record. The total finished design output consists of the device, its packaging and labeling, and the device master record.

design review—A documented, comprehensive, systematic examination of a design to evaluate the adequacy of the design requirements, to evaluate the capability of the design to meet these requirements, and to identify problems.

design validation—Establishing by objective evidence that device specifications conform with user needs and intended use(s).

design verification—The process of confirming at each design stage that the design output conforms to defined design input requirements for that stage.

device failure—The failure of a device to perform or function as intended, including any deviations from the device's performance specifications or intended use.

device for self-testing—Any device intended by the manufacturer to be used by laypersons in a home environment.

device history record (DHR)—A compilation of records containing the production history of a finished device.

device intended to be implanted in the human body for more than one year—A device that is intended to be placed into a surgically or naturally formed cavity of the human body for more than one year to continuously assist, restore, or replace the function of an organ system or structure of the human body throughout the useful life of the device. The term does not include a device that is intended and used only for temporary purposes or that is intended for explantation in one year or less.

device master record (DMR)—A compilation of records containing the procedures and specifications for a finished device.

directions for use—Directions under which the practitioner or layman (for example, patient or unlicensed healthcare provider), as appropriate, can use the device safely and for the purposes for which it is intended. Directions for use also include indications for use and appropriate contraindications, warnings, precautions, and adverse reaction information. Directions for use requirements applicable to prescription and over-the-counter devices appear throughout 21 CFR Part 801 and, in the case of in vitro diagnostic products, under 21 CFR § 809.10.

distributes—Any distribution of a tracked device, including the charitable distribution of a tracked device. This term does not include the distribution of a device under an effective investigational device exemption in accordance with Section 520(g) of the FD&C Act and 21 CFR Part 812, or the distribution of a device for teaching, law enforcement, research, or analysis as specified in 21 CFR § 801.125.

distributor—Any person who furthers the distribution of a device from the original place of manufacture to the person who makes delivery or sale to the ultimate user, that is, the final or multiple distributor, but who does not repackage or otherwise change the container, wrapper, or labeling of the device or device package.

dosimeter—A device or system having a reproducible, measurable response to radiation, which can be used to measure the absorbed dose in a given material.

environmental controls—Those controls and standardized procedures used in manufacturing areas to control bioburden levels. Such controls may include air filters, fluid filters, use of surface disinfectants, personnel gowning or uniforms, and personnel training.

establish—Define, document (in writing or electronically), and implement.

establishment (21 CFR § 807.3 (c))—A place of business under one management at one general physical location at which a device is manufactured, assembled, or otherwise processed.

F value—A measure of the effectiveness of a heat sterilization process to inactivate living microorganisms. The F value is calculated by determining the lethal rate per minute at each process temperature using the z value of the microorganisms.

F_0 value—The F value of a heat sterilization process calculated at 121.1 °C with a z value of 10 °C and a D value of one minute.

final distributor—Any person who distributes a tracked device intended for use by a single patient over the useful life of the device to the patient. This term includes, but is not limited to, licensed practitioners, retail pharmacies, hospitals, and other types of device user facilities.

finished device—Any device or accessory to any device that is suitable for use or capable of functioning, whether or not it is packaged, labeled, or sterilized.

general purpose reagent (GPR)—A chemical reagent that has general laboratory application, is used to collect, prepare, and examine specimens from the human body for diagnostic purposes, and is not labeled or otherwise intended for a specific diagnostic application.

HCT/P—Human cells, tissues, or cellular or tissue-based products.

importer—The initial distributor of an imported device who is required to register under section 510 of the FD&C Act and 21 CFR § 807.20. "Importer" does not include anyone who only performs a service for the person who furthers the marketing, that is, brokers, jobbers, or warehousers.

in vitro diagnostic (IVD) accessory—An article that, while not being an in vitro diagnostic medical device, is intended specifically by its manufacturer to be used together with an IVD device to enable that device to be used in accordance with its intended purpose.

in vitro diagnostic (IVD) medical device—Any medical device that is a reagent, reagent product, calibrator, control material, kit, instrument, apparatus, equipment, or system, whether used alone or in combination, intended by the manufacturer to be used in vitro for the examination of specimens, including blood and tissue donations, derived from the human body, solely or principally for the purpose of providing information: (1) concerning a physiological or pathological state, (2) concerning a congenital abnormality, (3) to determine the safety and compatibility with potential recipients, or (4) to monitor therapeutic measures.

Specimen receptacles are considered to be in vitro diagnostic medical devices. Specimen receptacles are those devices, whether vacuum-type or not, specifically intended by their manufacturers for the primary containment and preservation of specimens derived from the human body for the purpose of in vitro diagnostic examination.

Products for general laboratory use are not in vitro diagnostic medical devices unless such products, in view of their characteristics, are specifically intended by their manufacturer to be used for in vitro diagnostic examination.

initial importer (21 CFR § 807.3 (g))—Any importer who furthers the marketing of a device from a foreign manufacturer to the person who makes the final delivery or sale of the device to the ultimate consumer or user, but does not repackage, or otherwise change the container, wrapper, or labeling of the device or device package.

installation qualification (GHTF.SG3.N99-10)—Establishing by objective evidence that all key aspects of the process equipment and ancillary system installation adhere to the manufacturer's approved specification and that the recommendations of the supplier of the equipment are suitably considered; demonstrating by objective evidence that equipment is correctly installed.

installation qualification—A step in the validation process that establishes, using appropriate studies and records, that the process equipment can perform within its design specifications.

intended uses (21 CFR § 801.4)—The term "intended uses" refers to the objective intent of the persons legally responsible for the labeling of the device. The intent is determined by their expressions or may be shown by the circumstances surrounding the distribution of the device. This objective intent may, for example, be shown by labeling claims, advertising matter, or oral or written statements by such representatives. It may be shown by the offering or the using of the device, with the knowledge of such persons or their representatives, for a purpose for which it is neither labeled nor advertised.

label (FD&C Act § 201(k))—A display of written, printed, or graphic matter upon the immediate container of any article.

- The term "immediate container" does not include package liners. Any word, statement, or other information appearing on the immediate container must also appear "on the outside container or wrapper, if any there be, or the retail package of such article, or be easily legible through the outside container or wrapper."

labeling (FD&C Act § 201(m))—Includes all labels and other written, printed, or graphic matter: (1) upon any article or any of its containers or wrappers, or (2) accompanying such article.

- The term "accompanying" is interpreted liberally to mean more than physical association with the product. It extends to posters, tags, pamphlets, circulars, booklets, brochures, instruction books, direction sheets, fillers, etc. "Accompanying" also includes labeling that is brought together with the device after shipment or delivery for shipment in interstate commerce.

lead auditor—An auditor designated to manage an audit (also known as an audit team leader).

licensed practitioner—A physician, dentist, or other healthcare practitioner licensed by the law of the state in which he or she practices to use or order the use of the tracked device.

life-supporting or life-sustaining device (used outside a device user facility)—A device that is essential, or yields information that is essential, to the restoration or continuation of a bodily function important to the continuation of human life that is intended for use outside a hospital, nursing home, ambulatory surgical facility, or diagnostic or outpatient treatment facility. Physicians' offices are not device user facilities and, therefore, devices used therein are subject to tracking if they otherwise satisfy the statutory and regulatory criteria.

linearity—Extent to which a measuring instrument's bias varies along its full operating range with the measured quantity. In a gage R&R study, linearity is the difference in the bias values throughout the expected operating range of the gage.

lot or batch—One or more components or finished devices that consist of a single type, model, class, size, composition, or software version that are manufactured under essentially the same conditions and are intended to have uniform characteristics and quality within specified limits.

lot tolerance percent defective (LTPD)—See rejectable quality level (RQL).

management system—A system to establish policy and objectives and to achieve those objectives.

management with executive responsibility—Senior employees of a manufacturer who have the authority to establish or make changes to the manufacturer's quality policy and quality system.

manufacturer (FDA)—Any person who designs, manufactures, fabricates, assembles, or processes a finished device. Manufacturer includes, but is not limited to, those who perform the functions of contract sterilization, installation, relabeling, remanufacturing, repacking, or specification development and initial distributors of foreign entities performing these functions.

manufacturer (ISO)—The natural or legal person with responsibility for the design, manufacture, packaging, and labeling of a device before it is placed on the market under his or her own name, regardless of whether these operations are carried out by that person or on his or her behalf by a third party. The obligations of this directive to be met by manufacturers also apply to the natural or legal person who assembles, packages, processes, fully refurbishes, and/or labels one or more ready-made products and/or assigns to them their intended purpose as devices with a view to their being placed on the market under his or her own name. This subparagraph does not apply to the person who, while not a manufacturer within the meaning of the first subparagraph, assembles or adapts devices already on the market to their intended purpose for an individual patient.

manufacturing material (FDA)—Any material or substance used in or used to facilitate the manufacturing process, a concomitant constituent, or a byproduct constituent produced during the manufacturing process that is present in or on the finished device as a residue or impurity not by design or intent of the manufacturer.

MDR—Depending on context, may in this book refer to: (1) Medical Device Report or Reportable (as in a type of post-market incident, see 21 CFR 803), or (2) Medical Device Regulation, as in Regulation (EU) 2017/745 of the European Parliament and of the council of 5 April 2017 on medical devices.

medical device (FDA)—An instrument, apparatus, implement, machine, contrivance, implant, in vitro reagent, or other similar or related article, including a component part or accessory that is:

- Recognized in the official National Formulary, or the U.S. Pharmacopoeia, or any supplement to them,
- Intended for use in the diagnosis of disease or other conditions, or in the cure, mitigation, treatment, or prevention of disease, in man or other animals, or
- Intended to affect the structure or any function of the human body of or body of other animals, and which does not achieve any of its primary intended purposes through chemical action within or on the body of a human or other animals and which is not dependent upon being metabolized for the achievement of any of its primary intended purposes.

medical device (MDD)—Any instrument, apparatus, appliance, software, material, or other article, whether used alone or in combination, including the software intended by its manufacturer to be used specifically for diagnostic and/or therapeutic purposes and necessary for its proper application, intended by the manufacturer to be used for human beings for the purpose of:

- Diagnosis, prevention, monitoring, treatment, or alleviation of disease
- Diagnosis, monitoring, treatment, alleviation of or compensation for an injury or handicap
- Investigation, replacement, or modification of the anatomy or of a physiological process
- Control of conception

and which does not achieve its principal intended action in or on the human body by pharmacological, immunological, or metabolic means but which may be assisted in its function by such means.

microbiological challenge—A population of known microorganisms, such as biological indicators, biological indicator test packs, or inoculated product, that can be used to test a sterilization cycle.

multiple distributor—Any device user facility, rental company, or any other entity that distributes a life-sustaining or life-supporting device intended for use by more than one patient over the useful life of the device.

nonconformity—The nonfulfillment of a specified requirement.

objective evidence—Verifiable information or records pertaining to the quality of an item or service or to the existence and implementation of a quality system element that is based on visual observation, measurement, or test.

official correspondent (21 CFR § 807.3 (e))—The person designated by the owner or operator of an establishment as responsible for the following: (1) the annual registration of the establishment; (2) contact with the FDA for device listing; (3) maintenance and submission of a current list of officers and directors to the FDA upon the request of the commissioner; (4) the receipt of pertinent correspondence from the FDA directed to and involving the owner or operator and/or any of the firm's establishments; and (5) the annual certification of MDRs required by section 804.30 of this chapter or forwarding the certification form to the person designated by the firm as responsible for the certification.

operational qualification (GHTF.SG3.N99-10)—Establishing by objective evidence process control limits and action levels that result in product that meets all predetermined requirements; demonstration that a process will produce acceptable results and establish process limits (worst case parameters).

owner or operator (21 CFR § 807.3 (f))—The corporation, subsidiary, affiliated company, partnership, or proprietor that is directly responsible for the activities of the registering establishment.

parametric release—A method of declaring that a product is sterile based on a review of the process data rather than based on sample testing or biological indicator results.

performance qualification (GHTF.SG3.N99-10)—Establishing by objective evidence that the process, under anticipated conditions, consistently produces a product that meets all predetermined requirements; established long-term process stability.

permanently implantable device—A device that is intended to be placed into a surgically or naturally formed cavity of the human body to continuously assist, restore, or replace the function of an organ system or structure of the human body throughout the useful life of the device. The term does not include any device that is intended and used for temporary purposes or that is intended for explantation.

power of test—The probability of not making a Type II, or β, error. Power is the probability of correctly accepting a "good" lot. Power is quantified as 1- β.

preconditioning—A step in the sterilization process prior to exposure to the sterilizing gas mixture, designed to bring the product to specified conditions of temperature and relative humidity. This step may be accomplished within the sterilization vessel, in an external area, or in both.

presterilization count—The population of viable microorganisms on a product or package prior to sterilization.

preventive action—An action taken to eliminate the cause of a potential nonconformity or other undesirable potential situation. Preventive action is taken to prevent occurrence of a nonconformity.

primary operating function—A function that involves user interaction that is either frequently used or related to the safety of the medical device.

process qualification (sterilization)—Obtaining and documenting evidence that the sterilization process will produce acceptable products.

process validation—Establishing by objective evidence that a process consistently produces a result or product meeting its predetermined specifications.

process performance qualification (PPQ)—Establishing by objective evidence that the system, under anticipated conditions, consistently produces a product that meets all predetermined requirements.

producer's risk—The alpha (α) risk of rejecting a lot that is truly acceptable according to the desired quality level. This risk can lead to an error called alpha error or Type I error, which is the error of rejecting a good lot. The producer's risk is commonly set to 0.05.

product—Components, manufacturing materials, in-process devices, finished devices, and returned devices.

prospective validation—Establishing documented evidence, prior to process implementation, that a system performs as is intended, based on preplanned protocols.

pyrogen—A biological or chemical agent that produces a fever in mammals.

qualification—The documented verification that all aspects of a facility, utility, or equipment that can affect product quality operate as intended throughout all anticipated ranges.

quality—The totality of features and characteristics that bear on the ability of a device to satisfy fitness for use, including safety and performance.

quality audit—A systematic, independent examination of a manufacturer's quality system that is performed at defined intervals and at sufficient frequency to determine whether both quality system activities and the results of such activities comply with quality system procedures, that these procedures are implemented effectively, and that these procedures are suitable to achieve quality system objectives.

quality audit observation—A statement of fact made during a quality audit and substantiated by objective evidence.

quality policy—The overall intentions and direction of an organization with respect to quality, as established by management with executive responsibility.

quality system—The organizational structure, responsibilities, procedures, processes, and resources for implementing quality management.

quality system record—Procedures and the documentation of activities required by this part that are not specific to a particular device(s), including but not limited to the records required by 21 CFR § 820.20.

recovery efficiency—Measure of the ability of a specific technique to remove and culture microorganisms from a test article.

regulatory requirements—Any part of a law, ordinance, decree, or other regulation that applies to quality systems of medical device manufacturers. Guidelines, guidance documents, notes, draft documents, or the like should not be used as regulatory documents and are not to be construed as such unless formally promulgated.

rejectable quality level (RQL) or lot tolerance percent defective (LTPD)—The maximum defective rate or quality level having a "low" probability of being accepted, typically a 10 percent probability. RQL lots would therefore be routinely rejected by the sampling plan. RQL is associated with the Type II, or β, error.

remanufacturer—Any person who processes, conditions, renovates, repackages, restores, or does any other act to a finished device that significantly changes the finished device's performance or safety specifications or intended use.

repeatability—The variation in measurements obtained when one measurement device is used several times by the same person to measure the same characteristic on the same product.

reproducibility—The variation in measurements made by different people using the same measuring device to measure the same characteristic on the same product.

rework—Action taken on a nonconforming product so it will fulfill the specified requirements before it is released for distribution.

retrospective validation—Validating a system that has been operating for some time. There are various schools of thought on how to approach retrospective validation. Some may feel that a full-blown validation is required to assure the system is functioning properly.

revalidation—Repeating the original validation effort or any part of it that also includes investigating and reviewing existing performance data.

serious adverse health consequences—Any significant adverse experience related to a device, including device-related events that are life-threatening or that involve permanent or long-term injuries or illnesses.

simulated product load—A sterilization vessel load that is as difficult to sterilize as the actual product load.

specification—Any requirement with which a product, process, service, or other activity must conform.

stability—(1) Of a gage: it is the ability of a gage to retain its accuracy over time and usage; (2) of a process: a process is said to be stable if it shows no recognizable pattern of change.

sterile—Free from living microorganisms. In practice, sterility is expressed as a probability function. For example, sterility may be expressed as the probability of a surviving microorganism being one in a million (10^{-6}).

sterility assurance level (SAL)—The probability of a nonsterile product after sterilization. The SAL is usually expressed as 10^{-n}.

sterilization—The process used to remove all living microorganisms on a product.

sterilization dose—The minimum absorbed dose of radiation required to achieve the specified sterility assurance level.

temperature distribution study—A study to determine the temperature profile within a sterilizing chamber during a sterilization cycle.

terminal sterilization—The process in which the product is rendered free of microorganisms at the last stage(s) of the manufacturing process. In the case of ethylene oxide and radiation sterilization, the product is typically sterilized in the final packaging, including the shipping containers. In the case of moist heat sterilization, the product is sterilized in the primary container with subsequent label application and final packaging.

training elements—Topics within a training program that describe the content for addressing a particular training need.

U.S. agent (21 CFR § 807.3(r))—A person residing in or maintaining a place of business in the United States whom a foreign establishment designates as its agent. This definition excludes mailboxes, answering machines, services, or other places where an individual acting as the foreign establishment's agent is not physically present.

usability—Characteristic of the user interface that establishes effectiveness, efficiency, ease of user learning, and user satisfaction.

usability specification—Documentation defining the user interface requirements related to usability.

user interface—Means by which the user and the medical device interact.

user profile—Summary of the mental, physical, and demographic traits of an intended user population, as well as any special characteristics that can have a bearing on design decisions, such as occupational skills and job requirements.

validation—Confirmation by examination and provision of objective evidence that the requirements for a specific intended use can be consistently fulfilled.

validation (sterilization)—A written procedure for developing, recording, and interpreting the data required to determine that a process will consistently yield product that complies with established specifications. In the case of sterilization cycles, validation includes commissioning (demonstrating that the equipment to be used conforms to specifications) and performance qualification (demonstrating that acceptable product will be produced when the commissioned equipment is used in accordance with documented procedures).

verification—Confirmation by examination and provision of objective evidence that specified requirements have been fulfilled.

verification (sterilization)—Evaluation to assure current operation or applicability for use of a system. For example, although a set of thermocouples has been calibrated, a single-point check of the thermocouples in the temperature range to be measured is considered a verification of the correct functioning of the equipment prior to and after use in developing a sterilization cycle. In other words, it is a confirmation that specified requirements have been met.

where appropriate—When a requirement is qualified by "where appropriate," it is deemed to be appropriate unless the manufacturer can document justification otherwise.

z value—The number of degrees of temperature required for a 1-logarithm change in the D value. A z value can be obtained from a thermal resistance curve. D values are plotted against temperature and the reciprocal of the slope is determined as the z value.

Appendix B

Certified Medical Device Auditor (CMDA) Body of Knowledge (2020)

The topics in this body of knowledge (BoK) include additional detail in the form of subtext explanations and cognitive level. These details will be used by the Exam Development Committee as guidelines for writing test questions and are designed to help candidates prepare for the exam by identifying specific content within each topic that may be tested. The subtext is not intended to limit the subject matter or be all-inclusive of what might be covered in an exam but is intended to clarify how the topics relate to a medical device auditor's role. The descriptor in parentheses at the end of each entry refers to the maximum cognitive level at which the topic will be tested. A more comprehensive description of cognitive levels is provided at the end of this document.

I. Auditing Fundamentals (12 Questions)

A. Types of audits

1. Audits by purpose. Identify and distinguish between audits by purpose: organizational effectiveness, system efficiency, business performance, process effectiveness, risk management, regulatory compliance, supplier qualification, compliance with standards (certification and surveillance), design history file compliance, and for-cause audit. (Analyze)

2. Audits by method. Identify and distinguish between audits by method: product, process, system, first-party, second-party, third-party, internal, external, desk, management, department, and function. (Analyze)

B. Audit roles and responsibilities. Explain key functions and responsibilities of various audit participants including audit team members, lead auditor, client, auditee, etc. (Understand)

C. Ethical, legal, and professional issues

1. Professional conduct and responsibilities. Define and apply the ASQ Code of Ethics, concepts of due diligence and due care with respect to confidentiality and conflict of interest, and various factors that influence audit credibility, including auditor independence, objectivity, and qualifications. (Apply)

2. Legal consequences and liability. Identify potential legal and financial ramifications of improper auditor actions (carelessness, negligence, etc.) in various situations, and anticipate the effect that certain audit results can have on an auditee's liability. (Apply)

3. Data privacy. Demonstrate the importance of maintaining confidentiality of personal information reviewed during audits. (Apply)

II. Auditing and Inspection Processes (28 Questions)

A. Audit preparation and planning

1. Elements of the audit planning process. Determine and implement steps in audit preparation and planning, such as verifying audit authority, establishing the purpose, scope, and type of audit, audit criteria, and the resources necessary, including the size and number of audit teams. (Evaluate)

2. Auditor selection. Identify and examine various internal or outsourced auditor selection criteria, such as education, experience, industry background, and subject-matter expertise, and the characteristics that make auditors effective, such as interpersonal skills, problem-solving skills, attention to detail, cultural sensitivity, and ability to work independently as well as in a group or on a team. (Evaluate)

3. Audit-related documentation. Identify sources of pre-audit information and examine audit-related documentation, such as reference materials and prior audits. (Evaluate)

4. Auditing tools. Identify the sampling plan or method and procedural guidelines to be used for the specific audit. Select and prepare working papers (checklists, log sheets, etc.) to document the audit. (Create)

5. Auditing strategies. Identify and use various tactical methods for conducting an audit, such as forward and backward tracing, discovery, etc. (Apply)

6. Logistics. Identify and organize various audit-related logistics, such as travel, safety and security considerations, the need for escorts, translators, confidentiality agreements, and clear right of access. (Apply)

B. Audit performance

1. Opening meeting. Manage the opening meeting of an audit, including identifying the audit's purpose and scope, describing any scoring, rating, or classification criteria for potential audit findings, creating a record of the attendees, reviewing the audit schedule, and answering questions as needed. (Apply)

2. Data collection and analysis . Select and apply various data collection methods, such as observing work activities, taking physical measurements, examining paper and electronic documents, etc. Evaluate the results to determine their importance for providing audit evidence. (Evaluate)
3. Data integrity principles. Examine record-keeping requirements for data acquisition systems to ensure data integrity. Evaluate the data collected during an audit to ensure they are attributable, legible, contemporaneous, original, and accurate (ALCOA). (Evaluate)
4. Communication techniques. Define and apply appropriate interviewing techniques (for example, when to use various question types, the significance of pauses and their length, when and how to prompt a response), in various situations, including when supervisors are present, when conducting multiple interviews, and when using a translator. Identify typical conflict situations and use appropriate techniques to resolve them. (Apply)
5. Organization and analysis of objective evidence. Identify and differentiate sources of objective evidence, such as observed, measured, confirmed, and documented. Classify evidence in terms of significance, severity, frequency, and level of risk. Evaluate the evidence for its potential impact on product, process, system, and cost of quality. Determine whether additional investigation is required to meet the scope of the audit. (Evaluate)
6. On-site audit management. Interpret situations throughout audit performance to determine whether time is being managed well and when changes need to be made, such as revising planned audit team activities, reallocating resources, and adjusting the audit plan. Communicate with the auditee about any changes or other events related to the audit. (Analyze)
7. Exit/closing meeting. Formally manage these meetings: reiterate the audit's purpose, scope, scoring, rating, or classification criteria, and create a record of the attendees. Present the audit results and obtain concurrence on evidence that could lead to an adverse conclusion. Discuss the next steps in the process (follow-up audit, additional evidence-gathering, etc.), and clarify who is responsible for performing those steps. (Apply)

C. Audit report

1. Basic elements. Define, plan, and apply the steps in generating an audit report, including reviewing and finalizing results, organizing details, obtaining necessary approvals, and distributing the report. (Create)
2. Effective audit reports. Report observations and nonconformances accurately; cite objective evidence, procedures, and requirements; and develop and evaluate various components, such as executive

summaries, prioritized data, graphic presentation, and the impact of nonconformances. (Create)

3. Record retention. Identify and apply record retention requirements, including the type of documents and storage considerations. (Apply)

D. Audit follow-up and closure

1. Elements of corrective and preventive action (CAPA). Identify and apply the elements of these processes, including problem identification, prioritizing actions based on risk, assignment of responsibility, root cause analysis, and establishing a plan to verify effectiveness of corrective actions to prevent recurrence. (Analyze)
2. Review of corrective action plan. Use various criteria to evaluate the acceptability of corrective action plans. Identify and apply strategies for negotiating changes to unacceptable plans. (Apply)
3. Conducting audit follow-up. Use various methods to verify and evaluate the effectiveness of corrective actions taken, such as re-examining procedures, observing revised processes, and conducting follow-up audits or reaudits. Develop strategies when corrective actions are not implemented or are not effective, such as communicating to the next level of management, re-issuing the corrective action request, etc. (Evaluate)
4. Audit closure. Identify and apply various elements of, and criteria for, audit closure. (Evaluate)

E. Audit procedural references

1. International guidelines for auditing quality systems . Understand general auditing principles as described in ISO 19011 and the Medical Device Single Audit Program (MDSAP) audit model. (Understand)
2. Quality System Inspection Technique (QSIT) and FDA CPG 7382.845. Understand QSIT auditing requirements and its various subsystems. Explain the purpose and scope of FDA criteria for taking regulatory action on the basis of quality system audit results. (Understand)

III. Medical Device Quality Management System Requirements (38 Questions)

A. Regulatory laws and requirements

1. FDA—Code of Federal Regulations (CFR) Title 21. Identify, define, and apply the following FDA requirement parts: 4—Regulation of combination products, 7—Enforcement policy, 11—Electronic records; signatures, 58—Good laboratory practice for nonclinical laboratory studies, 801—Labeling, 803—Medical device reporting, 806—Medical devices; reports of corrections and removals, 807—Establishment registration and device listing for manufacturers and

initial importers of devices, 820—Quality system regulation, 821—Medical device tracking requirements, and 830—Unique device identification. (Apply)

2. U.S. requirements (FD&C Act, 201, 301-304, 501-502, 510, 513, 518, 522, 704). Identify how the FD&C Act defines and differentiates between device classifications and premarket requirements. Recognize the implications of misbranding and adulteration. (Apply)
3. EU MDR 2017/745. Recognize requirements of the directive and the key differences between this and U.S. regulations. (Apply)
4. Health Canada. Recognize current requirements of the Canadian Medical Device Regulation SOP/98-282 and the key differences between this and U.S. regulations. (Apply)
5. Other international agencies. Recognize requirements enforced by international agencies such as Therapeutic Goods Administration (TGA) and Japanese Pharmaceutical and Medical Device Agency, etc. (Understand)

B. Requirements for in vitro diagnostic (IVD) devices. Recognize the requirements of 21 CFR 809 and IVDR 2017/746 as they apply to in vitro diagnostic (IVD) devices. (Understand)

C. International standards for quality systems. Evaluate the selection and use of the following quality system standards: ISO 9001, ISO 13485, and ISO 17025. (Evaluate)

D. Quality System Regulation (QSR) requirements (21 CFR 820—parts as shown)

1. Management responsibility (Parts 20, 22, 25). Assess management's responsibility in establishing and maintaining the quality system: organizational structure and management representative, quality planning/objectives, resources, management reviews, quality audits, personnel training and education, and control of customer property. (Evaluate)
2. Design controls (Part 30). Evaluate the scope, purpose, and implementation of controls and their elements, including design and development planning, input, output, review, verification, validation, transfer, changes, and design history file. (Evaluate)
3. Document (Part 40) and record control (Parts 180-186). Describe and review elements of a document and change control system, including approval processes, retention policies, communication procedures and maintenance of device master records (DMRs), device history records (DHRs), and quality system records. (Analyze)
4. Purchasing controls and acceptance activities (Parts 50, 80, 86). Describe supplier qualification and purchasing control requirements

for products, components, and services. Describe appropriate identification and acceptance activities, including inspection, test, and verification processes used for incoming products. (Apply)

5. Identification and traceability (Parts 60, 65). Use appropriate methods for identifying and tracing products during all stages of receipt, production, distribution, and installation. (Apply)
6. Production and process controls (Parts 70, 75). Assess production and process controls, including process validation, monitoring, control of materials, equipment, environment, contamination, and software validation for automated processes. (Evaluate)
7. Inspection, measuring, and test equipment (Part 72). Determine the suitability and calibration of inspection equipment. Ensure calibration is traceable to national or international standards. (Evaluate)
8. Nonconforming product (Part 90). Determine the adequacy of procedures, processes, and records established for the control and disposition of nonconforming product. (Evaluate)
9. Corrective and preventive action (CAPA) system (Part 100). Assess analysis of quality data sources to determine the need for CAPA. Define and distinguish between corrective action and preventive action. Review CAPA procedures, processes, and records to evaluate the effectiveness of the system. (Evaluate)
10. Product handling, storage, distribution, and installation (Parts 140-170). Determine the adequacy of procedures, processes, and records established for these aspects of product control to ensure product integrity. (Analyze)
11. Complaint files (Part 198). Determine adequacy of complaint handling procedures, including investigation and determination of Medical Device Reporting. (Evaluate)
12. Servicing (Part 200). Determine the adequacy of procedures, processes, and records established for products that require servicing activities such as troubleshooting and repair. Evaluate service reports for events that must be reported to the FDA to ensure that they are included in the complaint handling process. (Analyze)
13. Statistical techniques (Part 250). Determine the adequacy and validity of statistical techniques and sampling plans used to measure process capability and acceptability of product characteristics. Evaluate the rationale for statistical techniques used in quality systems, including design verification and validation, acceptance sampling, etc. (Analyze)

E. Post-market surveillance. Determine the appropriateness of the procedures, processes, and records established for the control of post-market surveillance activities. Define and describe vigilance, medical device reporting (MDR), and adverse event reporting (AER) requirements. Review the adequacy of requirements and processes for product recall, corrections, removals, and tracking. (Analyze)

IV. Technical Medical Device Knowledge (42 Questions)

A. Risk management

1. ISO 14971. Describe the principles of risk management, including risk analysis, evaluation, control, benefit-risk analysis, and the incorporation of production and post-production information. (Evaluate)

2. IEC 62366. Determine whether the processes used for identification of known or foreseeable hazards are suitable in both normal and fault conditions, including hazards arising from device use. Verify that risk control measures have been implemented in design and production. (Evaluate)

3. ISO 13485. Describe and assess the risk-based controls for appropriate processes needed for the quality management system. (Evaluate)

B. Design control

1. Human factors and usability engineering. Evaluate human factors and usability studies performed during design and development. (Evaluate)

2. Biological evaluation. Describe material characterization and the principles of biocompatibility test selection rationale as described in ISO 10993-1 and FDA-related guidance. Understand the differences between cytotoxicity, sensitization, and irritation. (Understand)

3. Packaging. Interpret the appropriate standards for sterile and nonsterile product packaging per ISO 11607, and referenced standards including, ASTM D4169 (Distribution) and ASTM F1980 (Aging). (Understand)

4. Device shelf life. Explain how a device's useful life/shelf life is determined and discuss the various parameters that determine the length of time a device will remain within acceptable specifications (for example, sterility or package integrity). (Understand)

5. General safety and performance requirements. Identify the elements of General Safety and Performance Requirements, per EU MDR 2017/745. (Remember)

C. Software development and maintenance for products. Identify principles of product software life cycle in accordance with FDA General Principles of Software Validation Guidance and IEC 62304. Describe the software development life-cycle model, including V&V, cybersecurity considerations, change control methods, and the risk management process. (Understand)

D. Labeling. Identify labeling requirements for devices, instructions for use (IFU), and promotional/marketing material (per 21 CFR 801). Understand the use of symbols (per ISO 15223) and UDI/GTIN/UPC (per 21 CFR 830). (Understand)

E. Controlled environments and utility systems

1. Controlled environments. Identify and interpret controlled environment specifications (per ISO 14644), qualifications, validations, and monitoring (bioburden and endotoxins). Review housekeeping, disinfection, and sanitization processes in terms of controlled environment specifications and classifications. Verify that appropriate training and personnel practices are used in controlled environments. (Analyze)

2. Utility systems. Describe utility setups in medical device manufacturing facilities for water, compressed gas, heating, ventilation, and air conditioning (HVAC) systems, including whether they require qualification, validation, or maintenance. (Understand)

F. Sterile medical devices

1. Definitions. Describe and distinguish between aseptically processed products and terminally sterilized products. (Understand)

2. Methods. Identify basic elements of sterilization for dry heat, steam, electron beam, ethylene oxide (EtO), and radiation. (Remember)

3. Process controls and validation for ethylene oxide (EtO) and radiation. Determine appropriate validation, process controls and monitoring (for example, dose audits, parametric release, process challenge device (PCD), residuals, etc.) are properly implemented to ensure Sterility Assurance Level (SAL). Ensure the process is documented in accordance with industry standards: ISO 11135, ISO 11137. (Apply)

G. Laboratory testing and failure analysis. Assess procedures and records used for laboratory test methods and determine whether they are appropriate. (Evaluate)

H. Validation. Define and evaluate elements of different types of validations such as process (IQ/OQ/PQ per GHTF/SG3/N99-10), cleanliness, test method, and rework. (Evaluate)

I. Reprocessing/reuse and cleaning of medical devices. Identify elements of reprocessing and cleaning validations in accordance with the FDA Guidance on Reprocessing of Reusable Devices. (Understand)

J. Common medical device directives and standards. Define and describe elements of various standards and directives as they relate to medical devices. (Understand)

1. IEC 60601-1
2. Restriction of Hazardous Substances (RoHS) directive
3. Registration, Evaluation, Authorization and Restriction of Chemicals (REACH)

K. Sources for new and evolving standards. Describe the sources for standards and guidance documents that form the basis for industry norms and standards, such as the FDA Recognized Consensus Standards Database, the Harmonised Standards Listing, Medical Device Guidances (MEDDEV), Notified Body Operating Group (NBOG), and Europa. (Remember)

V. Quality Tools and Techniques (15 Questions)

A. Quality control and problem-solving tools. Identify, interpret, analyze, and draw conclusions based upon: 1) Pareto charts, 2) cause and effect diagrams, 3) flowcharts, 4) statistical process control (SPC) charts, 5) check sheets, 6) scatter diagrams, 7) histograms, 8) root cause analysis, 9) plan-do-check-act (PDCA), 10) Setting Alert and Action Levels, 11) 5 Whys, 12) Is/Is Not (Kepner-Tregoe). (Analyze)

B. Process improvement techniques

1. Process capability. Identify and interpret various process capability indices, such as Cp, Cpk, Pp, and Ppk. Recognize how these metrics are used in relation to established requirements and the effect on PPM. (Understand)
2. Six Sigma. Identify and define the Six Sigma DMAIC phases: define, measure, analyze, improve, and control. (Understand)
3. Lean tools. Identify and define various lean tools: 5S, standard operations, kanban (pull), error-proofing, value-stream mapping, etc. (Understand)
4. Measurement system analysis (MSA). Identify and define various MSA terms (bias, linearity, stability, accuracy, precision, repeatability, reproducibility, etc.) and describe how these elements affect measurement systems. (Understand)
5. Cost of quality (COQ). Define and describe the four basic COQ categories: prevention, appraisal, internal failure, and external failure. (Understand)

C. Data types and sampling

1. Qualitative and quantitative analysis. Describe qualitative data in terms of the nature, type, or other characteristics of an observation or condition. Describe how quantitative data are used to detect patterns or trends. Identify how such analyses can indicate whether a problem is systemic or isolated. (Analyze)

2. Attributes and variables data. Determine whether to use an attributes sampling plan or variables sampling plan in various situations such as process monitoring and control, receiving inspection, auditing, etc. (Analyze)
3. Sampling. Identify and interpret sampling plans. Determine if sampling plans are based on risk and statistically valid rationale. (Evaluate)

LEVELS OF COGNITION BASED ON BLOOM'S TAXONOMY—REVISED (2001)

In addition to content specifics, the subtext for each topic in this BoK also indicates the intended complexity level of the test questions for that topic. These levels are based on "Levels of Cognition" (from Bloom's Taxonomy—Revised, 2001) and are presented below in rank order, from least complex to most complex.

Remember

Recall or recognize terms, definitions, facts, ideas, materials, patterns, sequences, methods, principles, etc.

Understand

Read and understand descriptions, communications, reports, tables, diagrams, directions, regulations, etc.

Apply

Know when and how to use ideas, procedures, methods, formulas, principles, theories, etc.

Analyze

Break down information into its constituent parts and recognize their relationship to one another and how they are organized; identify sublevel factors or salient data from a complex scenario.

Evaluate

Make judgments about the value of proposed ideas, solutions, etc., by comparing the proposal to specific criteria or standards.

Create

Put parts or elements together in such a way as to reveal a pattern or structure not clearly there before; identify which data or information from a complex set is appropriate to examine further or from which supported conclusions can be drawn.

Appendix C
Certified Medical Device Auditor (CMDA) References (2020)

All reference materials listed below cover the parts of the Body of Knowledge. The ASQ Certification Board does not endorse any one particular reference source.

Publicly available:

ASQ Code of Ethics

Brazilian Health Regulatory Agency (Anvisa)

Directive 2012/19/EU of the European Parliament and of the Council of 4 July 2012 on waste electrical and electronic equipment (WEEE)

FDA—Food, Drug, and Cosmetic (FD&C) Act, Sections 201, 301-4; 501-2; 510; 513; 518; 522; 704

FDA—Code of Federal Regulations (CFR) Title 21 Part: 4; 7; 11; 58; 201 Subpart A; 801 Subpart A; 803; 806; 807; 820; 821; 830

FDA—9-Sep-99, Guidance for Industry, FDA Reviewers and Compliance on Off-The-Shelf Software Use in Medical Devices

FDA—11-Jan-02, General Principles of Software Validation Final, Guidance for Industry and FDA Staff

FDA—6-Jan-2017, MDSAP AU P0002.004, Medical Device Single Audit Program & Companion Document

FDA—Guidance for the Content of Premarket Submissions for Software Contained in Medical Devices

FDA—Guidance Document for Applying Human Factors and Usability Engineering to Medical Devices

FDA—Guidance Document for Shelf Life of Medical Devices

GHTF/SG3/N99-10: 2004, Quality Management Systems—Process Validation Guidance

GHTF/SG4 Guidelines for Regulatory Auditing of Quality Management Systems of Medical Device Manufacturers

Health Canada—SOR/98-282 Medical Devices Regulations

REACH—Regulation (EC) No 1907/2006 of the European Parliament and of the Council of 18 December 2006 concerning the Registration, Evaluation, Authorization and Restriction of Chemicals (REACH)

Regulation (EU) 2017/745 of the European Parliament and of the Council of 5 April 2017 on medical devices

RoHs—Restriction of the use of certain hazardous materials in electrical and electronic equipment directive 2011/65/EU: EU Directive for Restriction of the use of certain hazardous materials in electrical equipment

Standards:

IEC 62304: 2006: Medical device software, software life cycle processes.

IEC 62366-1: 2015 Medical devices—Application of usability engineering to medical devices

IEC 80001-1:2010 Application of risk management for IT-networks incorporating medical devices

ISO 13485:2016, Medical devices—Quality management systems—Requirements for regulatory purposes

ISO 9001:2015, Quality management systems—Requirements

ISO/IEC 17025: 2017, General requirements for the competence of testing and calibration laboratories

ISO 11137-1:2006, Sterilization of health care products—Radiation—Part 1: Requirements for development, validation, and routine control of a sterilization process for medical devices

ISO 11607-1: 2006, Packaging for terminally sterilized medical devices—Part 1: Requirements for materials, sterile barrier systems, and packaging systems

ISO 10993-1: 2018, Biological evaluation of medical devices—Part 1: Evaluation and testing within a risk management process

ISO 14644-1: 2015, Classification of air cleanliness, cleanrooms, and associated controlled environments

ISO 14937: 2009, Sterilization of health care products—General requirements for characterization of a sterilizing agent and the development, validation, and routine control of a sterilization process for medical devices

ISO 14971: 2019, Medical devices -Application of risk management to medical devices

ISO 15223-1: 2016, Medical devices—Symbols to be used with medical device labels, labelling and information to be supplied—Part 1: General requirements

ISO 17665-1:2006, Sterilization of health care products—Moist heat—Part 1: Requirements for the development, validation, and routine control of a sterilization process for medical devices

ISO 19011:2018 Guidelines for auditing management systems

Books:

Arter, Dennis R. 2003. *Quality Audits for Improved Performance,* third edition. Milwaukee: ASQ Quality Press.

Brassard, Michael, and Diane Ritter. 2010. *The Memory Jogger 2,* second edition. Methuen, MA: Goal/QPC. ISBN 978-1-57681-113-9.

Crawford, Heather, and ASQ Biomedical Division. 2017. *The Biomedical Quality Auditor Handbook,* third edition. Milwaukee: ASQ Quality Press.

De Feo, Joseph A. 2017. *Juran's Quality Handbook,* seventh edition. New York: McGraw-Hill Publishing Co.

Griffith, Gary K. 2013. *The Quality Technician's Handbook,* sixth edition. New Jersey: Pearson Education.

Gryna, Frank M., Richard C. H. Chua, and Joseph A. Defeo. 2007. *Juran's Quality Planning and Analysis for Enterprise Quality,* fifth edition. New York: McGraw-Hill.

Parsowith, Scott B. 1995. *Fundamentals of Quality Auditing.* Milwaukee: ASQ Quality Press.

Russell, J. P., ed. 2013. *The ASQ Auditing Handbook,* fourth edition. Milwaukee: ASQ Quality Press.

Sayle, Allan J. 1997. *Management Audits,* third edition. Brighton, MI: Allan Sayle Associates. ISBN 0951173901

Tague, Nancy R. 2004. *The Quality Toolbox,* second edition. Milwaukee: ASQ Quality Press.

Note: For the latest version of the above referenced standards, regulations, and guidance, visit:

ISO standards @ www.iso.org

FDA regulations @ www.ecfr.gov

FDA guidance @ https://www.fda.gov/regulatory-information/search-fda-guidance-documents

End Notes

Chapter 2

1. https://www.who.int/medicines/publications/pharmprep/WHO_TRS_996_annex05.pdf?ua=1

Chapter 4

2. A History of Medical Device Regulation & Oversight in the United States | FDA, accessed March 2020, https://www.fda.gov/medical-devices/overview-device-regulation/history-medical-device-regulation-oversight-united-states
3. USFDA Current Good Manufacturing Practice Requirements for Combination Products, January 2017, https://www.fda.gov/regulatory-information/search-fda-guidance-documents/current-good-manufacturing-practice-requirements-combination-products
4. USFDA Initiation of Voluntary Recalls Under 21 CFR Part 7, Subpart C, April 2019, https://www.fda.gov/safety/recalls-market-withdrawals-safety-alerts/industry-guidance-recalls
5. USFDA What is a Medical Device Recall? accessed March 2020, https://www.fda.gov/medical-devices/medical-device-recalls/what-medical-device-recall
6. USFDA Part 11, Electronic Records; Electronic Signatures — Scope and Application, August 2003, https://www.fda.gov/regulatory-information/search-fda-guidance-documents/part-11-electronic-records-electronic-signatures-scope-and-application
7. USFDA The Applicability of Good Laboratory Practice in Premarket Device Submissions: Questions & Answers, August 2013, https://www.federalregister.gov/documents/2013/08/28/2013-20916/the-applicability-of-good-laboratory-practice-in-premarket-device-submissions-questions-and-answers
8. Richardson, Eric, Medical Device Labeling, FDA Small Business Regulatory Education for Industry (REdI), September 2015.
9. USFDA Unique Device Identification: Direct Marking of Devices, November 2017, https://www.fda.gov/regulatory-information/search-fda-guidance-documents/unique-device-identification-direct-marking-devices
10. USFDA Unique Device Identification System: Small Entity Compliance Guide, August 2014, https://www.fda.gov/regulatory-information/search-fda-guidance-documents/unique-device-identification-system-small-entity-compliance-guide
11. USFDA UDI Basics, accessed March 2020, https://www.fda.gov/medical-devices/unique-device-identification-system-udi-system/udi-basics

12. USFDA Medical Device Reporting (MDR): How to Report Medical Device Problems, accessed March 2020, https://www.fda.gov/medical-devices/medical-device-safety/medical-device-reporting-mdr-how-report-medical-device-problems
13. Freeman, Anike, Overview of Medical Device Reporting , CDRHLearn, August 2018, http://www.fda.gov/CDRHLearn
14. Chang, Isaac, Medical Device Reporting for Manufacturers, November 2016 webinar, http://www.fda.gov/training/cdrhlearn
15. USFDA Medical Device Reporting for Manufacturers, November 2016 https://www.fda.gov/regulatory-information/search-fda-guidance-documents/medical-device-reporting-manufacturers
16. Instructions for completing Form 3500A: http://www.fda.gov/downloads/Safety/MedWatch/HowToReport/DownloadForms/UCM387002.pdf.
17. USFDA Recalls, Corrections and Removals (Devices), April 2019, https://www.fda.gov/medical-devices/postmarket-requirements-devices/recalls-corrections-and-removals-devices
18. Tartal, J., Device Establishment Registration & Listing, August 2014, http://www.fda.gov/medicaldevices/deviceregulationandguidance/howtomarketyourdevice/registrationandlisting/default.htm
19. USFDA The 510(k) Program: Evaluating Substantial Equivalence in Premarket Notifications [510(k)], July 2014, https://www.fda.gov/regulatory-information/search-fda-guidance-documents/510k-program-evaluating-substantial-equivalence-premarket-notifications-510k
20. USFDA Premarket Notification 510(k), accessed March 2020, https://www.fda.gov/medical-devices/premarket-submissions/premarket-notification-510k
21. Evaluating Substantial Equivalence in Premarket Notifications, FDA Guidance, July 28, 2014, Appendix A. 510(k) Decision-Making Flowchart
22. USFDA Medical Device Tracking, March 2014, https://www.fda.gov/medical-devices/postmarket-requirements-devices/medical-device-tracking
23. USFDA Medical Device Tracking, accessed March 2020, https://www.fda.gov/medical-devices/postmarket-requirements-devices/medical-device-tracking
24. USFDA Unique Device Identification: Direct Marking of Devices, November 2017, https://www.fda.gov/regulatory-information/search-fda-guidance-documents/unique-device-identification-direct-marking-devices
25. USFDA Unique Device Identification System: Small Entity Compliance Guide, August 2014, https://www.fda.gov/regulatory-information/search-fda-guidance-documents/unique-device-identification-system-small-entity-compliance-guide
26. USFDA UDI Basics, accessed March 2020, https://www.fda.gov/medical-devices/unique-device-identification-system-udi-system/udi-basics

Chapter 5

27. 21 USC § 321(h) (Pub. L. 94-295, § 3(a)(1)(A).
28. Id.
29. 21 USC § 360(i); Publ L. 94-295 §6(a).
30. FD&C Act § 513(i), 21 USC § 360c(i), 21 CFR § 807.100.
31. 21 USC § 360aaa-aaa-1 (2001).
32. FDA—Jan-2009, Good Reprint Practices for the Distribution of Medical Journal Articles and Medical or Scientific Reference Publications on Unapproved New uses of Approved Drugs and Approved or Cleared Medical Devices. Accessible at: http://www.fda.gov/RegulatoryInformation/Guidances/ucm125126.htm

33. 21 USC § 360bbb (2001).
34. 21 USC § 331.
35. 21 USC § 351(a)(1) (2001).
36. 21 USC § 351(h) (2001).
37. 21 USC § 360(j)(1)(A) (2001).
38. 21 USC § 351(a)(3) (2001).
39. Id.
40. 21 USC § 351(a)(2)(A) (2001).
41. 21 USC § 351(e)(1)-(2) (2001).
42. 21 USC § 351(f)(1)(B)(i)-(ii); 351(f)(1)(C) (2001).
43. 21 USC § 352(o), 360(j) (2001).
44. 21 USC § 352(b), 352(0) (2001).
45. 21 USC § 352(o), 360(b) (2001).
46. 21 USC § 352(o), 360(j) (2001).
47. 21 USC § 352(o), 360(k), 360(d), 360(e) (2001).
48. 21 USC § 352(a), 352(q) (2001).
49. 21 USC § 352(j) (2001).
50. 21 USC § 352(q) (2001).
51. 21 USC § 60(j)(1)(B)(ii) (2001). The FD&C Act distinguishes between "label" and "labeling." A "label" refers to written, printed, or graphic statements that appear upon "the immediate container" of an article. "Labeling" encompasses all labels, as well as additional written, printed, or graphic statements appearing upon any container or wrapper for the article, the article itself, or any material accompanying the article.
52. 21 USC § 360(j)(1)(A), 360(j)(1)(B)(i) (2001).
53. 21 USC § 360(j)(1)(A) (2001).
54. 21 USC § 352(b) (2001).
55. 21 USC § 352(b), 352(0), 360(e) (2001).
56. 21 USC § 352(c) (2001).
57. 21 USC § 352(f) (2001).
58. 21 USC § 352(s), 260d(2)(C) (2001).
59. 21 USC § 352(r) (2001).
60. Id.
61. Id.
62. 21 USC § 352(t), 360(h) (2001).
63. 21 USC § 352(t), 360(l) (2001).
64. 21 USC § 360h.
65. 21 USC § 360ll.
66. MDA, Pub. L. No. 94-295, 90 Stat. 539 (1976), codified at 15 USC § 55 (1994); 21 USC § 301, 331, 334, 351, 352, 358, 360, 374, 379, 381.
67. Pub. L. No. 101-629, 104 Stat. 4511 (1990), codified at 21 USC § 301 note, 321, 333, 333 note, 351, 353, 360, 360c, 360c note, 360d-i, 360i notes, 360j, 360j note, 3601, 360gg-hh, 360hh note, 360ii-ss, 383, 383 note; 42 USC § 263b-n (Supp. 1991).
68. Pub. L. No. 102-300, 106 Stat. 238 (1992), 21 USC § 301 note, 321, 331, 334, 346a, 352, 353, 356, 357, 360c-d, 371, 372, 372a, 376, 381; 42 USC § 262.
69. See 21 CFR 810 (effective May 19, 1997).
70. FD&C Act § 518(a), 21 USC § 360h(a).
71. H.R. Cong. Rep. No. 1090, 94th Cong. 60, 2nd Sess. (1976) (reprinted in 1976 U.S.C.C.A.N. 1112-13).
72. FDA's site posts safety alerts that can be used to develop sample forms. http://www.fda.gov/safety/recalls/EnforcementReports/default.htm. An individual can also subscribe to email notification through the website.

73. FD&C Act § 518(b), (c), 21 USC § 360h(b), (c).
74. H.R. Rep. No. 953, 94th Cong., 2nd Sess. (1976).
75. By "serious, adverse health consequences," Congress meant "any significant adverse experience attributable to a device, including those which may be either life-threatening, or involve permanent or long-term injuries, but excluding those non-life-threatening injuries that are temporary and reasonably reversible" [S. Rep. No. 513, 101st Cong., 2nd Sess. (1990)].
76. S. Rep. No. 513, 101st Cong., 2nd Sess. 19 (1990).
77. 21 CFR § 810.2(h).
78. 61 Federal Register 59,004, 59,005 (1996).
79. 21 CFR § 810.10(a).
80. 21 CFR § 810.10(b).
81. 21 CFR § 810.10(c).
82. 21 CFR § 810.11(a).
83. 21 CFR § 810.10(e), (f); 810.11(b).
84. 21 CFR § 810.11 (a), (e).
85. 21 CFR § 810.11(e), 810.12(c).
86. 21 CFR § 810.13(b), (d); 810.14.
87. FD&C Act § 518(e) (2) (B) (i) (I), (II); 21 USC § 360h(e) (2) (B) (i) (I), (II).
88. 21 CFR § 810.15(b).
89. 21 CFR § 810.14(C)(2).
90. 21 CFR § 810.14(C)(3).
91. 21 CFR § 810.15(d).
92. 21 CFR § 810.17(a).
93. 21 CFR § 810.17(b).
94. 21 USC § 374.
95. FD&C Act § 704(a)(1)(A), (B); 21 USC § 374(a)(1)(A), (B).
96. FD&C Act § 510(h); 21 USC § 360(h).
97. FD&C Act § 704(a)(1), 21 USC § 374(a)(1).
98. United States v. Crescent-Kelvan Co., 164 F.2d 582 (3rd Cir. 1948); United States v. Arnold's Pharmacy, Inc. 116 F. Supp. 310 (D.N.J. 1953); Golden Grain Macaroni Co. v. United States, 209 F.2d 166 (9th Cir. 1953).
99. FD&C Act § 304, 21 USC § 374.
100. Marshall v. Barlow's, Inc., 436 U.S. 307, 313 (1978), citing Colonnade Catering Corp. v. United States, 397 U.S. 72, 77 (1970) and United States v. Biswell, 406 U.S. 311, 316 (1972).
101. Jamieson-McKames Pharmaceuticals, Inc., 651 F. 2d 532 (8th Cir. 1981), cert. denied, 455 U.S. 1016 (1982).
102. Id. at 538.
103. Marshall v. Barlow's, Inc., 536 U.S. at 313.
104. Id., citing Almeida-Sanchez v. United States, 413 U.S. 266, 271, (1973).
105. Id.
106. United States v. Jamieson-McKames Pharmaceuticals, Inc., 651 F. 2d 532, 537 (8th Cir. 1981), citing McDermott v. Wisconsin, 228 U.S. 115 (1913).
107. United States v. Thriftimart, Inc., 429 F. 2d 1006 (9th Cir. 1970); United States v. Jamieson- McKames Pharmaceuticals, Inc., 651 F. 2d 532 (8th Cir. 1981), cert. denied, 455 U.S. 1016 (1982).
108. FDA Investigation Operations Manual 2013, at 5.2.5 and 5.2.6.
109. The full manual can be found at https://www.fda.gov/inspections-compliance-enforcement-and-criminal-investigations/inspection-references/investigations-operations-manual.

110. Sample form accessible at https://www.fda.gov/downloads/ICECI/Inspections/IOM/UCM497756.pdf.
111. FD&C Act § 704(a)(1)(A), 21 USC § 374(a)(1)(A).
112. FD&C Act § 301(e), (f); 21 USC § 331(e), (f).
113. FD&C Act § 704(a)(1), 21 USC § 374(a)(1).
114. FD&C Act § 703, 21 USC § 373.
115. FD&C Act § 704(c), 21 USC § 374(c); see Attachment 3, form FDA 484.
116. FD&C Act § 702(b), 21 USC § 372(b).
117. FD&C Act § 301(k), 21 USC § 331(k).
118. FD&C Act § 304(c), 21 USC § 334(c).
119. Investigation Operations Manual, 5.2.9.1.
120. 5 USC § 552.
121. FDA Field Management Directive, Procedure for Release of Establishment Inspection Report (April 1, 1997).
122. FD&C Act § 704(b), 21 USC § 374(b).
123. Investigation Operations Manual, 5.2.7.
124. FD&C Act § 74, 21 USC § 374.

Chapter 10

125. 109. 21 USC § 351, 352, 360, 360c, 360d, 360e, 360h, 360i, 360j, 360l, 371, 374, 381, 383.
126. https://www.fda.gov/files/drugs/published/Process-Validation--General-Principles-and-Practices.pdf
127. 21 CFR § 820.90.
128. 21 CFR § 820.100.
129. 21 CFR § 820.198.
130. 21 CFR § 820.198(c) and (d).
131. 21 CFR § 820.198(g).

Chapter 11

132. 21 CFR § 7.3(g).
133. FD&C Act § 518(e), 21 USC § 360h(e).
134. 21 CFR § 810.10.
135. 21 CFR § 810(d).
136. 21 CFR § 7.40.
137. 21 CFR § 7.3(m).
138. 21 CFR § 7.41.
139. 21 CFR § 7.41.
140. 21 CFR § 7.41(a).
141. 21 CFR § 7.40(c).
142. 21 USC § 7.45.
143. 21 CFR § 7.46(b).
144. 21 CFR § 7.48(d).
145. 21 CFR § 7.46.
146. 21 CFR § 7.46(a).
147. 21 CFR § 7.42(a).
148. 21 CFR § 7.42(b).
149. 21 CFR § 7.3.
150. 21 CFR § 7.42(a)(1).
151. 21 CFR § 7.42(a)(2).

152. 21 CFR § 7.42(a)(1).
153. 21 CFR § 7.49(a).
154. 21 CFR § 7.49(b).
155. 21 CFR § 7.49(c).
156. 21 CFR § 7.49(c).
157. 21 CFR § 7.42(b)(2).
158. 21 CFR § 7.50.
159. 21 CFR § 7.42(b)(3).
160. 21 CFR § 7.53.
161. 21 CFR § 7.53(b).
162. 21 CFR § 7.53(c).
163. 21 CFR § 7.55.

Chapter 13

164. Adapted from fda.gov, originally credited to Redmill and Rajan, 1997.

Chapter 14

165. https://www.fda.gov/regulatory-information/search-fda-guidance-documents/use-international-standard-iso-10993-1-biological-evaluation-medical-devices-part-1-evaluation-and

Chapter 17

166. https://www.fda.gov/regulatory-information/search-fda-guidance-documents/shelf-software-use-medical-devices
167. https://www.fda.gov/regulatory-information/search-fda-guidance-documents/content-premarket-submissions-management-cybersecurity-medical-devices
168. https://www.fda.gov/regulatory-information/search-fda-guidance-documents/postmarketmanagement-cybersecurity-medical-devices
169. https://www.nist.gov/publications/framework-improving-critical-infrastructure-cybersecurity-version-11

Chapter 20

170. 21 CFR § 820.70(c).
171. 21 CFR § 820.70(d).
172. 21 CFR § 820.70(e).
173. 21 CFR § 820.70(f).
174. 21 CFR § 820.70(g).
175. 21 CFR § 820.70(h).
176. 21 CFR § 820.70(i).
177. 21 CFR § 820.72.
178. https://www.fda.gov/regulatory-information/search-fda-guidance-documents/submission-and-review-sterility-information-premarket-notification-510k-submissions-devices-labeled
179. ISO 11135-1:2014.

Chapter 22

180. Carlberg, D. M., *Cleanroom Microbiology for the Non-Microbiologist,* second edition (New York: CRC Press, 2005).
181. Adapted from GHTF Study Group 3, 2004. Quality Management Systems – Process Validation Guidance, second edition.
182. Durivage, Mark A., *Practical Attribute and Variable Measurement Systems Analysis (MSA)* (Milwaukee: Quality Press, 2016).
183. Durivage, Mark A., *Practical Attribute and Variable Measurement Systems Analysis (MSA)* (Milwaukee: Quality Press, 2016).
184. Durivage, Mark A. *Practical Attribute and Variable Measurement Systems Analysis (MSA)* (Milwaukee: Quality Press, 2016).

Chapter 23

185. https://www.fda.gov/regulatory-information/search-fda-guidance-documents/reprocessing-medical-devices-health-care-settings-validation-methods-and-labeling

Chapter 24

186. https://echa.europa.eu/guidance-documents/guidance-on-reach

Chapter 25

187. https://www.accessdata.fda.gov/scripts/cdrh/cfdocs/cfstandards/search.cfm
188. https://www.fda.gov/regulatory-information/search-fda-guidance-documents/submission-and-review-sterility-information-premarket-notification-510k-submissions-devices-labeled
189. https://ec.europa.eu/growth/single-market/european-standards/harmonised-standards/medical-devices_en
190. https://ec.europa.eu/growth/sectors/medical-devices/current-directives/guidance_en

Chapter 26

191. Rooney, James J., and Lee N. Vanden Heuvel, "Root Cause Analysis for Beginners" Quality Progress 37, no. 7 (2004): 45-53.

Chapter 27

192. Kubiak, T. M., and Donald W. Benbow, *The Certified Six Sigma Black Belt Handbook,* second edition (Milwaukee: ASQ Quality Press, 2009): 7–8.
193. Walker, H. Fred, Ahmad Elshennawy, Bhisham C. Gupta, and Mary McShane Vaughn, *The Certified Quality Inspector Handbook,* second edition (Milwaukee: ASQ Quality Press, 2013): 120–121. Reference noted: Automotive Industry Action Group, Measurement Systems Analysis (MSA) Work Group, Measurement Systems Analysis Reference Manual, Third Edition (Dearborn, MI: Automotive Industry Action Group Press, 2002).
194. ReVelle, Jack B. *Quality Essentials: A Reference Guide from A to Z* (Milwaukee: ASQ Quality Press, 2004): 27–28.

Index

Note: Page numbers in *italics* indicate figures and tables.

B

C

D

E

F

I

J

K

L

M

N

O

P

About the Editor

Scott A. Laman

Scott A. Laman has 35 years of experience in applying quality and statistical principles to research; product and process development; quality and reliability engineering; and risk management in the chemical, plastics, and medical industries. He has executed multi-site organizational changes, led corrective and preventive projects to improve quality systems, implemented new global and local quality system processes, and executed numerous manufacturing improvement projects as a hands-on quality manager and engineer. He is currently Senior Manager, Quality Engineering and Risk Management at Teleflex, Inc. in Wyomissing, PA and leads a multi-functional department that supports new product development, sustaining engineering, compliance, and post-market surveillance.

Scott holds B.S. and M.S. degrees in Chemical Engineering from Syracuse University. He is a PMI-certified Project Management Professional (PMP), Fellow of the American Society for Quality (ASQ), and holds ASQ certifications of Quality Engineer, Reliability Engineer, Manager of Quality/Organizational Excellence, Six Sigma Black Belt, Quality Auditor, Medical Device Auditor, and Supplier Quality Professional.

As a member of ASQ, he is a Past Chair of the Certification Board and led the development of a complete documentation system for the board's policies, procedures, and forms. He is also a Past Chair of the Professional Ethics and Qualifications Committee and led the development of the current ASQ Code of Ethics and committee operating procedures. He is an active member of the *Quality Progress* (QP) journal Administrative Committee with responsibility for editorial reviews and manuscript disposition. His 30 published contributions to QP include several feature articles and columns of various types.

NOTES

NOTES

NOTES

NOTES